BREADTIME STORIES

A Cookbook for Bakers and Browsers

BREADTIME STORIES

A Cookbook for Bakers and Browsers

by

Susan Jane Cheney

Illustrated by
Kathy Miller Brown

TEN SPEED PRESS
BERKELEY, CALIFORNIA

TEN SPEED PRESS
Box 7123
Berkeley, California 94707

Illustrations © 1990 by Kathy Miller Brown
Cover design by Fifth Street Design
Text design by Paula Schlosser
Composition by Wilsted & Taylor, Oakland, California

LIBRARY OF CONGRESS CATALOGING-IN-PUBLICATION DATA
Cheney, Susan.
  Breadtime stories.

  Includes indexes.
  1. Bread.   I. Title.
TX769.C42   1989   641.8′15   89-4993
ISBN 0-89815-315-8

First printing, 1990

5   4   3   2   1   —   94   93   92   91   90

Manufactured in the United States of America

*To the memory of my mother, Jane E. Cheney, and
her mother, Emma M. Ettinger,
in whose kitchens my culinary odyssey began.*

CONTENTS

▝▝▝▝▝▝▝▝▝▝▝▝▝▝▝▝▝▝▝▝▝▝▝▝▝▝▝▝▝▝▝▝▝▝▝

ACKNOWLEDGMENTS

I WISH TO THANK David Arbeit, my husband and dearest friend, for his willingness to taste anything and everything, and his careful and honest critiques and invaluble technical assistance. His unwavering support and confidence in me made this book possible.

I would also like to express my appreciation to my father, Lee C. Cheney, for teaching me by example how to work hard at the things I find interesting and for reminding me to "have a little fun every day."

My sincere thanks too to other family members and to friends scattered far and wide: their enthusiasm and encouragement spurred me on far more than they know. Special thanks to Sue Taylor for her editorial aid at a critical juncture and to Ray Bard for his help in getting this project off the ground.

I am grateful to Jackie Wan, my editor. Her expertise and considered advice have greatly enhanced the book.

Many thanks to Kathy Miller-Brown for lending her creative spirit to the artwork and for translating my mental images of illustrations into the fine drawings in this book.

Once Upon a Time

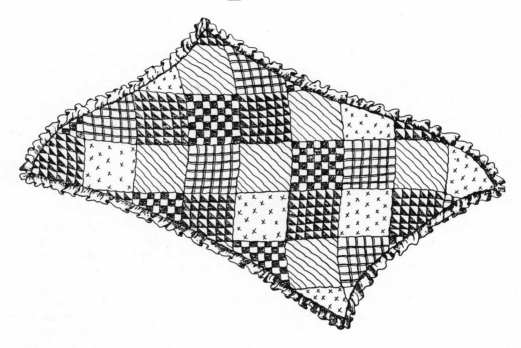

THE LITTLE RED HEN was one of my favorite childhood stories. It tells the tale of bread making to illustrate that those who work will receive their just rewards and those who don't won't. On her own, the Little Red Hen sows, grows, harvests, and mills a crop of wheat and prepares a batch of bread. Her fellow barnyard inhabitants ignore her requests for assistance until she asks: "And who will help me *eat* this bread?" Then everyone is eager to participate, but the Little Red Hen keeps all the bread for herself. I was not so much impressed by the story's moral as I was fascinated by the activities described, and age hasn't quelled my enthusiasm. Fresh grains and flour, thick ceramic bowls, wooden spoons, smooth marble work surfaces—all the ingredients and implements for baking—enthrall me. Measuring, mixing, and kneading invigorate rather than tire me. I faithfully peruse the cookbook sections of bookstores and libraries, ponder uses for every new discovery in cookware shops, and make pilgrimages to bakeries as though they contained rare works of art.

Are people born with compelling interests? As a toddler, I was once caught in the act of sprinkling flour throughout the first floor of the house. I think I recall the shocked expression on my mother's face before she broke into laughter at my antic. I no doubt enjoyed the soft, satiny feel of Pillsbury's All-Purpose Blend sifting through my fingers. This incident foretold my intensely "breadridden" years to come. I have been known to cart a bowl of dough around in my car so I could punch it down at the appropriate times, and, even when I was employed as a cook, I would hurry home to my own kitchen and happily start cooking again. Baking and cooking have a firm grip on me and they won't let go.

I'm sure I was influenced by my grandmother, whom I shadowed at the kitchen counter, sink, and stove. I still feel her presence daily as I use her finely crocheted pot holders, flowered china, and shiny copper-bottomed pots and pans. Granny baked and cooked and took pride in her excellence as a homemaker, but she didn't pursue these endeavors as sciences and arts as I do. My approach more closely resembles my dad's absorption in organic chemistry. I'm not satisfied simply turning out attractive, delicious culinary products—I want to know why they were successful or how they can be varied; I'm never merely disappointed in flops—I want to understand what went wrong.

This book reflects my years in the kitchen. Its primary focus is baking, as is my own; I'm an avid cook but a fervent baker. But it is not just another bread book. My special interest is the intermingling of baking and cooking, whereby breads fit into a healthful yet satisfying pattern of eating. I view baking and cooking as a cooperative adventure, and I like to explore the synergy between them.

The recipes were inspired by loaves and dishes I have tasted or read, heard or dreamed about, or just imagined, devised, and refined through extensive testing in my "lab," as my husband long ago labeled the kitchen. They incorporate a variety of whole grains and whole grain products, legumes and soy foods, vegetables, fruits, nuts, seeds, and occasionally eggs. They don't contain meat, fowl, or fish, and milk products appear only as options. These recipes are for you bread lovers aware of health issues who don't want to give up baked goods but are resolute about consuming a wholesome diet. They are for you whole grain enthusiasts who are weary of adjusting recipes that include refined flours. And you vegetarians and those of you who avoid milk products or refined sweeteners for any reason will happily discover answers to your special needs without going through a tedious translation process. But these recipes will appeal to anyone who savors wholesome food and the art of preparing it.

Regardless of their dietary persuasion, most people are cognizant of the close relationship between diet and health. Many of my meat-eating and dairy-loving friends and acquaintances are heeding the advice of doctors and the Surgeon General and looking for ways to cut down on salt and fatty, high-cholesterol foods and to consume more fiber. Vegetarians as well as meat-eaters are adjusting their diets, since many traditional meat substitutes, notably cheese and eggs, are high in cholesterol and don't jibe well with new dietary guidelines. Whole grains, beans, and soy products are healthier choices. Tofu and tempeh in particular can fill the role of meat. Tofu readily stands in for ricotta and cottage cheese, and can serve the binding function of eggs in baked goods. Blended with a bit of lemon juice and oil, it substitutes for sour cream. Soy milk replaces milk. Once you've incorporated these ingredients into your culinary repertoire, you may well wonder how you've managed without them.

Like most experienced bakers and cooks, I usually refer to recipes casually, as skeletal outlines, and toss in intuitive rather than carefully measured quantities of ingredients. In the interest of clear communication, I have disciplined myself and specified amounts here. Still, I view baking and cooking as flexible, expressive mediums, and I encourage you to do so too. Once you have the gist of a recipe, you can substitute seasonings and make alterations to reflect your personal taste. When you approach baking and cooking this way, you'll likely find that ideas for new recipes and revisions of existing ones roll into your mind like a wave. By far the most difficult aspect of writing this book was capturing recipes at a point in time before some new idea inspired me to alter them yet again. My goal here is to build a foundation for creative bakers and cooks as opposed to rote recipe followers, to provide a guide for a new breed in the kitchen.

The book is organized into four major parts. **Part One**, **Getting Ready for Bread**, lays the groundwork for all that is to follow. It introduces grains and other key bread ingredients, describes bread-making utensils, and offers tips on organization. Consider this a storeroom of ideas that you'll want to refer back to periodically. **Part Two**, **The Breadroom**, covers bread-making techniques and includes a large selection of bread recipes. **Part Three**, **Getting into Bread**, explores the collaborative possibilities between baking and cooking, combining a variety of toppings and fillings with breads, doughs, and batters in numerous ways. **Part Four**, **Breadfellows**, addresses another aspect of the close relationship between baking and cooking. Here, three chapters offer choice salads and dressings, soups and vegetable stews, and desserts—cookies, cakes, and pies—that can be served with breads and bread-based dishes to round out a meal. Finally, there is a glossary of ingredients and techniques.

To effectively utilize the book, I suggest you read the text that precedes the recipe first, then read the recipe through completely before assembling the ingredients and getting to work. At the top of each recipe, I have noted the yield and preparation times; both are approximate, depending upon appetites and individual working pace, respectively. Notes at the end of recipes offer additional explanations and possible substitutions in ingredients and techniques. Grasp the fundamentals, explore the recipes, open your imagination, and you'll be well on your way to creating your own breadtime stories happily ever after.

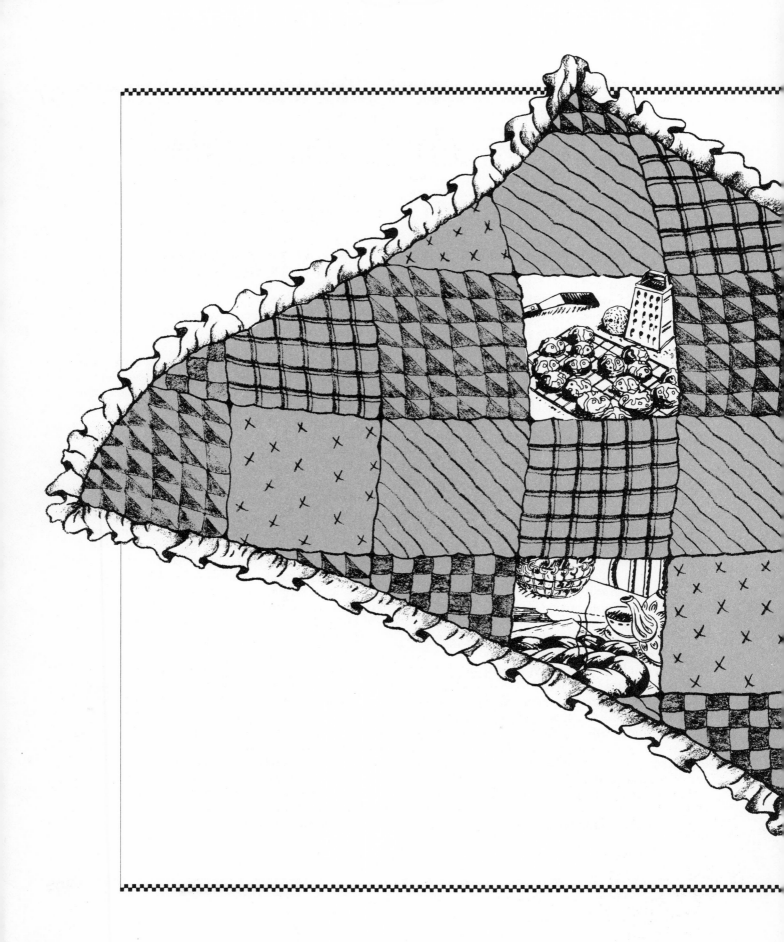

THE BREADROOM:
BREADS AND
BREAD MAKING

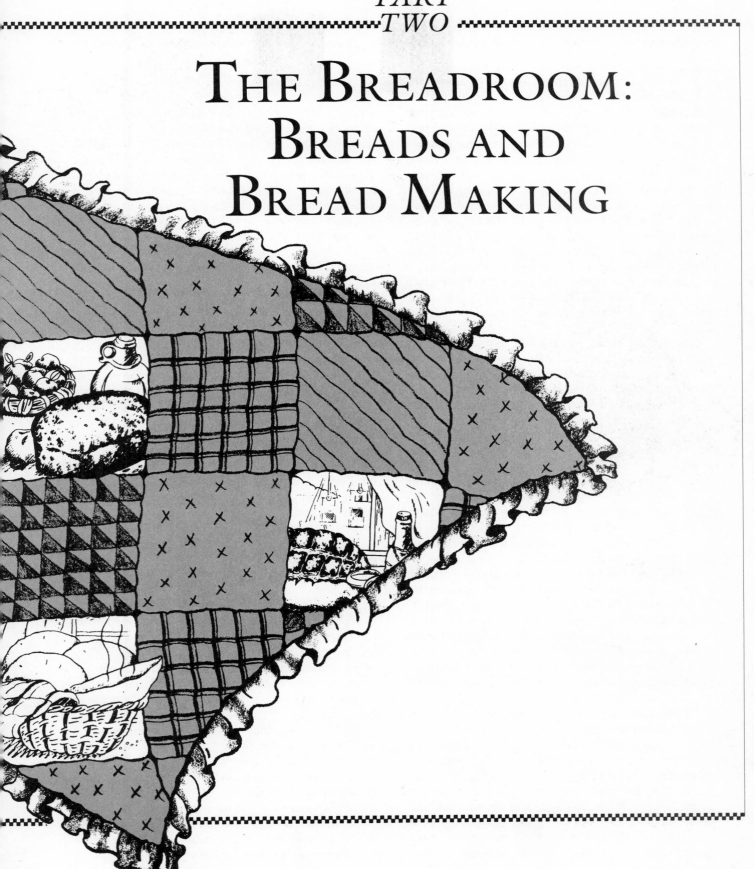

I ONCE TAUGHT KINDERGARTEN in New York City and was amazed to discover that the children didn't have the slightest idea where bread came from. The only child who ventured a guess suggested that slices grew on trees! Needless to say, our next lesson was about bread—what it is, what it is made from, how it is put together, and which tools are used to make it. We mixed and kneaded a dough, baked and sliced a loaf of bread, and enjoyed our just rewards. Sometimes, I find myself imagining the children of those children pondering the mystery of where bread comes from—and learning the answer from their enlightened parents, who remember their kindergarten project.

Regardless of age, every competent baker must possess a basic understanding of bread, the grains and other ingredients that compose it, and the tools of the trade.

No doubt bread evolved as a series of happenstances, the consequence of early peoples' attempts to make grains palatable and digestible. I imagine these people pounding and soaking grains to soften the seed coats. At some point, a pulverized, soaked mass of grain was left out in the sun or over a fire and baked into a solid chunk which could be picked up and likely tasted somewhat different, maybe better, than its wetter form. Risen bread was probably a further chance happening. Most likely, a moist grain mixture sat around in a warm place long enough to attract wild yeast from the air. These organisms initiated fermentation in the dough and it rose into a light loaf.

The specific history of bread making remains obscure, but, over time, this ongoing endeavor has resulted in countless breads and techniques for making them. Variations in breads around the world reflect regional grains, different culinary methods and customs, and, especially, the diversity of individuals—their tastes and creative impulses. Despite this variety, the fundamental nature of bread hasn't changed much at all; in its most elementary form, bread remains a mixture of grain, usually ground, and liquid that is cooked in some way to form a compact whole.

Most modern bread originates far from human hands and homes—hence the ignorance of my kindergartners. In Western society at least, technological developments have transformed most bakeries into factories and most breads into the crustless, squishy white loaves that line store shelves today. This high-tech bread is typically tasteless and short on nutrients and character.

Many people in America have never tasted really good bread, making their take-it-for-granted and take-it-or-leave-it attitudes toward bread understandable. Furthermore, we have become so used to the appalling absence of sustaining qualities in modern bread that we consider it to be dispensable high-calorie starch rather than a valuable contribution to health. No wonder we consider bread to be little more than an accessory to a meal rather than an integral part of it. Yet the word *bread* is synonymous, at least in English, with food in general, and, beyond edible sustenance, to livelihood; a *breadwinner* is a provider, and the term radiates strength and nurturance.

The timing seems right for an upgrading of bread among modern consumers. Not all of us are sold on soft white bread, and recently, as health professionals have recognized the value of complex carbohydrates, their dietary recommendations for whole grain products are on the upswing. Whole grain bread appears to be gaining a new respect in the American diet.

Unfortunately, good and good-for-you commercial bread isn't always easy to find. One solution is to make it yourself. If you do, you'll discover rewards even beyond a delicious, nutritious final product. Bread dough is an artistic medium and manipulating it affords sensual pleasure comparable to working with clay or playing with mud. Bread making can be an engrossing, calming, meditative activity. This may be stretching it, but I think that by making your own bread rather than buying bread that you don't really care much for, you might just eventually have some impact on quality in society as a whole.

Whatever your particular motivations, a thorough baking education will allow you to most effectively pursue your objectives. It's my intention to dispel the mystique shrouding bread making without doing away with its delights. Comprehending baking principles won't squelch your wonder at the process or your appreciation of the finished product, just as a grasp of biology doesn't preclude awe at the miracle of pregnancy and a newborn child. Baking knowledge will drive away apprehension, inhibition, and anxiety—major stumbling blocks to the adventures awaiting you in bread making.

Begin your education by familiarizing yourself with grains—the staff of the "staff of life." Move on to learn about other key components of breads, including liquids, leavens, salt, fats, and sweeteners. Next, collect the appropriate utensils. Baking implements aren't particularly specialized, so you don't have to make a large dollar investment to get going. One thing you do need to commit is some time, but baking isn't too demanding in this respect either. Let's get started.

CHAPTER 1

Grains

GLASS JARS OF GRAINS form an earthy colored collage in my kitchen cupboards. In them I store everything from whole wheat berries to rye, barley, oats, millet, and rice. In a sense, I have the whole world in my cupboard because grains just like these have nourished people all over the world for eons.

Grains are the primary raw materials of bread. And bread, of course, is virtually a universal food. The particular grains used to make a bread largely determine its flavor, texture, and nutrition. As you stock your kitchen to get ready for baking, look to this primer for information on buying, storing, and cooking grains as well as for a rundown on grains most commonly used in making bread, ranging from ancient ones like wheat and barley to high-tech developments such as triticale.

In my cooking, I use only unrefined whole grains. I do this because whole grains are far superior in flavor and texture. A taste test comparing white and brown rice, white and whole wheat pasta, pearled and hull-less barley dramatically reveals the impact of refinement on grains. Anyone accustomed to refined grains and flours would probably be astounded at the whole grains' dis-

tinct flavors and definite textures. These grains and grain products aren't just vehicles for sauces and spreads; they have personalities of their own. I remember the first time my father-in-law, who is notoriously skeptical of natural foods, tasted brown rice. After the first bite, he exclaimed, "How come our rice at home doesn't taste this good!"

The other reason I favor whole grains is that they are higher in nutritive value than refined ones. No doubt you've been hearing a lot lately about complex carbohydrates. Grains are loaded with them, which makes grains of all types superb energy sources. But unrefined grains provide other valuable nutrients as well, including proteins, fats, vitamins, and minerals. Also, whole grains supply fiber or roughage, which benefits our bodies all the way from our teeth and facial muscles to our large intestines.

Though grains differ in look and taste, they all have basically the same makeup, and it helps to understand their components to comprehend what refinement takes away. Each kernel contains a nutrient-packed minuscule seed for a rudimentary plant; this is called the germ. Adjacent to this is the endosperm, much larger and consisting mostly of complex carbohydrates encased in protein, designed to sustain the germ in the early stages of its growth. A multi-layered hard covering which is termed the bran protects the grain embryo and its storehouse until moisture and light bring it to life. The innermost layer of bran contains minerals, vitamins, oil, and additional proteins, including enzymes, special proteins which act as catalysts for accessing the nutrients. In essence, each kernel of grain is a system unto itself, including, in the correct proportions, both nutrients and the agents required to release them.

Early milling technology consisted of the simple process of rubbing whole grains between two stone surfaces until the resulting product reached a desired fineness—grits, meal, or flour. Small-scale, mechanized stone-wheel milling is still used to produce some of the whole grain flour available today. This technique maintains a low temperature and low humidity in the grain, conditions thought to preserve its flavor, nutrients, and freshness. In addition, stone milling disperses the oil quite evenly throughout the flour, which retards spoilage. The vitamin E in ground grain serves as a preservative, but only for a couple of months.

Modern mills use steel rollers. For 100 percent whole grain products, whole grains entering the mill are merely pulverized and leave the mill changed only in physical form. However, modern milling is capable of a much more complicated process in which the grain is ground and select portions are removed. The flour is then usually subjected to various treatments, such as bleaching with chemical gases. It is often enriched with vitamins and minerals, but many more substances are removed than are added back, and those that are replaced aren't put back in their original proportion in the whole grain. Refinement also robs whole grains of their wonderful capacity for natural fermentation in bread making. To remedy this, chemical conditioners are added to white flour. My big objection to grain refinement can be summed up in one phrase: "If it isn't broken, why fix it?" Why not leave grains intact in the first place?

Historically, the attraction to refined flour is threefold. First, for ages, the color white has been associated with cleanliness and purity. Early white flour was simply picked free of dirt and other foreign matter—an expensive, tedious task to accomplish. Later, through sifting or "bolting," the darker portions of the grain, the bran and germ, were removed and discarded, and whitening agents—even chalk—were added to further lighten the flour. Only the wealthy could afford refined flour, so the color of one's flour came to signify social position. Finally, the diminished vulnerability of white flour to spoilage once the germ and bran were removed

enabled early travelers to carry it long distances and shopkeepers to stock it for extended periods. The difference between then and now is—or should be—that we are aware that the convenience of long storage is paid for with lost nutrition and taste.

Storing Grains

I keep my jars of grains, tightly closed, on my lowest, coolest shelves and enclose a few fresh bay leaves in each container or affix a cotton swab dipped in bay oil to the underside of the lid to discourage insects, notably Indian meal moths. Careless, casual storage of grains can result in some expensive disasters. Some friends of mine suddenly realized that they had a "living" cupboard; the bugs went after everything—from whole grains and flour to raisins and shelf paper!

Pick the driest, coolest, darkest spot in your house for grain storage. If you live in a cold place, use an unheated dry room or porch. If it's open to the outside, be sure your containers are impervious to predators such as mice and squirrels. Where temperature and humidity fluctuate a lot, it's best either to buy grains in small quantities and use them up quickly or to store them, well wrapped, in the refrigerator or freezer. In any case, always use up the oldest grains first.

Intact kernels of grain with their hard protective coats keep much better than broken or pulverized grains. As soon as a grain is cracked open and its natural oils are exposed to the air, it becomes susceptible to rancidity. Corn and oats are especially vulnerable. Taste a little bit of grain or flour to check freshness; rancid grains have a bitter flavor. I buy milled grains—cracked and rolled and meals and flours—in relatively small quantities, wrap them airtight, and keep them in the refrigerator or freezer.

I would love to have an effective grain grinder always at the ready. Then I would keep only whole grains on hand. The flavor of freshly ground grains is truly incomparable! I know a family that grinds rice or cornmeal almost every morning for a scrumptious hot breakfast cereal. They grind fresh flour for bread and other baked goods. I have a hand grinder but no space to leave it set up all of the time—which is the only efficient arrangement. Besides, grinding enough grain for a batch of bread would take considerable time and energy with my particular mill.

Shopping for Grains

Organically grown grains (and beans and produce) have become a real priority for me because they are more nutritionally sound and their production isn't detrimental to farm workers or to the environment. I look for merchants who share that concern, and who are committed to quality and know how to maintain that quality. I'm fortunate to have three quality-conscious natural foods supermarkets in the city where I live. Smaller natural foods stores, food cooperatives, and natural foods sections in regular supermarkets may be other good sources for quality grains.

One of the problems in shopping for grains is that it's usually impossible to know how old they are. Unless whole wheat flour turns over quickly, it should be refrigerated. To ensure freshness, I buy some grains through the mail. The two reputable companies I'm most familiar with are Walnut Acres Natural Foods (Penns Creek, Pennsylvania 17862; 1-800-433-3998) and Mountain Ark Trading Company (120 South East Avenue, Fayetteville, Arkansas 72701; 1-800-643-8909).

Bulk bins may give natural foods stores an appealing, old-time country store ambience, but they can be risky in the insect department. Many markets now seem to be switching to limited access Plexiglas chute-style bins. But if you see any tiny moths fluttering around in any store, flee and buy your grains elsewhere. Heat any suspect grain for about 30 minutes in a 140- to 150-degree oven and cool it thoroughly before putting it away. Freezing grain is another way to both head off and remedy insect infestation. Many good quality grains are also sold in hermetically sealed bags.

Next, let's go over the different grains used in baking, beginning with the most common of all, wheat.

WHEAT

Without a doubt, wheat is the most important grain for making bread. A high proportion of wheat flour is generally incorporated into any yeast-raised bread because wheat contains gluten, a protein prevalent in and pretty much unique to it. When activated by beating and kneading, gluten forms an elastic network that expands with the carbon dioxide gas produced by yeast activity. Oven heat sets this gas-filled structure, maintaining the shape of a loaf.

For baking, all wheat is not the same. Wheats are classified on the basis of their hardness or strength as determined by their gluten content: the more gluten, the "harder" or "stronger" the wheat. High-gluten or hard wheat flours produce a springy, resilient texture in breads. Low-gluten or soft wheat flours contain less protein than hard ones and give baked goods a tender, cakey crumb. Hard wheats are often referred to as bread wheats and soft wheats as pastry wheats. Bread flours are slightly granular in texture; pastry flours have a soft, silky feel to them. Gluten content can be too high for yeasted breads. For instance, durum wheat, an exceptionally high-gluten variety, is too hard for most bread making. It is superlative for making pasta, however.

You will probably hear several other terms in regard to wheat: spring wheat and winter wheat, red wheat and white wheat. Spring wheats are planted in the spring and harvested in the fall; winter wheats are sown in the fall and reaped late the following spring. Spring wheats are generally higher in gluten than winter wheats. Wheats are also identified as "red" or "white," based on kernel color. Red wheats are higher in gluten than white wheats. I find hard red spring wheat flour ideal for kneaded breads.

I also prefer to use finely ground flour, particularly for kneaded breads. Because it is a hard material, the bran in any whole grain flour tends to abrade the gluten strands that are forming as a dough is mixed and kneaded. The mixing and kneading processes themselves strengthen the gluten, but the finer the bran fragments in the flour, the less damage the bran will do to the developing gluten. Finely ground high-gluten whole wheat bread flour yields the lightest, highest-rising whole grain loaves.

All-purpose flour is a blend of hard and soft wheats and is advertised as suitable for any type of baking. However, this label doesn't specify the relative proportions of hard and soft wheats present. I find that selecting identifiable strong flour for kneaded breads and weak flour for quick breads and pastries is a much surer way to successful baking. All-purpose flour simplifies the pantry but also may compromise the excellence of baked goods.

One more thing in regard to wheat flour. You've probably heard of gluten flour. Gluten can be isolated by washing everything else out of wheat flour—refined wheat flour in the case of commercial gluten flour. The pure gluten is dried, ground, and usually mixed half and half with refined white flour to prepare gluten flour. Combined with low-gluten flours, gluten flour will increase the rise of breads—but at the expense of flavor, texture, digestibility, and keeping quality. I don't recommend using this highly refined product.

The nutty flavor of whole wheat comes through no matter what its form. Cook whole berries to dryness for a chewy pilaf or grain salad base, or incorporate them into bread dough. Cracked wheat is quick to cook and requires only soaking in boiling water before going into a bread mix. Bulgur, whole wheat which has been steamed and dried before cracking, readily softens when soaked in hot water. Rolled wheat makes a satisfying cereal which can also substitute for part of the liquid in bread dough. Uncooked wheat flakes add texture to doughs. Sprouted wheat is surprisingly sweet tasting. Chopped and mixed into bread dough, wheat sprouts add flavor, texture, and moistness to the crumb; they also contain active enzymes that enhance rising.

Whole wheat products are rich in iron, magnesium, calcium, phosphorus, many trace minerals, vitamin E, and B vitamins. Since many nutrients are concentrated in wheat germ and bran, adding extra amounts of these to baked goods augments nutritive value. Bran contributes extra fiber as well.

BARLEY

Probably my first taste of barley was in canned soup, and I remember the mushy white grains as bland and undistinguished. When I discovered whole grain barley, its distinctive, sweet flavor was an exciting surprise. Most commercially available barley is pearled, or run through a sander-type device called a pearler, which takes off the chaff and most of the nutrient-filled, fiber-rich germ and bran with it. Hull-less barley is far superior. This is barley with only the chaff removed and the bran and germ intact. Look for it in natural foods stores. Whole barley takes longer to cook than pearled barley, but soaking it beforehand shortens cooking time somewhat. You can also pressure-cook it.

Barley flour lends a wonderfully sweet flavor to bread, which prior roasting intensifies. It also contributes moistness and a cakelike texture to baked goods. Don't include a lot or you'll have a dense loaf. If you have a mill, grind your own flour from hull-less barley or buy the darkest barley flour you can find—its darkness indicates it was ground from whole or minimally pearled grain. For chewy sweetness, add cooked whole barley to bread dough. Barley is my favorite grain for natural-rise breads (see pages 102, 105-6, and 107).

BUCKWHEAT

I don't think anyone is lukewarm about buckwheat or *kasha*, its Russian name. You're either drawn to or revolted by its distinctive flavor and aroma. I'm one of its most enthusiastic fans!

Though used as a grain, buckwheat is actually a member of the rhubarb family. Hulled buckwheat groats are cream-colored and turn reddish brown when toasted. Roasting accentuates buckwheat's flavor.

Nutritionally, buckwheat resembles wheat. It contains generous amounts of iron, B vitamins, and calcium. Buckwheat also contains rutic acid, which

benefits circulation. The darker buckwheat flour is, the more of the lysine-rich hull has been included in it. Lysine is one of several amino acids, the building blocks of proteins, that the human body cannot synthesize and must obtain from diet; these are called essential amino acids. Lysine is scarce in most grains.

Buckwheat flour is gluten-free; it contributes heft and compactness as well as its unusual flavor to baked goods. A little bit goes a long way in both flavor and texture. I like to add toasted, softened buckwheat groats to bread dough and muffins. Thoroughly cooked groats lend flavor and moistness to bread, though they don't add much texture to its crumb. Buckwheat flour makes fine thin crêpes.

CORN

Corn is indigenous to the Americas, though its cultivation has spread to Europe: in a Romanian village, I was treated to *mamaliga*, a traditional cornmeal porridge; *polenta* is cornmeal mush in northern Italy. Here, we eat sweet corn as a vegetable and cook dried field corn whole or, more often, grind it into grits, meal, or flour.

Corn varieties differ in protein, starch content, and color—from familiar yellow and white ears to red, blue, brown, and black ones. Corn (especially the yellow varieties) is high in carotene, a compound which the body transforms into vitamin A. Phosphorus and potassium are also abundant in corn.

Freshly ground corn is sweet; stale meal has a strong bitter taste. Buy cornmeal as freshly ground as possible in small quantities and keep it tightly wrapped in the freezer.

In breads, cooked whole kernels of sweet or dried corn show up as chewy sweet spots. Uncooked cornmeal produces a somewhat crunchy and crumbly texture in breads. Cooked cornmeal adds moistness.

Sprinkled on the baking sheet, cornmeal keeps pizzas and freestanding loaves and rolls from sticking.

MILLET

A common ingredient in birdseed, millet is probably more familiar to domestic and wild birds than to humans in the United States. Millet for birds and people is sold hulled; each grain is a tiny yellow sphere. You'll find "people" millet in natural foods stores.

The protein in millet is particularly well endowed with the scarcer essential amino acids, and millet contains an abundance of iron—more than any other grain except amaranth.

Millet cooks relatively quickly to a light, fluffy consistency. It has a delicately sweet, nutty flavor, which is enhanced by lightly toasting the dry grains before cooking them in a liquid. Sautéing raw millet in a small amount of oil also keeps the cooked grains from clumping together.

Cooked millet adds moisture, a slight chewiness, and a subtly sweet flavor to breads. Uncooked millet in dough contributes a pleasant crunchiness and an appealing speckled pattern to slices. Millet flour doesn't promote rise, but it gives a soft, cakelike crumb to baked goods.

OATS

In this country, oats connote breakfast—from steaming bowls of hot oatmeal to Cheerios to crunchy granola. The abundance of polyunsaturated fats in oats makes them a good source of long-lasting energy. Their high fat content does make oats especially vulnerable to rancidity, so store milled oat products with care—in the freezer if possible. Oats are also high in protein, B vitamins, iron, phosphorus, and calcium. Oat bran is the new dietary hero because of its capacity for absorbing cholesterol and transporting it out of the body.

Steel-cut oats are made by slicing up whole oats into smaller pieces. Rolled oats are flattened oat grains, and instant rolled oats are oat grains which have been cut up and steamed before being rolled very thinly. Oat flour can be ground from either of the above or from whole oats. Rolled oats are soft enough to grind to flour in a blender.

All forms of oats are good in breads. Cooked whole, cut, or rolled oats give breads a moist and chewy, yet light texture and a slightly sweet flavor. Uncooked oat flakes appear as light-colored specks in breads and add chewiness to the crumb. Since they will absorb liquid, add them to an extra wet mix. Oat flour also contributes to moistness and sweetness in breads. Oat breads keep well and make superlative toast.

RICE

Rice sustains more people worldwide than any other grain or food of any kind. In some Oriental languages, the words for rice and meal are synonymous. Rice is a familiar though not particularly important food to most Americans, and much of the rice eaten here is highly refined. Polished rice is depleted of most of its protein, fat, minerals, vitamins, and fiber—to say nothing of flavor and texture. Brown rice tastes mildly sweet and is chewy; white rice is almost characterless in both respects. Since the rice plant is especially susceptible to diseases and pests, all but organically grown rice in the United States is heavily doused with pesticides.

Varieties of brown rice are differentiated by grain length and classified as short-, medium-, or long-grain. These cook up a bit differently but are similar nutritionally. The starch in short-grain rice causes it to cook slightly stickier and chewier than medium- or long-grain rices. These cook to a fluffier consistency since the individual grains remain more separate. Both short- and medium-grain rice tend to have a more pronounced flavor than regular long-grain rice. Basmati rice, a long-grain Indian variety, has an exotic, alluring flavor and aroma. Don't mistake sweet rice for short-grain; sweet rice, also known as glutinous rice, cooks to an almost gluey consistency—an advantage for certain preparations but not for general use.

Whole grain rice of any length contributes its subtly sweet flavor to baked goods. Cooked whole brown rice adds a moist and chewy texture to breads; I think it's at its best in sourdough and natural-rise breads (see pages 104, 105, 107). Rice grits produce crunchiness. Rice flour fosters a moist, compact, smooth crumb; pre-toasting augments its flavor. It doesn't contain gluten though, so go easy on the amount you add to yeasted breads. Most commercial rice flour is ground from polished rice; for a more nutritious and tasty alternative, either search for brown rice flour or grind your own from the whole grain. Like wheat bran and germ, rice bran and polishings (the inner bran layers) provide extra fiber and enrichment.

RYE

Rye berries are darker and slightly longer and narrower than wheat grains. Rye has a unique, hearty flavor. Somewhat intense by itself, it mingles agreeably with the nutty taste of whole wheat. Nutritionally, whole rye resembles whole wheat; it is especially rich in minerals, notably potassium, and in B vitamins, particularly riboflavin.

Rye ferments readily, producing a desirable sourness in breads. Although rye contains some gluten, it differs from the gluten found in wheat and can't be developed into a strong, elastic structure in dough. Predominantly rye doughs tend to be soft and sticky. Breads containing rye flour have a fine-grained, compact crumb. Caraway and fennel or anise seeds, orange zest, and molasses all blend well with the flavor of rye and are frequently included in rye baked goods.

TRITICALE

Triticale is a 20th century, man-made grain, created by genetically manipulating and crossing wheat and rye. Its name is derived from the Latin terms *triticum*, which means wheat, and *secale*, meaning rye. This hybrid represents an attempt to marry the plentiful protein and gluten content of wheat with the heartiness and prolific nature of rye. Triticale berries have the color of wheat and the shape of rye. The grain is also available as rolled flakes or flour.

Triticale has a subtly rye-ish flavor; it is milder than rye but not quite as nutty-flavored as wheat. This new grain is higher in protein than either of its parent plants and is particularly well endowed with the amino acid lysine.

Although triticale does contain a significant amount of gluten, it differs from the gluten in wheat and in rye. Doughs in which triticale flour predominates do best with a minimum of gentle handling rather than vigorous kneading; give them one rather than multiple rising periods. A small amount of triticale in any form is an agreeable addition to wheat doughs.

AMARANTH

Amaranth is not a new grain; it was a staple of the Aztecs in Mexico and Central America. Interest in amaranth has been rekindled recently as research has revealed its high nutritional value. Other pluses for amaranth are that it is fast-growing and high-yielding even in exceedingly dry areas.

Unlike most other grains, amaranth isn't a grass; it's a broad-leafed plant in the same family as spinach, chard, and beets. Both its leaves and tiny round yellow seeds are edible. The seeds are high in protein, including lysine and other amino acids typically scarce in grains. Amaranth also contains more iron and calcium than most other grains.

Amaranth has a nutty, sometimes spicy or peppery flavor. Toasting brings out its flavor—and also pops it like minuscule popcorn! Cooking gives amaranth a rather gelatinous texture, but you can cook some along with other grains—say, buckwheat, millet, or rice—without a noticeable effect and take advantage of its flavor and nutrition. Use 1 part amaranth to 3 parts of the other grain. Substitute amaranth flour for about a quarter of the flour in a basic whole wheat bread recipe.

Amaranth seed and flour is available in many natural foods stores and from mail order sources.

QUINOA

Quinoa is another "new" old grain. It was an important food for the Incas in ancient Peru. Quinoa is related to amaranth and has a similar nutritional profile. If anything, it is even more nutritious.

Raw quinoa resembles pale grains of millet. Cooked, the small round grains look like miniature tapioca pearls and have a fluffy texture.

Quinoa is covered with a bitter substance called saponin, which provides natural protection from insects. Be sure to rinse even packaged grain thoroughly with cool water before cooking to eliminate the unpleasant flavor of this beneficial cloak. Rinse and dry it before grinding into flour. Use your blender and figure on ¾ cup grain for each cup of flour.

Rid of the saponin, quinoa has a unique, pleasant flavor. Pan-toast it lightly for a nuttier taste. Quinoa cooks quickly; in 15 to 20 minutes it swells to four to five times its original volume. The cooked grain adds moisture and texture to breads. Since quinoa lacks gluten, combine a small amount of quinoa flour with wheat flour in yeasted breads to maintain a light texture. You can use more in quick breads or flat breads.

Look for quinoa in natural foods stores or order it through the mail.

SORGHUM

Presently, most of the sorghum grown in this country is used for animal feed, and the feed store is where you're most likely to find this grain. If you buy it there, be sure it is pesticide-free. Look for it from mail order sources too. It is sometimes called milo.

Nutritionally, sorghum is similar to corn. Physically, it resembles millet, although different varieties vary in size and color. Sorghum has an appealing sweet flavor. A mineral-rich syrup produced from sorghum stalks was widely used in the South before sugar was readily available.

Sorghum can be cooked whole or ground into meal or flour. It lacks gluten, so combine it with wheat flour in raised breads.

Cooking Grains

Specific cooking directions for different grains vary, but some fundamental principles apply to all of them:

- In general, the more finely ground the grain, the quicker it will cook: whole grain berries take longest, grain meals the least.

- Most packaged grains have been cleaned quite thoroughly. Bulk grains may have small twigs or stones in their midst. Spread suspect grain in a single layer on a tray or baking sheet and check carefully for inedible particles. Rinse whole grains thoroughly before cooking by swirling them in a bowl of water and draining in a fine-mesh strainer.

- Match pot size and the quantity of grain to be cooked as closely as possible. Grains require suf-

ficient room to expand, but a small amount of grain in a large pot won't cook evenly and thoroughly no matter how long it simmers. Use a 1- to 2-quart pot for a cup of dry grain.

- When increasing the quantity of grain to be cooked, you don't need to increase the liquid proportionately. For example, use about 1¾ cups of water for 1 cup of rice and 3 cups of water for 2 cups of rice.

- Grains are often salted during cooking, but salt is an optional ingredient, added solely for seasoning. If you add a salted grain to bread, reduce the salt in the recipe.

- Grains continue to cook after the heat under the pot is turned off. When cooking grains to dryness, remove the pot from the heat and leave it covered for at least several minutes—preferably longer—to allow the grain to steam gently. The grain will be fluffier and less sticky than grain that is served immediately.

- It's difficult to give an absolute ratio of liquid to grain or an exact cooking time, since a number

GRAIN PREPARATION
(See text for specific directions)

GRAIN	WATER PER CUP OF GRAIN	PREPARATION TIME	APPROXIMATE YIELD
Whole Grains			
Wheat Berries	3 cups	About 1 hour	3 cups
Rye Berries	3 cups	45 to 60 minutes	3 cups
Triticale Berries	2½ cups	About 40 minutes	3 cups
Oats	3 cups	30 to 40 minutes	3 cups
Barley	3½ to 4 cups	45 to 60 minutes	3 cups
Brown Rice	1¾ cups	40 minutes	4 cups
Millet	2 cups	30 minutes	4 cups
Buckwheat	1¾ cups	30 minutes	4 cups
Quinoa	2 cups	15 to 20 minutes	4 cups
Cracked Grains			
Cracked Wheat	2 cups	25 to 30 minutes	4 cups
Cracked Rye	2 cups	25 to 30 minutes	4 cups
Grits (any grain)	4 cups	15 to 30 minutes	3 to 4 cups
Bulgur	1½ cups	30 minutes	2½ cups
Rolled Grains			
All grains	2 to 3 cups	10 to 20 minutes	2 to 3 cups
Grain Meals			
All grains	3 to 5 cups	10 to 20 minutes	3 cups

of factors influence the cooking process: the age of the grain—older grain may require a bit more liquid and take a little longer to cook; the pot—grains cook more efficiently in heavy, well-insulated pots with snug lids; and even personal taste, since "just right" for you might be underdone or overdone for me and vice versa. So, tune in to your particular supplies, utensils, and preferences, and use the following directions as a guide.

WHOLE GRAINS

Soaking cuts down cooking time for **wheat**, **rye**, and **triticale berries**, **barley**, and **oats**. After rinsing the grain, pour boiling water over it in a pot (see chart), cover, and let it soak at least until the water cools and preferably several hours or overnight. Bring to a simmer, cover, reduce the heat to low, and cook until the grain has absorbed the liquid and is tender (see approximate times). Add more water if it cooks away before the grain is done. If liquid remains when the grain is tender, drain it and reserve for stock. If it's just a bit of liquid, uncover and cook to dryness.

Rice, **millet**, **buckwheat**, and **quinoa** all cook relatively quickly without presoaking. To enhance flavor, sauté them in a small amount of oil first. Then add water (see amounts) and a pinch of salt if you wish, bring to a boil, stir, reduce the heat to low, cover tightly, and cook (see times). When the time is up, remove the pot from the heat but leave the lid in place for 10 minutes and preferably longer to allow the grain to finish steaming.

Any whole grain can be cooked with additional water for a longer period of time to achieve a softer consistency, such as for a hot breakfast cereal.

CRACKED GRAINS

Cracked grains are generally cooked either as a pilaf—with a light, fluffy texture—or as a thick, creamy porridge. Coarse particles of grain are best for pilaf; use grits (any finely cracked grain) for a smooth porridge.

Cracked wheat, **rye**, or **triticale** can all be used for pilaf. Cook by the method for rice, etc., above.

Bulgur is available in varying degrees of fineness. It has been precooked, so it only needs to be soaked. Pour boiling water as specified in the chart below (add a pinch of salt if you wish) over the dry bulgur in a bowl, cover, and leave it to steep for about 30 minutes. To keep the grains more separate, toss the dry bulgur with a teaspoon of oil before adding the water.

Cook **grits** of any grain by slowly sprinkling them into boiling water, stirring constantly. Simmer over low heat, stirring often, until the mixture is smooth and the consistency you prefer.

ROLLED GRAINS

Cook **rolled oats**, **wheat**, **rye**, **triticale**, **barley**, and **rice** by the method for grits described above, or combine the flakes and water in a pot, bring to a simmer, and cook, stirring occasionally, until done. Remove from the heat and let sit, covered, for several minutes and the cereal will hardly stick to the pot. Use 1 part grain to 2 to 3 parts water, depending on the consistency you want; more liquid produces a creamier texture. For a nuttier flavor, toast the flakes first—in a dry pan or with a little oil.

GRAIN MEALS

For a grain mush (corn, for instance), very gradually sprinkle the grain meal into rapidly boiling water while stirring constantly. Reduce the heat to low and cook, stirring constantly or at least frequently, until it reaches the desired consistency. The longer the grain cooks and the more vigorously you stir, the smoother and creamier it will be. For another method, stir the meal with an equal amount of cold water and then gradually add this paste to 3 parts boiling water, stirring constantly. Either technique should avoid a lumpy texture. One cup meal cooked in 4 cups water yields 3 to 6 servings, depending on appetites.

▼▼▼▼▼▼▪▪▪▪▪▪▪▪▪▪▪▪▪▪▪▪▪▪▼▼▼▼▼▼

Other Bread Ingredients

AFTER I DISCOVERED a delicious, wonderfully crusty, naturally-leavened bread in a market in Amherst, Massachusetts, I was eager to visit the bakers who had made it and learn some of their secrets. I found the bakery in a rural area west of Boston, and one of the two baker/owners showed me around. They were baking their bread in a brick oven, and that explained the superb crusts of their loaves. The baker told me that he and his partner had learned their craft from a master baker in Belgium. Their teacher had stressed that the most important determinant of good bread was top quality ingredients. Heeding his advice, they had left Boston, where the water was not to their liking, and chosen this site on the basis of water quality studies. Even before this visit, I was already committed to good quality ingredients, but I had taken water pretty much for granted. Now I began to take a closer look at everything in my baking larder.

Aside from grains, water or another liquid is the predominant ingredient in breads, and, without its binding function, there wouldn't be bread. Other more or less key bread components include leavens, salt, fats, and sweeteners. We've already covered grains in the previous chapter; now let's talk about some of these other ingredients. I'll also discuss textural and flavorful additions to baked goods, including dried fruits, nuts, seeds, herbs, spices, vanilla, and citrus zest.

Liquids

WATER

Water is the most elemental of liquids—and many fine breads contain nothing more than plain water for the liquid component. Depending on its source, water differs considerably in flavor, due to minerals and other substances dissolved in it. Most public utility systems treat water supplies with chemicals, such as chlorine and fluorine, and both public and private water supplies are increasingly contaminated with all sorts of toxic waste products, some of which even the treatment systems do not touch. To avoid unwelcome elements, I use reputable spring water or filtered water. You can rid tap water of chlorine by boiling it and leaving it uncovered for a day or overnight. Chlorine-free water is especially important for sourdough and natural-rise doughs.

Some minerals in water are beneficial to bread dough, but both extremely hard water and very soft water can have a detrimental effect on dough development. Since distilled water is the softest water there is, don't use it for bread dough.

MILK AND MILK SUBSTITUTES

Milk is often called for in bread recipes. Always scald milk before adding it to a dough mix to destroy proteins that might interfere with gluten development. Compared to water, milk and other milk products, such as yogurt, buttermilk, and cottage cheese, impart a lighter, softer character to the crumb and crust of a bread, and they also prolong its freshness. This is particularly true of those products with a higher fat content. You can substitute milk in a recipe that calls for water, but still use water for proofing the yeast.

I avoid milk products because of an allergy, but I sometimes use soy milk instead. As you'll see in the recipes that follow, you can substitute soy milk directly for cow's milk. Soy milk too should be scalded before adding it to bread mixes to destroy any bacteria it is hosting. I find that the soy milk I purchase in a plastic container keeps better if I scald it and transfer it to a glass jar before storing it in the refrigerator. Soy milk will produce a lustrous dark brown crust and light crumb resembling those of egg breads.

Nut "milks" can also substitute for milk. Blend 1 part cashews or blanched, peeled almonds with 4 parts water, strain if you wish, and season with a pinch of salt. For sesame milk, substitute sesame seeds. Like whole dairy products, these liquids also contain a significant amount of fat as well as other nutrients.

OTHER LIQUIDS

Vegetable or bean stocks, grain or noodle cooking water, teas, coffee, roasted grain beverages, fruit or vegetable juices, beer, and even blended leftover soups are other possibilities for bread liquids. Mildly acidic liquids, such as potato water and some fruit juices, have a somewhat accelerating effect on yeasted doughs. Raw or cooked fruits and vegetables function as liquid ingredients in breads and double as natural sweeteners too. Cooked grains and beans add moisture as well as flavor to doughs and batters.

EGGS

Eggs should be counted as a liquid ingredient in bread doughs or batters. I recommend you use fresh yard eggs from free-ranging hens because they are far superior to commercially produced eggs: the yolks are yellower, the whites firmer and less watery, and the flavor infinitely better. Test the freshness of eggs by putting them into water; eggs that float are not fresh. When adding eggs to anything, I follow a practice I learned from my dad: I break each egg into a cup or saucer to check its freshness before combining it with other ingredients—including other eggs. Eggs add loft and richness to breads. A high proportion of whole eggs in bread causes the crumb to dry out quickly; extra fat is often added to egg breads to compensate for this.

Leavens

A leaven is any substance which promotes rising of baked goods. The simplest leaven is steam, caused by the interaction of oven or pan heat and moisture in a dough or batter. Other leavening agents include yeasts, baking soda and baking powder, and beaten eggs.

YEAST

Yeast is actually a type of fungus. It thrives and proliferates in a warm, wet environment if it has starch available for nourishment. As it feeds on sugars, it multiplies; it also produces alcohol and carbon dioxide. This is what makes bread dough balloon up. In a cold, dry state, yeast remains dormant; too much heat, over about 130 degrees Fahrenheit, will kill it.

There are yeasts in the air around us all the time, and these are available for bread raising. They are the leavens for sourdough and natural-rise breads. Saved sourdough starters perpetuate the life of certain yeast strains. Natural-rise breads are leavened with whatever yeasts are present as the dough rests.

Commercial baking yeast is a particular isolated strain of yeast. It is available as compressed solid cakes or as dried granules. The best way to keep either type is to wrap it well and freeze it; the compressed form should last for three or more months; dried yeast will remain viable for three years or longer if frozen. Thawed, compressed yeast should be a tan color, have a fresh, yeasty smell, and be moist, compact, and smooth; it is probably impotent if it is dry, crumbly, and gray. To test the viability of yeast, dissolve a teaspoonful in 2 tablespoons lukewarm water, sprinkle with a teaspoon of flour, cover, and place in a warm spot; if it becomes foamy within 10 minutes, the yeast is still alive. This is known as proofing the yeast, and I recommend you do this every time you make a batch of bread.

For convenience, I use active dry yeast. Dried yeast is at least twice as active as compressed yeast, and keeps longer. I buy a reputable brand, usually Red Star, in bulk from a natural foods market. Active dry yeast is also available in ¼-ounce packets and 4-ounce jars. These sometimes contain unnecessary preservatives or accelerators, so check before you buy them. Bulk yeast is substantially less expensive than packaged yeast. Purchase yeast that has been kept in a cool, dry location and, if it isn't stamped with an expiration date, buy from a source with relatively quick turnover.

BAKING SODA AND BAKING POWDER

Both baking soda and baking powders are activated by liquid, and most baking powders have a further burst of activity when warmed. Baking soda must be combined with an acidic liquid, such as sour milk or fruit juice, to be activated; baking powders already contain both acidic and alkaline components and simply require a liquid to prompt leavening. As with yeasted breads, the risen structure of chemically leavened breads is set by the heat of baking.

You shouldn't need more than 1 teaspoon baking soda or baking powder per cup of flour in a recipe, if that much. Overuse of these leavens can cause a bitter flavor in baked goods and also diminishes their nutritional worth. Despite the surer effectiveness of baking powders containing aluminum compounds, I avoid them because of the potentially detrimental impact of aluminum on health. Instead, I use Rumford Baking Powder, an all-phosphate type. Replace your supply of baking soda and baking powder periodically to ensure a fresh flavor and effective rise in baked goods. If you can't find nonaluminum baking powder, prepare your own by combining 2 parts cream of tartar, 1 part baking soda, and 2 parts arrowroot powder. If you're also trying to cut down on sodium, substitute potassium bicarbonate (from your pharmacist) for the baking soda.

Due to decreased barometric pressure, chemical leavens possess more leavening power at high altitudes.

To counteract this effect, decrease the quantity of baking soda or baking powder approximately ¼ teaspoon for each teaspoon in the recipe for every 2500 feet over 5000 feet of altitude.

EGGS

Vigorously beaten whole eggs in a batter can cause a leavening effect: for instance, popovers and oven pancakes puff up dramatically upon contact with high oven heat. Stiffly beaten egg whites alone leaven spoonbread, and they give pancakes and other quick breads an extra boost.

Salt

Although there is very little salt in bread doughs, it serves several significant functions, and, if absent, is sorely missed. Salt brings out the flavors of the other ingredients in a bread. It promotes moisture retention and the development of a crisp crust. It also serves a preservative role in the dough by helping to prevent the growth of unwelcome bacteria.

Regular table salts all look and taste pretty much alike. Everything other than pure sodium chloride has been refined out of them, and then substances have been added to make them pure white and free running. Most table salt is fortified with potassium iodide, since iodine, an element essential for human health, may be lacking in a typical daily diet, especially in certain geographical regions.

You can also buy natural salts. Sea salts are a product of the evaporation of salt waters; other salts are mined from the earth. Natural salts vary in color, crystal size, and saltiness; they also differ somewhat in composition. Natural salts have a mild, pleasantly salty taste unlike the burning harshness of refined table salt.

For its minerals and trace elements, I use natural sea salt produced by sun-drying unpolluted sea water. Lima Sea Salt, imported from Belgium, is a good brand. You can get it at natural foods stores or from mail order sources. To minimize caking, store salt in a tightly closed container in a cool, dry spot.

The amount of salt to add to bread dough depends to some extent on individual taste preferences. However, with yeasted doughs, keep in mind that salt will slow the action of the yeast, and consequently the development of the dough. Also, be sure to take into account the saltiness of other ingredients that you are incorporating into the bread. Miso or tamari may substitute for salt altogether.

Whether to add the salt to the flour or to dissolve it in some of the liquid first depends on the size of the salt crystals. Any fine-grained salt can go directly in with the flour; a large-crystal salt needs predissolving, since the crystals will not dissolve in the dough despite mixing.

Fats

Fats are optional in breads, but contribute richness, tenderness, smoothness, and moistness to the crumb. They also prevent bread from drying out quickly. Too much fat, however, gives a bread a heavy, sticky texture and a greasy taste. Some breads, such as French bread, are traditionally fat-free.

Any form of fat has pretty much the same effect on dough, though there are valid reasons for selecting one type over another. One criterion is health; for most recipes, liquid vegetable oils are preferable to butter and margarine, which contain a greater proportion of saturated fats. However, these solid fats do excel at producing flakiness in biscuits and pastries.

I use minimally refined oils because oil refinement may involve high heat and various chemicals which deplete nutrients; mechanically extracted or "coldpressed" oils are nutritionally superior to highly refined ones. I choose an oil for a particular bread mainly on the basis of taste: a light, delicate oil when I want a subtle flavor; a stronger tasting oil when I want a more heavy-handed effect—olive oil in Italian bread, for instance. For solid fat, I favor preservative-free, unsalted soy margarine. Salted butter and margarine tend to be too salty for my taste. If you substitute salted butter or margarine in a recipe which specifies unsalted fat or vice versa, remember to adjust the salt in the recipe accordingly.

Whatever fat you use, freshness is absolutely essential. As soon as fat is exposed to air, oxidation begins, and fat that is the least bit rancid cannot hide in breads any more successfully than anywhere else in cooking. Buy oils in relatively small quantities and keep them securely closed in a consistently cool pantry or in the refrigerator to preserve freshness. Keep surplus butter and margarine in the freezer.

Sweeteners

Fresh whole grains have subtly sweet flavors. The fermentation that takes place in yeasted breads enhances this intrinsic sweetness. Added sweeteners tend to mask the natural sweetness of grains and even to counteract the flavor-inducing effects of fermentation. Since yeast will feed on simple sugars before breaking down the starch of grains, added sweeteners accelerate the yeast's activity and promote swift rising of dough, which causes it to be underdeveloped in both texture and flavor. An overabundance of sweetener in yeasted dough will actually slow down both the activity of the yeast and the development of the gluten, so that especially sweet breads take longer to make than usual. The trend toward adding sweeteners to breads likely paralleled the escalation of grain refinement, which not only strips grains of much of their intrinsic sweetness but also hinders fermentation. Quick breads don't have the benefit of fermentation for flavor, so sweeteners have a more significant role to play when these are meant to taste sweet.

To prepare sweet breads of any kind, I often prefer to add sweet-tasting spices, such as cinnamon, cardamom, and coriander, or dried fruits or sweet-tasting fresh fruits or vegetables rather than a lot of a sweetener. Unsweetened yeasted doughs can be combined with sweet fillings, and, of course, baked breads can be served with sweet toppings.

When I do add a sweetener to bread, I do it in a small quantity and always consider the flavor and nutritional quality of the sweetener. Added sweeteners do promote browning and a tender crumb, but even a modest amount of a strong-flavored sweetener such as molasses or buckwheat honey will dominate the flavor of a bread. I favor honey, maple syrup, molasses, barley malt, or rice syrup over any type of refined sugar; I keep refined sugar on hand only for feeding hummingbirds and freshening cut flowers. I recently discovered a totally unrefined sugar called Sucanat, short for "sugar cane natural," which is simply the dehydrated juice from organically grown sugar cane. I like to use it or date sugar, which is ground-up pitted dried dates, for streusel toppings and cinnamon buns.

HONEY

There's a lot more to honey than clover! Bees gather the nectar of a wide variety of flowering plants, and, as honey connoisseurs readily attest, honeys vary greatly in color and flavor and these characteristics come through in baked items. Honey in bread helps to maintain moistness, and unrefined honeys supposedly function as natural preservatives in bread. Store honey in tightly closed jars in a cool cupboard. To convert crystallized honey back to a liquid form, remove the lid and place the jar in a pan of water over low heat. Honey and other liquid sweeteners are easier to measure accurately if the jar is heated in a water bath first.

MAPLE SYRUP

Unlike honey, maple syrup maintains all of its nutrients even at high oven temperatures. Less expensive Grade B syrup contributes a more assertive flavor than Grade A syrup; I prefer Grade B for all uses. Keep opened containers of maple syrup in the refrigerator to prevent fermentation or molding. For economy, I purchase maple syrup by the gallon. Immediately after opening the container, I heat the syrup, pour it into hot, sterile canning jars, and cap them with sterile canning lids; I check to be sure the lids have sealed before storing the cooled jars in a cupboard.

MOLASSES

I use unsulfured molasses to avoid sulfur, an agent of sugar refinement, which is questionable healthwise. Blackstrap molasses contributes little sweetness but a dark color and unique flavor to breads.

GRAIN SYRUPS

Grain syrups are other sweeteners for breads. Rice syrup is sweet but mild. It won't crystallize, though it may harden if cold; soften it the same way you decrystallize honey. Since it has a high proportion of complex carbohydrates, rice syrup doesn't cause a sugar rush like that of sweeteners composed of simple sugars. Barley malt syrup is made from whole barley which has been sprouted, then roasted and extracted as a liquid. It is very thick and sticky and has a somewhat sweet, rich flavor. Look for grain syrups in natural foods markets. Store them in a cool, dark cupboard.

Special Ingredients

DRIED FRUITS

Dried fruits, particularly if they are presoaked or cooked, contribute moisture as well as flavor to breads, and their flavor is intensified if you use their soaking or cooking water as part of the liquid. Dried fruits also provide sweetness and texture. Add them in a diced form or as smooth purées. Some dried fruits are treated with sulfur in the process of preserving them; I avoid sulfured fruits for the same reasons I steer clear of sul-

fured molasses. Many unsulfured, even organically grown, dried fruits are readily available now. Store dried fruits in a cool pantry or in the refrigerator.

HERBS AND SPICES

Flavoring with herbs and spices requires a careful hand and nose; a little bit goes a long way and, while the right amount of an herb or spice can have a sublime effect, too much can be dreadful. Also keep in mind that the flavor of herbs and spices tends to become stronger with time in baked goods. Combining the flavors of different herbs and spices is another aspect of the art of seasoning which is best learned through experience and experimentation. Indian curry powders are examples of intricate, subtle spice blends. In addition to flavor and aroma, herbs and spices may also contribute to the texture of baked goods.

I generally use about twice the amount of a fresh herb as a dried one, since drying concentrates the flavor. Pick or strip the leaves off the stems of fresh herbs and mince them to enhance and distribute the flavor effectively; crush or grind dried ones for the same purpose. Sautéing or toasting herbs and spices intensifies their flavor; I like to roast cumin, caraway, fennel, and other seeds before adding them to doughs or batters.

To prolong their freshness, stand the cut end of bunches of fresh herbs in water in a container, cover loosely with a plastic bag, and refrigerate. Dried herbs and spices keep best in tightly closed jars in a dry, cool, relatively dark location. Unground herbs and spices maintain their zestiness longer than ground ones. Buy small amounts and use them up within a few months.

One of the great pleasures for me in living in different regions of the country has been discovering indigenous herbs and vegetables. In the Southeast, there were lessons in greens, beans, and peas. In Texas, I've received an education in peppers, and cilantro and pericon, also called sweet marigold or Texas tarragon, have become two of my favorite seasonings.

NUTS AND SEEDS

Nuts and seeds may be added to bread doughs and batters whole, chopped, or ground, as smooth nut or seed butters, or as "milks" (see page 16). For yeasted breads, it's usually best to knead nuts and seeds into the dough after a sponge stage and perhaps a bowl rise as well; by then, the dough is strong and stretchable enough so that it can rise well despite these additions. Nuts are also used in fillings for breads, and seeds are attractive, tasty garnishes on loaves and rolls. Whatever their form, nuts and seeds add to the nutritional value as well as the fat content of breads and other baked goods.

Light roasting crisps seeds and nuts, amplifies their flavor, and renders them more digestible. I toast nuts on a baking sheet in a 300- to 350-degree oven and roast seeds in an ungreased iron skillet over low to moderate heat on top of the stove, stirring or agitating the pan frequently. In either case, watch closely to prevent burning!

Like other ingredients containing a high percentage of fat, nuts are especially prone to rancidity. Uncracked nuts will keep fresh for a long period, particularly if they are stored in a cool, dry place, but shelled nuts should be tightly wrapped and refrigerated. Nuts freeze well, though their vitamin E is sacrificed in the process.

Nuts from different sources can differ in quality. Many undergo bleaching and other processes which improve their cosmetic appeal but may adversely affect flavor and nutritional value. Organically grown and mechanically hulled nuts and seeds are gradually becoming available in retail outlets.

VANILLA

Pure vanilla extract is prepared from vanilla beans, the seed pods of certain tropical orchids. Though more expensive than synthetically produced vanilla flavorings, pure vanilla extract is far superior in flavor and aroma. To preserve its potency, store it in a tightly closed, dark glass bottle in a closed cupboard.

CITRUS ZEST

The outermost rind of citrus fruits, called the zest, adds piquancy to breads and other baked goods. Since these fruits are often injected and sprayed with various chemical substances, use organically grown ones and rinse them well. Rub the peel lightly on the finest shredding surface of a stainless steel grater to prepare zest.

CHAPTER 3

Breadtime Tools

W ITHIN A SHORT PERIOD of time, I learned firsthand about the two extremes of a faulty oven. I was visiting friends and planned to prepare a special meal for them, including yeasted rolls. I made up the dough, oversaw its risings, and cut and shaped it into rolls; after they rose, I popped them into the preheated oven and set the timer. When the buzzer went off and I opened the door, I couldn't believe my eyes: grapefruit-sized balloons of semi-raw dough filled the oven! Unbeknownst to my hosts, an electric element of their range had expired; this revelation explained several other recent baking flops as well.

Not long after this experience, I moved into a new apartment and was eager to make my first batch of bread—a symbolic settling act for me. I contentedly prepared the dough, then turned on the oven and waited for it to come up to temperature. I arranged the risen loaves inside and set the timer. A few minutes later, I heard a small explosion and whirled around to see flames leaping out from under the gas burners; the oven had never stopped heating! The simple moral of these accounts is that ovens can and do fail, and a mal-adjusted oven throws a severe kink into a baking day.

Basic Tools

▪ A **reliable oven** is one of several fundamental items that you cannot happily manage without. Old timers who baked successfully with wood-burning stoves acquired the knack for stoking them effectively. Those of us who depend upon modern gas or electric ranges must also be vigilant. As my anecdotes illustrate, any oven is susceptible to malfunctions.

One way to keep tabs on the accuracy of your oven is to place a **high-quality oven thermometer** inside and check to see that its reading matches the temperature you set. It isn't unusual for oven mechanisms, such as thermostats or heating coils, to fail gradually; with an accurate thermometer, you can determine when something is out of kilter.

▪ A **large, thick-sided ceramic bowl** is an asset for bread making since it retains warmth and insulates dough from drafts as it rises; also, its weight helps to keep it in place during mixing. You don't have to invest a lot; I found my three "Real McCoy" bowls in graduated sizes at a hardware store and the five-and-dime. Stainless steel bowls are another alternative, though they aren't as effective insulators as ceramic ones. Be sure your bowl will accommodate a lot of dough expansion; a dough should be able even to triple in size without reaching the top. My bowls have capacities of about 3 quarts, 5 quarts, and 8 quarts, respectively; I use the middle-sized one the most—for two- to three-loaf batches of bread.

▪ At least one **large, sturdy wooden mixing spoon** is essential; stirring bread dough requires a durable implement. I have a collection of wooden spoons of various shapes and sizes; I reserve a few of them for non-garlic and non-onion projects since these flavors persist in the wood.

▪ **Measuring cups** for dry and liquid ingredients and **measuring spoons** are conveniences—with a good eye, you might get by without them, as many of our ancestors may have done. I have 1-, 2-, and 4-cup glass measures, a couple of sets of ¼- to 1-cup stainless steel measuring cups, and multiple stainless steel measuring spoons. I find it's handier to separate cups or spoons which come fastened together on a ring so that I don't have to wash them all when I use one.

▪ **Dough scrapers** are extraordinarily simple yet invaluable baking tools. A plastic U-shaped scraper with one rounded and one straight edge is especially effective for removing bread dough and scraps from the bowl before kneading. A metal dough scraper—a square of sheet metal with a wooden grip along one side—is extremely helpful for clearing the work surface when kneading dough and rolling pastry and also for cleaning up.

▪ For kneaded breads, a **kneading surface** of some type is indispensable. Ideally, it should be at least 2 feet square. I prepare dough on my baking table, a small, sturdy maple table. Just under the top surface it has two pull-out boards that cannot withstand kneading but expand the table surface to hold baking sheets, pans, and other lightweight items while I work; beneath the table extenders are two shallow drawers for small utensils. Originally, there were large flour bins underneath the drawers, but they were gone before I acquired the table. The wooden surface of the table is now covered with a piece of marble, cut to size from a large slab purchased from a New England family that had owned a drug store for several generations. The marble was formerly the front panel of an elegant soda fountain; I suspect that many older pharmacies have these valuable remnants of past lives collecting dust in their basements. The smooth, cool surface is splendid for kneading dough, rolling out pastry, cutting biscuits, and other baking activities.

The most charming account of a marble work surface I have heard was the recollection of Katherine Tucker Windham on National Public Radio about the marble pastry slab in her Southern childhood home. She remembered that most kitchens in the town were equipped with a marble slab, salvaged when the decor of the drugstore's old soda fountain was updated. But her family's marble surface was unique, because it was a tombstone! For everyday projects, such as bread, biscuits, and pie dough, the smooth back of the stone faced up. However, when a special occasion came along, the stone was turned over and its delicate rosebuds, leaves, doves, and other intricate carvings were pressed into service for decorating candy or fancy cakes or pastries.

Any stable wooden table surface, particularly one that has been planed, sanded, and oiled, is fine to knead on, as is a large wooden breadboard, which can be temporarily anchored to a table or counter by placing a damp towel or rubber mat underneath. Again, since wood is an absorbent material, avoid chopping strongly flavored foods, such as onions and garlic, on your kneading surface, unless you don't mind these flavors permeating all of your breads. Rub oil into the wood periodically to prevent it from drying out.

A kneading surface should just fit under your fully outstretched arm; measure to the heel of your hand, not to your finger tips. You want to be able to work from above the dough without bending much at the waist. If the only available surface, such as a counter top, is too high, find something to stand on: a shallow wooden box or milk crate—something that will bring you up to the appropriate height. A surface that is too low is more of a problem since it is difficult to adjust and to adjust to; bending over it may strain your lower back. Working on a surface of optimum height for you may make a significant difference in your kneading technique and ultimately in your bread.

- In lieu of a flour sifter, I use a medium-sized **fine-mesh stainless steel strainer** for sifting. This implement is much easier to clean than a regular flour sifter and serves a lot of other culinary functions as well. I also have a smaller strainer for sifting lumps out of small measures of salt, baking powder, baking soda, and spices; this one doubles as a tea strainer.

- You'll need a **rolling pin** for biscuits, English muffins, and kneaded flat breads, and to prepare filled doughs. My rolling pin is slender and graceful but surprisingly heavy, fashioned from rosewood by a woodworker in Vermont; just holding it gives me pleasure.

- A **blender** is just about unbeatable for achieving absolutely smooth liquid combinations such as popover and crêpe batters. A really basic machine is fine; until recently, I used my mother's original, one-speed Waring model, which began its long career making milkshakes in the early 1950s.

- You'll need several **unnapped muslin or linen tea towels** for covering doughs to protect them from moisture loss throughout the bread-making process. In fabric stores and mill-end outlets, you may find this kind of toweling sold by the yard; cut towels to the length you desire and hem the ends.

- **Baking sheets** and **pans** are required, but you may exercise a lot of flexibility here, since bread can be baked in a wide variety of containers, including pottery or Pyrex casseroles, assorted baking dishes, and stainless steel or enamel mixing bowls. Springform cake pans permit especially easy removal of baked loaves, though an adequately baked loaf in a sufficiently greased pan should slip out readily anyway. There is nothing mandatory or magical about rectangular bread pans; they simply mold loaves that can be cut easily into traditional square slices. Also, several rectangular pans may fit more efficiently into the oven than those of other shapes.

Breads baked in sided containers will have straighter, less crusty sides than freestanding items. Since I'm a crust fan, I often bake freestanding loaves and rolls on stainless steel, tinned steel, or blackened steel baking sheets or in pie plates. All you really need for these unpanned items is an ovenproof flat surface. Clay oven tiles and baking stones give breads wonderful bottom crusts.

My prize loaf pan is a very long and narrow tinned steel one made by my great-great-grandfather, who was a tinsmith in the Midwest. Well-seasoned tinned steel pans of any shape conduct and hold heat well and therefore promote desirable browning on the bottoms and sides of loaves. Allow these pans to darken with age; don't try to scrub them back to shiny newness. Wash them gently and put them in a warm oven to dry.

I try to avoid aluminum pans altogether, because of aluminum's potentially harmful effects on health. Another drawback to aluminum is that it tends to reflect rather than absorb heat, especially when it is shiny, causing burned bottoms on freestanding breads and poor browning on panned ones. I would also advise against using tin cans for baking or steaming breads, though many of us delighted in their versatility in the past. I changed my mind because of the possibility that the lead solder used to seal can seams may leach into doughs and batters.

- You may want to invest in some particularly useful specialized baking pans. **Muffin tins** can be used for yeasted rolls and even small popovers as well as regular muffins; I prefer tinned steel muffin tins with either six or twelve 3-inch cups. Tinned or blackened steel **popover pans** definitely make the best popovers and also work well for large muffins. A **decorative tube pan**, such as a fluted kugelhopf pan, makes fancy sweet breads or coffee cakes even fancier. A **14- to 15-inch shallow, round pan** is just right for large round loaves, pizzas, and turnovers arranged back-to-back; my blackened steel pan produces great bottom crusts.

- You can line baking pans with **baking parchment**, a special type of paper that generally comes on a roll, 20 or more feet long and 15 inches wide—the length of a standard home-sized baking sheet. It eliminates the need for greasing pans—and also for scrubbing them later; freestanding loaves, rolls, biscuits, cookies, and other items bake directly on the paper without sticking. One piece of parchment can be reused for several bakings. Look for it in cookware shops.

- For stove-top breads such as pancakes, crumpets, tortillas, and chapatis, you'll need a **griddle** and a **shallow skillet** or two. I prefer cast-iron pans, since they are economical, even-heating, and versatile—they can be used in the oven as well as on top of the range, and they require little greasing once they are well seasoned. My kitchen somehow inherited an **electric frying pan**, which I find especially useful for cooking English muffins.

- **Waffle irons** come in many makes and models. Mine is a Scandinavian cast-iron type which heats on top of the stove. It works well on a gas burner; I would

guess that it would be more difficult to regulate on an electric range, since most everything is.

▪ A **sturdy, long-bladed serrated bread knife** with a wavy, not toothed, cutting edge is best for cutting bread. Saw gently back and forth rather than pressing down hard as you cut. I have an American-made knife with an oak handle and a stainless steel blade that continues to slice well even after more than ten years of daily use. A **heavy Chinese-style cleaver** is my preference for cutting pizza and flat breads; slide them onto a cutting board first.

▪ Probably the most specialized baking utensil I have is a **baking cloche**. This ingenious device functions as a pan and miniature brick oven rolled into one. It consists of two pieces of unglazed earthenware: the base is a round, 10-inch flat dish with a 1-inch lip around the edge; the top is a high bell-shaped piece that rests on the lip of the base to form a closed container. Although the dimensions limit the size and shape of the loaf that it can accommodate, the baking cloche is a terrific contraption. A loaf baked in it emerges superbly browned and crusty in comparison to one made from the same dough baked in an open container.

You can improvise a baking cloche by inverting an earthenware bowl over a loaf on a baking sheet or on baking tiles, but the surface of a glazed bowl may suffer from the high oven heat. Another improvisational possibility is to turn a large, unglazed plant pot without a drainage hole in the bottom over the bread. The advantages of the cloche over these alternatives are the snug fit of the base and top and the handle on top of the bell with which it can be lifted off easily; the latter is a distinct safety feature. When not in use for baking, the cloche can serve as a bread box.

Other Useful Tools

A number of other small items are less essential for successful baking but play significant bit parts in making various breads. These are mostly common kitchen or household utensils that you may already have around.

Their order of appearance in the following list doesn't indicate greater or lesser importance.

▪ A **food or "chef's" thermometer** consists of a thin metal spike with a round temperature dial on one end. It gives an almost instant reading and can reassure you about the temperature of the water for the yeast; you can also use it to measure the temperature of other ingredients and doughs.

▪ A **portable room thermometer** may sound like a strange bread-making tool, but room temperature is a key factor in the rising of yeasted doughs. By moving a dough to a warmer or cooler spot—as determined by the thermometer—you can regulate the length of time it will take to rise.

▪ A **scale** that goes up to at least 5 pounds is useful for portioning dough for loaves, rolls, and so on, as well as for weighing pasta and vegetables; now I wonder how I managed without one in my kitchen.

▪ A **timer** helps keep track of baking times; you may have one built into your oven already. An extra timer is an asset when more than one project is underway at the same time.

▪ A **ruler** is useful for determining the dimensions of pans and of rolled doughs; my kitchen ruler is an easily washed flexible plastic one.

▪ An **atomizer** or plant mister is handy for dampening towels and spraying loaves before and during baking to promote crisp crusts. Be sure to use one that has had only water in it—no plant fertilizers, etc.

▪ **Plastic or rubber spatulas** in different sizes make it possible to retrieve everything to the last drop. Use only heat resistant scrapers for hot substances to avoid consuming plastic compounds.

▪ **Tongs** are a safe means of holding chapatis over a burner to encourage them to puff up.

▪ A **ladle** is my favorite way of transferring batter from bowl to griddle, though a glass measuring cup, pitcher, or gravy boat serves the same purpose.

▪ A **pancake turner** or **metal spatula** is necessary for turning griddle-baked items.

▪ **Pastry brushes** work well for applying glazes to breads and rolls and oil to griddles. Use soft bristles or feather brushes on risen dough.

▪ A **wire whisk** combines liquid ingredients and whips up egg whites in a jiffy. Whisks are available in assorted sizes.

■ I use my **electric mixer** for preparing batters and beating egg whites and my **food processor** for purée-ing, preparing biscuit and pastry doughs, and many other bread-related and cooking tasks, but I don't make yeasted doughs in either one. I'm not philosophically opposed to mechanical mixing; in fact, I think it is the only sensible approach to baking in large quantities. For home baking though, I prefer to mix and knead by hand. Neither machine can handle more than a small batch of dough, but more to the point, using them for kneading would deprive me of one of the aspects of home bread making that I enjoy the most. If you do try machine kneading, take care not to overwork the dough, and handle the dough at the end in order to feel its condition.

■ Aside from a food processor, a **pastry blender** is the most efficient way to cut butter or margarine into flour for biscuits or pastry dough.

■ A **cake tester**—a fine, rigid wire about 6 inches long with a loop on one end—provides a reliable way to test the readiness of quick loaves, muffins, biscuits, and scones, as well as cakes; when it is inserted into the center of a baked item and comes out without any bat-ter or dough adhering, the item is sufficiently baked. A clean broomstraw can serve the same function.

■ A **stainless steel grater** with a variety of grating surfaces is an effective and space-saving device for pre-paring lemon or orange zest, fresh ginger, nutmeg, and raw vegetables or fruits for bread doughs and batters.

■ **Sharp-edged metal cutters** give biscuits and English muffins a clean edge which promotes even ris-ing. Biscuits are usually 2 to 3 inches in diameter and English muffins are typically 4 inches across.

■ **Crumpet rings** are necessary for making these teatime treats. Buy stainless steel ones in a cookware shop or improvise by cutting both ends out of squat 4-inch cans, such as the kind tuna fish comes in; try to find cans without lead-soldered seams.

■ A **mortar and pestle** or a **spice grinder** brings out the best in dried herbs and spices.

■ Sharp **razor blades** are best for slashing loaves and rolls before baking. Double-edged blades require a bit more care to use safely but they do last twice as long as single-edged ones.

■ **Wire or slatted wooden cooling racks** are ideal for cooling all types of breads since they allow air cir-culation on all sides.

■ You'll need a **steamer** of some kind—or an effec-tive makeshift one—for steamed breads; this is also a good way to warm bread and add a bit of moisture too.

■ Lastly, keep **potholders** handy for hot pans.

Perhaps the Most Critical Tool of All

So, bread making doesn't require much in the way of specialized equipment, though certain items are almost indispensable. Others make baking tasks easier or more enjoyable or the final product more aesthetically pleas-ing. Still, no amount of equipment can make up for a lack of forethought and planning, which may be the most important tool of all.

Because many utensils serve multiple purposes in the kitchen, you'll need to check to be sure that neces-sary or preferable items for bread making are in good condition and clean and available. Your large ceramic bread bowl may be filled with a mixture of grains for a batch of granola; the casserole that molds such a nicely shaped loaf may be in the refrigerator holding the left-overs of last evening's main dish; your kneading sur-face, alias the kitchen table, may be littered with break-fast dishes, library books, assorted mail and such.

A small amount of planning and preparation may prevent annoying interruptions and delays and keep your bread making moving along smoothly. Properly equipped and organized, you will be freer to enjoy the activity and to approach it more creatively.

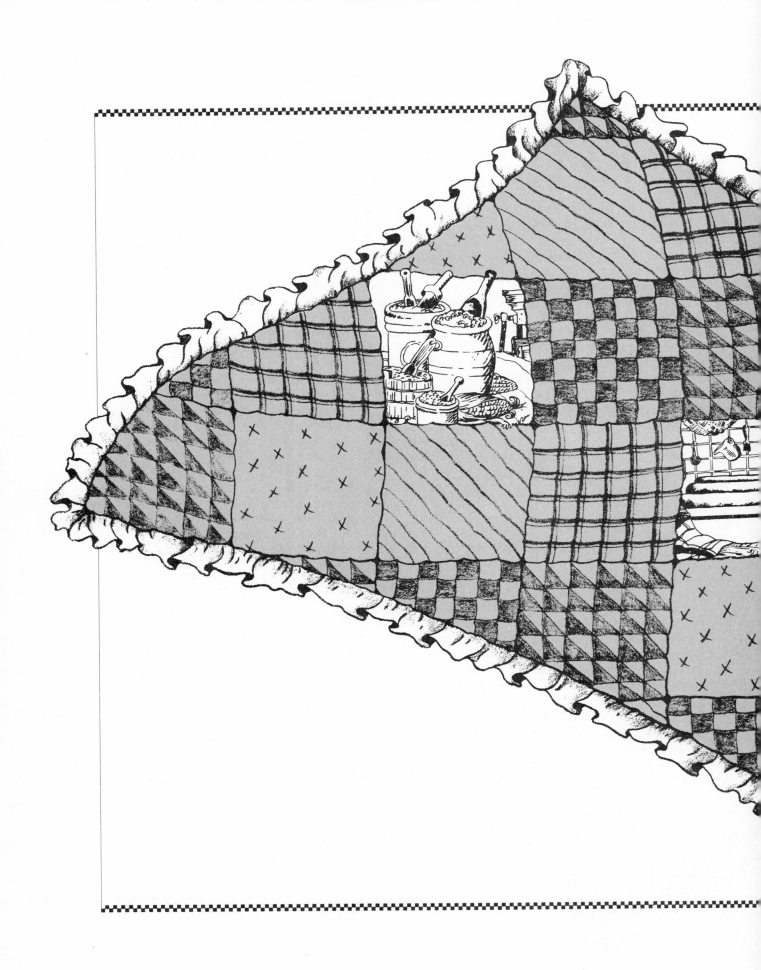

GETTING READY FOR BREAD

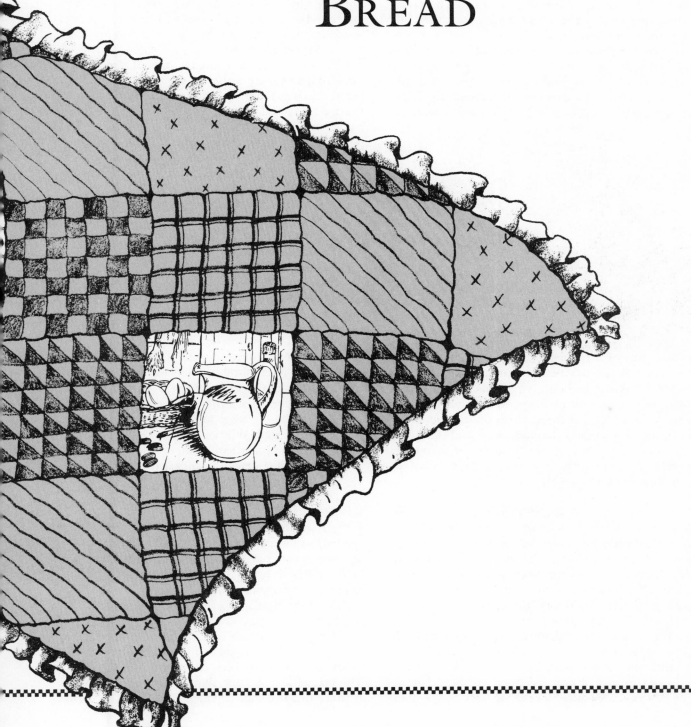

▼▼▼

IDIDN'T GROW UP EATING splendid, warm-from-the-oven, yeasted loaves or even fresh bakery bread, but because of my parents' preferences, I was spared an exclusive diet of the white balloon bread which became prevalent in the '50s and '60s. There was always some whole wheat bread in our house; the kind I remember in particular was Monks' bread, a somewhat coarse-grained, nutty-flavored loaf, which somehow seemed less commercial than other packaged brands. Its name alone held an exotic appeal for me; I envisioned silent, heavily robed men kneading, shaping, and baking the dough in a secluded monastery.

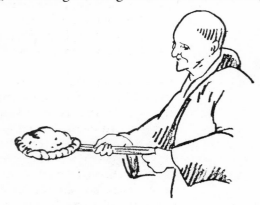

Over the years, I've experienced a multitude of breads, many of them memorable. I've found them in all sorts of places: bakeries, restaurants, and cafes, of course; but also at the homes of friends and friends of friends and through my own experimentation. Each experience has added something to my understanding of bread, and I like to think that each new bread I discover contributes to my baking education. In the following chapters, I'll retrace my experiences with breads and share what I've learned with you.

The homemade breads familiar to me as a child were all quick breads. We had pancakes or waffles for breakfast on weekend mornings, hardly thinking of them as breads at all. Economical dinners paired cornbread with hearty soups. Biscuits with honey or dumplings accompanied beef stews. Banana or date-nut bread served as dessert or Sunday night supper. These breads became my first baking projects.

The summer after I graduated from high school, I waitressed in an Italian restaurant on Mackinac Island, a picturesque resort in northern Michigan. A large family from Chicago owned and operated the business. Iggy Palermo, the patriarch, and his oldest son, Frank,

made the pizza dough for the Sunday night special. On Wednesday evenings, the locals gathered for hoagies on their fresh long rolls; the aroma of the just-baked dough was overwhelmingly enticing, and the other waitresses and I always managed to sneak a few warm loaves and some butter and jam back to our rooming house quarters. This was my introduction to fresh homemade yeasted bread.

The next year, my eyes were opened wide to the extraordinary variety and exquisite flavors possible in baked goods as I journeyed about eastern and western Europe for several months. I traveled from one baked marvel to another: chewy, thick-crusted sour ryes and pumpernickels; long, crisp baguettes; flaky croissants and golden brioche; paper-thin crêpes folded around delectable fillings; delicate pastries; and even East Indian flat breads in London.

My initial hands-on experience with yeasted doughs came a couple of years later, while spending several weeks with my college roommate on her parents' farm, where making yeasted coffee cakes, or buns as they called them, was routine. Ann and her mother showed me how to prepare yeasted dough and, along with her father and brother, provided me with my first critiques.

After college, settled in my own apartment, I began to explore baking in earnest, and my repertoire of both quick and yeasted breads expanded. At the same time, the emerging health foods movement changed the way I thought about ingredients. I was amazed by the natural foods supermarkets and whole grain bakeries that I came upon during a trip to California; I had no idea such places existed. When I returned home, I joined others who had made similar discoveries and became involved with the newly organized Ithaca Real Food Co-op.

A friend shared her sourdough starter with me, and this gift catapulted me into another realm of baking. First, I incorporated starter into quick breads and yeasted breads for added flavor; later, I began to use sourdough batter as the sole leaven in breads. I discovered sourdough baking to be a family legacy when my father told me that his mother maintained a "sour" for the bread she regularly baked on their fruit farm near Salt Lake City, Utah.

A move to western Massachusetts exposed me to natural-rise baking. A tiny Amherst restaurant served sandwiches on thin slices of natural-rise rice bread. This bread had a pleasant, slightly sour flavor and a satisfying substance and chewiness, and unlike the bricklike unleavened breads I had tasted in the '60s, it had risen. When a friend offered me a piece of even better natural-rise rice bread from a bakery in Boston, I was so impressed that I traveled to spend a day with the baker and observe the process. Then I began experimenting. First I developed an unpasteurized cider and rice bread; the fermenting liquid gave the fermenting grain an extra boost. I went on to work out breads that relied only on the natural fermentation of simple doughs for rise. Most recently, I've been making natural-rise breads boosted with a special cultured grain.

My experiences with flat breads don't fit into the chronological picture quite so neatly; they have slipped in around the edges of my exploration of other techniques. I've been making all kinds of them a lot since I've been living in warm climates, as they require minimal baking or can be cooked on top of the stove.

Looking back, I see that my bread-making endeavors evolved from breads requiring the use of modern day leavenings to those that are fundamentally primitive—sort of like moving backward in time. I began with quick breads, then progressed to commercially yeasted, sourdough, natural-rise, and flat breads. Perhaps ironically, my earliest breads, quick breads, depended more upon advances in bread-making technology than technique, while breads which came later, such as natural-rise breads, relied much more on tech-

nique than technology. This was a logical learning sequence. By following the course of my own learning pattern, the next five chapters are designed to gradually develop the technical proficiency necessary for you to master each successive bread-making challenge. One thing I should make clear: I haven't given up on one kind of bread as I've added another; I'm still making breads that I started with as a child in addition to trying out new ones.

As you read on, bear in mind that masterful baking of any kind requires more than recipes. In a modest Greek restaurant in Toronto, I was served the most delectable baklava I had ever tasted. I excitedly asked if I might have the recipe. The cook sent it out with the waitress, along with an admonition that "it wouldn't come out the same." A skilled professional baker I met refuses to divulge her recipes for breads and pastries at all. Like the Greek baker, she feels that lists of ingredients and instructions don't guarantee quality replications of her excellent products.

Rest assured, you'll gradually feel at home with bread-making techniques. But for genuine understanding, delve beyond the physical methods and ask questions. For instance: what is actually happening in the bread batter or dough to make it rise? What are the effects of including particular ingredients, using certain utensils and methods? What effects do external factors such as time, temperature, humidity, and altitude have on your bread? The answers will draw the various aspects of baking together into a meaningful whole for you. On a tangible level, this integrated body of knowledge may differentiate between mediocre and truly remarkable baked goods. So, try out these recipes, but keep attuned to the larger context of information accompanying them. Hopefully, it will both assure your success with these particular breads and also serve as a springboard for your own creative baking.

CHAPTER 4

Quick Breads

As a small child, I would help my mother and grandmother measure and sift ingredients, stir up batters and spoon them into loaf pans and muffin tins, roll and cut out biscuits, and ladle batter onto the griddle for pancakes. Sometimes they gave me leftover batter and bits of dough to make miniature muffins and quarter-sized biscuits in my toy baking tins. Later, I made the life-sized items on my own from start to finish and basked in my family's praise.

My first breads were all quick breads because these were the breads that were made in my home. Quick breads are a good starting point for any beginning baker because they can be made in a hurry, entail only simple and straightforward processes, and provide almost immediate gratification. But even experienced bakers find it pays to have quick breads in their repertoires so they can produce breads on short notice.

Most quick breads are leavened with baking soda and/or baking powder; these include loaves, muffins, pancakes, waffles, biscuits, and scones. These chemically leavened breads are the youngsters in baking history. They became popular in the United States in the last half of the nineteenth century when baking pow-

ders first became readily available. These leavens, long-keeping and easy to use, obviated the need for maintaining starters and fussing with live yeasts. No doubt their time-saving features were highly appealing. Quick breads have since carved out a permanent niche in home baking.

INGREDIENTS FOR QUICK BREADS

Soft, low-gluten or pastry wheat flour is preferable for quick breads. Other low-gluten flours, such as oat, corn, barley, buckwheat, rice, or millet flour, are appropriate as well and provide variety in flavors and textures. Bread flour may be included but tends to cause a tough texture if used exclusively. If you can't find whole wheat pastry flour, an all-purpose whole wheat flour is the best alternative.

Any liquid may be used in quick breads if you're using baking powder for leavening, but baking soda must be combined with an acidic liquid for effective leavening. Fruit juices are one option; try to find organically grown citrus fruits, particularly if you are using the zest as well as the juice. Eggs add moisture, richness, and cohesiveness, and are leavening agents too, especially when they have been separated and the whites beaten. If you add extra fresh fruits, vegetables, and cooked grains, take into account their moisture content and reduce the amount of liquid specified in the recipe. Conversely, add a bit more liquid if you increase the proportion of solids by adding extra nuts or other dry ingredients.

Salt's only role in quick breads is to enhance flavor. Chemical leavens containing sodium also taste salty, so a small amount of salt suffices. One teaspoon of baking soda or baking powder per cup of flour in a recipe is adequate for leavening purposes and isn't likely to produce a bitter or metallic taste which can result from adding too much.

Through much experimentation, I have found that it is possible to make quick breads that are healthful yet still delicious. They don't have to be laden with fat, cholesterol, and refined sweeteners to taste good. I generally use liquid vegetable oils rather than butter and other solid fats, and I have found that only modest amounts are needed for good flavor and texture. I use honey, maple syrup, molasses, rice syrup, barley malt, and Sucanat rather than refined sugar for quick breads that are reasonably but not cloyingly sweet. Fresh and dried fruits, fruit juices, and even some vegetables—carrots, winter squash, and yams, for instance—also contribute sweetness to these breads. Nuts and seeds add richness and crunch. I sometimes use tofu in lieu of eggs as a binding agent and soy milk in place of milk; these provide nutrients yet cut down on fat and cholesterol. Low-fat milk and yogurt and buttermilk are healthier dairy choices than sour cream or cream. Keep these things in mind when you want to modify recipes for traditional quick breads to make them more wholesome.

MIXING THE BATTER

Precise measurements are important for success in making quick breads, and improvising is best limited to simple substitutions of like ingredients. Bring all of the ingredients to room temperature before mixing to ensure that the bread bakes evenly; this is especially crucial for loaves.

Putting together most quick breads involves three swift procedures. First, sift together the dry ingredients, stirring the bran back into the mixture if it separates out in the sifting process. If they are at all lumpy, sift the salt, baking soda and/or baking powder, and any ground spices through a small, fine-mesh strainer before sifting them along with the flour. Next, in a separate container, blend or beat together the liquid ingredients. Finally, combine the dry and wet mixtures all at once and stir gently and briefly—just enough to form a slightly lumpy batter. Overmixing tends to make quick breads heavy and tough.

Once the batter or dough is made, it should be used at once; don't try to store or hold it. Leavening begins as soon as the dry ingredients have been moistened and will quickly run its course; for optimum rising, bake immediately after mixing. For almost instant quick breads, you can prepare the dry ingredients and wet ingredients separately ahead of time and then combine them just before baking.

Loaves and Muffins

Quick loaves and muffins are made from relatively thick batters that can be used interchangeably. That is, a loaf batter can generally be baked up as muffins and vice versa. Prepare the batter by following the basic three-step procedure outlined above. Stir any coarse dry ingredients, such as grain flakes, thoroughly with the sifted mixture. Add dried fruits and nuts as you mix the dry and wet mixtures together. The batter should resemble a thick porridge; if it is too thick or thin, correct the consistency by adding a little liquid or flour.

Immediately spread the mixture evenly in a greased loaf pan or divide it among greased or paper-lined muffin tins. Loaf pans should be two-thirds to three-quarters full to allow for rising. For especially large, capped muffins, fill the cups level with the top; be sure to grease the tin around the top of the muffin cups. If the amount of batter is insufficient for all of the cups in the muffin tin, partially fill the empty cups with hot water. This prevents unfilled greased cups from burning, and the extra steam will benefit the muffins' texture too.

Rectangular pans are not essential for loaves; any ovenproof pan with about the same volume will do. Certain quick breads, such as corn bread, are traditionally baked in shallow square or round cake pans, or even pie plates or cast-iron frying pans. Other batter breads can be nonconformists, too; follow your inclinations in choosing pans.

In any case, put the filled pan directly into a preheated oven. Loaves generally require a moderate baking temperature (325 to 350 degrees) and bake in about an hour, depending on pan size. Bake muffins at a higher temperature (375 to 400 degrees) for 20 to 30 minutes.

To check for doneness, insert a cake tester, broom straw, or skewer into the center and see if it comes out clean—that is, without any uncooked batter adhering to it. The top of the bread or muffin should be browned and firm yet resilient to a light touch, and the sides should have shrunk slightly from the sides of the pan. An exemplary quick loaf or muffin has a moist and tender cakelike crumb. The texture is even, though perhaps somewhat crumbly.

Quick loaves and muffins are rather fragile, especially when they are still hot; they become firmer as they cool. It is best to cool them in the pan for a few minutes before turning them out onto a cooling rack. You may eat muffins right away. Quick loaves can be cut while they are still warm, but they slice much better after they have cooled completely.

Quick loaves keep quite well. Wrap them well after they have thoroughly cooled and store them in a cool, dry location. It's best to refrigerate particularly moist, fruity loaves after a couple of days to prevent an off flavor. Slices are good heated, toasted, or steamed even when a loaf is past its prime. Muffins can be perked up with a light steaming or by warming them in the oven in a covered container.

CORN BREAD
▗▖▗▖▗▖

Hot corn bread is wonderful with bean or pea soups. It's also a perfect partner for chili, baked beans, or marinated bean salads. Warm up leftovers and serve with apple butter for breakfast.

YIELD: 1 8-inch square or 1 9-inch round bread

PREPARATION TIME: 20 minutes to prepare; 20 minutes to bake

> 2 tablespoons wheat germ or bran, or sesame, poppy, chia, or ground sunflower seeds
> 1½ cups milk or soy milk
> 1½ tablespoons lemon juice or vinegar
> 1½ cups whole wheat pastry flour
> 1½ cups cornmeal (yellow, blue, white, etc.)
> ¾ teaspoon sea salt
> 1½ teaspoons baking soda
> 3 tablespoons vegetable oil
> 3 tablespoons maple syrup, mild-flavored honey, or rice syrup (optional)
> 2 eggs

Preheat the oven to 400 degrees. Grease the pan and coat the inside with the wheat germ or bran or seeds. Combine the milk and lemon juice and set aside to curdle.

Sift the flour, cornmeal, salt, and baking soda into a medium-sized bowl.

In a second bowl, whisk the oil and sweetener. Beat in the eggs. Whisk in the curdled milk.

Make a well in the center of the dry ingredients.

Pour in the wet mixture and stir gently, just until the two are combined. Spread the batter in the prepared pan. Bake in the preheated oven 20 minutes or until the top is browned and a tester inserted in the center comes out clean. Cool briefly and serve warm.

NOTES

- For a slightly finer-grained corn bread, substitute rye flour for all or part of the whole wheat pastry flour.

- For especially crusty bread, bake it in a preheated, greased 9-inch cast-iron frying pan.

- Stir 1 cup fresh corn kernels into the batter.

- If you don't have lemon juice or vinegar to sour the milk, substitute 1½ cups buttermilk or beaten yogurt; or use uncurdled milk or soy milk and substitute either 1½ teaspoons baking powder or ¾ teaspoon baking soda plus ¾ teaspoon cream of tartar for the baking soda in the recipe.

- For a different flavor, add the finely grated zest of an orange to the liquid mixture; substitute orange juice for all or part of the milk or soy milk and omit the lemon juice.

- Use this batter to make 10 to 12 large muffins. Omit the wheat germ or bran or seeds. Bake at 400 degrees for 20 minutes.

BANANA BREAD
▗▖▗▖▗▖

I associate banana bread with Mrs. Wilson, an elderly baby-sitter from my childhood. The four of us often gave other sitters a tough time, but never this surrogate grandmother; her stays with us were special. Though firm, she exercised some practical indulgence, such as her homemade banana bread.

YIELD: 1 medium-sized loaf

PREPARATION TIME: 25 minutes to prepare; 1 hour to bake

> 2 tablespoons poppy seeds
> ⅔ cup milk or soy milk

2 teaspoons lemon juice or vinegar
⅓ cup sunflower oil
⅓ cup maple syrup
1 egg
2 cups whole wheat pastry flour
½ teaspoon sea salt
1 teaspoon baking soda
1 teaspoon baking powder
1 cup mashed ripe banana
1 cup lightly toasted walnuts or pecans, coarsely chopped

Preheat the oven to 350 degrees. Grease an 8½ × 4½-inch loaf pan. Sprinkle in the poppy seeds and tilt the pan to coat the bottom and sides.

Combine the milk and lemon juice, and set aside to curdle.

In a medium-sized bowl, whisk the oil and syrup. Beat in the egg. Stir in the curdled milk.

Sift the flour, salt, baking soda, and baking powder. Add half this mixture and half the banana to the bowl and stir gently. Add the remaining dry ingredients and banana and stir just until a thick batter forms. Fold in the nuts with a few strokes. Spread the batter in the prepared pan. Bake in the preheated oven 1 hour or until a tester inserted in the center comes out clean. Cool in the pan 10 to 15 minutes, then turn out onto a rack. The loaf will slice best when it has thoroughly cooled.

NOTES
- For an eggless version, omit the milk or soy milk, lemon juice, and egg. Thoroughly blend 4 ounces tofu with ¾ cup unsweetened apple juice; whisk this mixture with the oil and syrup.

- Use the batter to make 10 large muffins. Omit the poppy seeds. Bake at 400 degrees for 20 minutes.

PEANUT-BANANA BREAD
▾▾▾

Peanut butter contributes to the flavor and moistness of this subtly spiced, fine-grained quick bread.

YIELD: 1 loaf

PREPARATION TIME: 20 minutes to prepare; 50 to 60 minutes to bake

3 tablespoons sesame seeds
½ cup unsalted peanut butter
2 tablespoons sesame oil
6 tablespoons mild-flavored honey
2 eggs
1 cup mashed ripe banana
2 cups sifted whole wheat pastry flour

½ teaspoon sea salt
1 teaspoon baking powder
1 teaspoon baking soda
1 teaspoon ground coriander
1 teaspoon ground ginger

Preheat the oven to 325 degrees. Grease an 8½ × 4½-inch loaf pan and coat the inside with 2 tablespoons of the sesame seeds.

In a medium-sized bowl, whisk the peanut butter, oil, and honey. Thoroughly whisk in the eggs. Whisk in the mashed banana.

Sift the flour, salt, baking powder, baking soda, coriander, and ginger. Add to the wet mixture and stir gently, just until a thick batter forms. Spread it in the prepared pan and sprinkle the remaining sesame seeds on top. Bake immediately in the preheated oven 50 minutes, or until it tests done. Cool in the pan 10 to 15 minutes, then turn out onto a rack.

NOTES
- Use this batter to make 8 large muffins. Omit the 2 tablespoons sesame seeds for coating the pan. Bake at 400 degrees for about 20 minutes.

FRUIT SAUCE-RAISIN BREAD
▾▾▾

Set aside a cup of apple sauce or pear sauce to make this wonderfully spicy loaf. Serve it for tea, dessert, or breakfast.

YIELD: 1 loaf

PREPARATION TIME: 20 minutes to prepare; 1 hour to bake

2 tablespoons bran or wheat germ
2 cups whole wheat pastry flour
½ teaspoon sea salt
1 teaspoon baking soda
½ teaspoon cinnamon
¼ teaspoon ground cloves
¼ teaspoon freshly grated nutmeg
¼ cup sunflower oil
¼ cup maple syrup
1 egg
1 cup APPLE SAUCE or PEAR SAUCE (page 136)
⅔ cup raisins
⅔ cup lightly toasted pecans, coarsely chopped

Preheat the oven to 350 degrees. Grease an 8½ × 4½-inch loaf pan and dust the inside with the bran or wheat germ.

Sift the flour, salt, baking soda, cinnamon, cloves, and nutmeg.

In a medium-sized bowl, whisk the oil and syrup. Whisk in the egg. Stir in the fruit sauce and raisins. Add the dry mixture and stir gently, just until a thick batter forms. Fold in the nuts.

Evenly spread the batter in the prepared pan. Bake in the preheated oven about 1 hour—until a tester inserted in the center comes out clean. Let cool in the pan 10 minutes, then turn out onto a rack.

NOTES

- Substitute walnuts for the pecans.

- Use the batter to make 10 large muffins. Omit the bran or wheat germ. Bake at 400 degrees for 20 minutes.

SPICED SQUASH BREAD
▼▼▼

As it bakes, this bread will fill your whole house with a festive fragrance. Substitute other varieties of winter squash or pumpkin, sweet potatoes, yams, or carrots for the butternut squash.

YIELD: 1 loaf

PREPARATION TIME: 25 minutes to prepare; 55 minutes to bake

> 2 tablespoons bran or wheat germ
> 1/3 cup sunflower oil
> 1/3 cup maple syrup
> 1 egg
> 1 cup mashed cooked butternut squash
> 1 2/3 cups whole wheat pastry flour
> 1 1/2 teaspoons baking soda
> 1/2 teaspoon sea salt
> 1/2 teaspoon freshly grated nutmeg
> 1/2 teaspoon cinnamon
> 1/4 teaspoon cloves
> 1 cup lightly toasted walnuts, coarsely chopped

Preheat the oven to 350 degrees. Grease an 8 × 4-inch loaf pan and dust the inside with the bran or wheat germ.

In a blender or food processor fitted with the metal blade, thoroughly blend the oil, syrup, egg, and squash. Transfer to a medium-sized bowl.

In another bowl, sift the flour, soda, salt, and spices. Add to the blended mixture and stir gently to form a thick batter. Fold in the nuts.

Immediately spread the batter in the prepared pan. Bake in the preheated oven 55 minutes or until a tester inserted in the center comes out clean. Cool in the pan 10 minutes, then turn out onto a rack.

NOTES

- Substitute chopped pecans or whole pine nuts for the walnuts.

- Use the batter to make 8 large muffins. Omit the bran or wheat germ. Bake at 400 degrees for 20 minutes.

DATE BREAD
▼▼▼

Dainty date-nut bread sandwiches have always seemed to me like the ultimate in tearoom fare. Medjool dates are my favorite. Spread thin slices of this loaf with TAHINI-MISO SPREAD *(page 132).*

YIELD: 1 loaf

PREPARATION TIME: 25 minutes to prepare; about 1 hour to bake

> 2 tablespoons bran or wheat germ
> 1 orange
> 1 cup unsweetened apple juice, or as needed
> 4 ounces tofu
> 1/4 cup sunflower oil
> 1/4 cup maple syrup, rice syrup, or mild-flavored honey
> 1 cup chopped dates
> 2 cups whole wheat pastry flour
> 1 teaspoon baking soda
> 1 teaspoon baking powder
> 1/2 teaspoon sea salt
> 1 cup lightly toasted pecans, coarsely chopped

Preheat the oven to 350 degrees. Grease and lightly dust the inside of an 8 1/2 × 4 1/2-inch loaf pan with the bran or wheat germ.

Grate the zest from the orange into a medium-sized bowl. Juice the orange and measure the juice. Add apple juice to equal 1 1/4 cups. In a blender, thoroughly blend the juice with the tofu. Whisk the oil, syrup, and blended mixture with the zest. Stir in the dates.

In another bowl, sift the flour, baking soda, baking powder, and sea salt. Add to the wet mixture and stir gently, just until a thick batter forms. Fold in the pecans.

Spread the batter in the prepared pan. Bake in the preheated oven 1 hour or until the bread tests done. Cool in the pan 10 to 15 minutes, then turn out onto a rack.

NOTES

- Substitute walnuts or other nuts for the pecans.

- For an egg/milk variation of this recipe, omit the tofu. Substitute milk or soy milk for the apple juice. Beat 1 egg and the milk/orange juice mixture with the oil and syrup.

- Bake the bread in an 8 × 8 × 2-inch pan at 350 degrees for 40 minutes. Top the cooled bread with *LEMON GLAZE* or *ORANGE GLAZE* (page 112).

- Use the batter to make 8 to 10 large muffins. Omit the bran or wheat germ. Bake at 400 degrees for about 20 minutes.

CRANBERRY-NUT BREAD
⬥⬥⬥

My feet were cold and damp, my fingers were numb, I was chilled all over, yet I still felt honored to be sharing the secret of a New York cranberry bog. We had chosen to go on a late autumn afternoon when we figured the berries would be ripe to pick. Dismal gray clouds hung over us and daylight was rapidly waning as we squatted in our rubber boots and combed our fingers through the icy water, feeling for firm berries. Only mental images of the cranberry-nut bread which would soon follow this expedition kept my sense of adventure from freezing over.

Red cranberries interspersed throughout this bread provide a pleasant contrast in flavor as well as bright spots of color. Make this one for winter holidays.

YIELD: 1 loaf

PREPARATION TIME: 25 minutes to prepare; 50 to 60 minutes to bake

> 2 tablespoons bran or wheat germ
> 1 orange
> 2/3 cup unsweetened apple juice, or as needed
> 4 ounces tofu
> 1/3 cup sunflower oil
> 1/3 cup mild-flavored honey (orange blossom honey is especially good in this bread)
> 2 cups whole wheat pastry flour
> 1/2 teaspoon sea salt
> 1 teaspoon baking soda
> 1 teaspoon baking powder
> 1 cup fresh cranberries, picked over, rinsed, and well drained
> 1 cup lightly toasted walnuts or pecans, coarsely chopped

Preheat the oven to 350 degrees. Grease an 8½ × 4½-inch loaf pan and dust the inside with the bran or wheat germ.

Finely grate the zest of the orange into a medium-sized bowl. Juice the orange and measure the juice. Add apple juice to equal 1 cup. In a blender, blend the tofu and a small amount of the juice. With the machine running, gradually add the remainder of the juice and blend until the mixture is thoroughly smooth. Whisk the oil and honey with the zest. Whisk in the blended mixture.

In another bowl, sift the flour, salt, baking soda, and baking powder. Add to the wet mixture and stir gently, just until a batter forms. Fold in the cranberries and nuts.

Spread the batter in the prepared pan. Bake immediately in the preheated oven 50 to 60 minutes, until the bread is well browned and a tester inserted in the center comes out clean. Cool in the pan 10 minutes, then turn out onto a rack.

NOTES

- Substitute unthawed frozen cranberries for the fresh ones.

- Substitute ½ cup raisins for half the nuts for a loaf with sweet and tart spots throughout.

- Use the batter to make 10 large muffins. Omit the bran or wheat germ. Bake about 20 minutes at 400 degrees.

ST. PATRICK'S IRISH SODA BREAD
⬥⬥⬥

This bread is made from a biscuit-type dough. The oil and honey are optional; adding them will make the bread a bit richer. Cutting the top allows for even expansion as the bread rises in the oven. One St. Patrick's Day, I delivered fresh, warm loaves of this bread to three generations of Ryans and Kellys.

YIELD: 1 round loaf

PREPARATION TIME: 20 minutes to prepare; 45 minutes to bake

> 1 cup milk or soy milk
> 1 tablespoon lemon juice or vinegar
> 1 cup whole wheat pastry flour
> 1 cup whole wheat bread flour
> 1/2 teaspoon sea salt
> 1 teaspoon baking soda
> 1½ teaspoons caraway seeds, coarsely ground

½ cup currants or raisins
2 tablespoons sunflower oil (optional)
2 tablespoons honey (optional)

Preheat the oven to 350 degrees. Lightly grease or line a baking sheet with baking parchment.

Combine the milk and lemon juice; set aside to curdle.

In a medium-sized bowl, sift the flours, salt, and baking soda. Stir in the caraway seeds and currants.

If you are adding the oil and honey, whisk them into the curdled milk.

Make a well in the center of the dry mixture. Pour in the wet mixture and stir gently, just until a soft dough forms. Turn the dough out onto a floured surface and knead the dough gently and briefly—just a few turns. Round the dough into a ball and place it on the prepared sheet. Dip a razor blade or sharp knife in flour and cut a deep cross in the top of the loaf.

Bake in the preheated oven 45 minutes or until a tester comes out clean. Set the loaf on a rack and cover it loosely with a tea towel. Leave it to cool at least 30 minutes before cutting it into wedges or slices.

NOTES
- Add the grated zest of a lemon or orange to the liquid ingredients before combining them with the dry mixture. If you add orange zest, you may also juice the orange and combine the juice with enough milk or soy milk to equal 1 cup of liquid; omit the lemon juice.

- Substitute buttermilk or yogurt for the milk or soy milk and omit the lemon juice.

- For an especially moist yet crusty bread, bake it in a baking cloche.

STREUSEL COFFEE CAKE
▾▾▾

Quick coffee cakes are usually loaded with butter, sour cream, eggs, and sugar. Here's an eggless, nondairy alternative that is still plenty rich and sweet. Serve it for breakfast or dessert.

YIELD: 1 8-inch square or 9-inch round coffee cake

PREPARATION TIME: 25 minutes to prepare; 40 minutes to bake

    4 tablespoons lightly toasted fine whole grain
          bread crumbs
    1 teaspoon cinnamon
    2 tablespoons date sugar or Sucanat
    ½ cup lightly toasted chopped pecans
    4 ounces tofu

    1 cup unsweetened apple juice
    ⅓ cup sunflower oil
    ⅓ cup maple syrup
    1 teaspoon pure vanilla extract
    2 cups sifted whole wheat pastry flour
    ½ teaspoon sea salt
    1 teaspoon baking soda
    ½ teaspoon freshly grated nutmeg

Preheat the oven to 350 degrees. Grease an 8-inch square or 9-inch round baking pan and lightly dust the inside with 2 tablespoons of the bread crumbs.

In a small bowl, thoroughly mix the remaining 2 tablespoons crumbs, ½ teaspoon cinnamon, sugar, and pecans with a fork. Set this streusel mixture aside.

In a blender, blend the tofu, gradually adding the apple juice, until the mixture is thoroughly smooth. Whisk the oil, syrup, and vanilla together in a medium-sized bowl. Whisk in the blended tofu.

In another bowl, sift the sifted flour, salt, baking soda, ½ teaspoon cinnamon, and nutmeg. Add this to the wet mixture and stir gently, just until a batter forms. Spread half the batter in the prepared pan and sprinkle half the streusel mixture over it; repeat these two layers.

Bake immediately in the preheated oven 40 minutes or until a tester inserted in the center comes out clean. Serve warm or at room temperature.

OATMEAL-RAISIN MUFFINS
▾▾▾

These moist, raisiny muffins are low in fat and cholesterol and high in fiber—a great way to start your day.

YIELD: 10 to 12 large muffins

PREPARATION TIME: 20 minutes to prepare; 20 minutes to bake

    1½ cups unsweetened apple juice
    ¾ cup raisins
    6 ounces tofu
    3 tablespoons sunflower oil
    3 tablespoons maple syrup
    1¼ cups whole wheat pastry flour
    1 cup rye flour
    ¾ teaspoon sea salt
    1½ teaspoons baking soda
    ¾ cup rolled oats

Heat the apple juice just to a simmer and pour it over the raisins. Preheat the oven to 400 degrees. Grease 10 to 12 muffin cups.

When the juice has cooled to lukewarm, drain the raisins, saving the liquid. In a blender, thoroughly blend the reserved liquid with the tofu. In a medium-sized mixing bowl, whisk the oil and syrup. Whisk in the blended mixture and stir in the raisins.

In another bowl, sift the flours, salt, and baking soda. Thoroughly stir in the oats. Add to the liquid mixture, stirring gently just until a thick batter forms.

Fill the prepared muffin cups. Bake immediately in the preheated oven 20 minutes or until the muffins are lightly browned and test done. Cool briefly and serve warm.

NOTES

- For a finer texture, grind the oats to a flour and sift with the other dry ingredients.

- For variety, fold ¾ cup lightly toasted, coarsely chopped walnuts or pecans into the batter.

- To make a loaf, spread the batter in an 8½ × 4½-inch loaf pan and bake at 350 degrees about an hour.

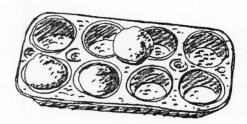

MELLOW MUFFINS
▾▾▾

On summer Sunday mornings, I like to make a batch of these muffins, cut up juicy seasonal fruits, grab the newspaper, and head for the natural spring pool in my town for a swim and breakfast picnic. TAHINI-MISO SPREAD (page 132) goes well with these muffins.

YIELD: 8 or 9 large muffins

PREPARATION TIME: 25 minutes to prepare; 20 minutes to bake

> *1 orange*
> *⅔ cup milk or soy milk, or as needed*
> *1 cup whole wheat pastry flour*
> *½ cup barley flour*
> *½ teaspoon sea salt*
> *1 teaspoon baking soda*
> *½ cup rolled oats*
> *¼ cup sunflower oil*
> *¼ cup maple syrup*
> *1 egg*
> *½ cup chopped dates*
> *½ cup lightly toasted, coarsely chopped pecans*

Preheat the oven to 400 degrees. Grease the muffin cups.

Grate the zest from the orange into a medium-sized mixing bowl. Juice the orange. Measure the juice, add milk to equal 1 cup of liquid, and set aside to curdle.

In another bowl, sift the flours, salt, and baking soda. Stir in the oats.

Add the oil and syrup to the zest and whisk thoroughly. Whisk in the egg and curdled milk. Stir in the dates. Add the dry mixture and stir gently, just until a thick batter forms. Fold in the nuts.

Fill the prepared cups. Bake in the preheated oven 20 minutes or until the muffins test done. Cool briefly and serve warm or at room temperature.

NOTES

- For finer-textured muffins, grind the rolled oats to a coarse flour (in a blender, etc.) before mixing them with the other dry ingredients.

- Omit the orange zest and juice; add the zest of one lemon and 1 tablespoon lemon juice plus milk or soy milk to equal 1 cup.

- To make a loaf, spread the batter in an 8½ × 4½-inch loaf pan and bake at 350 degrees about 50 minutes.

GOT THE BLUES MUFFINS
▾▾▾

Blue cornmeal, ground from blue corn, has long been a staple for the Pueblo Indians of the Southwest. I became acquainted with the unique flavor and unusual color it imparts to quick breads and tortillas a decade ago when a friend brought me several pounds from New Mexico. Now it is not so difficult to find in other regions of the country. Substitute yellow or white cornmeal if you don't have the blue variety. Frozen blueberries can replace the fresh ones in these muffins; use them straight out of the freezer or drain off extra liquid if they're already thawed.

YIELD: 8 large muffins

PREPARATION TIME: 20 minutes to prepare; 20 minutes to bake

> *⅓ cup blue cornmeal*
> *1⅓ cups whole wheat pastry flour*
> *½ teaspoon sea salt*
> *1 teaspoon baking soda*
> *4 ounces tofu*
> *⅔ cup unsweetened apple juice*
> *¼ cup sunflower oil*
> *¼ cup maple syrup*
> *1 cup blueberries*

Preheat the oven to 400 degrees. Grease 8 muffin cups.

Sift the cornmeal, flour, salt, and baking soda.

In a blender, blend the tofu and gradually add the apple juice. Add the oil and syrup and blend until the mixture is thoroughly smooth. Pour it into a medium-sized mixing bowl. Add the dry mixture and stir gently, just until a thick, slightly lumpy batter forms. Fold in the blueberries.

Fill the prepared muffin cups. Bake in the preheated oven 20 minutes or until a tester inserted in the center comes out clean. Cool the muffins briefly and serve warm.

NOTES

- Instead of making muffins, spread the batter in an 8-inch square or 9-inch round baking pan; bake about 20 minutes at 400 degrees.

VERY BERRY MUFFINS
▾▾▾

Only slightly sweet, these chewy muffins are good for lunch or dinner as well as breakfast. Serve them with a soup or salad.

YIELD: 8 large muffins

PREPARATION TIME: 20 minutes to prepare; 20 minutes to bake

> ¾ cup milk or soy milk
> 1 tablespoon lemon juice
> 2 tablespoons sunflower oil
> 2 tablespoons maple syrup
> 1 egg
> 1½ cups whole wheat pastry flour
> ½ teaspoon sea salt
> 1 teaspoon baking soda
> ½ teaspoon baking powder
> 1 cup cooked wheat berries (see page 13–14)
> ½ cup currants

Preheat the oven to 400 degrees. Grease 8 muffin cups.

Combine the milk and lemon juice; set aside to curdle. In a medium-sized bowl, whisk the oil and syrup. Whisk in the egg and curdled milk.

In another bowl, sift the flour, salt, baking soda, and baking powder. Add to the wet mixture and stir gently, just until a batter forms. Fold in the wheat berries and currants.

Fill the prepared muffin cups. Bake in the preheated oven 20 minutes or until the muffins test done. Cool briefly and serve warm or at room temperature.

NOTES

- Substitute another cooked grain, such as rice, rye berries, or millet, for the wheat berries.

- Add ½ cup lightly toasted, coarsely chopped walnuts.

- Omit the currants.

- For a loaf, spread the batter in an 8 × 4-inch loaf pan; bake about 50 minutes at 350 degrees.

MAPLE BRAN MUFFINS
▾▾▾

These basic bran muffins are wide open for variation. Look at the notes for some possibilities or try out some of your own.

YIELD: 9 large muffins

PREPARATION TIME: 20 minutes to prepare; 20 minutes to bake

> 1½ cups milk or soy milk
> 1½ tablespoons lemon juice
> 3 tablespoons vegetable oil
> 3 tablespoons maple syrup
> 2 eggs
> ¾ cup raisins
> 1½ cups whole wheat pastry flour
> ¾ teaspoon sea salt
> 1½ teaspoons baking soda
> 1½ cups bran

Preheat the oven to 400 degrees. Grease the muffin cups.

Combine the milk and lemon juice and set aside to curdle. In a medium-sized mixing bowl, beat the oil and syrup. Thoroughly beat in the eggs. Stir in the curdled milk and the raisins.

In another bowl, sift the flour, salt, and baking soda. Stir in the bran. Add to the wet mixture. Fold gently, just until a thick batter forms.

Fill the prepared muffin cups. Bake in the preheated oven 20 to 25 minutes, until the muffins are browned and test done. Cool briefly and serve warm.

NOTES

- Substitute honey or unsulfured molasses for the maple syrup.

- Substitute chopped dates, prunes, or soaked dried apricots for the raisins.

- Substitute all or half of the raisins with lightly toasted, coarsely chopped walnuts or pecans.

- Substitute buttermilk or yogurt for the milk or soy milk and omit the lemon juice.

- For eggless, nondairy muffins, omit the egg, milk, and lemon juice; blend 6 ounces tofu with 1½ cups unsweetened apple juice, and whisk this mixture with the oil and sweetener.

- To make a loaf, spread the batter in an 8½ × 4½-inch loaf pan; bake about an hour at 350 degrees.

BUCKWHEAT MUFFINS

At our house, we refer to these moist muffins as "Gussie muffins" after my husband's Grandma Gussie, who always stuffed him with kasha when he visited. Buckwheat is one of my favorite grains too, and I relish its unique flavor in breads.

YIELD: 8 large muffins

PREPARATION TIME: 20 minutes to prepare; 25 minutes to bake

> ⅔ *cup milk or soy milk*
> 2 *teaspoons lemon juice or vinegar*
> 2 *tablespoons vegetable oil*
> 3 *tablespoons honey*
> 1 *tablespoon blackstrap molasses*
> 1 *egg*
> 1 *cup cooked toasted buckwheat groats (see page 13–14)*
> ½ *cup raisins*
> 1½ *cups whole wheat pastry flour*
> ½ *teaspoon sea salt*
> 1 *teaspoon baking soda*
> ½ *teaspoon baking powder*

Preheat the oven to 375 degrees. Grease 8 muffin cups.

Combine the milk and lemon juice and set aside to curdle.

In a medium-sized bowl, beat the oil, honey, and molasses. Thoroughly beat in the egg. Stir in the curdled milk, buckwheat groats, and raisins.

In another bowl, sift the flour, salt, baking soda, and baking powder. Add to the wet mixture all at once and stir gently, just enough to form a thick batter.

Fill the prepared muffin cups. Bake in the preheated oven about 25 minutes, or until the muffins have browned and a tester inserted in the center comes out clean. Cool briefly and serve warm.

NOTES

- Substitute ¼ cup lightly toasted chopped walnuts for half the raisins.

- Substitute barley malt or rice syrup for the honey and molasses.

- Substitute buttermilk or yogurt for the milk or soy milk and omit the lemon juice.

- For eggless, nondairy muffins, omit the egg, milk, and lemon juice; blend 4 ounces tofu with ¾ cup unsweetened apple juice, and whisk this mixture with the oil, honey, and molasses.

- Instead of making muffins, spread the batter in an 8-inch square or 9-inch round baking pan; bake at 375 degrees 25 to 30 minutes or until the bread tests done.

Pancakes and Waffles

Though they are generally interchangeable, waffle batters are usually a bit thicker than pancake batters and contain a larger amount of fat to prevent them from sticking in the waffle iron. Follow the basic instructions for making quick bread batters on page 31.

Bake pancakes on a hot, lightly greased griddle. My cast-iron one is well seasoned and requires very little greasing. As I learned from *The Laurel's Kitchen Bread Book*, a combination of one part soy lecithin to two parts vegetable oil is an especially effective pan-greasing substance, although butter or margarine or oil alone will do. I use liquid soy lecithin whisked with sesame or sunflower oil and keep a little container of this mixture handy in the refrigerator. One caution: I have found that safflower oil promotes sticking. Turn a pancake when the top is well bubbled and the edges are beginning to firm up. When you lift the edge, the bottom should appear golden. Cook it for a shorter time on the second side. Cooking time will vary for different batters. A pancake is ready when it is light and puffy and browned on both sides.

Specific directions for waffles depend on the particular waffle iron. You will soon tune in to yours regarding the amount of batter to use and the timing. Mine is a cast-iron, Scandinavian, top-of-the-stove type that makes circular waffles with a design of five little hearts. Whatever kind of waffle iron you have, always preheat and grease it lightly but thoroughly before ladling in the first batch of batter; try the lecithin and oil formula above. Merely closing the lid will spread the batter evenly, unless the batter is unusually thick. A waffle is done when it is golden and crisp on both sides. If the iron was preheated and greased sufficiently, the waffle should lift out easily. Avoid opening the iron before the waffle is likely to be ready or you may tear the waffle apart.

Pancakes and waffles are best eaten hot off the griddle, but if necessary they can be kept warm in a low oven. To keep waffles crisp, place them directly on the oven rack; they become soggy on a plate. If you have extra waffle batter, make up the waffles and freeze them; you can warm them briefly in a moderate oven or toaster oven for a quick breakfast.

LIGHT LEMONY PANCAKES
▼▼▼

Lemon zest and nutmeg add a special touch to these basic whole wheat pancakes, and a beaten egg white makes them extra light. Serve fresh berries or other seasonal fruits alongside.

YIELD: About 1 dozen 3-inch pancakes

PREPARATION TIME: 15 minutes to prepare; about 5 minutes to cook each batch

    Grated zest of 1 lemon
1 tablespoon sunflower oil
1 tablespoon maple syrup
1 egg, separated
1 cup milk or soy milk
1 tablespoon lemon juice
1 cup whole wheat pastry flour
1/2 teaspoon sea salt
1 teaspoon baking soda
1/2 teaspoon freshly grated nutmeg

Heat a griddle until water dropped on it sizzles immediately.

In a medium-sized bowl, whisk the lemon zest, oil, and syrup. Thoroughly beat in the egg yolk.

Combine the milk and lemon juice; set aside to curdle.

Sift the flour, salt, baking soda, and nutmeg.

Beat the egg white until it is stiff but not dry.

Whisk the curdled milk into the yolk mixture. Add the dry ingredients and stir gently to form a batter. Gently fold in the beaten egg white.

Lightly grease the hot griddle and ladle on batter. Cook until bubbles appear on the tops of the pancakes and their undersides are golden brown. Flip the pancakes and cook briefly, until light brown on the bottom. Serve them hot off the griddle, drizzled with a bit more maple syrup.

NOTES

- If you're in a hurry, don't bother separating the egg; beat the whole egg into the oil and syrup.

- For waffles, add an extra tablespoon of oil to the batter.

ORANGE-POPPY SEED PANCAKES
▼▼▼

Toasted poppy seeds add flavor and crunch to these zesty pancakes.

YIELD: About 1 dozen 3-inch pancakes

PREPARATION TIME: 20 minutes to prepare; about 5 minutes to cook each batch

2 tablespoons poppy seeds
1 orange
2/3 cup milk or soy milk, or as needed
1 tablespoon sunflower oil
1 tablespoon maple syrup
1 egg, separated
1 cup whole wheat pastry flour
1/2 teaspoon sea salt
1 teaspoon baking soda

Heat a dry skillet over moderate heat. Add the poppy seeds and cook, agitating the pan or stirring often, until lightly toasted; set aside.

Heat a griddle until water dropped on it sizzles immediately.

Grate the zest of the orange into a medium-sized mixing bowl. Juice the orange and measure the juice. Add milk to equal 1 cup of liquid; set aside to curdle. Add the oil and syrup to the zest and whisk thoroughly. Beat in the egg yolk. Whisk in the curdled milk.

Beat the egg white until it is stiff but not dry.

Sift the flour, salt, and baking soda. Add this all at once to the wet mixture and stir gently to form a batter. Stir in the toasted poppy seeds. Gently fold in the beaten egg white until it is just incorporated.

Lightly grease the hot griddle and ladle on batter. Cook until the tops of the pancakes bubble and the bottoms are golden. Flip and cook briefly, until the other side has browned. Serve the pancakes hot off the griddle or keep them warm in a low oven until serving. Top with maple or orange syrup.

NOTES

- If you're in a hurry, don't separate the egg; beat the whole egg into the oil and syrup.

- For waffles, add another tablespoon of oil to the batter.

CORNCAKES
▼▼▼

These griddlecakes are delicate steaming rounds of corn bread. Use blue cornmeal for purple pancakes!

YIELD: About 1 dozen 3-inch pancakes

PREPARATION TIME: 15 minutes to mix; about 5 minutes to cook each batch

 1 cup milk or soy milk
 1 tablespoon lemon juice or vinegar
 ½ cup cornmeal
 ½ cup whole wheat pastry flour
 1 teaspoon baking soda
 ¼ teaspoon sea salt
 1 egg, separated
 1 tablespoon sunflower oil
 1 tablespoon maple syrup

Heat a griddle until water dropped on it sizzles immediately.

Combine the milk and lemon juice and set aside to curdle.

Sift the cornmeal, flour, baking soda, and salt.

Beat the egg white until it is stiff but not dry.

In a medium-sized bowl, whisk the oil and syrup. Thoroughly whisk in the egg yolk. Whisk in the curdled milk. Add the dry ingredients all at once and stir just until a batter forms. Gently fold in the beaten egg white.

Lightly grease the hot griddle. Ladle on batter and cook until bubbles appear on the tops of the pancakes and the bottoms are golden. Turn and cook briefly, until the second side has browned.

Serve the pancakes hot off the griddle or keep them warm in a low oven. Top them with maple syrup or fruit butter.

NOTES

- Substitute buttermilk or yogurt for the milk or soy milk, and omit the lemon juice.

- For waffles, add another tablespoon of oil to the batter.

GOLDEN GRIDDLECAKES
▼▼▼

Sweet butternut squash is superb in these pancakes, but you can substitute other varieties of winter squash or use pumpkin, carrot, sweet potato, or yam. Top the pancakes with apple sauce, pear sauce, or **APPLE** *or* **PEAR BUTTER** *(see page 135-36).*

YIELD: About 1 dozen 3-inch pancakes

PREPARATION TIME: 15 minutes to mix; about 5 minutes to cook each batch

 1 egg, separated
 1 tablespoon sunflower oil
 ½ cup mashed cooked squash
 1 cup milk or soy milk
 1 cup whole wheat pastry flour
 ½ teaspoon sea salt
 1 teaspoon baking powder

Heat a griddle until water dropped on it sizzles immediately.

Beat the egg white until stiff but not dry and set aside. In a medium-sized bowl, thoroughly whisk the egg yolk, oil, squash, and milk.

In a separate bowl, sift the flour, salt, and baking powder. Gently stir the dry mixture into the wet mixture, just enough to form a batter. Carefully fold in the beaten egg white.

Lightly grease the hot griddle. Ladle batter onto it. Cook until bubbles form on the tops of the pancakes and their undersides are golden brown. Turn and cook briefly, until the other side has browned. Serve the pancakes hot off the griddle or keep them warm in a low oven.

NOTES

- For a sweeter batter, whisk a tablespoon of maple syrup or another sweetener into the liquid mixture.

- For waffles, add an extra tablespoon of oil to the batter.

APPLE FLAPJACKS
▼▼▼

Nudge your household awake with the spicy aroma of these light pancakes. Nobody will miss the eggs and milk products.

YIELD: About 1 dozen 3-inch pancakes

PREPARATION TIME: 15 minutes to mix; about 5 minutes to cook each griddleful

4 ounces tofu
1 cup unsweetened apple juice
1 tablespoon sunflower oil
1 tablespoon maple syrup
1 cup whole wheat pastry flour
½ teaspoon sea salt
1 teaspoon baking soda
¼ teaspoon freshly grated nutmeg
¼ teaspoon cinnamon

Heat a griddle until water dropped on it sizzles immediately.

Put the tofu in a blender with about ¼ cup of the apple juice. Blend and, with the machine running, gradually add the remaining juice. Blend until thoroughly smooth.

In a medium-sized bowl, whisk the oil and syrup. Thoroughly whisk in the blended mixture.

In another bowl, sift the flour, salt, baking soda, nutmeg, and cinnamon. Add to the wet ingredients and stir gently, just enough to form a batter.

Lightly grease the hot griddle. Ladle tablespoons of the batter onto it. Cook until the tops of the pancakes bubble and dry a bit and the bottoms have browned. Turn and cook briefly, until golden. Serve immediately.

NOTES
- For waffles, add another tablespoon of oil to this batter.

Biscuits and Scones

Both biscuits and scones should be tender and flaky on the inside and browned and slightly crusty on the outside. They are basically the same, except that scone recipes sometimes call for richer ingredients than those used in most biscuits. Also, scones are usually triangular in shape.

The secret to making light biscuits and scones is to follow the light-handed, rapid mixing principles described earlier. If the recipe calls for cold fat, as most do, use a pastry blender or a food processor fitted with a metal blade to cut the chilled butter or margarine into the dry mixture until it reaches an even, mealy consistency. If you use a food processor, transfer the mixture to a bowl. Add the liquid all at once and mix slowly with a long-tined fork, wooden spoon, or rubber spatula until the liquid is just incorporated and a soft dough forms. Turn the dough out onto a lightly floured work surface and knead it gently—just a few times around—until it holds together and isn't sticky. Too much handling will toughen and flatten the end product.

For biscuits, pat or lightly roll the dough ½ to ¾ inch thick. Cut out biscuits with a cutter of any shape or a sharp knife—biscuits do not have to be round! Dip the cutter or knife into flour before cutting each biscuit. Don't twist a round cutter or the biscuits will rise unevenly and bake up lopsided.

To make triangular scones, round the dough into a ball, flatten it to approximately ¾ inch thick, and then cut this round into equal wedges. You can make circular scones or some other shape if you prefer.

Place biscuits and scones an inch or so apart on an ungreased sheet and bake them immediately in a preheated 450-degree oven. Or use a preheated, medium-hot griddle and turn them once the first side is browned and firm. Test by inserting a cake tester in the middle.

Drop biscuits are prepared from a thick batter rather than a dough; they are similar to rolled biscuits except that they contain less flour. Small portions of the batter are simply dropped from a spoon onto a lightly greased or parchment-lined baking sheet. Bake these in the oven at a high temperature for a short time.

Biscuits and scones continue to cook after they come out of the oven or off the griddle. To avoid an uneven, doughy consistency, cool them on a wire rack, loosely draped with a dry tea towel, for 20 to 30 minutes before serving.

BASIC BISCUITS
▼▼▼

These flaky little breads are tender and full-flavored; keep them simple or dress them up. For the lightest biscuits, handle the dough gently and as little as possible. They will be soft-sided if baked close together, crusty if spaced farther apart.

YIELD: 8 small biscuits

PREPARATION TIME: About 45 minutes, including baking

½ cup milk or soy milk
1½ teaspoons lemon juice or vinegar
1½ cups whole wheat pastry flour
¼ teaspoon sea salt
½ teaspoon baking soda
1 teaspoon baking powder
3 tablespoons cold unsalted soy margarine or butter

Preheat the oven to 450 degrees.

Combine the milk and lemon juice; set aside to curdle.

Sift the flour. Measure 1½ cups of the sifted flour back into the sieve; set aside the remaining sifted flour for kneading and shaping. Sift the measured flour, salt, baking soda, and baking powder into a medium-sized mixing bowl. Using a pastry blender, cut the cold margarine or butter into the sifted ingredients until the mixture resembles a coarse meal. Or do this in a food processor fitted with the metal blade, and transfer the mixture to a bowl. Make a well in the center of the dry ingredients. Add the curdled milk all at once and stir gently with a fork just until a soft dough forms.

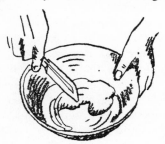

Sprinkle some of the reserved flour onto a work surface and turn the dough out onto it. Knead gently, adding additional flour as necessary, just until the dough comes together well and is not sticky. Pat or roll the dough ½ to ¾ inch thick. Cut out biscuits. Gently rework the dough scraps and cut additional biscuits.

Arrange the biscuits on an ungreased or parchment-lined baking sheet. Bake in the preheated oven 10 to 15 minutes, until the tops have browned and a tester inserted in the center comes out clean. Place on a cooling rack, cover loosely with a tea towel, and cool 15 to 30 minutes before serving.

NOTES

- If you don't have lemon juice or vinegar to curdle the milk, omit the baking soda and increase the baking powder to 1½ teaspoons; or substitute buttermilk for the milk or soy milk and lemon juice.

- For *SPICED LEMON BISCUITS*, add the grated zest of 1 lemon to the curdled milk and sift ½ teaspoon freshly grated nutmeg with the dry ingredients.

- For *ORANGE BISCUITS*, omit the lemon juice; grate the zest from an orange. Then squeeze the orange and measure the juice. Add milk to equal ½ cup of liquid and stir in the zest. Substitute this mixture for the ½ cup milk and proceed with the recipe.

SWEET POTATO PECAN BISCUITS
▼▼▼

Sweet potatoes or yams baked in their skins, split open, and sprinkled with toasted pecans are superbly sweet. Bake an extra one and set it aside for this further treat. Serve the biscuits with apple butter or orange marmalade.

YIELD: 9 large biscuits

PREPARATION TIME: 30 to 40 minutes, including baking

> 1 orange
> ⅓ cup milk or soy milk, or as needed
> 2 cups whole wheat pastry flour
> ½ teaspoon sea salt
> 1½ teaspoons baking powder
> ½ teaspoon baking soda
> ½ cup lightly toasted pecans, coarsely chopped
> ¾ to 1 cup mashed baked sweet potato or yam
> 3 tablespoons sunflower oil
> 1 tablespoon maple syrup
> Maple syrup for glazing

Preheat the oven to 450 degrees.

Finely grate the orange zest into a medium-sized bowl. Juice the orange and measure the juice. Add milk to equal ⅔ cup of liquid; set aside to curdle.

Sift the flour. Measure 2 cups of the sifted flour back into the sieve; set aside the remaining sifted flour for kneading and shaping. Sift the measured flour, salt, baking powder, and baking soda into another bowl. Stir in the chopped pecans.

Add the mashed sweet potato, oil, and syrup to the orange zest and mix thoroughly. Beat in the curdled mixture.

Make a well in the center of the dry ingredients. Pour in the wet ingredients all at once and mix gently, just until a soft dough forms. Turn the dough out onto a lightly floured surface and knead gently a few times. Pat or roll the dough about 1 inch thick. Cut out biscuits and arrange them on an ungreased or parchment-lined baking sheet.

Bake 15 minutes or until the biscuits have browned and a tester inserted in the center comes out clean. Place them on a cooling rack and lightly brush the tops with maple syrup. Cool about 15 minutes before serving.

ANITA'S DROP BISCUITS
▼▼▼

Anita and I lived in a large cooperative house back in the '70s and we did a lot of the cooking. These multi-grain drop biscuits of hers are especially quick to prepare. They go well with both sweet and savory spreads and add a special touch to any meal of the day.

YIELD: 6 large biscuits

PREPARATION TIME: 15 minutes to prepare; 10 to 15 minutes to bake

> ⅔ cup milk or soy milk
> 2 teaspoons lemon juice or vinegar
> ½ cup rolled oats

½ *cup whole wheat pastry flour*
½ *cup rye flour*
¼ *teaspoon sea salt*
½ *teaspoon baking soda*
1 *teaspoon baking powder*
3 *tablespoons cold unsalted soy margarine or*
   butter

Preheat the oven to 450 degrees. Lightly grease a baking sheet or line it with baking parchment.

Combine the milk and lemon juice; set aside to curdle.

In a blender or a food processor fitted with the metal blade, grind the oats to a flour. Sift this with the other flours, salt, baking soda, and baking powder into a medium-sized mixing bowl. Using a pastry blender, cut the margarine or butter into the dry mixture until it resembles a coarse meal. Or do this in a food processor fitted with the metal blade, and transfer the mixture to a bowl. Make a well in the center and pour in the curdled milk. Stir gently with a fork just until a soft dough forms.

Drop equal-sized mounds of the dough onto the prepared baking sheet. Bake in the preheated oven 10 to 15 minutes, until the biscuits have browned and a tester inserted in the center comes out clean. Place them directly on a cooling rack, cover loosely with a tea towel, and cool 15 to 20 minutes before serving.

NOTES
- Substitute buttermilk or beaten yogurt for the milk or soy milk and omit the lemon juice.

SCONES
▼▼▼

There's a fine line between biscuits and scones; scones are often richer and are usually wedge-shaped. Serve these basic scones for breakfast or an impromptu tea party.

YIELD: 8 scones

PREPARATION TIME: 30 to 40 minutes, including baking

   Cornmeal or rice flour
¾ *cup milk or soy milk*
1 *tablespoon lemon juice or vinegar*
2 *cups whole wheat pastry flour*
½ *teaspoon sea salt*
1 *teaspoon baking soda*
2 *tablespoons cold, unsalted soy margarine or*
   butter
⅓ *cup currants or raisins*

Preheat the oven to 450 degrees. Dust a baking sheet with cornmeal or rice flour.

Combine the milk and lemon juice; set aside to curdle.

Sift the whole wheat flour, salt, and baking soda into a medium-sized bowl. Using a pastry blender, cut in the margarine or butter until the mixture reaches the consistency of coarse meal. Or do this in a food processor fitted with the metal blade, and transfer the mixture to a bowl. Stir in the dried fruit. Make a well in the center and pour in the curdled milk. Stir slowly just until a soft dough forms.

Turn the dough out onto a lightly floured surface and knead gently and briefly—just several times around. Cut the dough in half and form each piece into a ball; press each ball into a round about ½ to ¾ inch thick. Cut each round into quarters and place these wedges an inch or so apart on the prepared baking sheet.

Bake in the preheated oven 15 to 20 minutes, until lightly browned and a tester inserted in the center comes out clean. Transfer to a cooling rack, cover loosely with a tea towel, and cool several minutes. Serve warm.

NOTES
- Substitute buttermilk or yogurt for the milk or soy milk and omit the lemon juice; or substitute uncurdled milk or soy milk and either replace all of the baking soda with baking powder or use ½ teaspoon cream of tartar and ½ teaspoon baking soda.

- For a lemony variation, add the finely grated zest of 1 lemon to the milk along with the lemon juice.

- Cook the scones on a moderately hot, ungreased griddle rather than in the oven. Turn after the first side has browned. The crust and crumb will be slightly different than oven-baked scones.

Egg-Leavened Quick Breads

Several other breads that are quick to make depend solely upon the combination of beaten eggs and high oven heat for leavening; popovers, oven-baked pancakes, and spoonbreads fall into this group.

POPOVERS
▼▼▼

An airy, egg-rich mixture, popover batter should be smoothly blended and about the consistency of heavy cream. In a hot oven, it swells up into hollow rolls. These small bread balloons should be crusty on the outside and soft on the inside.

I find that a large proportion of whole wheat bread flour is necessary for successful popovers. Used exclusively, pastry wheat and other low-gluten flours result in less puffy, muffinlike popovers. Prepare the batter with room temperature ingredients.

You can bake popovers in greased custard cups or muffin tins, but special popover pans are especially effective baking containers. Grease and preheat them before pouring in the batter. Fill all pans half to two-thirds full of batter.

Most popover recipes specify baking at a high temperature (425 to 450 degrees) for 15 minutes and then lowering the temperature to 325 to 350 degrees for 20 minutes more. This method works fine, but the two stages of baking present a problem if you want to start a second batch of popovers as soon as the first batch comes out of the oven, since you must first reheat the oven to the high temperature again. I have discovered that baking at 450 degrees for 25 minutes also produces good results, and a second batch can go directly into the oven; the popovers are done sooner, too.

Popovers are best right out of the oven, but if you must wait to serve them, remove each popover from its baking cup and puncture it with the tip of a sharp knife to release the steam inside. Turn off the oven, put the popovers (out of the pan) back inside, and prop the door partially open.

Serve popovers with preserves and fruit for breakfast or with soup and salad for lunch or supper. You can also prepare a dainty entrée by stuffing popovers with a savory filling.

YIELD: 6 large popovers

PREPARATION TIME: 35 to 40 minutes, including baking

> 1 cup whole wheat bread flour
> ¼ teaspoon sea salt
> 3 large eggs
> 1 cup milk or soy milk
> 1 tablespoon vegetable oil
> 2 teaspoons unsalted soy margarine or butter

Preheat the oven to 450 degrees.

Sift together the flour and salt onto a piece of waxed paper.

Break the eggs into a blender and blend, gradually adding the sifted mixture alternately with the milk. Add the oil and continue to blend until thoroughly smooth, scraping down any flour that clings to the sides of the blender jar.

If you are using a tinned or blackened steel popover pan, oil each cup lightly and preheat the pan for a few minutes. Cut the margarine or butter into 6 equal pieces and add a piece to each cup. Return the pan to the oven briefly—until the margarine or butter is sizzling. Or grease and lightly dust with flour 6 custard cups and arrange them in a baking pan.

Fill the prepared pans about half full of batter and put them into the oven immediately. Bake 25 minutes—without opening the oven door!

Remove the popovers from the pan; they should have crusty tops and sides and lift out of the pan easily. Serve them right away.

NOTES

- Blend herbs or spices into the batter; heavier additions, such as dried or fresh fruits or nuts, tend to interfere with rising.

- There are lots of possible variations, such as the following:

  Substitute ¼ cup rye flour for ¼ of the cup whole wheat bread flour.

  Substitute ¼ cup cornmeal for ¼ of the cup whole wheat bread flour.

  Before baking, sprinkle about ¼ teaspoon sesame seeds on top of each popover.

  Sift ½ teaspoon freshly grated nutmeg with the flour and salt and blend the finely grated zest from 1 lemon (about 1 teaspoon) into the batter.

  Blend 1 teaspoon finely grated orange zest into the batter and, just before baking, sprinkle about ¼ teaspoon poppy seeds on top of each popover.

OVEN PANCAKES
◆◆◆

These large, light, puffy pancakes are baked in the oven rather than on top of the stove. Use an ovenproof skillet and preheat it on top of the stove. Since you'll usually be making more than one pancake, it's helpful to have more than one skillet, but you can bake pancakes one after the other in the same pan, too.

The batter for oven pancakes is rich in eggs, like that for popovers, but is somewhat thicker. Pastry flour gives them a tender texture.

Serve these airy pancakes immediately, either whole

or cut in half or in wedges. *Maple syrup, marmalade, fruit sauces or fruit butters, and fresh fruit are good toppings for breakfast or brunch; I like them with blackberries, raspberries, or sliced strawberries or peaches. For a quick lunch or supper dish, top the pancakes with seasoned sautéed vegetables, such as spinach or mushrooms, or a savory sauce.*

YIELD: 2 10-inch pancakes

PREPARATION TIME: About 30 minutes—or 45 minutes if you can bake only one pancake at a time

> 1 cup whole wheat pastry flour
> ¼ teaspoon sea salt
> ¼ teaspoon freshly grated nutmeg
>   Grated zest from 1 lemon
> 4 eggs
> 1 cup milk or soy milk
> 2 teaspoons sunflower oil

Preheat the oven to 425 degrees and preheat two 10-inch ovenproof skillets on top of the stove over moderate heat.

Sift together the flour, salt, and nutmeg.

In a medium-sized bowl, thoroughly whisk the lemon zest and eggs. Whisk in the milk. Add the dry mixture and whisk until smooth.

Coat the inside of the hot skillets with the oil and divide the batter between them. Bake in the preheated oven 15 to 20 minutes, until puffed and browned. Serve immediately.

NOTES

- There are many possible variations on these pancakes: for example, substitute another flour for some or all of the whole wheat pastry flour, or omit the nutmeg and substitute finely minced fresh herbs.

SPOONBREAD
▪▪▪

Spoonbread is actually a cornmeal soufflé. Egg yolks are beaten into a smooth cornmeal porridge, then this mixture is lightened by carefully folding in stiffly beaten egg whites. High oven heat encourages the foamy batter to climb up the straight sides of a soufflé dish to form a crusty golden crown.

The texture of spoonbread is a bit denser than that of the lightest soufflés; it doesn't rise quite as dramatically, but it is also less susceptible to falling. Like a soufflé, spoonbread is meant to be eaten with a fork—or a spoon—rather than with fingers.

Serve this light custardy bread for breakfast or brunch with maple syrup or fruit butters. Spoonbread is also good for lunch or dinner; try it with sautéed greens and baked sweet potatoes.

YIELD: 2 generous servings

PREPARATION TIME: About 1 hour, including baking

> ½ cup cornmeal, plus extra for dusting the pan
> 1½ cups milk or soy milk
> 1 tablespoon unsalted soy margarine or butter
> ½ teaspoon sea salt
>   Freshly ground black pepper, to taste (optional)
> 2 large eggs at room temperature
>   Pinch of cream of tartar

Preheat the oven to 375 degrees. Grease the bottom and sides of a small soufflé dish and dust it lightly with cornmeal.

Heat the milk in a saucepan over medium heat. Gradually whisk in the ½ cup cornmeal, and stir constantly with a wire whisk or wooden spoon until the mixture becomes thick and smooth. Reduce the heat and stir in the margarine or butter and seasonings. Cook, stirring, for several minutes. Remove from the heat and set aside to cool somewhat.

Separate the eggs. In a small deep bowl, beat the whites and cream of tartar until stiff but not dry.

Beat the yolks in a medium-sized bowl. Add the cornmeal mixture and stir thoroughly. Gently fold in the egg whites.

Spread evenly in the prepared dish and smooth the top with a spatula. Bake 35 to 40 minutes, until the spoonbread is puffed and browned. Serve immediately from the baking dish.

NOTES

- For 4 to 6 servings, double this recipe.

- Add minced fresh herbs: try about a tablespoon of dill, chives, or parsley, or about ¼ teaspoon thyme, rosemary, or sage. Ground cumin and coriander are other interesting additions.

- Stir ½ cup grated cheddar cheese into the cornmeal/egg yolk mixture.

CHAPTER 5

Yeasted Breads

WE HAD BEGUN TAKING buses without having a destination as a way to both rest our exhausted feet and at the same time explore new areas of Paris. But this morning, our bus ride was purposeful and, despite the grayness of the day, I was filled with excited anticipation. The drizzle escalated into a downpour as we alighted from the bus, and as we walked up the steep street, we sidestepped rivulets that rushed down toward us. Suddenly, we were peering through a broad expanse of windows filled with artistic arrangements of breads, stalks of wheat, and flowers, into Bernard Ganachoud's bakery. We had arrived! Shortly before leaving for France, I had read an article that described Monsieur Ganachoud as one of the few remaining master bakers in Paris who had maintained a traditional approach to bread making. His breads were made from top quality ingredients; they were thoroughly fermented, baked in wood-fired brick ovens, and sold at their freshest and only from his shop. One wall and a long counter below it held an immense array of breads of many shapes and sizes, and we stood almost mesmerized by the sight and smell of these wonderful breads. Eating the ones we selected turned out to be fully as pleasurable as looking at them.

I don't know how many times I've been disappointed when I've admired a beautiful yeasted loaf in a bakery, bought it, and taken it home, only to discover that, despite its appearance, its taste and texture were less than admirable. The crumb might be too open or uneven, the flavor bland or yeasty. . . . It was just not what I was expecting or hoping for. Both delightful experiences, such as the visit to Ganachoud's bakery, and other, less positive experiences with breads have spurred me on to learn just what it takes to make an excellent bread, and I've gleaned some important insights along the way.

Many people who bake yeasted breads regularly and proficiently have only a vague understanding of what actually happens to transform a mass of ingredients into a finished bread. As often as not, they seem to regard the whole process as a bit of magic, and because of this, the results of their efforts are often inconsistent—sometimes outstanding, other times just okay. Many factors affect the process and outcome of yeasted breads, including ingredient proportions, mixing and baking techniques, temperature, and timing. You need to understand these cause-and-effect relationships in order to make the bread that you want. I'm going to tell you what I do and why.

FERMENTATION

While practice is essential for mastering basic baking techniques, knowing a little chemistry is also important for consistently producing the best yeasted breads. In short, when grain or flour is combined with liquid and live yeast organisms in the absence of oxygen, it undergoes fermentation, chemical changes which convert the grain's carbohydrates into simple sugars and produce carbon dioxide gas and alcohol. The gas leavens the dough, particularly when the grain composing it contains a large proportion of gluten proteins, since these can be developed into an elastic and expandable structure. The alcohol evaporates as the dough is handled; this is crucial, as its presence would ultimately do in the yeast. Finally, baking the bread permanently fixes the gluten web, kills the yeast when it is no longer useful, and drives off any remaining alcohol.

Leavening may be the most dramatic outcome of dough fermentation, but fermentation also benefits bread in other more subtle but significant ways. During fermentation, the grain is broken down both physically and enzymatically, softening it and releasing its natural sweetness. Fermented adequately, bread dough becomes slightly acidic, and this improves its flavor and digestibility. The gluten becomes stronger and stretchier, contributing to nicely shaped and evenly textured bread. Bread that is fermented well ends up moister and keeps longer. Adequate fermentation also enhances the bread's nutritional profile by freeing calcium, iron, zinc, and other important minerals that are bound up in the grain.

The primary requirement for dough fermentation is time—and this is the very thing it seems many bread recipes try to minimize. Yeast growth and leavening can be accelerated in various ways, but not without compromising the final product. Overly rapid rising of dough results in poor texture, a flat flavor, decreased digestibility, unavailable nutrients, and a short duration of freshness in the finished loaf. Patience is the secret ingredient for exceptional yeasted breads.

To allow for optimum fermentation, it is necessary to rein in the yeast's development. Since yeast multiplies readily in the right environment, you should start with a modest quantity in the dough, as it will set a desirable pace for dough development. You'll be surprised at how effectively a small amount of yeast will leaven a sizable quantity of dough if given sufficient time and appropriate conditions. Including a sponge stage and multiple risings of the dough at a moderate temperature (70 to 75 degrees) gives the yeast a chance to develop gradually.

TIMING

Whether you make a yeasted bread quickly or leisurely, the actual hands-on working of dough remains about the same and does not take long. The time you add to achieve a well-developed dough is mostly waiting time, which you can mesh with your other activities. Making a yeasted bread, unlike preparing a quick bread, isn't an uninterrupted start-to-finish project. You must keep attuned to the dough, but it does a lot of the work on its own.

I recall my early experiences in making yeasted bread and how cloaked in unknowns the process seemed. Though the veil of mystery has been lifted as I've learned about each of the many steps of the breadmaking process, there is still suspense in working with live ingredients. Like me, you too will become increasingly comfortable with the procedures and timing the more you bake. Gradually, besides developing finely tuned judgment and physical skills, you'll recognize improvisation and flexibility creeping into your baking routines. You'll begin substituting ingredients you have on hand rather than following recipes exactly, and you'll fit baking into your schedule rather than deferring all other activities when you bake. Eventually, your breads will become truly your own rather than simply replications of someone else's recipes.

One more thing. Probably the most familiar breads—to Americans at least—are yeasted breads, everything from plain wheat bread to braided egg bread to croissants, but few people realize that sourdough and natural-rise breads are also yeasted breads. Since these breads require some specialized techniques, we will cover them in later chapters. Still, much of the information in this chapter applies to them too.

Making a Basic Yeasted Bread

We could go on and on talking about bread making, but the best way to learn about it is to do it, so let's get into the kitchen and start with a really basic yeasted bread. This detailed recipe is the prototype for the variations that follow it: stick to this basic recipe until you've mastered the techniques. The recipe yields about 3½ pounds of dough—enough for two good-sized loaves.

In both the basic bread and the variations, I follow the "sponge method" of making dough. This includes an initial step in which the yeast, some or all of the remaining liquid, and part of the flour are combined and left to sit until light and spongy, before finishing up the dough and kneading it.

The sponge method takes a little longer than the other major alternative known as the straight dough method, but, given identical ingredients and conditions, bread made with a sponge has better flavor, texture, keeping qualities, and digestibility. During the sponge stage, the yeast multiplies and fermentation gets under way. The gluten begins to develop and strengthen as it is stretched by the activity of the yeast. This is especially important when making a bread containing some low-gluten flour; in that case, prepare the sponge with high-gluten flour and incorporate the weaker flour into the dough later.

ASSEMBLING INGREDIENTS AND UTENSILS

Plan ahead. Before your last pre-baking marketing trip, inventory your bread-making supplies so you won't have to run out to shop for an ingredient that you thought you had on hand but don't. (But remember too that shopping isn't the only way to cope with a missing or inadequate amount of an ingredient. Many ingredients serve similar functions and are possible substitutions in bread. By using your imagination—and your leftovers—you may come up with something extraordinary. In fact, bits of things of all sorts in my refrigerator and cupboards often stimulate me to bake.)

Generally, home-scale baking proceeds more smoothly if the major ingredients are all at room temperature; cold liquid and flour inhibit leavening as effectively as a cool draft. Remove flour from cold storage early enough so that it warms up to room temperature, or warm it briefly in the oven set on low heat. You don't want too much heat either, so if you are scalding milk, for instance, be sure it has cooled to lukewarm before you add it to the dough.

Okay, for this basic bread, you'll need the following ingredients and utensils:

INGREDIENTS
    3 *cups spring water*
    ¾ *teaspoon active dry yeast*
    7½ *to 8 cups whole wheat bread flour*
    2½ *teaspoons sea salt*
    2 *tablespoons oil*

UTENSILS
Measuring spoons
Liquid measuring cup
Dry measuring cup
Large (ceramic) mixing bowl
Large wooden spoon
Rubber scraper or plastic dough scraper
Kneading surface
Metal dough scraper
Unnapped tea towels
2 loaf pans
Razor blade

PROOFING THE YEAST

The first thing to do is prove that the yeast is lively—proofing the yeast. Heat ¼ cup of the water to lukewarm. It should be cool enough so that you can comfortably rest your finger in it or drop it on your wrist without it feeling hot. If you are uncertain about the water temperature, measure it with a thermometer; it should be between about 100 and 115 degrees Fahrenheit.

Next add the yeast. Oh-oh! I can imagine some quizzical expressions at "¾ teaspoon active dry yeast" in this recipe. You're probably assuming this is a misprint, and you're preparing to increase the yeast. Don't! Honestly, this is enough yeast and actually better than more. Less is best for good bread. Remember the discussion earlier in the chapter? Yeast is a live organism and it will multiply by feeding off the other ingredients. Just be sure to give the dough adequate time to develop.

Let's proceed. I measure yeast directly out of a jar that I keep in the freezer and add it to the warm water. Sprinkle in about a teaspoon of flour to provide food for the yeast. Cover the cup and place it in a warm, draft-free spot. If you have a gas oven with a pilot light, that's a good place. In 5 to 10 minutes, the surface should appear slightly bubbly. Stir with your finger to be sure the yeast has thoroughly dissolved before proceeding. If you feel granules, return the cup to the warm spot for a few more minutes and then check it again.

If bubbling does not occur within a reasonable length of time, there may be something wrong with the yeast—it may be too old or the water may have been too cold or too hot. Try stirring in a little more flour for food and give it another 5 to 10 minutes. If there is still no sign of life, throw out the mixture and begin again. Always keep extra yeast on hand.

PREPARING THE SPONGE

Combine the yeast solution and the remaining 2¾ cups water in the bowl. Gradually add about 3½ cups of the flour to form a somewhat thick batter. If the flour is packed down, fluff it up as you measure it. With the wooden spoon, beat the batter in one direction about 100 strokes. Cover the bowl with a dampened towel and a large plate or other solid cover and set it in a draft-free spot for a couple of hours—or longer—until the yeast has obviously multiplied and caused the batter to become active and bubbly.

A bread sponge does not have rigid time constraints. Even though it is preferable to catch a sponge at the pinnacle of its rise, it can rise to its limit and fall back without unduly damaging the gluten. Though it is best to wait for a sponge to fully develop, the bread will benefit even if you move ahead with bread making before it reaches that point. We're using the sponge here to get the yeast and gluten off to a good start.

MIXING THE DOUGH

Stir in the salt; avoid lumps by sifting it first if necessary. Add the oil and beat well—about 100 times. Add 2 cups of flour, a cup at a time, stirring well after each. Before adding more flour, beat this batter energetically in one direction until it appears stringy, which is visible evidence that the gluten is developing. The beating will be easier if you set the bowl upon a folded tea towel, dampened on both sides to anchor it, and hold the spoon in an almost vertical position with both hands. I stir in a clockwise direction. To put less strain on your back, bend your knees slightly or put one foot up on a stool. Stir with your whole body rather than just with your arms or wrists.

Continue to add flour, a cup at a time, stirring well after each addition. The batter will soon become too stiff to stir easily, but add part of another cup of flour and continue mixing. As flour coats the dough, it will pull away from the sides of the bowl and ball up in the center. Clean off the spoon with the scraper. If the flour was readily absorbed and the dough remains really sticky, add a bit more flour and mix again. But remember, the dough should be on the sticky rather than the dry side at this point.

Lightly sprinkle flour on the kneading surface and turn the dough out onto it. Scrape any bits of dough or flour remaining in the bowl on top of the dough. Cover the dough with a tea towel and leave it for 5 to 10 minutes to allow the gluten to relax before you begin to knead. Meanwhile, wash out the bowl and fill it with hot water.

KNEADING THE DOUGH

Begin to knead the dough. Right-handed, I press down on the center of the dough mass with the heel of my right hand; I push down and out—away from myself—simultaneously giving the dough about a quarter turn counterclockwise. At the end of the push, the fingers of my right hand pull the dough back over itself as it turns. My left hand assists this process, serving sort of a guid-

ing function in the pulling over and turning motion. For me, kneading is an integrated motion, during which the dough is pushed, pulled, and turned as my entire body rocks forward and back. This dissected description of kneading sounds a lot more complicated than the activity actually is, and each individual really must find a personal way with it. Watching a skilled baker knead may help you to gain aptitude, but there is no single correct way to knead dough.

Once the surface of the dough seems somewhat sticky, sprinkle a small amount of flour under it and continue kneading. Be sure to add flour in small amounts; you don't want the dough sliding around under your hands in a sea of flour or to add more than the dough requires. As you pause in kneading, scrape the kneading surface clean with your dough scraper. If the dough sticks to the kneading surface, it can take more flour. The quantity of flour specified in a bread recipe is always a ballpark figure, as any container of flour will differ in moisture content from day to day.

Fitting Yeasted Bread Making into Your Schedule

CLEARLY, YOUR BREAD-MAKING routines must depend to some extent on your life-style and schedule. It's always pleasant to set aside a day, or most of a day, for bread making, and this is probably a good way to start, so that you get a clear, concentrated sense of the sequence of events and all. Actually, since the hands-on activities of bread making take so little time, what you're gaining is a day to accomplish some things at home in addition to a batch of fresh homemade bread. But waiting for a free day every time you want to make bread may mean that you rarely do it.

Of all breads, yeasted breads do require the most considered timing; but they are much more flexible than you might imagine, adaptable enough to fit around a wide variety of scheduling constraints. While carrying a bowl of dough around in the trunk of your car is one possibility, there are better alternatives. It comes down to your exerting control over the dough so that it rises optimally within a given time frame. Remember that "optimal rising" means that the dough rises to its utmost potential but does not go beyond that point. If dough doesn't rise enough, it will be underdeveloped and heavy; if it overrises and collapses, its gluten will be damaged and unable to stretch to its full potential again. You have two options: to slow down the dough or speed it up, and there are various ways to do either. You can also get a jump on bread making by giving the yeast and gluten development a head start in a sponge stage. As I mentioned earlier, unlike finished doughs, bread sponges can even fall back without much harm to the eventual dough.

Generally, stretching out bread making within reason results in bread with better flavor, texture, digestibility, nutrition, and keeping quality, and I would recommend this approach. Bread made in a hurry isn't likely to be a complete disaster on any front, though; it will certainly be fresher and probably taste better than most that you can buy. However, it will have a rather airy texture and undistinguished flavor, it won't have quite as much nutritional worth as a longer-fermented bread, and it will dry out rapidly. Still, you may prefer fast-rising bread to any that you can buy. Try out different timings and decide for yourself which results you like the best.

So, what can you do to regulate rising? The two major variables influencing the length of time a dough or sponge takes to rise are the amount of yeast you start with and the temperature of the dough as it rises. Even if you start with a small amount of yeast, you'll eventually end up with a lot of it in the dough if the conditions for its growth are favorable—mainly that it isn't so cold that it stays dormant. The warmer the dough is, the faster the yeast will multiply—up to about 130 degrees, which will kill it.

If you want decently developed bread in a really short time—say, 3 hours or less, follow the straight dough technique and use a large amount of yeast (3 to 4 teaspoons for the basic whole wheat bread recipe) and keep the dough very warm (85 or so degrees). It's still best to give the dough two bowl rises as well as a shaped rise, and be sure it rises fully each time—that is, wait until it doesn't rebound when pressed before you deflate it after each rise. Plan to keep close tabs on the dough, since short rising doughs are much more rigid in terms of timing than longer rising doughs. The same is true of short rising sponges.

To move towards longer rising bread, decrease the initial amount of yeast and/or the rising temperature. If you want extremely well-developed dough, start with a very small quantity of yeast (as little as ¼ teaspoon) and keep the dough especially cool—even down to 50 degrees or less. Find a spot that matches your desired rising pace—an unheated room or porch or the refrigerator. Always cover doughs and sponges tightly to keep them from drying out—and anything from getting in! Experiment and figure out a timing routine that yields the bread you prefer and suits your schedule. The dough or sponge itself is your guiding light; if it isn't rising at a desirable rate, move it to a warmer or cooler spot and make a note to start with more or less yeast on your next try. This may take a while to work out just right.

Some other factors figure into rising behavior too, which you should take into account and manipulate as necessary. Salt puts the brakes on rising, so don't add it to sponges that you want to rise rather quickly, and vice versa. A moderate amount of sweetener accelerates rising, but an excess will have the opposite effect. Cold liquids will slow down rising and warm ones speed it up—but always use warm water for dissolving yeast unless indicated otherwise and don't add hot liquids to yeast once it has proofed. Dough or sponge consistency influences the pace of rising: a soft dough or thin sponge will rise faster than the same dough or sponge made stiffer by incorporating more flour.

Whatever your timetable, be sure to deflate dough and stir down sponges as necessary to remove the carbon dioxide and alcohol that build up, to redistribute the yeast and reinvigorate the developing gluten; do this at least every eight hours. If you make a sponge the consistency of dough, don't knead it thoroughly or it will be more difficult to incorporate the remaining ingredients; it will get a thorough kneading later when you make the full dough. Also, don't include low-gluten flours in sponges, since a major purpose of the sponge is to build up the strength of the gluten; add low-gluten flours at the final dough stage. Finally, if you rise a dough cold, let it warm up thoroughly to room temperature before you shape it.

You can work with the same variables when you are faced with unexpected interruptions. If you're called away just as you finish mixing or kneading the dough or after its first bowl rise, put it in a cool place or in the refrigerator. When you get back to it, let it warm up thoroughly to room temperature before resuming where you left off. An exception to this is shaped loaves. Enclose them in plastic bags, allowing space for rising, and, if they have risen fully when you return, put them right into a preheated oven; you may have to bake them a bit longer to compensate for their cold start. Chilling shaped loaves is a good way to stagger bakings if you can't fit all of the loaves from a single batch of dough into the oven at the same time. Always remember, though, that chilling dough doesn't stop it in its tracks; it takes a while for a warm dough to become cool through and through and its rising pace will diminish gradually. So even when you refrigerate dough, especially on short notice, keep in touch with it if possible to see that it doesn't overrise. Sponges and doughs can't go on indefinitely; try to move them toward finished bread within a reasonable length of time—two to three days at the outside.

Think of kneading as stretching exercises for the dough. Eventually, the gluten strands will interconnect in an organized structure which is elastic enough to expand under the pressure of the carbon dioxide gas produced by the yeast. As you knead, the dough will become increasingly integrated and smooth, tensile, and less sticky. Since you're using whole wheat flour, the dough will feel a bit gritty, especially at first, compared to a dough made with refined flour.

Beginning bread bakers wonder how they will know when the gluten is adequately developed—when they have done enough kneading. How long it takes will depend on the quantity of dough, gluten content of the flour, duration of the sponge stage, and the effectiveness of your beating and kneading of the dough. Fifteen to twenty minutes of steady kneading will probably do it, but you should learn to judge by the feel of the dough. When you're done, the dough should be smooth, supple, and have a certain springy or bouncy quality. At this point, particularly with especially high-gluten doughs, you may see tiny blisters across the taut, smooth surface.

When you've finished kneading, scrape the work surface and sprinkle it lightly with flour, set down the dough, and cover it with a damp tea towel. Let the dough rest for about 10 minutes.

FIRST BOWL RISE

When the dough has relaxed, uncover it and give it 5 to 10 quick kneads to round it into a ball. The dough will feel great to handle—smooth, elastic, together. Empty the bread bowl and dry it. Grease the inside very lightly with margarine, butter, or oil, just enough to keep the dough from sticking to the bowl and from drying out. Put the dough into the bowl, smooth side down, and then flip it over to coat it lightly with oil. Cover the bowl with a damp tea towel and place a solid cover such as a large plate or tray on top; this will also help the dough remain moist. After you have situated the dough for rising, clean off the kneading surface.

Professionals put dough to rise in a specially designed cabinet called a proof box, which has temperature and humidity controls. Since homes lack this piece of equipment, home bakers must improvise. Your intention is to keep drafts out and some warmth in the dough, but not to heat it. The dough in the bowl should be surrounded by an even temperature rather than warmed from a single direction, which can cause uneven rising and, if the heat is intense enough, hardening of a portion of the dough.

I find that cool room temperature is plenty warm. It's a good idea to wrap the covered bowl in a large beach towel or a blanket if the room is especially cool and drafty. Wrapped up, the dough will be 5 to 10 degrees warmer than the room, since it is well insulated and yeast produces heat as it works. On hot days, look for cool spots for the dough, such as the basement, or set the bread bowl in a large container of cold water.

Several factors influence the length of the rising period and the rising potential of a particular dough: the temperature of the dough and of the room; the quantity and liveliness of the yeast; the amount of salt, oil, and sweetener; the type of flour; and how well you kneaded the dough. At high altitudes, dough rises more quickly; plan on an extra rise or two to develop it fully.

At a room temperature of 70 to 75 degrees, the first bowl rise of this dough will take about 2 hours. If you eliminated the sponge stage, it will take longer. The dough will approximately double in size, but determine if it has risen sufficiently by pressing a finger against the

surface. If the dough gives in to your finger pressure and the indentation remains, it has risen enough; if the dough springs back, it should rise longer. Take care not to let the dough overrise. It will become sour from the accumulation of the fermentation by-products, the yeast will exhaust its food source, and the gluten will stretch to the breaking point, causing the dough to collapse in a heap with a permanently weakened structure.

DEFLATING THE DOUGH

When the dough has risen adequately, it is time to "punch it down" or "knock it back" in baking lingo. You can give it a literal punch to knock the air out, but

a gentler touch is better for the dough. I turn it out onto the unfloured kneading surface and knead it gently a few times.

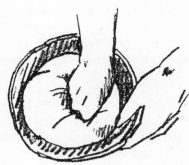

There are three reasons for doing this: first, to dispel the air, actually carbon dioxide gas and alcohol, which has accumulated in the dough during the fermentation process; second, to rearrange and reenergize the yeast organisms; and finally, to allow the gluten to retract and then stretch out again, thereby furthering its development.

SECOND BOWL RISE

Form the dough back into a ball and return it to the bowl. Cover and leave it to rise again. This rise may take slightly less time than the first one. Test it as you did the first time.

DIVIDING THE DOUGH

When the dough has risen adequately for the second time, turn it out onto the work surface and cut it in half; each piece will weigh about 1¾ pounds. Knead each piece briefly on an unfloured surface to expel gas and to round it into a ball. The dough should not feel at all sticky now, and you should not add flour at this point in the baking process.

Cover the dough and leave it to rest for a few minutes. It is important to continue to keep the dough covered with damp tea towels as much of the time as possible to preserve its moistness. During this resting period, the developed gluten will relax, enabling you to

Other Shapes for Breads

SHAPING IS THE beginning of the visual art phase of bread making. Loaves may be made in just about any shape and size, but some doughs are more suitable for particular manipulations than others. Smooth, strong wheat doughs work for any form of loaf. Doughs containing a large proportion of low-gluten flour are less strong and less tolerant of stretching than all-wheat doughs, and should always be formed into simple shapes.

In this country, the term "loaf" is virtually synonymous with a rectangular form. Perhaps the notion of a loaf is as stereotyped in other regions of the world as it is here, but the associated shape is likely different, such as long, thin baguettes in France. In some cultures, certain kinds of bread are associated with particular shapes, for instance, Jewish egg bread, or challah, which is usually braided. The shape of a loaf may also have symbolic meaning; this is often the case for special breads made for religious observances, festivals, or holidays.

ROUND LOAVES

To form a round loaf, take a piece of relaxed dough and knead it gently several times until it begins to round and the underside of the dough is smooth. Gather the edges, pinching them together in the middle to form a ball. Flip it over, smooth side up. With your hands gently cupping opposite sides of the ball and pressing inward, rotate it on the work surface in a clockwise direction several times until it is evenly rounded and the bottom is sealed. Now, forcefully drop the ball onto the kneading surface and then quickly repeat the rotating process; repeat this sequence once or twice more. Place the loaf on a parchment-lined, cornmeal-dusted, or lightly greased baking sheet or pie plate, or uniformly press it into a round metal, glass, or ceramic baking dish or bowl, filling about two-thirds of the pan's volume.

OVAL LOAVES

Oval loaves are elongated round loaves. To shape one, place both hands on the smooth top of a just-shaped round loaf, and, pressing gently, roll the dough back and forth until it becomes slightly elongated. Bake the loaf freestanding.

BRAIDING A LOAF

Braided loaves are most successfully made from a strong, glutenous dough. They can consist of three or more strands. Divide the dough cut for a single loaf into smaller pieces of equal weight. Knead each section briefly to expel all of the air, and let the dough rest a few minutes in order to relax the gluten. Form each piece into a strand by placing both of your palms, side by side, on top of the dough and, pressing down gently but firmly, rolling the dough back and forth as you move your hands apart, until the strand reaches the length and thickness you want. Be careful not to make the strands too thin, or they may tear apart as they rise, before or during baking.

Press together one end of each of the strands and braid them rather loosely to allow for the dough's expansion, then pinch together the opposite ends of the strands. Or, braid from the middle toward each end. Arrange the braid on a sheet or in a pan and tuck both ends under slightly.

Another way to form a three-strand braid begins with one long dough rope. Form a loop with two-thirds of the dough, overlapping the end slightly and pinching the point of overlap securely; leave the final third of the dough free. Turn the loop so that the free end is at the top. Drop the free end through the loop and pull the end to the left. Next, twist the loop clockwise and drop the free end through it again. Repeat this pattern until the braid is complete. Bernard Clayton describes this technique in his book *The Breads of France*.

WEAVING A BREAD BASKET

The same strands that are used for forming braided loaves may also be woven. For a Christmas dinner,

YEASTED BREADS ♦ 55

my husband and I baked a bread basket, lined it with a pretty cloth, and filled it with fresh rolls. It was on its second pass around the table before someone noticed that the basket itself was edible!

To weave a bread basket, grease the outside of an ovenproof bowl or pot and turn it upside down on a baking sheet. Lay an odd number, say 5 or 7, of rolled strands of dough of the same length equidistant from one another on the bottom and down the sides of the pot—like the spokes of a wheel. Press the ends together in the middle. These are the upright supports for the basket. Roll a long strand of dough and pinch one end of it under one of the support strands close to the middle of the pot. Weave it over and under the support strands, moving outward. Weave loosely, leaving ample slack to allow for the expansion of the dough as it rises. When the first weaving strand is used up, pinch another long one onto it and continue weaving. It's helpful to have one person rolling strands while another weaves. If you're working alone, roll several long strands before beginning to weave, so that you can continue uninterrupted. Leave an inch or so of the support strands to tuck into the woven portion to finish what will be the top edge of the basket.

work with the dough more easily and with less danger of tearing it. The more developed the dough is, the more crucial will be this resting period, since the potential for overstretching and tearing the gluten strands is greater. While the dough rests, wash the bread bowl and grease the pans with margarine, butter, or oil.

SHAPING AND PANNING LOAVES

To form a rectangular panned loaf, take a piece of the rounded, relaxed dough and gently press it out with your fingers into a thick oval or slightly rectangular shape, its width the length of the pan. Firmly roll the dough up into a cylinder, pinch the edge to form a seam, and pinch each end closed.

Place the rolled dough seam side down in the greased pan and press it evenly and firmly into the corners and against the sides. The dough should fill about two-thirds of the pan's volume.

SHAPED DOUGH RISE

Cover the shaped dough with a damp tea towel and set it in a draft-free spot at room temperature to rise again. Since the dough will continue to expand in the oven, this rise shouldn't be as complete as the two bowl rises, and it will take about three-fourths of the time for those—between 1 and 1½ hours. Near the end of this final rise, preheat the oven to 350 degrees.

When the dough rebounds slowly when pressed with a finger, it is ready to bake. The dough will be slightly rounded over the top of the pan; remember that it will rise more in the oven, so don't overdo it. Don't rush the dough at this stage, but do watch that it doesn't overrise.

SURFACE TREATMENTS: CUTTING AND GLAZING

Slash the top of the loaves with a razor blade held almost parallel to the surface of the dough. Make one or more cuts—¼ to ½ inch deep. Make one long slash down the center, an S-shaped cut, or two to three evenly spaced diagonal cuts.

Besides adding a decorative touch this permits the interior dough to expand after the crust has already become set by oven heat. Uncut loaves are likely to tear randomly on the top or sides. Docking, or piercing the surface of a loaf with a long-tined fork or a skewer, serves the same function for heavy textured, less glutenous doughs, such as rye breads.

Next, you can apply a glaze or another substance to the dough surface to influence the character of the baked crust (see page 56).

Slashing Patterns for Round Loaves and Rolls

THERE ARE LOTS of possibilities for cutting round loaves and rolls: for instance, C-shaped cuts (facing toward the center) on each side; additional parallel cuts in between the C-cuts; 3 or 4 pinwheel cuts around the crown; 3 or 4 long slashes from a single point on one side of the loaf; cuts in a crosshatch design on top of the loaf; or a circular cut all the way around the circumference.

BAKING THE BREAD

Arrange the prepared loaves in the preheated oven. Be sure to leave space between pans and between pans and oven walls so that the heat can circulate freely and evenly around the loaves. Especially in the early stages of baking, resist any urge to open the oven to check on the bread's progress. A window in my oven door has solved the curiosity problem for me and has provided many hours of enjoyable viewing.

If you know your oven heats unevenly, creating hot spots, you may wish to shift the pans around partway through baking. But wait until the loaves are at least half done and then rearrange them as quickly and efficiently as possible, since the oven temperature will drop rapidly with the door open and interfere with consistent baking.

Most home ovens are constructed of thin sheet metal and are generally not airtight, so they cannot hold in the steam produced during baking which gives bread a moist interior and crisp crust. I have tasted the difference in the bread baked in the brick ovens still used in some old bakeries and resurrected in some young bakeries, and I have fantasized for a long time about building, or at least using, a brick oven someday. At one time, I lined the bottom rack of my regular gas range with fire bricks and noticed some positive effect on my bread. The bricks' presence in the oven also affected the temperature of my apartment, since they took a long time to heat up and cool down; this was desirable during a cold winter but not when summer arrived! Now I simulate brick oven baking on a small scale by using a baking cloche, described on page 24 and 58.

These loaves will take about 50 minutes to bake. For future reference, keep in mind that baking time is influenced by dough composition, loaf size, container shape and material, baking temperature, and oven load. Denser, low-gluten breads take longer to bake than high-gluten ones, and they bake more thoroughly at a lower temperature for a longer period of time. Large loaves take longer to bake than small ones, given the same dough and oven temperature. The same amount of dough molded by a tall, narrow container will require a longer baking period than if it were spread out in a broad, shallow pan. Glass pans bake about 25 degrees hotter than metal ones; therefore, for glass, turn down the thermostat by 25 degrees or shorten the baking period. Cast-iron pans take longer to heat up and longer to cool down than either steel or glass ones. Of course, bread bakes more quickly at a higher rather than

---

Surface Treatments

- **Egg**—either the whole egg or just the egg yolk or egg white—can be brushed on as a glaze; any of these mixed with a little water becomes an egg wash. A beaten whole egg or egg yolk gives the baked bread a shiny, chewy crust and also securely holds sesame, poppy, caraway, or other seeds that you may want to sprinkle on for additional flavor and texture. Egg white makes the crust shiny and hard, and it, too, acts as a glue for seeds. Apply egg glazes or washes just before baking or 5 to 10 minutes before the end of the baking period.

- **Water**, brushed or sprayed onto the surface of the dough before and/or during baking, produces a hard, crisp crust. Incidentally, if you spray a loaf with an atomizer while it is in the oven, be careful not to hit the oven light, or you may end up with a glass-encrusted loaf; I learned this lesson the hard way. A little salt dissolved in the water, as well as an especially hot oven temperature, further enhances crustiness. Applying water to the dough surface simulates, to a degree anyway, the effect of steam injection in professional ovens.

- **Milk** or **melted butter** or **margarine** or **oil** brushed on the dough before and/or after baking produces a soft, tender crust.

- To get a shiny, chewy crust like that of commercial rye and pumpernickel breads, combine ½ teaspoon **potato starch** or **cornstarch** and about ¼ cup water, and boil it for several minutes until it is thick and clear. Half to three-quarters of the way through baking brush this on the bread, and again just before the bread is done.

Making Rolls and Other Small Breads

A ROLL IS JUST a small bread, usually an individual portion of bread, though one may not be enough! Rolls are usually somewhere between 2 and 4 ounces of dough, though they may be smaller or larger, depending on your intentions. I once made dozens of tiny "rollettes" to accompany dips at a friend's party. Yeasted rolls weighing about 3 ounces apiece will bake in 20 to 25 minutes in a moderate oven.

Rolls may be formed from any bread dough, and there are as many, if not more, roll shapes as loaf shapes. I was once charmed by walking into the kitchen of an acquaintance as she was helping her three-year-old son fashion a "doughfellow" out of a small piece of bread dough; they were pinching on his nose and ears as I arrived. It was a baking day ritual for them, and it was a special experience for me to observe it.

I have been asked, "How did you get these rolls so round?" It took me a while to learn an efficient rounding technique. Take a small, relaxed piece of dough and place it on the work surface with your hand cupped over it. With your palm resting on the dough, exert gentle downward pressure and simultaneously move your hand rapidly in a circular motion until the dough is evenly rounded and the bottom is sealed. For crusty round rolls, bake them a couple of inches apart; baked up against one another, they will have soft sides. Three or four tiny balls baked together in a muffin cup result in a cloverleaf roll.

Another roll-making technique involves rolling the dough into a flat sheet and cutting out squares or triangles, which are then rolled or folded in various ways. For crescent rolls, cut triangles and roll them from the base toward the point; arrange them on a sheet with the middle point lapped over in front just touching the sheet and the side points curled slightly inward. For pinwheel rolls, cut squares and then cut almost to the middle from each corner; fold every other point from each corner into the center and press firmly to seal. For envelope rolls, cut squares and fold each point into the center and seal.

For braided, spiraled, or knotted rolls, form compact dough strands from relaxed dough, twist them into single or double spirals, or knot or braid them. A high-gluten dough that isn't too grainy works best for these types of rolls.

Bread sticks are simply risen and baked rolled dough strands, usually glazed and seeded or else sprayed with water before and during baking for extra crunchiness. Bake them at 425 degrees for about 20 minutes.

Pretzels are dough strands that are dipped into a hot lye or baking soda solution (add about 1 tablespoon lye or baking soda to a quart of cold water and then heat it to very hot but not boiling) before they are knotted and left to rise on a baking sheet. Brush them with an egg wash and sprinkle on coarse salt before baking them in a preheated 400-degree oven for about 15 minutes.

Form **bagels** by looping dough ropes about 7 inches long into rings and securely pinching the ends together; or form balls and poke a hole through the center. Let them rest briefly and then boil them for a minute or two on each side in a pot of lightly salted water. Drain the bagels and place them on a greased baking sheet. Brush on an egg glaze, sprinkle on some seeds if you wish, and bake at 425 degrees for about 25 minutes—until browned.

Like rolls, **English muffins** may be made from any yeasted bread dough. After it has risen in the bowl, roll the dough with a rolling pin into an even sheet about ½ inch thick. Cover the dough with a damp tea towel and let rest for a few minutes. Roll the dough gently again, since it probably will have contracted a bit. Cut adjacent rounds—straight down without twisting—with a biscuit or muffin cutter. For uniformity, weigh the rounds and adjust the thickness of the dough if necessary, so that each round weighs about 2½ to 3 ounces. Place the rounds on a baking sheet sprinkled with cornmeal, cover them with a damp tea towel, and let them rise until they're light and puffy. Sprinkle cornmeal on the top of the rounds and gently flip them over, a few at a time, onto a preheated, ungreased griddle or skillet set over low heat or into an electric frying pan preheated to 250 degrees. Cook until the underside is lightly browned and the sides have firmed—about 10 minutes. Sprinkle the tops with cornmeal, turn carefully, and cook 5 to 10 minutes more, until the second side is lightly browned and the muffins sound hollow when tapped. To make more muffins from the dough scraps, knead these leftovers together into an integrated mass of dough; allow it to rest, covered with a damp towel, then begin the rolling and cutting procedure over again. Alternatively, use the dough scraps to make a loaf or rolls.

a lower temperature, and a loaf baked in an oven filled with several other loaves will take slightly longer to bake than if it was the only thing in the oven. Consider all of these factors when you estimate baking time.

TESTING THE BREAD

Bake the loaves until they have browned, all sides are firm, and they sound hollow when removed from the pan and tapped on the bottom. If the pans were adequately greased, the loaves should come out of the pans easily, usually by simply turning the pans over onto a rack. If the bread doesn't fall right out, thump the bottom of the pan in a couple of places and try again. A loaf that comes out of a pan easily is not necessarily done; check the brownness of the bottom and tap it for a distinctly hollow sound. Conversely, the bread may be done and may be sticking because the pan was greased insufficiently or unevenly. If you suspect this problem, run a long metal spatula around the loaf to attempt to loosen it from the pan. If you know you greased the pan thoroughly and you haven't baked the bread overly long, put the loaf back in the oven for a few more minutes; it may slide out of the pan easily the next time you check it.

Baking in a Cloche

LIGHTLY DUST THE base of the cloche with cornmeal. Shape a round loaf and place it in the middle of the base. Cover with a damp tea towel and set it aside to rise. Meanwhile, soak the bell portion in a sinkful of water. When the loaf has risen, slash the top, spray it with water or brush it with a glaze, and sprinkle on seeds if you wish. Remove the bell from the water and fit it on the base. Bake the bread at 450 degrees for 15 minutes, then turn the oven down to 400 degrees and bake 30 minutes longer. Remove the cloche from the oven and lift off the bell. Carefully run a pancake turner or metal spatula under the loaf to loosen it from the base. The bottom of the bread should be well browned and sound distinctly hollow when tapped. If it doesn't seem done, replace the bell and return it to the oven for 5 to 10 minutes or until the bread is ready.

COOLING AND SLICING THE BREAD

When the bread has tested done, immediately remove it from the pan and place it on a wire rack to cool. The crust will soften somewhat upon cooling. Brushing melted butter or margarine on it immediately after baking will accentuate this softening, as will covering the baked loaf with a towel or bowl as it cools—be sure to allow the loaf some air circulation, though. Be certain that a loaf has cooled completely, a several-hour process, before putting it away.

Cooled loaves slice much more evenly and thinly than hot ones, and the bread is more digestible since the cooking process is complete. The warmth of just-out-of-the-oven bread is enticing and the fragrance makes it almost irresistible, but the texture is doughy since the bread is really still baking. Making a portion of a batch of dough into small breads, such as rolls or English muffins, may provide a happy compromise for the cut-or-not-to-cut controversy which often ensues over freshly baked loaves. Small items cool much more quickly than large loaves and can be eaten sooner. See page 57–58 for directions for making rolls and other small breads.

A gentle back-and-forth sawing motion with a bread knife is the most effective way to slice bread.

STORING BREAD

The way you store your bread will have a definite effect on its continued good quality. The best method I've found for keeping yeasted breads is to put them in an earthenware bowl covered with a clean tea towel and an earthenware plate. Check the bread daily, and if it seems too moist, slide the plate over to allow a little more air to enter.

A pottery container would be an ideal bread box. Johanna, an art student friend of mine, set out to make one for me as a ceramics class project. She designed a wonderful art deco structure, complete with two chambers and sliding lids, and she prepared clay slabs and carefully connected them together. Unfortunately, the walls cracked and my unique bread box was never finished.

I sometimes wrap a small loaf that I know will be rapidly consumed in a clean, dry towel or place it in a brown paper or waxed paper bag, but I avoid plastic. From experience, I have concluded that plastic bags, wraps, and containers are least desirable for storing breads outside of the refrigerator; they prevent bread from breathing adequately and promote rapid molding. Plastic bags do keep bread from drying out when refrigerated, and refrigerator storage does inhibit mold growth, but bread stored properly at room tempera-

ture retains its moistness and fresh flavor longer than bread that is refrigerated.

I rarely freeze unsliced loaves of bread, since the texture of thawed bread is less satisfactory, more crumbly, than that of unfrozen bread. When I do freeze a whole or partial loaf, I slice it first, and take slices out of the freezer as I need them, generally to toast. Frozen slices thaw quickly and their flavor and texture remain relatively intact.

I often freeze baked small breads, such as rolls, English muffins, and bagels. Like bread slices, these items thaw quite quickly and maintain good texture and flavor. Wrap them well before freezing and use them up within several months.

Depending on time, I defrost bread items, wrapped, either in the refrigerator or at room temperature. It's best to let them thaw in the wrappings they were frozen in, since the frost inside will be reabsorbed, maintaining moisture in the bread. If you're really in a hurry, you can put the bread or rolls in a covered pan or wrap them in foil and heat them in a warm oven, but slower thawing produces a better texture.

Except for an occasional ball of dough intended for a future pizza, I don't freeze unbaked dough.

REHEATING BREAD

The best way I have found to reheat rolls is to lightly spray them all over with water from an atomizer and place them directly on the wire rack of a toaster oven or oven set at 325 to 350 degrees. This technique produces warm, crisp-crusted rolls in about 5 minutes. For soft-crusted rolls, heat them in a covered container. To heat and revitalize somewhat dry bread, steam it briefly.

Yeasted Bread Variations

Once you've mastered the basic whole wheat loaf, you'll no doubt want to expand your bread-making horizons. Variety is the spice of life and there are many possible variations on this bread which can enhance yours.

SUBSTITUTE GRAINS

For subtle variation in flavor and texture, replace some of the whole wheat bread flour with another flour, such as rye or triticale. To maintain a strong dough, though, still use at least two-thirds whole wheat bread flour. Add some cornmeal, rye meal, or bran for a coarser crumb. Soaked cracked grains and cooked whole grains contribute moistness and their own unique nubbliness. Refer back to chapter 1 for a description of different grains and their special contributions to breads.

Evaluating Yeasted Breads and Solving Problems

So, how should your bread have ended up? Beyond an intoxicating fragrance, the first impression of a bread is usually a visual one. To me, the quintessential yeasted loaf has a pleasing form and is a uniform shade of brown. Picked up, the bread has a promising heft indicating substance rather than either total airiness or dead weight. Pressed lightly, the loaf has firm yet slightly giving sides which reveal its resiliency. Cut open, the cross section reveals a thin, protective crust encasing an even-textured, compact interior that is moist and springy. The loaf slices thinly without crumbling. The texture is somewhat chewy and the flavor, reflecting the natural sweetness of the grains, is wonderfully complex.

If your bread didn't come out just this way, don't be discouraged. Check the following chart to see what might have gone wrong, and then try again soon.

Problem	Explanation	Solution
Bread is layered or streaked inside	Flour not absorbed by dough	Knead thoroughly and don't add a lot of flour at the end
Bread is heavy and dense	Too much flour in dough	Make dough less stiff
	Too much low-gluten flour	Use more high-gluten flour
	Dough didn't rise enough	Let dough rise longer or at higher temperature
	Too much salt, fat, or sweetener in dough	Adjust balance of ingredients
Crumb coarse and crumbly	Too much low-gluten flour	Increase proportion of high-gluten flour
	Dough not kneaded enough	Knead dough longer
	Dough rose too quickly	Use less yeast or more salt; rise in a cooler place
	Dough not properly developed	Dough probably hasn't had enough risings
	Dough overdeveloped—kneaded too much, risen too long, or not deflated well enough	Knead less and keep a closer eye on dough while rising
Crumb is uneven—compact in some areas and open in others	Dough overrose in pan	Bake loaf sooner next time
	Oven not hot enough	Increase baking temperature
	Not enough salt	Increase salt slightly
	Large difference between dough temperature and room temperature	Keep dough and room at a consistent temperature for final rise
Crust too hard and dry	Bread baked too long	Shorten baking time; for now, wrap loaf in towel as it cools or brush with melted margarine
	Oven temperature too high	Check oven
	Baked with too much steam	Spray less next time

Problem	Explanation	Solution
Crust too soft	Bread underbaked	Bake another 10 to 15 minutes
	Loaf needs surface treatment	Spray with water at beginning of baking or brush with egg white glaze first
Crust browned unevenly	Temperature varies in different areas of oven	Move pans around as bread bakes—after it has "set"
Sides and bottom are pale	Baking in shiny (probably aluminum) pans	Use tinned or blackened steel pans; for now, remove loaves from pans and bake another 5 to 10 minutes
Loaf splits along sides	Shaped loaf didn't rise long enough before baking	Let loaf rise until it springs back slightly when pressed
Freestanding loaf spreads out too much	Dough too soft	Use a stiffer dough or bake in a sided pan
Bread is flat/bland	Dough didn't develop long enough	Let dough ferment longer, deflating it as necessary
	Not enough salt	Add salt
Bread tastes yeasty	Dough rose too quickly	Start with cooler ingredients; rise dough in cooler spot
	Too much yeast	Reduce yeast

SUBSTITUTE LIQUIDS

You can substitute milk, soy milk, nut or seed "milks," vegetable stock, or fruit juices for all or part of the water. Potato cooking water makes light loaves with a wonderful flavor and texture. Beer lends an intriguing flavor—particularly to rye breads. For extra richness, protein, and loft, substitute some beaten eggs for part of the liquid. Puréed raw or cooked fruits or vegetables also count as liquid and often contribute a mellow sweetness. Apple or pear sauce and golden winter squashes and sweet potatoes are some of my favorites. Mashed cooked dried beans are a nourishing, flavorful, moisturizing addition to bread.

ADD SWEETENER

Honey, maple syrup, molasses, barley malt, rice syrup, or Sucanat are all options, but don't overdo it or you'll mask the natural sweetness of the grains themselves.

ADD DRIED FRUITS, GRATED VEGETABLES, NUTS, OR SEEDS

Raisins, currants, and other chopped dried fruits add chewy sweet spots. Seeds, chopped nuts, and sprouts provide a subtle crunch. Minced or grated vegetables or fruits also add textural interest as well as flavor. The bright orange flecks in carrot bread are outstanding!

SUBSTITUTE FATS

Replace the oil with nut or seed butter. Imagine—peanut butter or almond butter bread! You can also increase the oil by a tablespoon or two to make the bread richer and tenderer; don't go overboard, though, or it will be heavy and greasy tasting.

SPICE IT UP

Spices and herbs can inspire eyebrow-lifting appreciation. Caraway, dill, fennel, and anise are traditional accents in rye breads. Cumin, coriander, and oregano add an exotic touch to bean breads. Basil, rosemary, thyme, sage, and tarragon liven up a basic wheat loaf. Cinnamon, cloves, nutmeg, allspice, mace, and cardamom hint at festivity. Orange or lemon zest add zing.

Modify the basic recipe, try out the recipes that follow, and tap your own improvisational spirit to devise more. Soon you'll be making your own signature yeasted breads.

TRITICALE-WHEAT BREAD
▼▼▼

Though similar to whole wheat bread, the flavor of this bread is subtly different, with an appealing ruggedness. Making an all-wheat sponge before adding the triticale flour strengthens the dough. This dough works well for encasing savory fillings, such as in PIROSHKI (page 176) and KASHA KNISHES (page 177).

YIELD: 2 loaves

PREPARATION TIME: 2½ to 3 hours for sponge and dough; 5 hours for rising; 45 to 50 minutes to bake

  3   *cups spring water*
  ¾   *teaspoon active dry yeast*
  5   *cups whole wheat bread flour*
  2½ *teaspoons sea salt*
  2½ *tablespoons corn oil*
  2½ *cups triticale flour*

Heat ¼ cup of the water and cool it to lukewarm. Add the yeast and a teaspoon of wheat flour. Cover and set in a warm spot to proof. Add the remaining water and stir in about 3½ cups of the wheat flour to form a thick batter. Cover and set in a draft-free spot for about 2 hours, until a sponge develops.

Stir in the salt, oil, and triticale flour. Gradually stir in enough of the remaining wheat flour to form a dough.

Turn the dough out onto a lightly floured surface, cover, and let rest for several minutes. Knead until smooth and elastic, adding wheat flour as necessary to keep the dough from sticking.

Form the dough into a ball and put it in a lightly greased bowl. Cover and set aside for about 2 hours, until the dough has risen and does not spring back when pressed. Turn the dough out and knead it briefly. Return it to the bowl for a second rise.

Shape and pan the dough. Cover the loaves and set them aside to rise for about an hour or until the dough rebounds slowly when pressed.

Slash the tops of the loaves. Spray them with water or brush on an egg wash and sprinkle on some poppy seeds. Bake at 350 degrees for about 50 minutes—until the loaves are brown, have firm sides, and sound distinctly hollow when removed from the pans and tapped on the bottom.

Cool the bread thoroughly before slicing or storing it.

(For more detailed instructions, refer to the directions for BASIC YEASTED WHOLE WHEAT BREAD, beginning on page 48.)

NOTES
- For a heftier loaf, use half triticale flour (3¾ cups), but still start off with the wheat flour in the sponge to strengthen the dough.

ANADAMA BREAD
▼▼▼

There is an old story about a New Englander, his wife Anna, and a cornmeal bread which somehow originated from a spat between them: something about him growing tired of the cornmeal mush which she perpetually served him or her growing weary of serving him. In any case, the mush somehow got turned into a cornmeal-wheat bread called "anadama"—apparently a contracted form of his exasperated cursing, "Anna, damn her!" This is a moist, fine-textured bread with a subtle crunch. It is usually sweetened with molasses but you can omit it and a delicious, delicate corn flavor will come through. Use the freshest cornmeal you can find for this bread.

YIELD: 2 loaves

PREPARATION TIME: 2½ to 3 hours for sponge and dough; 5 hours for rising; 45 to 50 minutes to bake

  3   *cups spring water*
  ¾   *teaspoon active dry yeast*
  6¾ *cups whole wheat bread flour*
  1¼ *cups cornmeal*
  2½ *teaspoons sea salt*
  3   *tablespoons corn oil*
  3   *tablespoons molasses*

Heat ¼ cup of the water and cool it to lukewarm. Add the yeast and a teaspoon of flour. Cover and set in a warm spot to proof.

Sift together the cornmeal and 3¾ cups of the flour. Combine the proofed yeast and remaining water and stir in 3 cups or so of the sifted mixture to form a thick batter. Cover and set in a draft-free spot for about 2 hours or until it develops into a sponge.

Stir the salt, oil, and molasses into the sponge. Gradually stir in the remaining sifted mixture, and as much additional flour as necessary to form a dough.

Turn the dough out onto a lightly floured surface, cover, and let rest for several minutes. Knead until smooth and elastic, adding flour as necessary to keep the dough from sticking.

Form the dough into a ball and put it in a lightly greased bowl. Cover and set aside for about 2 hours, until the dough has risen and does not spring back when pressed. Turn the dough out and knead it briefly. Return it to the bowl for a second rise.

Shape and pan the dough. Cover the loaves and set

them aside to rise for about an hour or until the dough rebounds slowly when pressed.

Slash the tops of the loaves and spray them with water or brush on an egg wash. Bake at 350 degrees for about 50 minutes—until the loaves are brown, have firm sides, and sound distinctly hollow when removed from the pans and tapped on the bottom.

Cool the bread thoroughly before slicing or storing it.

(For more detailed instructions, refer to the directions for *BASIC YEASTED WHOLE WHEAT BREAD,* **beginning on page 48.)**

FINNISH RYE
▼▼▼

This moist, naturally sweet bread has a fine, even grain. It is traditionally shaped into round loaves. I often use part of the dough for the crust of a tart or for turnovers— see CABBAGE KUCHEN (page 173), KASHA KNISHES (page 177), and PIROSHKI (page 176).

YIELD: 2 loaves

PREPARATION TIME: 2½ to 3 hours for sponge and dough; 5 hours for rising; 45 to 50 minutes to bake

    3   cups spring water
    ¾   teaspoon active dry yeast
    4½ cups whole wheat bread flour
    1   tablespoon sea salt
    3   tablespoons corn oil
    3   cups rye flour

Heat ¼ cup of the water and cool it to lukewarm. Add the yeast and a teaspoon of wheat flour. Cover and set in a warm spot to proof. Add the remaining 2¾ cups water and gradually stir in about 3½ cups of wheat flour to form a thick batter. Cover and set in a draft-free spot for about 2 hours or until it develops into a sponge.

Stir the salt and oil into the sponge. Add the rye flour, a cup at a time. Gradually stir in as much additional wheat flour as necessary to form a dough.

Turn the dough out onto a lightly floured surface, cover, and let rest for several minutes. Knead the dough rather gently, since doughs containing rye flour are more fragile than all-wheat ones. Knead until the dough is smooth and resilient but stop as soon as it begins to feel sticky.

Form the dough into a ball and put it in a lightly greased bowl. Cover and set aside for about 2 hours, until the dough has risen and does not spring back when pressed. Turn the dough out and knead it briefly. Return it to the bowl for a second rise.

Shape and pan the dough. Cover the loaves and set them aside to rise for about an hour or until the dough rebounds slowly when pressed.

Dock or slash the tops of the loaves. Bake at 375 degrees for 40 to 50 minutes, until the loaves sound distinctly hollow when removed from the pan and tapped on the bottom.

Cool the bread thoroughly on a rack before slicing or storing it.

(For more detailed instructions, refer to the directions for *BASIC YEASTED WHOLE WHEAT BREAD,* **beginning on page 48.)**

BEER-RYE BREAD
▼▼▼

This rye bread is subtly sweet and tangy. I especially like the flavor imparted by dark beer. For WHOLE WHEAT BEER BREAD, substitute whole wheat bread flour for the rye flour. Set aside some of the dough for a CABBAGE or ONION KUCHEN (page 173) or a CRISSCROSS COFFEE CAKE (page 182).

YIELD: 2 loaves

PREPARATION TIME: 2½ to 3 hours for sponge and dough; 5 hours for rising; 45 to 50 minutes to bake

    ¾   cup spring water
    ¾   teaspoon active dry yeast
    4½ cups whole wheat bread flour
    2¼ cups beer, room temperature
    1   tablespoon sea salt
    3   tablespoons corn oil
    3   cups rye flour

Heat ¼ cup of the water and cool it to lukewarm. Add the yeast and a teaspoon of wheat flour, cover, and set in a warm place to proof. Add the remaining ½ cup water and the beer. Gradually stir in about 3½ cups of the wheat flour to form a thick batter. Cover and set in a draft-free spot for about 2 hours or until a sponge develops.

Stir the salt, oil, and rye flour into the sponge. Gradually stir in as much of the remaining wheat flour as necessary to form a dough.

Turn the dough out onto a lightly floured surface, cover, and let rest for a few minutes. Knead thoroughly but carefully until the dough is smooth and elastic. Stop if it begins to get sticky.

Form the dough into a ball and place it in a lightly greased bowl. Cover and set aside for about 2 hours, until the dough has risen and does not spring back when pressed. Turn the dough out and knead it briefly. Return it to the bowl for a second rise.

Shape and pan the dough. I usually make round loaves. Cover the loaves and set them aside to rise for about an hour or until the dough rebounds slowly when pressed.

Dock or slash the tops of the loaves. Bake at 375 degrees for 40 to 50 minutes—until the loaves sound distinctly hollow when removed from the pans and tapped on the bottom.

Cool the bread thoroughly before slicing or storing it.

(For more detailed instructions, refer to the directions for *BASIC YEASTED WHOLE WHEAT BREAD*, **beginning on page 48.)**

SPROUTED WHEAT BREAD
▾▾▾

When I taught preschool children, one of our projects was to sprout a variety of grains and beans. Surprisingly sweet wheat berry sprouts were always a favorite of even the most finicky three-year-olds. Wheat sprouts are extra-nutritious—very high in B vitamins and vitamins A, C, and E plus protein. They sweeten and moisten this bread and may even enhance its rising. I like to use part of the dough for English muffins. Begin sprouting ¼ cup hard wheat berries about three days before you want to make the bread; the sprouts should be about the same length as the grains of wheat.

YIELD: 2 loaves

PREPARATION TIME: 2½ to 3 hours for sponge and dough; 5 hours for rising; 50 to 60 minutes to bake

- 2¾ cups spring water
- ¾ teaspoon active dry yeast
- 6½ to 7 cups whole wheat bread flour
- 2¼ teaspoons sea salt
- 2 tablespoons corn oil
- 1½ to 2 cups wheat sprouts (see page 242)

Heat ¼ cup of the water and cool it to lukewarm. Add the yeast and a teaspoon of flour. Cover and set in a warm spot to proof. Add the remaining 2½ cups water. Stir in about 3 cups of the flour to form a thick batter. Cover and set in a draft-free spot for about 2 hours or until a sponge develops.

Stir the salt and oil into the sponge. Roll the sprouts in a tea towel to dry them, then coarsely chop them and stir them in. Gradually stir in enough of the remaining flour to form a dough.

Turn the dough out onto a lightly floured surface, cover, and let rest for several minutes. Knead until smooth and elastic, adding flour as necessary to keep the dough from sticking.

Form the dough into a ball and put it in a lightly greased bowl. Cover and set aside for 1½ to 2 hours or until the dough has risen and does not spring back when pressed. Turn the dough out and knead it briefly. Return it to the bowl for a second rise.

Shape and pan the dough. Cover the loaves and set them aside to rise for about an hour or until the dough rebounds slowly when pressed.

Slash the tops of the loaves and spray them with water or brush on an egg wash. Bake at 350 degrees for 50 to 60 minutes—the sprouts add moisture, so be sure you bake the bread long enough. The loaves should be well browned, have firm sides, and sound distinctly hollow when removed from the pans and tapped on the bottom.

Cool the bread thoroughly before slicing or storing it.

(For more detailed instructions, refer to the directions for *BASIC YEASTED WHOLE WHEAT BREAD*, **beginning on page 48.)**

NOTES
- Substitute milk or soy milk for the 2½ cups of water; scald and cool it to lukewarm before adding it to the proofed yeast.

VERY BERRY BREAD
▾▾▾

Cooked whole wheat berries give this bread a chewy, moist texture. Substitute rye berries for a different flavor. Use part of the dough to make excellent English muffins (see page 58).

YIELD: 2 loaves

PREPARATION TIME: 2½ to 3 hours for sponge and dough; 5 hours for rising; 50 minutes to bake

- 3 cups spring water
- ¾ teaspoon active dry yeast
- 7½ cups whole wheat bread flour
- 2¼ teaspoons sea salt
- 2 tablespoons corn oil
- 2 cups cooked wheat berries (see page 13–14)

Heat ¼ cup of the water and cool it to lukewarm. Add the yeast and a teaspoon of flour. Cover and set in a warm spot to proof. Add the remaining 2¾ cups water. Gradually stir in 2 to 3 cups of the flour to form a thick batter. Cover and set in a draft-free spot for about 2 hours or until a sponge develops.

Stir the salt, oil, and wheat berries into the sponge. Gradually stir in enough of the remaining flour to form a dough.

Turn the dough out onto a lightly floured surface,

cover, and let rest for a few minutes. Knead until smooth and elastic, adding flour as necessary to keep the dough from sticking.

Form the dough into a ball and put it into a lightly greased bowl. Cover and set aside for about 2 hours, until the dough has risen and does not spring back when pressed. Turn the dough out and knead it briefly. Return it to the bowl for a second rise.

Shape and pan the dough. Cover the loaves and set them aside to rise for about an hour or until the dough rebounds slowly when pressed.

Slash the tops of the loaves. Bake at 350 degrees for about 50 minutes—until the loaves are brown, have firm sides, and sound distinctly hollow when removed from the pans and tapped on the bottom.

Cool the bread thoroughly before slicing or storing it.

(For more detailed instructions, refer to the directions for *Basic Yeasted Whole Wheat Bread*, beginning on page 48.)

Sesame Bread
▾▾▾

The irresistible flavor and gentle crunch of roasted sesame seeds pervades this popular loaf.

YIELD: 2 loaves

PREPARATION TIME: 2½ to 3 hours for sponge and dough; 5 hours for rising; 45 to 50 minutes to bake

    3   cups spring water
   ¾   teaspoon active dry yeast
   7½ cups whole wheat bread flour
   ¾   cup sesame seeds
   2¼ teaspoons sea salt
   2   tablespoons sesame oil

Heat ¼ cup of the water and cool it to lukewarm. Add the yeast and a teaspoon of flour. Cover and set in a warm spot to proof. Add the remaining 2¾ cups water. Gradually stir in about 3½ cups of the flour to form a thick batter. Cover and set in a draft-free spot for 2 hours or until a sponge develops.

Meanwhile, roast the sesame seeds in a dry, heavy-bottomed skillet (cast iron works well) over moderate heat; agitate the pan or stir often to prevent the seeds from burning. Grind the seeds coarsely with a mortar and pestle or food processor.

Stir the salt, oil, and sesame seeds into the sponge. Gradually stir in enough of the remaining flour to form a dough.

Turn the dough out onto a lightly floured surface, cover, and let rest for about 10 minutes. Knead until

smooth and elastic, adding flour as necessary to keep the dough from sticking.

Form the dough into a ball and put it in a lightly greased bowl. Cover and set aside for about 2 hours, until the dough has risen and does not spring back when pressed. Turn the dough out and knead it briefly. Return it to the bowl for a second rise.

Shape and pan the dough. Cover the loaves and set them aside to rise for about an hour or until the dough rebounds slowly when pressed.

Slash the tops of the loaves; brush with an egg wash and sprinkle on whole sesame seeds. Bake at 350 degrees for about 50 minutes—until the loaves are brown, have firm sides, and sound distinctly hollow when removed from the pans and tapped on the bottom.

Cool the bread thoroughly before slicing or storing it.

(For more detailed instructions, refer to the directions for *Basic Yeasted Whole Wheat Bread*, beginning on page 48.)

NOTES
- Add the grated zest of a large lemon along with the salt, oil, and seeds.

- Substitute ¼ cup each of toasted poppy seeds and chopped sunflower seeds for ½ cup of the sesame seeds.

Pecan Bread
▾▾▾

Pecans are plentiful where I live in Texas and this bread is packed with them. You can substitute black walnuts, English walnuts, hazelnuts, or other nuts.

YIELD: 2 loaves

PREPARATION TIME: 2½ to 3 hours for the sponge and dough; 5 hours for rising; 45 to 50 minutes to bake

   ¼   cup spring water
   ¾   teaspoon active dry yeast
   6½ to 7 cups whole wheat bread flour
   2¾   cups milk or soy milk, scalded and cooled to warm
   2½   teaspoons sea salt
   2   tablespoons corn or sesame oil
   2   cups lightly toasted, coarsely chopped pecans

Heat the water and cool it to lukewarm. Add the yeast and a teaspoon of flour, cover, and set in a warm spot to proof. Add the milk and gradually stir in about 3½ cups of the flour to form a thick batter. Cover and set in a draft-free spot for about 2 hours or until a sponge develops.

Stir the salt and oil into the sponge. Gradually stir in enough of the remaining flour to form a dough.

Turn the dough out onto a lightly floured surface, cover, and let rest for several minutes. Knead until smooth and elastic, adding flour as necessary to keep the dough from sticking.

Form the dough into a ball and put it in a lightly greased bowl. Cover and set aside for about 2 hours, until the dough has risen and does not spring back when pressed. Turn the dough out and knead it briefly. Return it to the bowl for a second rise.

Turn the dough out onto an ungreased surface and press it out into a flat circle. Sprinkle two-thirds of the chopped nuts over the dough and lightly press them into it. Fold dough in half and press in the remaining nuts. Fold it in half again to enclose the nuts. Cover the dough and let it rest for a few minutes, until it has re-laxed. Gently knead the dough—initially, the nuts will tend to come to the surface but continue kneading until they seem to be evenly distributed. Rest the dough un-til it relaxes again.

Shape and pan the dough; I like to make round loaves. Cover the loaves and set them aside to rise for about an hour or until the dough rebounds slowly when pressed.

Slash the tops of the loaves; spray them with water or brush on an egg wash. Bake at 350 degrees for about 50 minutes—until the loaves are brown, have firm sides, and sound distinctly hollow when removed from the pans and tapped on the bottom.

Cool the bread thoroughly before slicing or stor-ing it.

(For more detailed instructions, refer to the di-rections for *Basic Yeasted Whole Wheat Bread,* **beginning on page 48.)**

NOTES
- Chop the nuts in small pieces for a finer texture.

Sweet Bread
▾▾▾

This rich, sweetened dough makes an exceedingly tender-textured bread. I especially like to use this dough for Sticky Buns *(page 180–81),* Apple Butter Buns *(page 180),* Cinnamon Swirl *(page 180), or* Fruit Sauce Pizza *(page 170–71).*

YIELD: 2 loaves

PREPARATION TIME: About 1 hour for sponge and dough; 5 hours for rising; 50 minutes to bake

   1/2 cup spring water
   3/4 teaspoon active dry yeast

   6 to 6 1/2 cups whole wheat bread flour
   1 1/2 cups milk or soy milk, scalded
   1/4 cup maple syrup
   2 teaspoons sea salt
   1/4 cup sunflower oil
   2 eggs, beaten (about 1/2 cup)

Heat the water and cool it to lukewarm. Add the yeast and a teaspoon of flour, cover, and set in a warm spot to proof. Stir in 1/2 cup of the flour, cover, and set in a draft-free spot for about 30 minutes, until a sponge develops.

Combine the hot milk, syrup, salt, and oil in a large bowl and set aside until the mixture cools to lukewarm. Reserve 1 teaspoon of the beaten egg for a glaze and whisk the rest of it and the sponge into the milk mix-ture. Gradually stir in enough of the remaining flour to form a dough.

Turn the dough out onto a lightly floured surface, cover, and let rest for several minutes. Knead until smooth and elastic, adding flour as necessary to keep the dough from sticking.

Form the dough into a ball and put it in a lightly greased bowl. Cover and set aside for about 2 hours, until the dough has risen and does not spring back when pressed. Turn the dough out and knead it briefly. Return it to the bowl for a second rise.

Shape and pan the dough. Cover the loaves and set them aside to rise for about an hour or until the dough rebounds slowly when pressed.

Slash the tops of the loaves. Whisk a little water with the reserved egg and brush it on the loaves. Bake at 350 degrees for about 50 minutes—until the loaves are brown, have firm sides, and sound distinctly hollow when removed from the pans and tapped on the bottom.

Cool the bread thoroughly before slicing or stor-ing it.

(For more detailed instructions, refer to the di-rections for *Basic Yeasted Whole Wheat Bread,* **beginning on page 48.)**

NOTES
- Substitute a mild-flavored honey for the maple syrup.

Spiced Honey Bread
▾▾▾

This light, spicy, fragrant bread is festive for holidays but appealing all year round. For breakfast, try it toasted and spread with Pear Butter *(page 135). This dough makes delicious English muffins (see page 58).*

YIELD: 2 round loaves

PREPARATION TIME: 1 hour for sponge and dough; 5 hours for rising; 45 to 50 minutes to bake

> ½ cup spring water
> ½ teaspoon active dry yeast
> 5½ to 6 cups whole wheat bread flour
> ¼ cup sesame oil
> ¼ cup honey
> 1 egg
> 1 tablespoon ground coriander
> ½ teaspoon cinnamon
> ¼ teaspoon ground cloves
> 2 teaspoons sea salt
> 1½ cups milk or soy milk, scalded and cooled to lukewarm

Heat the water and cool it to lukewarm. Add the yeast and a teaspoon of flour, cover, and set in a warm spot to proof. Stir in ½ cup of the flour, cover, and set in a draft-free spot for about 30 minutes, until a sponge develops.

In a large bowl, whisk together the sponge, oil, honey, egg, spices, salt, and milk. Gradually stir in enough of the remaining flour to form a dough.

Turn the dough out onto a lightly floured surface, cover, and let rest for several minutes. Knead until smooth and elastic, adding flour as necessary to keep the dough from sticking.

Form the dough into a ball and put it in a lightly greased bowl. Cover and set aside for about 2 hours, until the dough has risen and does not spring back when pressed. Turn the dough out and knead it briefly. Return it to the bowl for a second rise.

Shape two round loaves and put them in lightly greased pans or on a baking sheet lined with baking parchment. Cover the loaves and set them aside to rise for about an hour or until the dough rebounds slowly when pressed.

Slash the tops of the loaves; brush them with an egg wash if you wish. Bake at 350 degrees for 45 to 50 minutes—until the loaves are brown and sound distinctly hollow when tapped on the bottom.

Cool the bread thoroughly before slicing and storing it.

(**For more detailed instructions, refer to the directions for** *BASIC YEASTED WHOLE WHEAT BREAD*, **beginning on page 48.**)

GOLDEN HARVEST BREAD
▼▼▼

Make this subtly sweet bread in autumn when winter squashes are plentiful. Butternut squash is my favorite. Use a portion of the dough for a CRISSCROSS COFFEE *CAKE (page 182) or* APPLE BUTTER BUNS *(page 180).*

YIELD: 2 loaves

PREPARATION TIME: 2½ to 3 hours for sponge and dough; 5 hours for rising; 50 minutes to bake

> 2 cups spring water
> ¾ teaspoon active dry yeast
> 6 to 7 cups whole wheat bread flour
> 1½ cups mashed cooked winter squash
> 2 teaspoons sea salt
> 2 tablespoons corn oil

Heat ¼ cup of the water and cool it to lukewarm. Add the yeast and a teaspoon of flour, cover, and set in a warm spot to proof. Add the remaining 1¾ cups water and gradually stir in about 2½ cups of the flour to form a thick batter. Cover and set in a draft-free spot for 2 hours or until a sponge develops.

Stir the squash, salt, and oil into the sponge. Gradually stir in enough of the remaining flour to form a dough.

Turn the dough out onto a lightly floured surface, cover, and let rest for several minutes. Knead until smooth and elastic, adding flour as necessary to keep the dough from sticking.

Form the dough into a ball and put it in a lightly greased bowl. Cover and set aside for about 2 hours, until the dough has risen and does not spring back when pressed. Turn the dough out and knead it briefly. Return it to the bowl for a second rise.

Shape and pan the dough. Cover the loaves and set them aside to rise for about an hour or until the dough rebounds slowly when pressed.

Slash the tops of the loaves. Sometimes I brush these with an egg wash and sprinkle on sesame or poppy seeds. Bake at 350 degrees for about 50 minutes—until the loaves are brown, have firm sides, and sound distinctly hollow when removed from the pans and tapped on the bottom.

Cool the bread thoroughly before slicing or storing it.

(**For more detailed instructions, refer to the directions for** *BASIC YEASTED WHOLE WHEAT BREAD*, **beginning on page 48.**)

NOTES
- Substitute mashed cooked pumpkin, carrot, sweet potato, or yam for the squash.

- Substitute apple juice for the water.

- Add 2 tablespoons of a mild-flavored honey along with the squash, salt, and oil.

SPICY BEAN BREAD
▼▼▼

This dough is smooth and satiny and the baked bread is light and tender—perhaps not what you would expect from adding mashed cooked beans to bread. The beans add protein and give the bread a moist crumb. Ground roasted cumin seeds are a zesty complement to the subtly sweet flavor of the beans. You can substitute pinto beans, anasazi beans, or black turtle beans for the aduki beans.

YIELD: 2 loaves

PREPARATION TIME: About 1 hour for sponge and dough; 5 hours for rising; 50 minutes to bake

    1 cup spring water
    ¾ teaspoon active dry yeast
    7 cups whole wheat bread flour
    2 cups cooked aduki beans, mashed (see page 238)
    1½ cups bean stock (or spring water)
    2 teaspoons sea salt
    2 tablespoons sesame oil
    1 tablespoon roasted cumin seeds, coarsely ground

Heat ¼ cup of the water and cool it to lukewarm. Add the yeast and a teaspoon of flour, cover, and set in a warm spot to proof. Stir in the remaining ¾ cup of water and 1 cup of flour, cover, and set in a draft-free spot for about 30 minutes or until a sponge develops.

Stir together the beans and stock and warm slightly. Combine with the sponge, salt, oil, and ground seeds. Gradually stir in enough of the remaining flour to form a dough.

Turn the dough out onto a lightly floured surface, cover, and let rest several minutes, until relaxed. Knead until smooth and elastic, adding flour as necessary to keep the dough from sticking.

Form the dough into a ball and put it in a lightly greased bowl. Cover and set aside for about 2 hours, until the dough has risen and does not spring back when pressed. Turn the dough out and knead it briefly. Return it to the bowl for a second rise.

Shape and pan the dough. Cover the loaves and set them aside to rise for about an hour or until the dough rebounds slowly when pressed.

Slash the tops of the loaves. Bake at 350 degrees for about 50 minutes or until the loaves are brown, have firm sides, and sound distinctly hollow when removed from the pans and tapped on the bottom.

Cool the bread thoroughly before slicing or storing it.

(For more detailed instructions, refer to the directions for *BASIC YEASTED WHOLE WHEAT BREAD,* **beginning on page 48.)**

NOTES

- For a milder-flavored bread, omit the cumin and garnish the loaves with sesame seeds.

- Substitute olive oil for the sesame oil.

TOFU-HERB BREAD
▼▼▼

This moist, nutritious loaf has the lively flavor of fresh herbs and a compact crumb like that of a cottage cheese bread. Serve it with hot or chilled soups.

YIELD: 2 loaves

PREPARATION TIME: 2½ to 3 hours for sponge and dough; 5 hours for rising; 45 to 50 minutes to bake

    1½ cups spring water
    1 teaspoon active dry yeast
    6 to 6½ cups whole wheat bread flour
    1 pound tofu
    2 teaspoons sea salt
    ¼ cup lemon juice
    ¼ cup vegetable oil
    ¼ cup minced fresh dill weed
    ¼ cup minced fresh chives

Heat ¼ cup of the water and cool it to lukewarm. Add the yeast and a teaspoon of flour, cover, and set in a warm spot to proof. Combine with the remaining 1¼ cups water in a large bowl. Stir in about 2 cups of the flour to form a thick batter. Cover and set in a draft-free spot for about 2 hours or until a sponge develops.

In a blender or food processor fitted with the metal blade, blend the tofu, salt, lemon juice, and oil until thoroughly smooth. Stir this into the sponge along with the herbs. Gradually stir in enough of the remaining flour to form a dough.

Turn the dough out onto a lightly floured surface, cover, and let rest for several minutes. Knead until smooth and elastic, adding more flour as necessary to keep the dough from sticking.

Form the dough into a ball and put it in a lightly greased bowl. Cover and set aside for about 2 hours, until the dough has risen and does not spring back when pressed. Turn the dough out and knead it briefly. Return it to the bowl for a second rise.

Shape and pan the dough. I like to make round loaves. Cover the loaves and set them aside for about an hour or until the dough rebounds slowly when pressed.

Slash the tops of the loaves. Bake at 350 degrees for about 50 minutes—until the loaves are brown, have firm sides, and sound distinctly hollow when removed from the pans and tapped on the bottom.

Cool the bread thoroughly before slicing or storing it.

(For more detailed instructions, refer to the directions for *Basic Yeasted Whole Wheat Bread,* **beginning on page 48.)**

NOTES

- Substitute other fresh or dried herbs for the dill and chives. Gauge the amount by the potency of the herb (dill and chives are rather mild) and use about half as much of a dried herb as its fresh form.

CHALLAH
▼▼▼

Braided egg bread is traditional for the Jewish sabbath. With proper development, this dough will triple into light, airy loaves. Shape one large braid or, for an especially fancy bread, set two or three three-strand braids in graduated sizes atop one another. Of course, this dough does not have to be braided; it makes beautifully browned bread in any shape or size. You can also use a portion of the dough to make bread-crusted vegetable tarts (see pages 172–74), as I often do for dinner parties. Leftover challah makes exceptional French toast (page 185).

YIELD: 1 large loaf

PREPARATION TIME: About 2 hours for sponge and dough; 5 hours for rising; 40 to 50 minutes to bake

- 1²/₃ cups spring water
- ¹/₂ teaspoon active dry yeast
- 5¹/₂ to 6 cups whole wheat bread flour
- 3 large eggs, beaten (³/₄ cup)
- 2 teaspoons sea salt
- 3 tablespoons corn oil

Heat ¹/₄ cup of the water and cool it to lukewarm. Add the yeast and a teaspoon of flour, cover, and set in a warm spot to proof. Stir in the remaining water and about 2 cups of the flour and set in a draft-free spot for about an hour or until a sponge develops.

Reserve 2 to 3 teaspoons of the egg to use for a glaze. Stir the remainder of the egg and the salt and oil into the sponge. Gradually stir in enough of the remaining flour to form a dough.

Turn the dough out onto a lightly floured surface, cover, and let rest for several minutes. Knead until smooth and elastic, adding flour as necessary to keep the dough from sticking.

Form the dough into a ball and put it in a lightly greased bowl. Cover and set aside for about 2 hours, until the dough has risen and does not spring back when pressed. Turn the dough out and knead it briefly. Return it to the bowl for a second rise.

Shape the dough (see page 54 for braiding instructions). Set the braid on a lightly greased or parchment-lined baking sheet. Small braids may also be baked in loaf pans rather than freestanding. Cover and set aside to rise for about an hour or until the dough rebounds slowly when pressed.

Brush with the reserved egg and sprinkle with poppy seeds if you wish. Bake at 350 degrees for about 50 minutes, depending on the size of the loaf or loaves. The bread should be well browned, have firm sides, and sound distinctly hollow when removed from the pan and tapped on the bottom.

Cool the bread thoroughly before slicing or storing it.

(For more detailed instructions, refer to the directions for *Basic Yeasted Whole Wheat Bread,* **beginning on page 48.)**

GINGERY CARROT BREAD
▼▼▼

The pleasantly pungent aroma and zesty flavor of fresh ginger contribute to the special character of this orange-speckled bread. Cashews provide fat, contributing moistness as well as their subtle flavor. Use some of the dough for English muffins (see page 58). PEAR BUTTER *(page 135) is a terrific topping.*

YIELD: 2 loaves

PREPARATION TIME: 2¹/₂ to 3 hours for sponge and dough; 5 hours for rising; 50 minutes to bake

- 2¹/₂ cups spring water
- ³/₄ teaspoon active dried yeast
- 7 to 7¹/₂ cups whole wheat bread flour
- ¹/₃ cup lightly toasted cashews
- 2¹/₂ teaspoons finely grated fresh ginger root
- 2¹/₂ teaspoons sea salt
- 2¹/₂ cups lightly packed grated carrots (12 ounces)

Heat ¹/₄ cup of the water and cool it to lukewarm. Add the yeast and a teaspoon of flour, cover, and set in a warm spot to proof. Combine with 1³/₄ cups of the water in a large bowl. Stir in about 2¹/₂ cups of the flour to form a thick batter. Cover and set in a draft-free spot for about 2 hours or until a sponge develops.

Thoroughly purée the cashews and remaining ¹/₂ cup water in a blender and stir it into the sponge, along with the ginger, salt, and carrot. Gradually stir in enough of the remaining flour to form a dough.

Turn the dough out onto a lightly floured surface, cover, and let rest for several minutes. Knead until smooth and elastic, adding more flour as necessary to keep the dough from sticking.

Form the dough into a ball and put it in a lightly greased bowl. Cover and set aside for about 2 hours, until the dough has risen and does not spring back when pressed. Turn the dough out and knead it briefly. Return it to the bowl for a second rise.

Shape and pan the dough. Cover the loaves and set them aside to rise for about an hour or until the dough rebounds slowly when pressed.

Slash the tops of the loaves. Bake at 350 degrees for about 50 minutes—until the loaves are brown, have firm sides, and sound distinctly hollow when removed from the pans and tapped on the bottom.

Cool the bread thoroughly before slicing or storing it.

(For more detailed instructions, refer to the directions for *BASIC YEASTED WHOLE WHEAT BREAD,* **beginning on page 48.)**

NOTES

- Omit the cashews and add 2 tablespoons sesame oil; incorporate the extra ½ cup water and another ½ to ¾ cup flour in the sponge stage.

APPLE OR PEAR SAUCE BREAD
▼▼▼

This bread is fine grained and slightly sweet. In the pear-growing region of central France, bakers customarily add black pepper to pear bread dough. Follow their lead, or try allspice, nutmeg, freshly grated or ground ginger, lemon zest, or aniseed to accentuate the fruit flavor. Or let the fruit stand on its own as I have here. Refer to the recipe for PEAR BUTTER *(page 135); use the milled fruit sauce before it has been cooked down to fruit butter. Use part of this dough to make an* APPLICIOUS PIZZA *(page 171) or a* FRUIT SAUCE PIZZA *(page 170–71).*

YIELD: 2 loaves

PREPARATION TIME: 1½ to 2 hours for sponge and dough; 5 hours for rising; 50 minutes to bake

> 1¼ *cups spring water*
> ¾ *teaspoon active dry yeast*
> 7½ *cups whole wheat bread flour*
> 2½ *cups unsweetened apple sauce or pear sauce, at room temperature*
> 2½ *teaspoons sea salt*
> 2½ *tablespoons sesame or corn oil*

Heat ¼ cup of the water and cool it to lukewarm. Add the yeast and a teaspoon of flour, cover, and set in a

warm spot to proof. Combine with the remaining cup of water in a large bowl. Stir in a cup or so of the flour to form a thick batter. Cover and set in a draft-free spot for about an hour or until a sponge develops.

Stir the fruit sauce, salt, and oil into the sponge. Gradually stir in enough flour to form a dough.

Turn the dough out onto a lightly floured surface, cover, and let rest for several minutes. Knead until smooth and elastic, adding flour as necessary to keep the dough from sticking.

Form the dough into a ball and put it in a lightly greased bowl. Cover and set aside for about 2 hours, until the dough has risen and does not spring back when pressed. Turn the dough out and knead it briefly. Return it to the bowl for a second rise.

Shape and pan the dough. Cover the loaves and set them aside to rise for about an hour or until the dough rebounds slowly when pressed.

Slash the tops of the loaves and brush on an egg wash. Bake at 350 degrees for about 50 minutes—until the loaves are brown, have firm sides, and sound distinctly hollow when removed from the pans and tapped on the bottom.

Cool the bread thoroughly before slicing or storing it.

(For more detailed instructions, refer to the directions for *BASIC YEASTED WHOLE WHEAT BREAD,* **beginning on page 48.)**

NOTES

- Substitute 1¼ cups fruit butter blended with 1¼ cups water or unsweetened apple juice for the fruit sauce.

- For a special raisin bread, knead ¾ to 1 cup raisins into each loaf.

DATE-ORANGE BREAD
▼▼▼

Date purée seasoned with fresh orange zest and juice contributes sweetness to the flavor and moistness to the crumb of this bread. Medjool dates are my favorite. I like to make round loaves and garnish them with poppy seeds. This dough is a good choice for making STICKY BUNS *(page 180–81) and other coffee cakes.*

YIELD: 2 loaves

PREPARATION TIME: 1½ to 2 hours for sponge and dough; 5 to 6 hours for rising; 50 minutes to bake

> 2 *to* 2¼ *cups spring water*
> ¾ *teaspoon active dry yeast*
> 6 *to* 6½ *cups whole wheat bread flour*

1 orange
1 heaping cup dates (1/2 pound), pitted and
  chopped
2 teaspoons sea salt
2 tablespoons sesame oil

Heat 1/4 cup of the water and cool it to lukewarm. Add the yeast and a teaspoon of flour, cover, and set in a warm spot to proof. Combine with 3/4 cup of the water in a large bowl. Stir in 1 cup or so of the flour to form a batter. Cover and set in a draft-free spot for about an hour or until a sponge develops.

Meanwhile, finely grate the zest of the orange into a saucepan. Juice the orange, measure the juice, and add water to equal 1 cup. Add this and the dates to the saucepan. Simmer, covered, over low heat for about 30 minutes. Cool somewhat. Blend in a blender or food processor until smooth. Measure and add water to equal 2 cups.

Stir the date mixture into the sponge, along with the salt and oil. Gradually add enough of the remaining flour to form a dough.

Turn the dough out onto a lightly floured surface, cover, and let rest for several minutes. Knead until smooth and elastic, adding flour as necessary to keep the dough from sticking. Handle the dough carefully, since it tends to be somewhat tacky.

Form the dough into a ball and put it in a lightly greased bowl. Cover and set aside for about 2 hours, until the dough has risen and does not spring back when pressed. Turn the dough out and knead it briefly. Return it to the bowl for a second rise.

Shape and pan the dough. Cover the loaves and set them aside to rise for about an hour or until the dough rebounds slowly when pressed.

Slash the tops of the loaves. Brush on an egg wash and sprinkle on poppy seeds if you wish. Bake at 350 degrees for about 50 minutes—until the loaves are brown, have firm sides, and sound distinctly hollow when removed from the pans and tapped on the bottom.

Cool the bread thoroughly before slicing or storing it.

(For more detailed instructions, refer to the directions for BASIC YEASTED WHOLE WHEAT BREAD, beginning on page 48.)

NOTES

- Substitute a lemon for the orange—of course you will need more water to make up the cup of liquid for cooking the dates.

- Substitute other dried fruits—apricots, figs, or prunes—for the dates.

POPPY SEED BREAD
▼▼▼

This fine-grained bread is filled with the subtle flavor and crunch of poppy seeds. Use a half pound of the dough to make the crust for a CABBAGE KUCHEN (page 173).

YIELD: 2 loaves

PREPARATION TIME: About 1 hour for sponge and dough; 5 hours for rising; 50 minutes to bake

1/2 cup spring water
1/2 teaspoon active dry yeast
7 to 71/2 cups whole wheat bread flour
2 cups milk or soy milk
1/2 cup poppy seeds
1/4 cup mild-flavored honey
2 teaspoons sea salt
1/4 cup corn oil
2 eggs

Heat the water and cool it to lukewarm. Add the yeast and a teaspoon of flour, cover, and set in a warm spot to proof. Stir in 1/2 cup of the flour and set in a draft-free spot for about 30 minutes, until a sponge develops.

Scald the milk and pour it over the poppy seeds in a large bowl. Add the honey, salt, and oil and set aside until lukewarm. Beat the eggs and reserve a teaspoon or two for glazing. Beat the remaining egg and the sponge into the cooled mixture. Gradually stir in enough of the remaining flour to form a dough.

Turn the dough out onto a lightly floured surface, cover, and let rest for several minutes. Knead until smooth and elastic, adding flour as necessary to keep the dough from sticking.

Form the dough into a ball and put it in a lightly greased bowl. Cover and set aside for about 2 hours, until the dough has risen and does not spring back when pressed. Turn the dough out and knead it briefly. Return it to the bowl for a second rise.

Shape and pan the dough. Cover the loaves and set them aside to rise for about an hour or until the dough rebounds slowly when pressed.

Slash the tops of the loaves; brush on the reserved egg and sprinkle lightly with poppy seeds. Bake at 350 degrees for about 50 minutes—until the loaves are well browned, have firm sides, and sound distinctly hollow when removed from the pan and tapped on the bottom.

Cool the bread thoroughly before slicing or storing it.

(For more detailed instructions, refer to the directions for BASIC YEASTED WHOLE WHEAT BREAD, beginning on page 48.)

NUT BUTTER BREAD
▼▼▼

Definitely nutty tasting, this bread has a smooth, even texture. You can use a nut butter made with any kind of roasted nuts, and it can be chunky or smooth, as you wish. Try peanut butter in the bread and use part of the dough as the crust for HARVEST MOON *(page 174).*

YIELD: 2 loaves

PREPARATION TIME: About 2 hours for sponge and dough; 5 hours for rising; 50 minutes to bake

> 1⅓ cups spring water
> ¾ teaspoon active dry yeast
> 6 to 6¾ cups whole wheat bread flour
> 2 cups milk or soy milk
> ⅔ cup unsalted nut butter
> 2½ teaspoons sea salt

Heat ⅓ cup of the water and cool it to lukewarm. Add the yeast and a teaspoon of flour, cover, and set in a warm spot to proof. Combine with the remaining cup of water in a large bowl. Stir in 1½ to 1¾ cups of the flour to form a thick batter. Cover and set in a draft-free spot for about 1½ hours or until a sponge develops.

Meanwhile, scald the milk and gradually whisk it with the nut butter and salt. Cool to lukewarm.

Stir the milk mixture into the sponge. Gradually stir in enough of the remaining flour to form a dough.

Turn the dough out onto a lightly floured surface, cover, and let rest for several minutes. Knead until smooth and elastic, adding flour as necessary to keep the dough from sticking.

Form the dough into a ball and put it in a lightly greased bowl. Cover and set aside for about 2 hours, until the dough has risen and does not spring back when pressed. Turn the dough out and knead it briefly. Return it to the bowl for a second rise.

Shape and pan the dough. Cover the loaves and set them aside to rise for about an hour or until the dough rebounds slowly when pressed.

Slash the tops of the loaves; brush on an egg wash and sprinkle on sesame seeds or finely chopped nuts. Bake at 350 degrees for about 50 minutes—until the loaves are brown, have firm sides, and sound distinctly hollow when removed from the pans and tapped on the bottom.

Cool the bread thoroughly before slicing or storing it.

(For more detailed instructions, refer to the directions for BASIC YEASTED WHOLE WHEAT BREAD, **beginning on page 48.)**

NOTES
- Be sure to decrease the salt if you substitute salted nut butter.

CRACKED WHEAT BREAD
▼▼▼

Cracked wheat adds a pleasant crunchiness to this great bread. Coarse cracked wheat gives the best texture. You can substitute cracked rye, steel-cut oats, or toasted buckwheat groats. This dough makes wonderful rolls and English muffins (see page 58).

YIELD: 2 large loaves

PREPARATION TIME: About 1½ hours for sponge and dough; 5 hours for rising; 50 minutes to bake

> 2½ cups spring water
> 1 cup cracked wheat
> 1 cup milk or soy milk, scalded and cooled to lukewarm
> 1 tablespoon lemon juice
> ½ teaspoon active dry yeast
> 6 to 6½ cups whole wheat bread flour
> 2 teaspoons sea salt
> 4 tablespoons corn oil

Boil 2 cups of the water and pour it over the cracked wheat in a large bowl. Set it aside until lukewarm. Combine the milk and lemon juice and set aside to curdle.

Meanwhile, heat the remaining ½ cup of water and cool it to lukewarm. Add the yeast and a teaspoon of flour, cover, and set in a warm spot to proof. Stir in ½ cup flour, cover, and set in a draft-free spot for about 30 minutes, until a sponge develops.

Mix the sponge, curdled milk, salt, and oil with the soaked wheat. Gradually stir in enough of the remaining flour to form a dough.

Turn the dough out onto a lightly floured surface, cover, and let rest for several minutes. Knead until smooth and elastic, adding flour as necessary to keep the dough from sticking.

Form the dough into a ball and put it in a lightly greased bowl. Cover and set aside for about 2 hours, until the dough has risen and does not spring back when pressed. Turn the dough out and knead it briefly. Return it to the bowl for a second rise.

Shape and pan the dough. Cover the loaves and set them aside to rise for about an hour or until the dough rebounds slowly when pressed.

Slash the tops of the loaves; brush on an egg wash if you wish. Bake at 350 degrees for about 50 minutes—until the loaves are brown, have firm sides, and sound distinctly hollow when removed from the pans and tapped on the bottom.

Cool the bread thoroughly before slicing or storing it.

(For more detailed instructions, refer to the directions for BASIC YEASTED WHOLE WHEAT BREAD, **beginning on page 48.)**

NOTES
- Substitute a flavorful vegetable stock for the wheat-soaking water.
- Substitute 1 cup buttermilk or yogurt for the milk and lemon juice.

STEEL-CUT OATS BREAD
◆◆◆

Naturally sweet, moist, and chewy, this bread makes wonderful toast.

YIELD: 2 loaves

PREPARATION TIME: 1½ hours for sponge and dough; 5 hours for rising; 50 minutes to bake

    3   cups spring water
    1   cup steel-cut oats
    ½   teaspoon active dry yeast
    6   to 7 cups whole wheat bread flour
    2   tablespoons sesame oil
    2   teaspoons sea salt

Boil 2 cups of the water and pour it over the oats in a large bowl. Set aside until lukewarm.

Meanwhile, heat ¼ cup of the remaining water and cool it to lukewarm. Add the yeast and a teaspoon of flour, cover, and set in a warm spot to proof. Stir in the remaining ¾ cup water and a cup or so of the flour, cover, and set in a draft-free spot for about an hour or until a sponge develops.

Stir the sponge into the oats along with the oil and salt. Gradually stir in enough of the remaining flour to form a dough.

Turn the dough out onto a lightly floured surface, cover, and let rest for several minutes. Knead until smooth and elastic, adding flour as necessary to keep the dough from sticking.

Form the dough into a ball and put it in a lightly greased bowl. Cover and set aside for about 2 hours, until the dough has risen and does not spring back when pressed. Turn the dough out and knead it briefly. Return it to the bowl for a second rise.

Shape and pan the loaves. Cover the loaves and set them aside to rise for about an hour or until the dough rebounds slowly when pressed.

Slash the tops of the loaves. Brush them with an egg wash and sprinkle on sesame or poppy seeds if you wish. Bake at 350 degrees for about 50 minutes—until the loaves are brown, have firm sides, and sound distinctly hollow when removed from the pans and tapped on the bottom.

Cool the bread thoroughly before slicing or storing it.

(For more detailed instructions, refer to the directions for *BASIC YEASTED WHOLE WHEAT BREAD*, beginning on page 48.)

NOTES
- Add 2 to 4 tablespoons molasses to the hot oat mixture.

ROLLED OAT BREAD
◆◆◆

This oat bread has a finer texture than the preceding one. It's also great for toasting. For a delicious raisin bread, knead 2 cups of raisins into the dough before shaping it into loaves, or make one loaf with raisins and one loaf without.

YIELD: 2 loaves

PREPARATION TIME: About 1½ hours for sponge and dough; 5 hours for rising; 50 minutes to bake

    3   cups spring water
    1   cup rolled oats
    2   teaspoons sea salt
    2   tablespoons sesame oil
    ¾   teaspoon active dry yeast
    6   cups whole wheat bread flour

Boil 2 cups of the water and pour it over the oats in a large bowl. Add the salt and oil and set aside until lukewarm.

Heat ¼ cup of the water and cool it to lukewarm. Add the yeast and a teaspoon of flour, cover, and set in a warm spot to proof. Add the remaining ¾ cup of water and stir in about 1 cup of flour. Cover and set in a draft-free spot for about an hour or until a sponge develops.

Stir the sponge into the cooled oat mixture. Gradually stir in enough of the flour to form a dough.

Turn the dough out onto a lightly greased surface, cover, and let rest for several minutes. Knead until smooth and elastic, adding flour as necessary to keep the dough from sticking.

Form the dough into a ball and put it in a lightly greased bowl. Cover and set aside for about 2 hours, until the dough has risen and does not spring back when pressed. Turn the dough out and knead it briefly. Return it to the bowl for a second rise.

Shape and pan the dough. Cover the loaves and set them aside to rise for about an hour or until the dough rebounds slowly when pressed.

Slash the tops of the loaves. Bake at 350 degrees for about 50 minutes—until the loaves are brown, have firm sides, and sound distinctly hollow when removed from the pans and tapped on the bottom.

Cool the bread thoroughly before slicing or storing it.

(For more detailed instructions, refer to the directions for BASIC YEASTED WHOLE WHEAT BREAD, **beginning on page 48.)**

NOTES
- Add 2 tablespoons of maple syrup to the oats along with the salt and oil.

TRUE GRITS BREAD
▪▪▪

Bolster your fortitude with this slightly sweet and chewy bread. You may substitute another kind of grits—soy, rice, barley—for corn grits.

YIELD: 2 loaves

PREPARATION TIME: About 2½ hours to cook and cool the grits and prepare the sponge and dough; 5 hours to rise; 50 minutes to bake

> 3¼ cups spring water
> ½ cup corn grits
> ¾ teaspoon active dry yeast
> 6 to 6½ cups whole wheat bread flour
> 2 teaspoons sea salt
> 2 tablespoons corn oil

In a medium-sized saucepan, bring 1½ cups of the water to a boil. Slowly sprinkle the grits into the boiling water, stirring constantly. Reduce the heat to low, cover tightly, and cook 5 minutes, until the grits have thickened. Turn off the heat and leave the pot covered until the grits have cooled to lukewarm.

Heat ¼ cup of the water and cool it to lukewarm. Add the yeast and a teaspoon of flour, cover, and set in a warm spot to proof. Combine the proofed yeast with the remaining 1½ cups water in a large bowl. Stir in 2 cups or so of the flour to form a thick batter. Cover and set in a draft-free spot for about 2 hours or until it develops into a sponge.

Stir the cooled grits, salt, and oil into the sponge. Gradually stir in enough of the remaining flour to form a dough.

Turn the dough out onto a lightly floured surface, cover, and let rest for several minutes. Knead until smooth and elastic, adding more flour as necessary to keep the dough from sticking. This dough tends to be tacky and requires somewhat gentle kneading.

Form the dough into a ball and put it in a lightly greased bowl. Cover and set aside for about 2 hours, until the dough has risen and does not spring back when pressed. Turn the dough out and knead it briefly. Return it to the bowl for a second rise.

Shape and pan the dough. Cover the loaves and set them aside to rise for about an hour or until the dough rebounds slowly when pressed.

Slash the tops of the loaves. Brush the tops with melted margarine or butter. Bake at 350 degrees for about 50 minutes—until the loaves are brown, have firm sides, and sound distinctly hollow when removed from the pans and tapped on the bottom.

Cool the bread thoroughly before slicing or storing it.

(For more detailed instructions, refer to the directions for BASIC YEASTED WHOLE WHEAT BREAD, **beginning on page 48.)**

LIMPA RYE
▪▪▪

Fennel, caraway, and orange flavor this light, Swedish-style rye bread. You can substitute cracked wheat for the cracked rye.

YIELD: 2 round loaves

PREPARATION TIME: 2½ to 3 hours for sponge and dough; 5 hours for rising; 45 to 50 minutes to bake

> 2⅔ cups spring water
> ½ cup cracked rye
> 2 teaspoons sea salt
> ¾ teaspoon active dry yeast
> 3½ to 4½ cups whole wheat bread flour
> 1½ teaspoons fennel seeds
> 1½ teaspoons caraway seeds
> 1 to 2 tablespoons freshly grated orange zest
>   Juice of 1 orange (about ⅓ cup)
> 2 tablespoons corn oil
> 2 cups rye flour

Heat 1 cup of the water to boiling and pour it over the cracked rye and salt in a large bowl; set aside until lukewarm.

Heat ⅓ cup of the water and cool it to lukewarm. Add the yeast and a teaspoon of wheat flour, cover, and set in a warm spot to proof. Combine with the remaining 1⅓ cups water in a large bowl. Gradually stir in about 3 cups of the wheat flour to form a thick batter. Cover and set in a draft-free spot for about 2 hours or until a sponge develops.

In a heavy-bottomed, ungreased skillet over moderate heat, roast the fennel and caraway seeds, stirring or agitating the pan often to prevent them from burning. Grind the seeds to a coarse consistency with a mortar and pestle or spice grinder.

Stir the soaked rye, ground seeds, orange zest, orange juice, and oil into the sponge. Gradually stir in the rye flour and then enough of the remaining wheat flour to form a dough.

Turn the dough out onto a lightly floured surface, cover, and let rest for a few minutes. Knead until smooth and elastic, adding more wheat flour as necessary to keep the dough from sticking. Knead carefully and expect the dough to remain a bit tacky.

Form the dough into a ball and put it in a lightly greased bowl. Cover and set aside for about 2 hours, until the dough has risen and does not spring back when pressed. Turn the dough out and knead it briefly. Return it to the bowl for a second rise.

Shape and pan 2 round loaves. Cover the loaves and set them aside to rise for about an hour or until the dough rebounds slowly when pressed.

Dock or slash the tops of the loaves. Bake at 350 degrees for about 50 minutes—until the loaves have firm sides and sound distinctly hollow when removed from the pans and tapped on the bottom.

Cool the bread thoroughly before slicing or storing it.

(For more detailed instructions, refer to the directions for *Basic Yeasted Whole Wheat Bread,* **beginning on page 48.)**

PUMPERNICKEL-RYE BREAD
▾▾▾

Ironically, New York nightclub Fat Tuesday's is long and narrow, and a 14-piece jazz band was stretched out along practically the entire length of one wall of the club. The musicians were so close to us in the audience that my knees were almost bumping those of the sax player. He had music on his stand, but as he played, his eyes were transfixed on the partially consumed loaf of pumpernickel just about under his nose on the end of our table. And he blew up a storm of improvisational licks. When I reached out to cut another slice of bread, he lowered his horn and, with a glint in his eyes, cautioned me, "You'd better leave that fine-looking bread right where it is—it's my inspiration!"

I hope this dark, rich pumpernickel bread will be your inspiration!

YIELD: 2 large loaves

PREPARATION TIME: 2½ to 3 hours for sponge and dough; 5 hours for rising; 50 minutes to bake

> 3½ *cups plus 2 tablespoons spring water*
> ¼ *cup soy grits*
> 2 *tablespoons Cafix or other instant grain beverage*
> ¾ *teaspoon active dry yeast*
> 6 *cups whole wheat bread flour*
> 2 *tablespoons roasted carob powder*
> 2 *tablespoons blackstrap molasses*
>   *Grated zest of 1 orange*
> 2 *teaspoons sea salt*
> 4 *tablespoons corn oil*
> 1 *cup rye flakes, coarsely ground to the consistency of coarse meal*
> 1½ *cups rye flour*

Boil ½ cup of the water and pour it over the grits and Cafix. Set aside until lukewarm.

Heat ¼ cup of the water and cool it to lukewarm. Add the yeast and a teaspoon of wheat flour, cover, and set in a warm spot to proof. Add the proofed yeast to 2¾ cups of the water in a large bowl. Gradually stir in about 3½ cups of the wheat flour to form a thick batter. Cover and set in a draft-free spot for about 2 hours or until a sponge develops.

Mix the remaining 2 tablespoons of water and the carob powder to a smooth paste. Stir this, along with the soaked grits, molasses, orange zest, salt, and oil into the sponge. Stir in the rye meal and rye flour and then gradually stir in enough of the remaining wheat flour to form a dough.

Turn the dough out onto a lightly floured surface, cover, and let rest for several minutes, until relaxed. Knead until smooth and elastic, adding wheat flour as necessary to keep the dough from sticking. Handle the dough carefully and expect it to remain somewhat tacky.

Form the dough into a ball and put it in a lightly greased bowl. Cover and set aside for about 2 hours, until the dough has risen and does not spring back when pressed. Turn the dough out and knead it briefly. Return the dough to the bowl for a second rise.

Shape the dough; I make 2 or 3 round or oval free-standing loaves. Cover the loaves and set them aside to rise for about an hour or until the dough rebounds slowly when pressed.

Slash or dock the tops of the loaves. Bake at 350 degrees for about 50 minutes—until the loaves sound distinctly hollow when removed from the pans and tapped on the bottom. For a shiny crust, brush a cornstarch wash (see page 56) onto the loaves halfway through baking and again about 5 minutes before they are done.

Cool the bread thoroughly before slicing or storing it.

(For more detailed instructions, refer to the directions for *Basic Yeasted Whole Wheat Bread*, beginning on page 48.)

NOTES

- Substitute oat flakes or bran for the rye flakes.

- Add 1 tablespoon caraway seeds and omit the orange zest if you prefer.

- For *Pumpernickel-Rye Raisin Bread*, knead 1 to 2 cups of steamed raisins or currants into the dough before shaping.

Alan's French Bread
▼▼▞

The French would be loathe to lay claim to much of the "French" bread that is made in this country, since it lacks the well-developed flavor and crisp crust that characterize an exemplary French loaf. These signature traits depend on long, slow rises and a steamy, hot oven, respectively. Years ago, Alan Harris, a friendly baker in Massachusetts, taught me his French bread secrets, including an especially effective way to shape the long, thin loaves called baguettes. This is a whole grain version of Alan's French bread recipe. Following tradition, this French bread is oil-free. For a head start on the bread, you might want to mix the sponge and let it rise in the refrigerator overnight.

YIELD: 2 small loaves or 1 large one

PREPARATION TIME: 2½ to 3 hours for sponge and dough; 6 hours for rising; 40 to 50 minutes to bake

    1⅔ cups spring water
    ½ teaspoon active dry yeast
    4 cups whole wheat bread flour
    1½ teaspoons sea salt

Heat ⅓ cup of the water and cool it to lukewarm. Add the yeast and a teaspoon of flour and set in a warm spot to proof. Stir in the remaining 1⅓ cups water and about 2 cups of the flour to form a thick batter. Set in a draft-free spot for about 2 hours or until a sponge develops.

Stir the salt into the sponge. Gradually stir in enough of the remaining flour to form a dough.

Turn the dough out onto a lightly floured surface, cover, and let rest for several minutes, until relaxed. Knead until smooth and elastic, adding flour as necessary to keep the dough from sticking.

Form the dough into a ball and put it in a clean, ungreased bowl. Cover and set aside at cool room temperature for about 2 hours or until the dough has risen and does not spring back when pressed. Turn the dough out and knead it briefly. Return it to the bowl for a second rise.

Turn the dough out and cut it in two. Knead each piece briefly and round it into a ball. Set the balls on a lightly floured surface and cover with a damp towel.

When the balls have risen into puffy dough balloons, shape the loaves. To form baguettes, press the air out of the dough until you have a flat circle, fold the circle in half, and pound the edges together with your fist. Turn the straight edge to face you, pull the curved edge over to meet the straight edge, and pound the two edges securely all along the length to form a narrow cylinder. Place your hands on top of and in the middle of the dough, and, with a gentle but firm back-and-forth motion, roll the dough and move your hands toward the ends of the cylinder, expanding its length—just like making coils out of clay. Repeat until the dough is about 10 inches long (longer for a large baguette). For round loaves, shape as described on page 54.

Alan puts baguettes to rise, seam side up, between folds of heavy canvas dusted with flour. When they have risen, he carefully flips each one over onto a wooden paddle called a baker's peel, and transfers it to the floor of his oven to bake. If you have baking tiles or a baking stone, you can follow this technique. If you use long baguette pans or baking sheets, lightly sprinkle them with cornmeal before putting the loaves on them to rise. Let round loaves rise, seam side up, in baskets lined with flour-dusted cloth, on cornmeal-dusted sheets, or in round containers which you have greased and dusted with cornmeal.

Near the end of the rising period, which will take about 1 hour, preheat the oven to 450 degrees. If you are baking on tiles or a baking stone, allow extra time for preheating so that it will be hot. When the shaped loaves have risen and rebound slowly when pressed with a finger, slash the tops, spray with cold water, and place in the preheated oven. Spray the loaves every 5 minutes for the first 10 to 15 minutes of baking. Bake baguettes 20 to 25 minutes, until the crust is brown and crisp. Bake a large round loaf at 450 degrees for the first 15 minutes and then reduce the temperature to 350 degrees and bake 20 to 30 minutes longer—until it sounds distinctly hollow when tapped on the bottom.

NOTES

- In addition to spraying the loaves to create steam in the oven, place a pan of boiling water on the bottom of the oven for the first 15 minutes of baking. For even more effective steaming, put a preheated brick or flatiron into the water.

- French bread doesn't stay fresh very long; eat it up right away or freeze it, tightly wrapped, as soon as it has thoroughly cooled.

- Leftover French bread makes great French toast (see page 185).

- For a crusty, whole grain *ITALIAN BREAD*, add 2 tablespoons olive oil to the sponge along with the salt.

BRIOCHE
▾▾▾

Jaunty topknots characterize these rich French buns. Brioche are traditionally baked in special fluted tins which come in many sizes. If you don't have brioche pans, use Pyrex custard cups or muffin tins for small brioche or form the dough into a loaf—round with a topknot, braided, or some other shape. An egg wash gives brioche a deep brown crust; their crumb is soft and tender. Like other egg-rich breads, brioche tend to dry out quickly and they are best when freshly baked.

YIELD: 6 3½-inch brioche or 12 muffin-sized ones

PREPARATION TIME: 3 to 3½ hours for sponge and dough; at least 30 minutes for chilling the dough; 1½ to 2 hours for shaping and rising; 15 to 20 minutes to bake

> ¼ cup spring water
> 2 teaspoons active dry yeast
> 1⅔ to 2 cups whole wheat bread flour
> 4 eggs, room temperature
> 1 tablespoon honey
> ½ teaspoon sea salt
> ¼ pound unsalted soy margarine or butter, melted and cooled to lukewarm

Heat the water and cool it to lukewarm. Add the yeast and a teaspoon of flour, cover, and set in a warm spot to proof. Whisk the proofed yeast with 1 egg in a me-dium-sized mixing bowl. Beat in ⅔ cup of the flour to form a batter. Cover and set in a draft-free spot for 1½ to 2 hours—until a sponge has developed.

Beat the honey, salt, 2 eggs, and ⅔ cup flour into the sponge. Beating vigorously, gradually add the melted margarine. Add flour, ⅓ cup at a time, stirring well after each addition, to form a dough. Turn out onto a lightly floured surface, cover, and let rest for a few minutes. Wash the bowl and fill it with hot water.

Knead, lightly sprinkling flour under the dough as necessary to keep it from sticking. When it is smooth and elastic, form the dough into a ball. Dry the bowl and put in the dough, cover, and set in a draft-free spot for about an hour—until it is well risen.

Turn the dough out onto a lightly floured surface and pat it into a long rectangle. From the short side, fold in ⅓ of the dough and then fold in the opposite side. Sprinkle lightly with flour and wrap snugly with plastic wrap. Chill in the refrigerator for at least 30 minutes. If you want to wait several hours or overnight to shape the dough, place the wrapped dough in a container and set a weight on top to restrict its rising—I put it in a loaf pan with a small breadboard on top and an old flatiron on top of that. Wrapped and weighted, the dough will keep for up to three days.

For traditional individual brioche tins, 3 inches in diameter at the top, cut the dough into 12 equal pieces; for 3½-inch Pyrex custard cups, cut it into 6 pieces. Cut a small piece off each piece to use for the topknot. Follow the regular roll-making technique described on page 57 to form balls. For each brioche, place the large ball into a well-greased pan. Form a point about ½ inch long on the small ball. Dip a finger into flour and then poke a deep depression in the top of the large ball. Fit the small ball into the hole. Arrange the brioche pans on a baking sheet, cover lightly, and place in a draft-free spot for 1 to 2 hours—until the dough is well risen.

Preheat the oven to 425 degrees. Beat the remaining egg with a bit of water. Brush the top of the buns with this wash, then brush them a second time. Bake 5 minutes for small brioche or 10 minutes for larger ones. Turn the oven down to 375 degrees and bake 10 to 15 minutes longer—until the brioche are browned and a tester inserted into the center comes out clean. Remove from the pans and cool briefly. Serve warm.

CROISSANTS
🔺🔺🔺

I visited Paris for the first time when I was nineteen, and this is where I tasted my first croissants. Each morning, I joined Parisians at a bustling café counter and washed down two light, flaky rolls with a large, handleless cup of steaming café au lait and felt very French. Now, a bite of the fresh crusty crescents can transport me back to my adventuresome youth. The expansive texture of these delicate pastries results from the many alternate layers of dough and fat which puff apart when exposed to high oven heat. Besides enhanced nutrition, whole wheat croissants have a fuller flavor than those made from refined flour. If I plan on croissants for a late breakfast, I do everything but the shaping the day before, chill the dough overnight, and take it out for shaping and rising about 2½ hours before serving.

YIELD: 6 croissants

PREPARATION TIME: 2 hours to prepare and chill the dough; 30 to 40 minutes to layer the dough and several hours for chilling; 15 minutes to shape; 1½ to 2 hours for rising; 15 to 20 minutes to bake

>   ¾ cup milk or soy milk, scalded
>   1½ teaspoons honey
>   ½ teaspoon sea salt
>   ¼ cup plus 1 teaspoon spring water
>   1 teaspoon active dry yeast
>   ¼ cup whole wheat pastry flour
>   1¾ cups whole wheat bread flour
>   ¼ pound unsalted soy margarine
>   1 egg

Combine the milk, honey, and salt in a medium-sized bowl and set aside to cool to lukewarm.

Heat ¼ cup of the water and cool it to lukewarm. Add the yeast and a teaspoon of flour, cover, and set in a warm spot to proof.

Beat the proofed yeast and pastry flour into the milk mixture. Gradually stir in bread flour until a soft dough forms. Turn out onto a lightly floured surface and knead briefly—just a minute or two—until smooth. Developing the gluten too much will make the dough difficult to roll out later. Wash and dry the bowl and return the dough to it, cover with plastic wrap or a plastic bag, and refrigerate about 1½ hours.

Cut the stick of margarine in half crosswise and then cut each piece in half lengthwise. Lay the pieces adjacent to one another on a piece of waxed paper. Draw a 4×6-inch rectangle on another piece of waxed paper and center it on top of the margarine. Using the drawing as a guide, roll the margarine into a 4×6-inch rectangle. Refrigerate between the waxed paper.

On a lightly floured surface, roll the dough into a 6×11-inch rectangle. Peel the top piece of waxed paper off the margarine and position the margarine on one side of the dough, leaving a 1-inch border uncovered—the margarine will cover about two-thirds of the dough. Remove the other piece of waxed paper and, with the back of a knife, score the margarine in half parallel to the short side of the rectangle. Fold the uncovered third of dough over the center third and fold in the other side like a business letter. Place the short side of the folded dough parallel to the front edge of your work surface and carefully roll the dough into a 6×11-inch rectangle and once again fold it in thirds. Wrap the dough tightly with lightly floured plastic wrap and then in a plastic bag. Refrigerate, topped with a weight (I use an old flatiron). It's a good idea to put the wrapped dough in a loaf pan so that the weight will not topple off as the dough rises. Chill the dough for 1 hour—or up to several hours.

On a lightly floured surface, roll and fold the dough as above (but without adding more margarine) two more times. Wrap, refrigerate, and weight it. Chill for at least 2 hours and as long as overnight.

On a lightly floured surface, roll the dough into a 6×18-inch rectangle. Cut it into three 6-inch squares. Cut each square into two triangles. With the wide side of a triangle facing you, roll the dough so that you expand the triangle to approximately 8 inches on each side. Roll up the triangle starting from the base, encouraging the two base points to curl inward and ending with the top point lapped over the front just to the bottom of the roll but not tucked underneath. Shape the other croissants in the same manner.

Arrange the croissants on a parchment-lined or ungreased baking sheet. Whisk the egg and 1 teaspoon water and brush a dab under each of the overlapping points. Brush the croissants with the egg wash. Set the sheet in a warm, draft-free spot for 1½ to 2 hours—until the croissants are well risen.

Preheat the oven to 450 degrees. Give the croissants a second coat of egg wash. Bake 15 minutes—until they are deep brown and crusty. Cool briefly and serve warm.

NOTES
- Substitute spring water for the milk or soy milk.

- Substitute unsalted butter for half or all of the margarine.

DANISH PASTRIES

▼▼▼

Danish dough is made by a technique similar to that for croissants, but these pastries are even richer and flakier. Danishes can be shaped in a number of ways and stuffed with a variety of fillings; here I fill them with a sweet and spicy ground almond mixture. Though these pastries take some time to make, they're fun to fuss with for a special occasion. You can do everthing but shaping, rising, and baking the day before and chill the dough overnight; take the dough out 2 to 2½ hours before serving.

YIELD: 8 large individual pastries or 1 braid or coffee cake

PREPARATION TIME: 2 hours for the dough; 1 hour to layer the dough with 3½ hours of interspersed chilling; 1½ hours to shape and rise; 10 to 15 minutes to bake

> ¼ cup whole wheat pastry flour plus extra for rolling the dough
> 1¼ cups whole wheat bread flour
> 6 tablespoons plus 1 teaspoon spring water
> ¼ teaspoon ground cardamom
> 3 tablespoons mild-flavored honey
> ¼ teaspoon sea salt
> 1 tablespoon active dry yeast
> 3 eggs
> 5 ounces (1¼ sticks) unsalted soy margarine or butter, chilled
> Grated zest of 1 orange (about 1 teaspoon)
> ¼ teaspoon cinnamon
> ½ cup lightly toasted almonds, finely chopped

Sift together the ¼ cup pastry flour and the bread flour and set aside.

Heat 2 tablespoons of the water and whisk it with the cardamom, 1 tablespoon of the honey, and the salt in a medium-sized bowl; set this aside to cool.

Heat ¼ cup of the water and cool it to lukewarm. Add the yeast and a teaspoon of flour, cover, and set in a warm spot to proof.

Add the proofed yeast to the bowl along with 1 egg and whisk all together. Gradually beat in the flour to form a soft dough which will pull away from the sides of the bowl. Scrape down the sides of the bowl and cover tightly with plastic wrap. Refrigerate 1½ hours.

Roll the margarine between two pieces of waxed paper into a 4 × 6-inch rectangle. Refrigerate until firm.

Turn the dough out onto a work surface lightly sprinkled with pastry flour. Adding flour as necessary to keep the dough from sticking, roll it into a 6 × 11-inch rectangle. Peel the waxed paper off one side of the margarine and position the margarine on one end of the dough, leaving a 1-inch border on three sides—it will cover about two-thirds of the length of the dough.

Peel off the remaining wax paper and lightly score the margarine down the middle, parallel to the short side of the rectangle. Fold the uncovered third of the dough over the center third. Fold the other side in to totally encase the margarine.

Flour the work surface and carefully roll the dough into a 6 × 11-inch rectangle. Fold in thirds again. Wrap in lightly floured plastic wrap and then in a plastic bag. Refrigerate with a weight on top to prevent the gluten in the dough from stretching beyond its limits and breaking. Chill for 1 hour.

Position the dough on a floured work surface with its short edge closest to you. Roll it into a 6 × 11-inch rectangle. Fold in thirds and turn it so that the short edge is again in front. Repeat. Wrap, refrigerate, and weight the dough. Chill 2 hours.

Roll and fold the dough 2 more times. Chill, weighted, for 30 minutes.

To make the filling, in a small bowl whisk together the orange zest, 1 egg, the cinnamon, and the remaining 2 tablespoons honey. Thoroughly mix in the almonds. If the mixture is very stiff, juice the orange and add some of the orange juice; it should be moist but still hold its shape. Set this aside.

On a lightly floured surface, roll the dough into an 8 × 16-inch rectangle. With a sharp knife, cut off a narrow strip of dough along each side and discard it. Cut the rectangle into 4-inch squares. You may shape and fill these in different ways:

- Place ⅛ of the filling in the center of each square, fold one corner to the center and brush it with a bit of egg wash (the remaining egg beaten with the teaspoon of water), fold the opposite corner to the center, and press it onto the first one to seal it.

- For envelopes, follow the procedure above but fold all four corners in—or fold the corners of the dough in and place the filling on top.

- For cockscombs, fill half of each square and brush the edges with egg wash; fold in half to

enclose the filling, make cuts almost to the filling at ¾- to 1-inch intervals along the long sealed side, spread the pastry open along the cut side.

- For pinwheels, make a cut from each corner toward the center of the square (about an inch from the center), place filling in the center, fold the edge to the right of each corner into the center, pressing the points together in the middle.

- To form a coffee cake, leave the 8 × 16-inch rectangle intact and spread the filling evenly over the surface. Roll up the dough from the long side and pinch the edges together. Form this filled log into a ring, joining the ends. Slash the top at equal intervals to allow for expansion.

- For spiral pastries, form the filled log and cut it crosswise into 1-inch slices. Lay each slice on its side.

- For a crisscross coffee cake, follow directions on page 182.

Arrange pastries on a parchment-lined or lightly greased baking sheet. Cover loosely with a tea towel or lightly floured plastic wrap or waxed paper. Let pastries rise for 45 minutes or until they appear light and puffy.

Preheat the oven to 400 degrees. Lightly brush the pastries with the remaining egg wash. Bake 10 to 15 minutes, until well browned and crisp. Cool briefly and serve warm.

NOTES
- Fruit butters and dried fruit purées are good alternative fillings; see *PEAR BUTTER* (page 135) and *APRICOT-ALMOND BARS* (page 227). You can also use a cooked fruit filling, such as that for *CRISSCROSS COFFEE CAKE* (page 182).

KUGELHOPF
▼▼▼

There are many versions of this almond-studded bread and almost as many ways to spell its name, since several nations, including Austria and France, participated in its creation. Marie Antoinette may have been referring to kugelhopf when she declared, "Let them eat cake!" and ignited the French Revolution. The light, slightly sweet, raisin-and-nut-laced dough is often an unkneaded but vigorously beaten yeasted batter as it is here. For an elegant shaped bread, bake it in a traditional, decoratively fluted baking pan. Serve kugelhopf as a dessert with dry white wine or champagne or for breakfast plain, warmed, or toasted. PEAR BUTTER (page 135) is a delicious topping.

YIELD: 1 large bread

PREPARATION TIME: About 1 hour to prepare; 3 hours for rising; 50 minutes to bake

  ⅓ *cup dry white wine (such as a chardonnay)*
  ⅔ *cup raisins*
  ½ *cup spring water*
  ½ *teaspoon active dry yeast*
  3 *cups whole wheat bread flour*
  ¼ *cup sunflower oil*
  ¼ *cup mild-flavored honey*
  2 *to 3 eggs—to equal ½ cup*
  1 *cup milk or soy milk, scalded and cooled to lukewarm*
  1 *teaspoon sea salt*
  ⅓ *cup lightly toasted chopped almonds*
  1 *tablespoon unsalted butter or soy margarine, softened*
  2 *tablespoons bran*
16 *whole lightly toasted almonds*

Pour the wine over the raisins in a deep bowl and marinate for about an hour. Drain well and save the sweetened wine—it's good served on the kugelhopf.

Heat the water and cool it to lukewarm. Add the yeast and a teaspoon of flour, cover, and set in a warm spot to proof. Stir in ½ cup of the flour. Cover and set in a draft-free spot for about 30 minutes, until a sponge develops.

In a large bowl, whisk together the oil and honey. Whisk in the eggs and then the milk, salt, and sponge. Add the remaining flour, ½ cup at a time, beating well with a wooden spoon after each addition—the batter should become elastic as you develop the gluten in the flour. Stir in the raisins and chopped nuts. Scrape any dough on the sides of the bowl into the center, cover, and set in a draft-free spot for about 2 hours—until the batter has doubled.

Thoroughly grease a 9-inch, 10-cup kugelhopf tube pan (or a pan of comparable volume) with the softened butter or margarine. Dust with the bran. Arrange the whole almonds in the bottom. Evenly distribute the batter in the pan—it will be about half full. Cover with a damp towel and let rise for about an hour—until the batter has risen almost to the top of the pan.

Put it in a cold oven and and set the temperature to 350 degrees. Bake 50 minutes or until the bread is well browned and a tester inserted to the bottom of the pan comes out clean. Cool in the pan briefly. Turn out onto a rack to finish cooling.

NOTES
- Add the finely grated zest of 1 lemon—whisk it

into the liquid mixture before beating in the flour.

- Substitute lightly roasted hazelnuts for the almonds in the batter; rub the skins off the hot hazelnuts in a tea towel before chopping.

CRUMPETS
▾▾▾

Crumpets are made from a beaten rather than a kneaded yeasted dough and are cooked on a griddle. They are similar to English muffins (see page 58) but are somewhat more moist and porous.

YIELD: 6 4-inch crumpets

PREPARATION TIME: 30 to 40 minutes to prepare; 2 to 4 hours for rising; about 20 minutes to cook each batch

   ¾ *cup spring water*
   ½ *teaspoon active dry yeast*
   1 *cup whole wheat bread flour*
   ½ *cup milk or soy milk, scalded and cooled to lukewarm*
   ½ *teaspoon sea salt*
   ½ *cup whole wheat pastry flour*
   ¼ *teaspoon baking soda*

Heat ½ cup of the water and cool it to lukewarm in a medium-sized bowl. Add the yeast and a teaspoon of flour, cover, and set in a warm spot to proof. Stir in ½ cup of the bread flour, cover, and set in a draft-free spot for about 30 minutes—until the batter develops into a sponge.

Stir in the milk, salt, pastry flour, and remaining bread flour, beating well with a wooden spoon after each addition, to form a soft dough. Cover and set aside for 1 to 2 hours—until the dough has doubled.

Dissolve the baking soda in the remaining ¼ cup water and thoroughly stir it into the dough to achieve a batterlike consistency. Cover and let rise for 1 to 2 hours—until it doubles again.

Heat a griddle over moderate heat. Liberally grease the inside of the crumpet rings and lightly grease the surface of the hot griddle. Arrange crumpet rings on the griddle and spoon the dough into them, nudging it against the sides, to a depth of about ½ inch. Cook 10 to 15 minutes—until the top surface has bubbled and dried and the bottom has browned. Turn the crumpets and remove the rings. Cook 5 minutes or so—until the second side browns. Cool on a rack.

Carefully insert the tines of a fork around the edge of a crumpet and gently pull the halves apart. Toast the halves and top with margarine or butter and perhaps preserves, marmalade, or fruit butters.

NOTES

- If you don't have crumpet rings (metal rings 4 inches in diameter and ¾ inches high), remove the bottom from empty tuna or comparable cans—try to find cans without lead-soldered seams; add batter to a depth of about ½ inch.

YEASTED CORN BREAD
▾▾▾

This yeasted corn bread has a different texture than its chemically leavened cousins and it keeps better. Serve it with chili or soups.

YIELD: 1 8-inch square or 9-inch round pan

PREPARATION TIME: 15 to 20 minutes to prepare; 2 hours for rising; 30 minutes to bake

   ¼ *cup spring water*
   1½ *teaspoons active dry yeast*
   1 *cup whole wheat bread flour*
   1 *cup milk or soy milk, scalded*
   2 *tablespoons maple syrup*
   ½ *teaspoon sea salt*
   2 *tablespoons sunflower, sesame, or corn oil*
   1 *egg*
   1 *cup cornmeal*
   ¼ *cup whole wheat pastry flour*

Heat the water and cool it to lukewarm. Add the yeast and a teaspoon of the bread flour, cover, and set in a warm spot to proof.

In a medium-sized bowl, combine the hot milk, syrup, salt, and oil; set aside until lukewarm. Beat in the egg.

Sift together the cornmeal and bread and pastry flours.

Add the proofed yeast to the milk mixture and stir well. Vigorously stir in the dry mixture. Cover and set in a draft-free spot for about an hour—until the batter develops into a sponge.

Grease an 8-inch square or 9-inch round pan. Stir down the sponge and spread it evenly in the pan. Cover and set aside for 45 minutes or until the batter rises in the pan.

Preheat the oven to 350 degrees. Bake the bread 30 minutes—until it has browned and a tester inserted into the center comes out clean. Cool briefly and serve warm or at room temperature.

NOTES

- Omit the bowl rise if you're short on time.

- The egg is optional; add 2 to 4 tablespoons of additional liquid if the egg is omitted.

YEASTED BISCUITS
▼▼▼

Exceptionally light and tender, these biscuits also make excellent burger buns when cut with a 4-inch cutter.

YIELD: 6 to 8 large biscuits

PREPARATION TIME: 50 to 60 minutes to prepare; 1 hour to rise; 15 minutes to bake

> 1¼ cups whole wheat pastry flour
> 1 cup whole wheat bread flour
> ½ cup spring water
> 1 teaspoon active dry yeast
> ½ cup milk or soy milk, scalded
> 1 tablespoon honey
> ½ teaspoon sea salt
> 4 tablespoons cold unsalted soy margarine or butter

Sift together the 1 cup pastry flour and the bread flour.

Heat the water and cool it to lukewarm. Add the yeast and a teaspoon of flour, cover, and set in a warm spot to proof. Stir in ½ to ¾ cup of the sifted flour to form a batter. Cover and set in a draft-free spot for about 30 minutes—until a sponge develops.

Stir together the hot milk, honey, and salt. Set aside until lukewarm.

In a food processor fitted with the metal blade or in a medium-sized bowl with a pastry blender, evenly cut the margarine or butter into the remainder of the sifted flour until it reaches the consistency of coarse meal. If you use a processor, transfer the mixture to a bowl. Make a well in the center of the mixture.

Whisk the cooled milk into the sponge. Pour into the dry mixture and stir until a soft dough forms. Cover and set aside for about 5 minutes.

Sprinkle a bit of pastry flour over the dough in the bowl and turn it out onto a liberally floured surface. Knead briefly, just until the dough comes together and is smooth. Roll or pat ¾ to 1 inch thick. Cut out biscuits, dipping the cutter in flour each time and pressing straight down. Gently knead any scraps of dough together and resume cutting. Arrange on an ungreased or parchment-lined baking sheet and cover loosely with a damp tea towel. Set in a draft-free spot for about 1 hour—until the biscuits are well risen.

Preheat the oven to 400 degrees. Bake the biscuits 15 minutes or until they have browned and sound hollow when tapped on the bottom. Transfer to a rack, cover loosely with a dry tea towel, and cool 10 to 15 minutes. Serve warm.

NOTES
- Substitute maple syrup or another sweetener for the honey—or omit it altogether.

- Substitute oil for the margarine or butter.

FEATHERWEIGHTS
▼▼▼

As their name implies, these dual-leavened biscuits are especially light. Their tender texture is a pleasant cross between a chemically leavened biscuit and a yeasted roll.

YIELD: 9 biscuits

PREPARATION TIME: 50 to 60 minutes to prepare; 1 hour to rise; 10 minutes to bake

> 1 cup whole wheat pastry flour plus extra for the work surface
> 1 cup whole wheat bread flour
> ½ cup spring water
> 1 teaspoon active dry yeast
> ½ cup milk or soy milk, scalded
> 1½ teaspoons lemon juice
> 1 tablespoon honey
> ½ teaspoon sea salt
> ½ teaspoon baking soda
> 1½ teaspoons baking powder
> 4 tablespoons cold unsalted soy margarine or butter

Sift together the 1 cup pastry flour and the bread flour.

Heat the water and cool it to lukewarm. Add the yeast and a teaspoon of flour, cover, and set in a warm spot to proof. Stir in ½ cup of the sifted flour mixture. Cover and set in a draft-free spot for 20 to 30 minutes—until the batter develops into a sponge.

Combine the milk, lemon juice, and honey; cool to lukewarm.

Sift the remaining sifted mixture with the salt, baking soda, and baking powder. In a food processor fitted with the metal blade or in a bowl with a pastry blender, cut the margarine or butter into this dry mixture until it reaches the consistency of a coarse meal. If you use a processor, transfer the mixture to a bowl. Make a well in the center of the mixture.

Whisk together the sponge and curdled milk and pour into the well. Stir gently until a soft dough forms. Cover and set aside for 5 to 10 minutes.

Turn the dough out onto a surface sprinkled with pastry flour. Knead briefly, just until the dough is smooth. Roll or pat out about ¾ inch thick. Cut biscuits with a 2½-inch cutter—or a 4-inch cutter for bun-sized biscuits. Dip the cutter in flour before cutting each biscuit and press straight down without twisting. Knead dough scraps together and cut additional biscuits. Arrange biscuits on an ungreased baking sheet, cover, and set in a draft-free spot for about an hour, until the biscuits are well risen.

Preheat the oven to 450 degrees. Bake biscuits 10 minutes, until a tester inserted in the center comes out clean. Transfer to a cooling rack and cover loosely with a dry tea towel. Leave 10 to 15 minutes. Serve warm.

NOTES

- Substitute maple syrup or rice syrup for the honey—or omit it altogether.

- Substitute oil for the margarine or butter.

Yeasted Muffins
▾▾▾

When you want rolls but don't have the time and/or inclination to knead a dough, follow this simple formula for wonderfully nutty-tasting, crusty, breadlike muffins.

YIELD: 8 large muffins

PREPARATION TIME: 15 minutes to prepare; 1½ hours for rising; 25 to 30 minutes to bake

> ¼ *cup spring water*
> 1½ *teaspoons active dry yeast*
> 2 *cups whole wheat bread flour*
> 1¼ *cups milk or soy milk, scalded and cooled to lukewarm*
> ½ *teaspoon sea salt*
> 2 *tablespoons vegetable oil*

Heat the water and cool it to lukewarm. Add the yeast and a teaspoon of flour, cover, and set in a warm spot to proof.

Add the proofed yeast to the milk in a medium-sized mixing bowl. Stir in the salt and oil. Stir in the flour, a cup at a time, to form a thick batter. Cover and set in a draft-free spot for about an hour, until the batter develops into a sponge.

Stir the batter down and spoon it into 8 large, well-greased muffin tins or popover pans. Cover and set aside for 30 minutes, until the batter has risen.

Put the pan into a cold oven and set the temperature to 375 degrees. Bake 25 to 30 minutes—until the muffins are brown and crusty and sound hollow when removed from the pan and tapped on the bottom. Cool briefly and serve warm.

NOTES

- Before baking, brush the tops lightly with water, milk, or beaten egg or egg white and sprinkle on sesame, poppy, or other seeds.

- Use olive oil for an especially rich flavor.

- There are endless possible variations on this basic recipe: for example, substitute another flour—whole wheat pastry, oat, rye, barley, buckwheat, corn, etc.—for ½ to ⅔ cup of the whole wheat bread flour; substitute water, apple juice, or vegetable stock for the milk; add ½ cup steamed or soaked raisins or other chopped dried fruits, the grated zest of a lemon or orange, or fresh or dried herbs or spices to the batter.

Yeasted Pancakes
▾▾▾

These delicious griddlecakes have a slightly different texture than those leavened with baking powder and baking soda.

YIELD: About 1 dozen 3-inch pancakes

PREPARATION TIME: 1½ to 2 hours

> 1 *cup spring water*
> 1½ *teaspoons active dry yeast*
> ½ *cup whole wheat bread flour*
> 1 *cup whole wheat pastry flour*
> ½ *cup milk or soy milk, scalded and cooled to lukewarm*
> ½ *teaspoon sea salt*
> 1 *tablespoon corn oil*
> 1 *tablespoon maple syrup*

Heat the water and cool it to lukewarm in a medium-sized mixing bowl. Add the yeast and a teaspoon of flour, cover, and set in a warm spot to proof. Stir in the bread flour and ½ cup of the pastry flour. Cover and set in a draft-free spot for 20 to 30 minutes—until the batter develops into a sponge.

Stir in the milk, salt, oil, syrup, and remaining ½ cup pastry flour. Cover and set aside for about an hour—until the batter again develops into a sponge.

Heat a griddle until water dropped on it sizzles immediately; lightly grease the surface. Ladle on batter. Cook the pancakes until bubbles form on top and the bottoms are golden. Turn and cook several minutes—until browned. Serve hot off the griddle—or keep them in a warm oven until serving.

NOTES

- For *Yeasted Buckwheat Cakes*, substitute buckwheat flour for ¼ to ½ cup of the pastry flour added in the last stage of the batter; ½ cup will give the batter a pronounced rather than a subtle buckwheat flavor and a slightly heavier texture.

- Substitute cornmeal or other flours, such as oat, rye, or barley, for the final ½ cup of whole wheat pastry flour.

- For an even better flavor, and to speed up breakfast preparation, start the night before. Stir together the yeast (you may reduce it to ½ teaspoon), water, and ½ cup each whole wheat bread and whole wheat pastry flour; cover and set in a cool spot. Proceed with the recipe in the morning.

CHAPTER 6

Sourdough Breads

A FTER THE MENUS, the next thing to arrive at the table was a small round loaf of warm sourdough bread. Its satisfying aroma, flavor, and texture derived from its fresh sourdough leaven and many slow risings. This bread, with a chewy crust and a compact yet light crumb, was a trademark of Le Papillon, a restaurant once located in an elegant turn-of-the-century neighborhood in Atlanta. The modest Victorian structure was surrounded by picturesque flower and herb beds interspersed with fruit trees. Inside, in several spacious, high-ceilinged rooms, tables were set with fresh linens, seasonal bouquets, and stoneware dishes. The restaurant was as welcoming as a gracious home. But the little sourdough loaves especially beckoned.

"Sourdough" describes any bread leavened with a starter, a fermented mixture of flour and liquid that functions as a yeast culture in the dough. Some of the starter is used to make the bread, and a portion is saved and replenished with more flour and liquid, ready for the next batch. My own sourdough starters are like part of the family, having resided with me for almost 20 years. Like many other starters, mine boast a lineage; I

obtained them from friends, who had obtained them from friends, and so on. I like to imagine that each sourdough loaf I make contains a bit of history in addition to its unique subtly tangy flavor and chewy texture. I feel that I am preserving a bread-making tradition when I make this very special sort of bread.

SOURDOUGH STARTERS

The development of saved starters was a step forward from a baker's dependence on wild yeasts and a new and spontaneous fermentation for every batch of bread. A strong, properly maintained sourdough starter along with a proven bread formula ensured loaf after loaf of successful bread. Early American pioneers and prospectors in remote areas depended so greatly on sourdough starters for reliable leavening that they were even known as "sourdoughs." Over time, commercial yeasts were developed, first in the form of fresh yeast cakes and later as dried granules. Commercial yeasts simplified and standardized the baking process, and as these became widely available, the use of starters began to decline.

Nevertheless, breads leavened solely with commercial yeast can never really replace sourdough breads, since the two processes result in substantially different products. Sourdough breads tend to have a somewhat more compact and springy crumb and a chewier crust than yeasted breads, and their tangy aroma and taste are alluring to many bread lovers. The particular starter, specific recipe, degree of development of the dough, and baking technique all contribute to the uniqueness of sourdough breads.

The most foolproof means of acquiring a sound sourdough starter is to obtain it from a friend. Another relatively reliable source is commercially available dried starters which come to life when mixed with liquid and placed in a warm environment. Dried starters can often be found in cookware shops and mail order catalogs.

Although starters are easiest to get going in a bakery or a kitchen where bread is baked regularly, and they are adversely affected by air pollution, you don't have to live in a rural bakery to create your own starter that can be passed from generation to generation. Just stir together a cup of liquid and enough flour to make a medium-thick batter in a clean glass or ceramic container large enough to allow room for expansion. Cover it with a clean tea towel or piece of muslin. Leave the mixture at warm room temperature for several days and stir it occasionally. During this time, it will attract airborne wild yeasts which will feed on the grain starch and multiply, giving off carbon dioxide gas and alcohol. The starch mixture will also attract friendly bacteria which participate in the fermentation of the grain and contribute to the character of the starter. If its aroma becomes offensive rather than pleasantly piquant, the starter has probably spoiled and you should try again.

Wheat or rye flours are typically used to prepare starters, although flour from any grain will ferment. The particular flour you use will influence the flavor that the starter will pass on to bread; a flour may also affect the activity potential of the starter. Rye is particularly fermentable, and rye starters have long been popular with sourdough bakers around the world. Whatever flour you choose to use, fresh whole grain flours ferment more readily than refined ones.

SOURDOUGH STARTERS WERE so valuable, they were included in marriage dowries. They were taken to bed on cold nights and carried inside coats on winter treks. It's been said that early sourdough bakers found many other uses for starter too, from treating wounds to chinking holes in cabins to imbibing the "hooch" which separated out on top.

Like flour, the liquid in a starter also affects the flavor of baked goods made from it. I use spring water. A quality spring water is preferable for any bread that relies on natural fermentation for rising; distilled and purified waters lack the minerals which facilitate the process, and chemicals in tap waters often interfere with it. Alternative liquids for starters are milk and vegetable, bean, or grain stocks.

In the early days, additional starchy substances such as hops, malt (which is barley or some other grain that has been softened in water, sprouted, and then kiln-dried), potatoes, or the cooking water of any of them were sometimes added to starters to enhance their leavening potential. I have found that my plain flour-and-water starters maintain plenty of leavening power, but you may want to experiment with additional ingredients. I would advise setting aside a portion of your proven starter, however, so that all is not lost if an experiment doesn't work out.

Recipes for specialized starters appear in other sources and you may want to try them after you've mastered the basic technique. Potatoes, onions, and yogurt are some of the ingredients that are sometimes included. Although some starter recipes call for some commercial yeast, a starter begun with commercial yeast usually has less character initially, and may take longer to produce a characteristic sourdough flavor. All starters change over time, becoming increasingly complex in flavor so long as they are well cared for.

I have wheat and rye starters, and I keep about a cup of each refrigerated in pint-sized canning jars and alternate their use. When using or storing sourdough, always keep it in glass, ceramic, or wooden containers and stir it with a wooden spoon; metal and plastic can adversely affect its flavor. Allow enough room in the container for the starter to double in size; I have had an active starter blow the top off of an inadequate jar. A starter can be stored at room temperature, but you must provide space for it to *more* than double. In addition, you will have to use or refresh it daily, as it will otherwise fall victim to undesirable microbes. If you ever neglect your starter, wherever it's stored, and discover that it is covered with a colorful mold, it is probably unsalvageable and you should toss it out.

RENEWING AND EXPANDING THE STARTER

Refrigerated starter needs renewing every week or so if not used for baking. A dark liquid consisting of alcohol and water may have separated out on top; this is normal. Stir the starter in its container. Pour off about half of the starter and add fresh flour and water to replace what you discarded. For instance, if you generally keep about a cup of starter, throw out about ½ cup and stir in ⅓ to ½ cup of water and about ½ cup of flour to make a batter of the original consistency. I do this in a bowl, so that I can wash out my starter's jar as another preservative measure. Leave this refreshed starter at room temperature for several hours, until it is active and bubbly, then return it to its jar and refrigerate it.

When I know I'll be away from home for more than a couple of weeks or I move long distance, I freeze my starters. Though they will keep for several months this way, I try to use them again as soon as possible. Thoroughly defrost a frozen starter at room temperature before trying to bake with it, and expect it to take a while to regain its former vigor.

Bubbliness and a pungent aroma indicate that you have an effective starter, but they don't guarantee good bread; sometimes unpleasant-tasting microorganisms overpower desirable ones. Using the starter in a batch of bread is the ultimate test. The first step is to expand the starter so that you create a surplus to bake with. This is similar to renewing the starter, except don't discard any of the original starter. Simply empty it into a large bowl and stir in additional liquid and enough flour to achieve the same consistency as the original starter. Use the kind of flour that your starter contains. If you'll need 1 cup of starter for your bread recipe, add slightly less than a cup of water and a cup or so of flour to the original cup of starter. Cover the bowl with a plate and leave it in a draft-free spot at room temperature for several hours or until it has risen in the bowl and is definitely active. I leave it overnight if I plan to bake the following morning. The warmer the spot and the longer the starter sits, the more pungent and lively it will become. Stir down the mixture and measure the cup you need for baking. Pour the remainder into a clean jar and refrigerate it for future use; this is your new saved starter. Now you're ready to bake.

When my starters are in good shape, they leaven bread well on their own without giving it an overly sour flavor. Nevertheless, sometimes you may want to include a bit of commercial yeast, as I do in some cases.

Added yeast will speed up the leavening process and does make a somewhat lighter bread, which may be desirable when you're adding heavy ingredients such as cooked or soaked grains; it depends on the effect you want. Yeasted sourdough breads don't keep as well as those without added yeast, and they also generally have a less intense sourdough flavor. As you work with your sourdough starter, you'll become familiar with its behavior in baking and how to control it, with or without added yeast.

Instructions for making a basic sourdough whole wheat bread and a basic yeasted sourdough whole wheat bread follow. You may want to refer to these detailed accounts as you try out the recipes that come later. We'll finish the chapter with some small and specialty sourdough breads, such as muffins, biscuits, pancakes, and corn bread.

Basic Sourdough Whole Wheat Bread

To make this basic sourdough whole wheat bread, generally follow the procedures for making yeasted breads (pages 48 to 59), but replace the proofed yeast with sourdough starter. Either a straight dough or a sponge method may be used, though I prefer the latter since it gives the yeast a chance to multiply and strengthens the gluten before the salt, oil, and remaining flour are added. If you use the sponge method, plan on about 2½ to 3½ hours for the sponge and dough, 5 hours for rising, and 50 minutes to bake loaves. For the straight dough method, omit the sponge step. Instead, stir together the starter, water, salt, and oil, then add flour to form a dough and proceed as described here; expect the dough to take longer to rise, especially the first bowl rise.

Regardless of the method, you must first expand your saved starter (see above). Do this several hours ahead of time—the night before if you're starting your bread in the morning—and remember to divide the mixture and save a portion of it.

Next, assemble your equipment (see page 49) and the ingredients. For 2 large loaves (about 4 pounds of dough), you'll need:

1 cup sourdough starter
2 cups spring water
7 cups whole wheat bread flour
2 teaspoons sea salt
2 tablespoons oil (corn, sesame, etc.)

Now, proceed with the following steps to make the basic bread; they will also be referenced by many of this chapter's recipes:

1. Combine the starter and water in a large bowl and gradually stir in 2 to 3 cups of flour to form a thick batter. Cover and set in a draft-free spot for 2 to 3 hours, or until it has developed into a sponge. You can leave the sponge longer, but the longer it sits, the sourer it will become. If you do leave it longer, stir it down periodically.

2. Stir in the salt and oil. Add flour a cup at a time, stirring well after each addition, until a dough forms. The dough will pull away from the sides and ball up in the center of the bowl.

3. Turn the dough out onto a lightly floured surface, cover, and let rest about 10 minutes. Meanwhile, wash the bowl and fill it with warm water. Thoroughly knead the dough, adding flour as necessary to keep it from sticking. When it is smooth and elastic, form the dough into a ball. Dry and lightly grease the bowl. Put the dough inside, smooth side down. Now turn the dough ball over so that it is greased lightly on the top. Cover and set aside for about 2 hours—until a finger pressed into the dough leaves a depression.

4. Turn the dough out and knead it gently several times to deflate and round it. Return it to the bowl, cover, and set aside for about 2 hours or slightly less—until it has risen and does not rebound when pressed.

5. Divide the dough, then shape and pan the pieces. I often make freestanding round loaves. Cover and let rise for about an hour or until the dough springs back slowly when pressed.

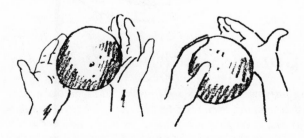

6. Slash the tops of the loaves. Spray with water or brush on an egg wash; sprinkle on seeds if you wish. Bake in a preheated 350-degree oven for about 50 minutes—until the loaves are brown, firm-sided, and sound hollow when removed from the pans and tapped on the bottom.

7. Thoroughly cool the bread on a rack before slicing or storing it.

Basic Yeasted Sourdough Whole Wheat Bread

This recipe for a basic yeast-boosted sourdough whole wheat bread also yields about 4 pounds of dough—enough for two large loaves. The flavor of this bread is slightly more complex than the basic yeasted whole wheat bread and a bit less tangy than the sourdough whole wheat bread without added yeast. Once again, generally follow the procedures for making yeasted breads (pages 48 to 59), but this time you'll use both sourdough starter and proofed yeast.

As with the basic yeasted and basic sourdough breads, you have a choice of using a straight dough or a sponge technique for this bread. If you decide on the sponge technique, you have an additional choice: you can set a sourdough sponge to develop before adding the yeast, or you can combine the sourdough starter and yeast in a sponge. I choose the first alternative, which gives the bread a more pronounced sourdough flavor. The second approach takes less time, if that is a consideration. Plan on between about 2 and 3½ hours for the sponge and dough, about 4 hours for rising, and 50 minutes to bake loaves.

If you want to omit the sponge step altogether, proof the yeast in ¼ cup of the water and combine with the remaining water and starter, stir in the salt and oil, add flour to form a dough, then proceed with kneading and subsequent steps.

Use the same equipment (see page 49) for this yeasted sourdough bread as you would for a basic yeasted or sourdough bread, and remember to expand your starter ahead of time.

Assemble the following ingredients:

> 1 *cup sourdough starter*
> 2 *cups spring water*
> 6½ *to 7 cups whole wheat bread flour*
> ¼ *teaspoon active dry yeast*
> 2 *teaspoons sea salt*
> 2 *tablespoons oil (corn, sesame, etc.)*

Proceed with the following steps to make the basic bread; refer back to them as you make the other yeasted sourdough breads in this chapter:

1. In a large bowl, stir together the starter and 1¾ cups water. Gradually stir in 2 to 2½ cups flour to form a thick batter. Cover and set in a draft-free spot for 2 to

3 hours, or until it has developed into a sponge.

2. Heat the remaining ¼ cup water and cool to lukewarm. Add the yeast and a teaspoon of flour, cover, and set in a warm spot to proof.

3. Add the proofed yeast to the sourdough sponge along with the salt and oil. Add flour, stirring well after each addition, until a dough forms. It will pull away from the sides and ball up in the center of the bowl.

4. Turn the dough out onto a lightly floured surface, cover, and let rest about 10 minutes. Meanwhile, wash the bowl and fill it with hot water. Thoroughly knead the dough, adding flour as necessary to keep it from sticking. When it is smooth and elastic, form the dough into a ball. Dry and lightly grease the bowl, put the dough inside, smooth side down, then turn it over. Cover and set aside for about 1½ hours or until a finger pressed into it leaves a depression.

5. Turn the dough out and knead it gently several times to deflate and round it. Return the dough to the bowl, cover, and set aside for 1 to 1½ hours, until it has risen and does not rebound when pressed.

6. Divide the dough and shape loaves. As with basic sourdough bread, I often make freestanding round loaves. Cover and let rise for about an hour—until the dough springs back slowly when pressed.

7. Slash the tops of the loaves. Spray with water or brush on an egg wash; sprinkle on seeds if you wish. Bake in a preheated 350-degree oven for about 50 minutes—until the loaves are brown, firm-sided, and sound distinctly hollow when removed from the pans and tapped on the bottom.

8. Thoroughly cool the bread on a rack before slicing and storing it.

VARIATIONS

You may think of sourdough bread as only the straightforward, unembellished loaves I've just described, but sourdough bread is as wide open to variations as are the yeasted breads in the previous chapter, and sourdough variations follow the same general pattern as those for yeasted breads. In either plain sourdough or yeasted sourdough bread, you can substitute flours or liquids or add flavorful and textural ingredients, such as cooked whole grains or soaked cracked ones, seeds, nuts, dried fruits, or raw fruits or vegetables or sprouts. Sourdough French bread is made from a simplified version of the basic recipe, but relies upon a specialized baking technique for its unique personality. Try the simple variations that follow before you go on to the recipes in the next section. Once you've mastered those, you'll be ready to invent your own.

- For **Multi-grain Sourdough Bread**, substitute 1 cup rye flour or rye meal (coarsely ground rye flakes)—or another flour, such as barley, rice, oat, or triticale—for 1 cup of the wheat flour. For dough strength, always use wheat flour in the sponge and add low-gluten flours after the sponge has developed.

- For **Sourdough Seed Bread**, knead ¼ cup toasted sesame seeds or flaxseed into each loaf after the first bowl rise or just before the shaped rise. Toast the seeds in a dry heavy skillet over low to moderate heat, agitating the pan often to keep the seeds from burning. Substitute other seeds or nuts.

- For **Sourdough Raisin Bread**, steam ¾ to 1 cup raisins for each loaf or pour hot water over the raisins, soak them for about an hour, and drain well. If you soak the raisins before you start the bread, use the soaking liquid in the dough. Knead the plumped raisins into the dough after the first bowl rise or just before the shaped rise. The raisins will come to the surface of the dough as you knead, but continue kneading them back in until they are well distributed throughout the dough. Substitute other dried fruits for the raisins.

- For **Italian Sourdough Bread**, substitute 2 tablespoons olive oil for the oil in the basic recipes. For an especially crisp crust, place a shallow pan of boiling water on the lowest rack of the oven for the first 15 minutes of baking and spray the loaves with water every 5 minutes during that same period. A baking cloche also gives this bread a terrific crust. These techniques work to crisp the crust of any sourdough bread.

GOLDEN SOURDOUGH BREAD
▼▼▼

Slightly sweet, barely sour, this harvest bread has a somewhat compact, even texture. You can substitute pumpkin, carrots, sweet potatoes, yams, or other varieties of winter squash for the butternut squash. I like to use part of the dough to make CINNAMON SWIRL *or* APPLE BUTTER BUNS *(see page 180).*

YIELD: 2 large loaves

PREPARATION TIME: 2½ to 3½ hours for sponge and dough; 5 hours for rising; 50 minutes to bake

> 2¼ cups spring water
> 1 cup sourdough starter
> 8½ to 9 cups whole wheat bread flour
> 1¼ cups mashed cooked butternut squash
> 2 teaspoons sea salt
> 2 tablespoons corn oil

Beat together 2 cups of the water, the starter, and 2½ cups flour in a large bowl, cover, and set in a draft-free spot for 2 to 3 hours, until a sponge develops.

Thoroughly blend the squash and remaining ¼ cup water and stir this into the sponge along with the salt and oil. Gradually stir in enough of the remaining flour to form a dough.

Follow steps 3 to 7 on page 87. I often brush the loaves with an egg wash and sprinkle on sesame or poppy seeds before baking.

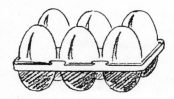

SOURDOUGH EGG BREAD
▰▰▰

This is a basic sourdough bread enriched with eggs—a sourdough challah! Like other egg-rich breads, this one has a fine texture. Make braided or unbraided loaves, freestanding or panned, or use a portion of the dough for sweet buns or a coffee cake.

YIELD: 2 loaves

PREPARATION TIME: 2½ to 3½ hours for sponge and dough; 5 hours for rising; 50 minutes to bake

> 2 cups spring water
> 1 cup sourdough starter
> 7 to 8 cups whole wheat bread flour
> 3 eggs
> 2 teaspoons sea salt
> 3 tablespoons sesame or corn oil

Beat together the water, starter, and 2 to 2½ cups of flour to form a thick batter. Cover and set in a draft-free spot for 2 to 3 hours, until it develops into a sponge.

Whisk the eggs and reserve about a tablespoon to use later for a glaze. Add the salt and oil to the rest of the beaten eggs and whisk well, then beat this mixture into the sponge. Gradually stir in enough of the remaining flour to form a dough.

Follow steps 3 to 7 on page 87.

FOCACCIA
▰▰▰

You need about half a recipe of Italian Sourdough Bread to make this savory flat herb bread. (You can also use a whole recipe of regular Italian bread—page 77.) Cut into strips, squares, or wedges, focaccia is a great addition to a buffet table and it enhances a simple soup-and-salad meal.

> About 2 pounds Italian Sourdough Bread dough
> 1 teaspoon finely minced fresh rosemary leaves
> 3 to 4 teaspoons olive oil
> Cornmeal

After the second bowl rise, on an unfloured surface, gently but thoroughly knead the rosemary into the dough. Form the dough into a ball, cover, and let rest a few minutes. Grease a large flat pan with a teaspoon or so of the olive oil and dust it lightly with cornmeal. I use a 15-inch blackened steel pizza pan.

On a lightly greased surface, roll the dough out into a 12-inch circle, about ½ inch thick. Transfer the dough to the pan, cover, and set in a draft-free spot for about an hour or until light and puffy.

Preheat the oven to 400 degrees. Using your fingertips, make light indentations over the surface of the dough. Drizzle the remaining olive oil over the surface. Bake 30 minutes, until the bread is well browned and crusty. Cool briefly on a rack, cut, and serve warm.

NOTES

- Substitute another herb, such as thyme or sage, for the rosemary—or use a compatible combination. If you use dried herbs, use half as much as the fresh.

- For *ONION FOCACCIA*, press thinly sliced rings from a medium-sized onion into the surface of the risen dough (with or without herbs kneaded in), drizzle on olive oil, and sprinkle a bit of sea salt over the top before baking.

NOTES

- Add 1 to 2 tablespoons of honey along with the salt, oil, and egg.

SOURDOUGH SPROUTED LENTIL BREAD

▾▾▾

The sprouts contribute rising power to this dough and add flavor, moistness, and a nutty quality to the baked loaves. Begin sprouting ¼ cup green lentils about three days before you plan to make the bread.

YIELD: 2 loaves

PREPARATION TIME: 2½ to 3 hours for sponge and dough; 5 hours for rising; 50 minutes to bake

> 1 cup sourdough starter
> 2 cups spring water
> 7½ to 8 cups whole wheat bread flour
> 2 to 3 cups lentil sprouts (see page 238)
> 2 teaspoons sea salt
> 2 tablespoons corn or sesame oil

Beat together the starter, water, and 2½ cups of the flour. Cover and set in a draft-free spot for 2 to 3 hours, until a sponge develops.

Coarsely chop the sprouts and stir them into the sponge along with the salt and oil. Gradually stir in enough of the remaining flour to form a dough.

Follow steps 3 to 7 on page 87.

NOTES
- Substitute other kinds of sprouts for the lentil sprouts.

SOURDOUGH GRITS BREAD

▾▾▾

Corn and soy grits add a subtle crunch to the compact texture of this fine bread; it's one that I never tire of. The grits are interchangeable: use all soy, all corn, half of each, or another grain altogether, such as rice or barley grits.

YIELD: 2 loaves

PREPARATION TIME: 1 hour to soak the grits; 2½ to 3½ hours for sponge and dough; 5 hours for rising; 50 minutes to bake

> 2½ cups spring water
> 2 tablespoons soy grits
> ¼ cup corn grits
> 1 cup sourdough starter
> 7½ to 8 cups whole wheat bread flour
> 2 teaspoons sea salt
> 2 tablespoons corn or sesame oil

Heat the water to boiling and pour it over the grits in a large bowl. Cover and set aside until lukewarm. Stir in the starter and 2½ cups of the flour to form a thick bat-ter. Cover and set in a draft-free spot for 2 to 3 hours, until a sponge develops.

Stir the salt and oil into the sponge. Gradually stir in enough of the remaining flour to form a dough.

Follow steps 3 to 7 on page 87.

HEARTY SOURDOUGH BREAD

▾▾▾

Substantially good! My father-in-law calls this stamina bread. Slice it thinly and savor its full flavor. Potato seems to enhance the rising of dough; it gives breads a moist crumb and adds flavor and nutrients.

YIELD: 2 loaves

PREPARATION TIME: 1 hour to soak the grain; 2½ to 3½ hours for sponge and dough; 5 hours for rising; 50 minutes to bake

> 2½ cups spring water
> 1 medium-sized potato, cubed
> 1 cup cracked wheat or rye
> 1 cup sourdough starter
> 7 to 8 cups whole wheat bread flour
> 2 teaspoons sea salt
> 2 tablespoons corn or sesame oil

Combine about ½ cup of the water and the potato in a blender and blend, gradually adding the remaining water, until the mixture is thoroughly smooth. Transfer to a saucepan and heat to boiling. Pour over the cracked grain in a large bowl. Cover and set aside until lukewarm.

Stir in the starter and 2 cups of the flour to form a thick batter. Cover and set in a draft-free spot for 2 to 3 hours or until the batter develops into a sponge.

Stir the salt and oil into the sponge. Gradually stir in enough of the remaining flour to form a dough.

Follow steps 3 to 7 on page 87.

SOURDOUGH MILLET BREAD

▾▾▾

This agreeable bread has a subtle sweet-and-sour flavor and a somewhat compact, moist, nubbly texture. Make extra millet for dinner and use it in this bread the next day. You can substitute cooked short-, medium-, or long-grain rice for the millet; my favorite is basmati rice. I like to use this rice dough for INDONESIAN PIZZA (page 167) or MEXICAN PIZZA (page 167).

YIELD: 2 loaves

PREPARATION TIME: 2½ to 3½ hours for sponge and dough; 5 hours for rising; 50 minutes to bake

2 cups cooled cooked millet (see page 13-14)
2 cups spring water
1 cup sourdough starter
7 cups whole wheat bread flour
2 teaspoons sea salt
2 tablespoons corn or sesame oil

Stir together the millet, water, starter, and 2 cups of the flour in a large bowl. Cover and set aside in a draft-free spot for 2 to 3 hours, until a sponge develops.

Stir the salt and oil into the sponge. Gradually stir in enough of the remaining flour to form a dough.

Follow steps 3 to 7 on page 87. I often brush the loaves with an egg wash and sprinkle on sesame seeds.

NOTES

- If the millet is on the dry side, add an extra ¼ to ½ cup water when you mix the batter.

- After the first bowl rise or just before shaping the dough, knead ¾ to 1 cup plumped raisins into each loaf. Steam the raisins or soak them in hot water and drain them well.

SOURDOUGH BERRY BREAD

▼▼▼

Cooked wheat berries give this bread a chewy, nutty texture and a delicious sweet taste. You can substitute cooked rye or triticale berries for the wheat berries.

YIELD: 2 large loaves

PREPARATION TIME: 2½ to 3½ hours for sponge and dough; 5 hours for rising; 50 minutes to bake

1 cup sourdough starter
2 cups spring water
7 cups whole wheat bread flour
2 cups cooked whole wheat berries (see page 13-14)
2 teaspoons sea salt
2 tablespoons corn oil

Stir together the starter, water, and 2 cups of the flour in a large bowl. Cover and set aside in a draft-free spot for 2 to 3 hours until a sponge develops.

Stir the wheat berries, salt, and oil into the sponge. Gradually stir in enough of the remaining flour to form a dough.

Follow steps 3 to 7 on page 87.

SOURDOUGH FRENCH BREAD

▼▼▼

This unique bread made San Francisco famous—or vice versa. With its hard crust, springy crumb, and well-developed flavor based on simple ingredients—flour,

water, salt, and yeast—it meets the requirements of any fine French bread. But the chewiness of its crust, its especially fine-grained and moist texture, and its distinctive tangy taste set this sourdough-leavened French bread apart as a special item. Finely ground flour will give your loaves extra oomph.

YIELD: 2 loaves

PREPARATION TIME: 2½ to 3 hours for sponge and dough; 5 to 6 hours for rising; 45 to 50 minutes to bake

1½ cups sourdough starter
1½ cups spring water
4½ cups whole wheat bread flour
1½ teaspoons sea salt

In a large bowl, stir together the starter, water, and 1½ cups of the flour. Cover and set in a draft-free spot for 2 to 2½ hours or until a sponge develops.

Stir in the salt. Gradually stir in additional flour to form a dough. Turn the dough out onto a lightly floured surface, cover, and let rest several minutes. Knead until smooth and elastic, adding flour as necessary to keep the dough from sticking.

Form the dough into a ball and put it in a lightly greased bowl. Cover and set aside for about 2 hours, until the dough has risen and does not spring back when pressed. Turn the dough out and knead it briefly. Return it to the bowl for a second rise.

Form round loaves or shape baguettes by the method described on page 76 and place them on cornmeal-dusted pans. Cover the loaves and set them aside to rise for about an hour or until the dough rebounds slowly when pressed.

Preheat the oven to 400 degrees. Slash the tops of the loaves and spray or brush them with cold water. Place a shallow pan of boiling water on the bottom rack of the oven and put the bread on the rack above it. After 5 minutes, open the oven door and quickly spray the loaves with cold water—remember to avoid spraying the oven light! Spray again after 5 minutes. After 5 more minutes (15 minutes into the baking), give the loaves one more spray and, before you close the oven door, remove the pan of water. Bake 30 minutes longer, until the bread is well browned and crusty and sounds hollow when tapped on the bottom.

NOTES

- Steaming is what gives any French bread a wonderful crust; the steaming tactics I employ here simulate professional steam injection devices. Baking in a cloche will also give the bread a great crust.

- If you have baking tiles or a baking stone, let the shaped loaves rise upside-down on a lightly floured surface—French bakers use cloth-lined baskets for round loaves and canvas for long ones. Preheat your tiles or stone when you preheat the oven. Turn a risen loaf over, right side up, onto a baking peel—a flat wooden shovel-like implement—and then quickly transfer it to the hot tiles or stone by pushing the peel forward and immediately pulling the peel out from under the loaf. You can improvise a peel with a thin board or piece of heavy cardboard. You can also just let the loaves rise on the tiles (arranged on a baking sheet) or baking stone outside of the oven. In either case, still use the pan of boiling water and spraying techniques too.

YEASTED SOURDOUGH CRACKED WHEAT BREAD
▬▬▬

This bread has a subtler sourdough flavor and less heft than its cousin, HEARTY SOURDOUGH BREAD (page 90).

YIELD: 2 large loaves

PREPARATION TIME: 2 to 3 hours for sponge and dough; 5 hours for rising; 50 minutes to bake

> 3 *cups spring water*
> 1 *cup cracked wheat*
> 1 *cup sourdough starter*
> 7½ *cups whole wheat bread flour*
> ¼ *teaspoon active dry yeast*
> 2 *teaspoons sea salt*
> 2 *tablespoons corn oil*

Heat 2 cups of the water to boiling and pour it over the cracked wheat in a large bowl. Cover and set aside until lukewarm. Stir in the starter and 2 cups of the flour to form a thick batter. Cover and set in a draft-free spot for about 2 hours until it develops into a sponge.

Meanwhile, heat ¼ cup of the water and cool it to lukewarm. Add the yeast and a teaspoon of flour, cover, and set in a draft-free spot to proof. Stir in the remaining ¾ cup water and 1 cup or so of flour to form a thick batter. Cover and set in a draft-free spot for 30 minutes to an hour, until it develops into a sponge.

Stir the yeast sponge into the sourdough sponge along with the salt and oil. Gradually stir in enough of the remaining flour to form a dough.

Follow steps 4 to 8 on page 88.

NOTES
- Substitute cracked rye or toasted buckwheat groats for the wheat.

YEASTED SOURDOUGH OAT BREAD
▬▬▬

Steel-cut oats contribute sweetness and a wonderfully chewy texture to this superb bread. It has an especially moist crumb and keeps particularly well. This dough makes delicious English muffins (see page 58).

YIELD: 2 large loaves

PREPARATION TIME: 2 to 3 hours for sponge and dough; 5 hours for rising; 50 minutes to bake

> 3 *cups spring water*
> 1 *cup steel-cut oats*
> 1 *cup sourdough starter*
> 8 *to 9 cups whole wheat bread flour*
> ¼ *teaspoon active dry yeast*
> 2 *teaspoons sea salt*
> 3 *tablespoons sesame oil*

Heat 2 cups of the water to boiling and pour it over the oats in a large bowl. Cover and set aside until lukewarm. Stir in the starter and 2 cups of the flour to form a thick batter. Cover and set in a draft-free spot for 2 to 3 hours, until it develops into a sponge.

Meanwhile, heat ¼ cup of the water and cool it to lukewarm. Add the yeast and a teaspoon of flour, cover, and set in a draft-free spot to proof. Stir in the remaining ¾ cup water and 1 cup or so of the flour, cover, and set in a draft-free spot for 30 minutes to an hour, until it develops into a sponge.

Stir the yeast sponge into the sourdough sponge along with the salt and oil. Gradually stir in enough of the remaining flour to form a dough.

Follow steps 4 to 8 on page 88.

NOTES
- For a sweeter dough, add 2 tablespoons maple syrup, honey, or rice syrup along with the salt and oil.

YEASTED SOURDOUGH BRAN BREAD
▬▬▬

This bread is dark and delectable and particularly high in healthful fiber. It's another good choice for making rolls and English muffins.

YIELD: 2 large loaves

PREPARATION TIME: 2 to 3 hours for sponge and dough; 5 hours for rising; 50 minutes to bake

> 3 *cups spring water*
> 1 *cup wheat bran*

1 *cup sourdough starter*
7 *to 8 cups whole wheat bread flour*
¼ *teaspoon active dry yeast*
2 *teaspoons sea salt*
¼ *cup corn oil*
2 *tablespoons blackstrap molasses*
2 *tablespoons honey or rice syrup*

Heat 2 cups of the water to boiling and pour it over the bran in a large bowl. Cover and set aside until lukewarm. Stir in the starter and 2 to 2½ cups of the flour to form a thick batter. Cover and set in a draft-free spot until it develops into a sponge.

Meanwhile, heat ¼ cup of the water and cool it to lukewarm. Add the yeast and a teaspoon of flour, cover, and set in a draft-free spot to proof. Stir in the remaining ¾ cup water and 1 cup or more of the flour to form a thick batter. Cover and set in a draft-free spot for 30 minutes to an hour, until a sponge develops.

Stir the yeast sponge into the sourdough sponge along with the salt, oil, molasses, and honey. Gradually stir in flour to form a dough.

Follow steps 4 to 8 on page 88. Brush the loaves with an egg wash and sprinkle on poppy seeds before baking.

NOTES

- Soak the bran in mild vegetable stock rather than water.

- Soak the bran in unsweetened apple juice and omit the sweeteners.

- Substitute oat bran or another kind of bran for the wheat bran.

*Y*EASTED *S*OURDOUGH *B*UCKWHEAT *B*READ
▼▼▼

This is a bread for kasha fans! Use part of the dough to make the crust for R*EUBEN'S* P*IZZA (page 168-69).*

YIELD: 2 loaves

PREPARATION TIME: 2 to 3 hours for sponge and dough; 5 hours for rising; 50 minutes to bake

2½ *cups spring water*
1 *cup sourdough starter*
7½ *cups whole wheat bread flour*
¼ *teaspoon active dry yeast*
2 *teaspoons sea salt*
2 *tablespoons corn or sesame oil*
2 *cups cooked toasted buckwheat groats (see page 13-14)*

Stir together 2 cups of the water and the starter in a large bowl. Stir in about 2½ cups of the flour to form a thick batter. Cover and set in a draft-free spot for 2 to 3 hours, until it develops into a sponge.

Meanwhile, heat the remaining ½ cup of water and cool it to lukewarm. Add the yeast and a teaspoon of flour, cover, and set in a draft-free spot to proof. Stir in about ½ cup of the flour to form a thick batter, cover, and return it to the draft-free spot for 30 minutes to an hour, until it develops into a sponge.

Stir the yeast sponge into the sourdough sponge along with the salt, oil, and buckwheat groats. Gradually stir in enough of the remaining flour to form a dough.

Follow steps 4 to 8 on page 88. Brush on an egg wash and sprinkle on poppy seeds before baking.

NOTES

- Substitute cooked brown rice or cooked millet (see page 13-14) for the buckwheat groats—or use a combination of cooked grains.

*S*OURDOUGH *R*YE *B*READ
▼▼▼

This bread is permeated with the unique sweetness of rye, and it has a compact texture that is perfect for thin slicing. Use part of the dough to make the crust for a cabbage or onion tart (page 173). For a truly all-rye bread, use a rye starter, though wheat starter will work just as well. For a lighter bread, substitute whole wheat bread flour for part of the rye flour, and, for best results, use the wheat flour in the sponge.

YIELD: 2 loaves

PREPARATION TIME: 3 to 3½ hours for sponge and dough; 5 hours for rising; 50 minutes to bake

1 *cup sourdough starter*
2 *cups spring water*
7 *to 7½ cups rye flour*
¼ *teaspoon active dry yeast*
2 *teaspoons sea salt*
2 *tablespoons corn oil*

Stir together the starter and 1½ cups of the water in a large bowl. Stir in about 2 cups of the flour to form a thick batter. Cover and set aside for 2 to 3 hours or until it develops into a sponge.

Meanwhile, heat the remaining ½ cup of water and cool it to lukewarm. Stir in the yeast and a teaspoon of flour, cover, and set in a draft-free spot to proof. Stir in about ½ cup of the flour to form a thick batter, cover, and set aside for 30 minutes to an hour, until it develops into a sponge.

Stir the yeast sponge into the sourdough sponge along with the salt and oil. Gradually stir in enough flour to form a dough. Knead gently—rye doughs tend to be stickier than predominantly wheat doughs and require more careful handling. Moistening your hands and the kneading surface with water may help to prevent the dough from becoming overly sticky or tearing. Knead less than you would a wheat dough. If the dough becomes sticky, stop kneading. The dough will become resilient but it will feel somewhat dense.

Form it into a ball and put it in a lightly greased bowl. Cover and set aside at cool room temperature for about 2 hours, until the dough has risen and does not spring back when pressed; it won't rise as much as a dough containing wheat flour. Turn the dough out and knead it briefly. Return it to the bowl for a second rise.

Shape and pan the dough. I recommend a sided container, since freestanding loaves made with this dough tend to spread out rather than rise up. Cover the loaves and set them aside to rise for about an hour or until the loaves have risen—these won't double in size.

Dock the loaves with a fork. Bake at 350 degrees for about 50 minutes, until the loaves have firm sides and sound distinctly hollow when tapped on the bottom. For a shiny crust, brush on an egg glaze before baking or apply a cornstarch glaze (page 56) when the bread is about half baked and then again about 5 minutes before it is done.

Cool the bread thoroughly before slicing or storing it.

PAIN POUR NICOL!
▼▼▼

Any bread that contains coarsely ground rye is generally called pumpernickel. My favorite story about the origin of this term is the one about Napoleon's horse Nicol. According to this tale, Nicol craved the dark rye bread customarily made by European peasants, and the imperial troops would scour the countryside, seeking pain pour Nicol— *"bread for Nicol." The appealing mix of flavors in this hearty bread satisfies human aficionados of pumpernickel too. Try it with* MUSHROOM PÂTÉ *(page 139). To prepare rye meal, grind or blend rye flakes to a coarse consistency.*

YIELD: 2 large loaves

PREPARATION TIME: 2½ to 3 hours for sponge and dough; 5 hours for rising; 50 minutes to bake

  1 *teaspoon freshly grated orange zest*
  1 *medium-sized potato, cubed*
3¼ *cups spring water*
 ½ *cup cornmeal*
1½ *teaspoons fennel seed, coarsely ground*

  1 *cup rye meal*
  1 *cup sourdough starter*
  7 *to 7½ cups whole wheat bread flour*
 ¼ *teaspoon active dry yeast*
 ¼ *teaspoon ground ginger*
  2 *tablespoons blackstrap molasses*
  3 *tablespoons corn oil*
2½ *teaspoons sea salt*
1½ *cups rye flour*

Combine the zest, potato, and ½ cup of the water in a blender. Blend, gradually adding 1 cup of water, until smooth. Transfer to a saucepan and stir in the cornmeal. Add 1½ cups boiling water and cook over moderate heat, stirring, until thick. Transfer to a large bowl and stir in the fennel seed and rye meal. Cool to lukewarm. Stir in the starter and 3 cups of wheat flour to form a thick batter. Cover and set in a draft-free spot for about 2 hours—until the batter develops into a sponge.

Meanwhile, heat the remaining ¼ cup of water and cool it to lukewarm. Add the yeast and about a teaspoon of wheat flour. Cover and set in a draft-free spot to proof. Stir in the ginger and ¼ cup of wheat flour. Cover and return to the draft-free spot for about 30 minutes—until it develops into a sponge.

Stir the yeast sponge into the sourdough sponge along with the molasses, oil, salt, and rye flour. Gradually stir in enough of the remaining wheat flour to form a dough.

Follow steps 4 to 8 on page 88. Spray the loaves with water or brush on an egg wash before baking or brush on a cornstarch glaze (page 56) halfway through baking and again about 5 minutes before the bread is done.

NOTES

- Substitute anise or caraway seeds for the fennel, and omit the orange zest if you prefer.

- Omit the yeast, ginger, and ¼ cup of both water and wheat flour; the dough might take slightly longer to rise and the final product will be a bit heftier.

SUPER SUNDAY SCONES
▼▼▼

These sourdough scones take a little longer to make than standard scones, but their unique flavor and texture is worth the extra time. Making them fits well into a relaxed weekend morning routine—mix the batter the night before and then let the scones rise while you leisurely read the paper or go out for a jog or swim before a late breakfast.

YIELD: 6 large scones

PREPARATION TIME: Several hours or overnight for sponge; 1 to 2 hours to shape and rise; 30 minutes to bake

> ½ cup sourdough starter
> ¾ cup milk or soy milk, scalded and cooled to lukewarm
> 1¼ to 1½ cups whole wheat pastry flour
> 3 tablespoons melted unsalted soy margarine or butter or light vegetable oil
> 2 tablespoons maple syrup
> ¼ cup raisins or currants
> ¼ teaspoon sea salt
> ½ cup rolled oats

In a medium-sized mixing bowl, stir together the starter, milk, and 1 cup pastry flour to form a thick batter. Cover and leave at room temperature for several hours or overnight—until it develops into a sponge.

Thoroughly stir 2 tablespoons of the melted margarine, the syrup, raisins or currants, and salt into the sponge. In a blender, grind the rolled oats to a coarse flour. Stir it into the sponge mixture to form a soft dough. Turn it out onto a lightly floured surface and knead gently and briefly, adding additional flour only as necessary to keep it from sticking. Pat the dough into a round about 1 inch thick. Cut it into 6 equal wedges.

Arrange the scones on a lightly greased or parchment-lined baking sheet or in a 10-inch pie plate. Brush with the remaining melted margarine. Cover and set in a draft-free spot for 1 to 2 hours—until light and puffy.

Place in a cold oven and set it to 375 degrees. Bake 30 minutes or until the scones have browned and a tester inserted into the center comes out clean. Transfer them to a cooling rack and cover loosely with a dry tea towel for 15 to 20 minutes. Serve warm.

NOTES

- Substitute ½ cup barley or rye flour for the rolled oats.

- Omit the syrup for less sweet scones.

- To hasten preparation, sift ½ teaspoon baking soda with the oat flour and salt and gently mix these dry ingredients into the risen sponge after you have stirred in the oil, syrup, and raisins or currants. Knead the dough as little and as lightly as possible, shape the scones quickly, and bake them immediately.

SOURDOUGH MUFFINS
▼▼▼

The sourdough starter contributes a slight tang to the flavor of these moist muffins. Baking soda leavens them, so they are quick to make. These are good keepers if there are ever any leftover.

YIELD: 10 to 12 large muffins

PREPARATION TIME: 20 minutes to prepare; 30 minutes to bake

> 1½ cups whole wheat pastry flour
> ½ cup rye flour
> ½ teaspoon sea salt
> 1 teaspoon baking soda
> ⅓ cup sunflower oil
> ⅓ cup maple syrup
> 1 egg
> ½ cup milk or soy milk, scalded and cooled to lukewarm
> Finely grated zest of 1 orange
> ¼ cup orange juice
> ¾ cup sourdough starter
> ½ cup raisins
> ½ cup lightly toasted, coarsely chopped pecans

Preheat the oven to 375 degrees. Grease the muffin cups.

Sift together the flours, salt, and soda.

In a medium-sized mixing bowl, whisk together the oil and syrup. Thoroughly beat in the egg. Whisk in the milk, orange zest and juice, and the starter. Stir in the raisins. Add the dry mixture and nuts and fold gently, mixing just enough to form a batter.

Fill the muffin cups. Bake in the preheated oven 30 minutes or until a tester inserted into the center comes out clean. Cool briefly and serve warm.

NOTES

- Omit the soda and let the batter rise in the pan before baking; in this case, fill the muffin cups only two-thirds full.

- Substitute more orange juice for part of the milk if the orange yields more than ¼ cup when squeezed.

- Substitute cornmeal for the rye flour; omit the

orange juice; add 1½ teaspoons lemon juice to the milk to curdle it; and increase the sourdough starter to 1 cup.

- Substitute oat flour or rolled oats for the rye flour and chopped dates for the raisins; omit the orange juice; add 1½ teaspoons lemon juice to the milk to curdle it; and use 1 cup starter.

SOURDOUGH CORN BREAD
▼▼▼

Tender and slightly tangy, this corn bread is an excellent complement to bean dishes and soups.

YIELD: 1 8-inch square or 9-inch round bread

PREPARATION TIME: About 2 hours for sponge and batter; 20 to 25 minutes to bake

> 1 cup sourdough starter
> 1 cup cornmeal
> ¾ cup milk or soy milk, scalded and cooled to lukewarm
> 2 tablespoons wheat germ, bran, or seeds (sesame, poppy, chia, or ground sunflower seeds)
> 1 cup whole wheat pastry flour
> ½ teaspoon sea salt
> ½ teaspoon baking soda
> ¼ cup vegetable oil or melted unsalted margarine or butter
> 2 tablespoons maple syrup, honey, or rice syrup
> 1 egg

In a large mixing bowl, stir together the starter, cornmeal, and milk. Cover and set aside for about 2 hours, until the batter has developed into a sponge.

Preheat the oven to 400 degrees. Grease an 8-inch square or 9-inch round baking pan. Add the wheat germ, bran, or seeds and tilt the pan to coat the bottom and sides.

Sift together the flour, salt, and soda.

Whisk together the oil and sweetener. Thoroughly whisk in the egg. Beat into the sponge. Gently fold in the dry mixture, mixing just enough to form a batter. Spread in the prepared pan.

Bake in the preheated oven 20 to 25 minutes—until the top is browned and a tester inserted into the center comes out clean. Cool briefly and serve warm.

NOTES

- For an especially crusty corn bread, bake in a preheated, greased 9-inch cast-iron frying pan.

- Sweetener is optional.

- You may omit the baking soda; let the batter rise in the pan before baking.

SOURDOUGH BANANA BREAD
▼▼▼

Only mildly sweet, this is definitely a bread rather than a dessert. Serve it with TAHINI-MISO SPREAD *(page 132).*

YIELD: 1 large loaf

PREPARATION TIME: 20 minutes to prepare; about 2 hours to rise; 1 hour to bake

> ¼ cup sunflower oil or other light vegetable oil
> ¼ cup honey, maple syrup, or rice syrup
> 1 egg
> 1 cup mashed ripe banana
> 1 tablespoon lemon juice
> 1 cup sourdough starter
> 2 cups sifted whole wheat pastry flour
> ½ teaspoon sea salt
> ¾ cup lightly toasted, coarsely chopped walnuts
> 2 tablespoons poppy seeds

In a large mixing bowl, whisk together the oil and sweetener. Beat in the egg. Whisk in the banana, lemon juice, and starter.

Sift together the flour and salt. Stir into the liquid mixture to form a thick batter. Fold in the walnuts.

Grease a 9×5-inch loaf pan and coat the bottom and sides with the poppy seeds. Evenly spread in the batter. Cover with a damp tea towel and set in a draft-free spot to rise for about 2 hours.

When the batter has risen almost to the top of the pan, place it in a cold oven and set the oven to 325 degrees. Bake 1 hour or until a tester inserted into the center comes out clean. Cool in the pan 15 to 20 minutes, then turn out onto a rack. This bread slices best after it has thoroughly cooled.

NOTES

- When this bread is a day or two old, I like to serve slices lightly toasted.

TRAIL BISCUITS
▾▾▾

These no-frills, slightly chewy sourdough biscuits are probably closest to those made by pioneer travelers and miners. My dad still has the gold scales that my great-grandfather used when he prospected in California during the Gold Rush. Most likely he attributed equal value to his sourdough.

YIELD: 6 2½-inch biscuits

PREPARATION TIME: 20 minutes to prepare; 30 to 60 minutes to rise; 30 minutes to bake

    1½ cups sourdough starter
    1½ teaspoons honey
    ½   cup whole wheat bread flour
    ½   cup whole wheat pastry flour
    ½   teaspoon sea salt
    ¼   teaspoon baking soda
    1   tablespoon unsalted soy margarine or butter, melted

In a medium-sized mixing bowl, whisk together the starter and honey.

Sift together the bread and pastry flours, salt, and soda. Gradually sift again into the liquid mixture and stir gently to form a soft dough. Turn it out onto a lightly floured surface and knead briefly until smooth.

Roll or pat out the dough about ¾ inch thick. Cut out biscuits, dipping the cutter into flour between each one. Knead dough scraps together and roll and cut more biscuits.

For crusty biscuits, arrange them about 1½ inches apart on an ungreased baking sheet. For soft-sided biscuits, place them close together in a lightly greased 9-inch round baking pan. Brush the tops of the biscuits with the melted margarine or butter. Set in a warm, draft-free spot for 30 to 60 minutes—until light and puffy.

Preheat the oven to 375 degrees. Bake the biscuits 30 minutes, until they are browned and a tester inserted into the center comes out clean. Cool directly on a rack loosely covered with a tea towel for about 15 minutes. Serve warm.

NOTES

- The baking soda neutralizes the acid sourdough, thereby sweetening the dough, and it also provides a bit of a leavening boost. You may leave out the soda; the biscuits will probably taste somewhat tangier and take longer to rise.

SOURDOUGH BISCUITS
▾▾▾

Leavened and flavored with sourdough, these flaky buns are a bit more breadlike than their quick bread counterparts.

YIELD: 6 2½-inch biscuits

PREPARATION TIME: 20 minutes to prepare; 30 to 60 minutes to rise; 15 minutes to bake

    ¼   cup milk or soy milk, scalded and cooled to lukewarm
    1½ teaspoons lemon juice
    ½   cup whole wheat pastry flour
    ½   cup whole wheat bread flour
    ¼   teaspoon sea salt
    ¼   teaspoon baking soda
    2   tablespoons cold unsalted soy margarine or butter
    ¾   cup sourdough starter

Combine the milk and lemon juice; set aside to curdle.

Sift together the pastry and bread flours, salt, and soda. In a food processor fitted with the metal blade or in a mixing bowl with a pastry blender, cut the margarine or butter into the dry mixture until it resembles a coarse meal. If you use a processor, transfer the mixture to a bowl. Make a well in the center of the mixture.

Whisk together the curdled milk and starter. Pour it into the well and stir gently until a soft dough forms. Turn it out onto a lightly floured surface and knead briefly—just 15 to 20 times—until smooth. Roll or pat out the dough ¾ inch thick. Cut out biscuits, dipping the cutter into flour between each one. Knead dough scraps together and roll and cut additional biscuits. For crusty biscuits, arrange them about 1½ inches apart on an ungreased baking sheet. For softer-sided biscuits, place them close together in a lightly greased 9-inch round baking tin. Cover with a damp tea towel and set in a warm spot for 30 to 60 minutes, until the dough is light and puffy.

Preheat the oven to 450 degrees. Bake the biscuits 15 minutes, until they are browned and a tester inserted into the center comes out clean. Transfer to a cooling rack, cover loosely with a tea towel, and cool about 15 minutes before serving.

NOTES

- The baking soda reacts with the acid sourdough, thereby neutralizing and sweetening the dough, and it provides a bit of a boost to the rising; you may omit the soda, but plan on a somewhat longer rising period.

SOURDOUGH FLAPJACKS
▚▚▚

Sourdough pancakes are a unique American griddle bread. This is a basic recipe; vary the flour for different flavors and textures. Add a cup of fresh berries or finely chopped fresh fruit or some lightly toasted chopped nuts or seeds to the batter just before cooking.

YIELD: About 1 dozen 4-inch pancakes

PREPARATION TIME: Several hours or overnight for the sponge; about 1 hour for the batter; 5 minutes to cook each batch

- ⅔ cup sourdough starter
- ⅔ cup plus 1 teaspoon spring water
- 1½ cups whole wheat pastry flour
- ¼ teaspoon sea salt
- 1 tablespoon maple syrup
- 1 tablespoon sunflower or other vegetable oil
- ½ cup milk or soy milk, scalded and cooled to lukewarm
- ¼ teaspoon baking soda

Stir together the starter, the ⅔ cup water, and 1 cup of the flour in a glass or ceramic bowl. Cover and leave at room temperature for several hours or overnight—until the batter rises into a sponge.

Beat in the salt, syrup, oil, milk, and remaining ½ cup flour. Cover and set aside for about 1 hour. Dissolve the baking soda in the 1 teaspoon water and stir it into the batter just before cooking.

Heat a griddle until water sprinkled on the surface sizzles immediately. Lightly grease the surface and ladle on batter. Cook the pancakes until the tops bubble and look somewhat dry around the edges and the bottoms are golden brown. Turn and cook briefly on the other side—just long enough to brown them.

Serve pancakes immediately or stack them on a plate, covered with a tea towel or inverted bowl and place them in a warm oven.

NOTES
- Substitute cornmeal or buckwheat, barley, rye, or oat flour for the ½ cup of flour that is added to the sponge.

- The baking soda is optional, but it does produce lighter pancakes.

- To make waffles, add another tablespoon of oil to the batter.

SOURDOUGH SWEET POTATO PANCAKES
▚▚▚

Serve these golden griddlecakes with maple syrup or **PEAR BUTTER** *(page 135).*

YIELD: About 1 dozen 4-inch pancakes

PREPARATION TIME: Several hours or overnight for the sponge; about 1 hour for the batter; 5 minutes to cook each batch

- ¾ cup sourdough starter
- ¾ cup plus 1 teaspoon spring water
- 1 cup whole wheat pastry flour
- ½ teaspoon sea salt
- 1 tablespoon maple syrup
- 1 tablespoon sunflower or corn oil
- ¾ cup milk or soy milk, scalded and cooled to lukewarm
- ½ cup mashed cooked sweet potato
- ½ cup cornmeal
- ¼ to ½ teaspoon baking soda

Stir together the starter, the ¾ cup water, and pastry flour in a glass or ceramic bowl. Cover and leave at room temperature for several hours or overnight—until the batter rises into a sponge.

Beat in the salt, syrup, oil, milk, sweet potato, and cornmeal. Cover and set aside for about 1 hour. Dissolve the baking soda in the 1 teaspoon water and stir it into the batter just before cooking.

Ladle batter onto a hot, lightly greased griddle. Cook the pancakes until the tops bubble and the bottoms are brown. Turn and cook briefly on the other side.

Serve the pancakes immediately or keep them warm in the oven.

NOTES
- The baking soda is optional, but it does lighten the pancakes.

- Add an extra tablespoon of oil to the batter for waffles.

CHAPTER 7

Natural-Rise Breads

THE ITHACA SEED COMPANY was a bookstore-restaurant located in an old cinder block garage down an alleyway just off the Cornell University campus in the late 1960s. I was drawn to the bookstore first. There were floor-to-ceiling shelves of counterculture titles to peruse, comfortable overstuffed chairs and sofas to sit on, and no pressure to buy. But the aroma of cooking foods and the clatter in the kitchen quickly diverted my attention. The restaurant only served dinners and there was a set menu each evening for a fixed price. Here I was introduced to a whole grain and bean-based cuisine and naturally-leavened bread. Actually, their loaves would more accurately have been described as *unleavened*, since they were invariably dense and bricklike. Despite their weightiness, there was something about those breads that intrigued me; though heavy and compact, the thick slices were chewy and flavorful.

For many people, the label "naturally-leavened" connotes weighty, unsliceable, deadbeat loaves. It may bring to their minds, too, those ponderous breads that appeared in early natural foods establishments like the Seed Company. Indeed some so-called natural-rise

breads really are lifeless loaves that plunge to the depths of your stomach as soon as you swallow, and a few experiences with such indigestible disasters would make anyone wary of the term.

But not all natural-rise breads deserve such a bad reputation. Given the opportunity, doughs prepared without commercial yeast or sourdough starters will rise into some of the most outstanding breads imaginable. When I first tasted a fine natural-rise bread, I felt that I had reached the end of a journey, a long, unconscious search for the ultimate in flavor and texture. No two batches ever emerge from the oven just alike, but there is something about skillfully made natural-rise bread that is extraordinarily satisfying. I have witnessed its broad appeal—even to whole grain skeptics who have dared to try it.

Naturally-leavened breads have a fine-grained crumb that is especially moist and flavorful. This is because thoroughly fermented dough absorbs liquid particularly well and also produces a subtle, complex mix of flavors that highlight the natural sweetness of grains. The chewy crusts of natural-rise loaves seal in both moisture and flavor, preserving freshness. Stored at room temperature, a natural-rise loaf will reach its peak in flavor and texture several days after baking as its crust softens and crumb mellows. You will be amazed at how easy it is to slice natural-rise breads thinly, and you'll find that a little of their hearty goodness goes a long way.

Natural-rise bread making is based on the principle that, given time and temperate, moist conditions, a dough made with fresh whole grains will undergo fermentation and rise without the addition of commercial yeast or sourdough starter. Left long enough in a slightly cool, draft-free spot, an unyeasted dough will attract ambient yeast and go through chemical changes analogous to those that take place in yeasted doughs or sourdoughs, but fermentation and rising will occur at a slower pace. As the carbohydrates are broken down during fermentation, a lot of other changes take place in the dough that develop the flavor and make nutrients more absorbable. In a sense, the grains in natural-rise doughs are partially digested during the long fermentation process, and therefore natural-rise breads are particularly nutritious and easy to digest.

In doughs leavened with commercial yeast, the yeast typically proliferates at such a rapid rate that the dough reaches its peak of elasticity well before it is fully developed in other ways. However, in natural-rise doughs, the yeast multiplies at a pace that is more compatible with full development. The rising process of a basic natural-rise bread might take up to 40 hours, but more often it is about 24 hours. "Two or three days to make bread!" I can imagine you exclaiming mentally or even shouting out loud. But wipe that skepticism off your face and trust me. Patience may be out of vogue, but this bread is truly worth the wait.

The long proofing period of natural-rise breads can even be advantageous timewise, since most of the time the dough is developing without any help from you. Because it allows large blocks of free time between dough-working tasks, this type of bread making may fit especially well into a busy schedule. You might prepare the dough one evening and bake it the following morning or evening or the morning after that, depending on the rate of dough development. Only a few quick kneading sessions are necessary between the two major activities of the process. In addition, making natural-rise breads in hot weather is appealing, since you can both work the dough and bake the bread in the cool of the evening or early morning. It bakes at a low temperature, too, which is another plus.

Creating natural-rise breads is more suspenseful and magical than any other type of bread making. Though mysterious, commercial yeast and sourdough starters are at least perceptible substances. Natural-rise doughs seem to expand by faith alone, and working with them challenges the confidence and patience of a baker. You'll probably find it helpful to become well versed in the techniques of yeasted baking before you tackle natural-rise breads.

With the exception of commercial yeast, a natural-rise bread is made with the same ingredients as a basic yeasted bread. There are important considerations, however. Fresh whole grain flour and pure spring water are especially crucial for successful natural-rise doughs. Whole grains contain all of the necessary elements for complete fermentation to occur; the less refined a flour, the better for naturally-leavened breads. The minerals in spring water facilitate fermentation, while chemicals typically found in tap water may impede it. Quality sea salt regulates fermentation and enhances flavor; it also fends off undesirable microorganisms. Include about ¼ teaspoon of salt for each cup of flour in a recipe. A small amount of good quality oil will make the crumb a bit more rich and tender.

I sometimes add a booster of some kind to speed up fermentation and rising of natural-rise breads. Unlike a sourdough starter, some of which is always saved for future bakings, a natural-rise booster only serves for a single batch of dough. It may be a fermented—or fermentable—liquid, such as preservative-free, unpasteurized apple cider or grape juice, or even, as I once discovered, leftover onion soup! Slightly soured cooked whole grains or porridge also provide a stimulus for rising. *Amasake*, a traditional Oriental fermented grain preparation, is another particularly effective and appealing booster for natural-rise breads; it adds sweetness to dough as well as leavening power. The addition of sprouted grains or beans and the substitution of dissolved miso for salt seem to accelerate dough development, too. Boosters such as these contribute to the flavor and texture of natural-rise breads as well as assisting leavening. Techniques for boosted natural-rise breads vary somewhat from the following basic natural-rise bread recipe.

Simply Natural-Rise Whole Wheat Bread

In general, natural-rise breads are made by the same methods used for making yeasted breads, and you might want to review the instructions in chapter 5 before you begin. The biggest difference is that rising periods for natural-rise breads are considerably longer than those for yeasted or sourdough breads. While natural-rise breads can be made with either a sponge or a straight dough method, I often eliminate the sponge step, since these doughs develop thoroughly without it. If you want to add a sponge step, mix the liquid with enough flour to form a batter, cover the bowl and set it aside for several hours. Then add the salt, oil, and enough flour to form a dough and proceed with kneading and so on. In general, I use sponges for natural-rise breads only when I am adding some kind of a booster, as you'll see in some of the recipes that follow this basic one.

Assemble the same utensils you use for yeasted or sourdough bread. As for ingredients, for one large loaf of a basic natural-rise whole wheat bread, you'll need:

> 2½ cups lukewarm spring water
> 1½ teaspoons sea salt
> 2 tablespoons corn or sesame oil
> 6 cups whole wheat bread flour

Proceed with the following steps:

1. Stir together the liquid, salt, and oil in the large bowl. Gradually add flour, a cup at a time, beating well after each addition, until the dough is too stiff to stir. (Another way preferred by some bakers to mix this type of dough is to start with the flour in the bowl. Mix in the oil with your fingers until it is evenly distributed throughout the flour, then dissolve the salt in the liquid and add it to the flour until a workable dough forms. You may have to adjust the flour or liquid slightly to achieve the correct dough consistency.)

2. Turn the dough out on a lightly floured surface, cover, and let it rest for several minutes.

3. Knead the dough until it is smooth and resilient. Natural-rise doughs tend to be a bit more difficult to work with than yeasted doughs or sourdoughs, so it may take a little extra time and effort to knead them thoroughly. I knead on a lightly floured surface. Some people find it easier to knead on a slightly wet surface. You might want to experiment with both alternatives.

4. When the dough is ready, form it into a ball. Wash out the bowl, grease it lightly, and place the dough inside, turning it to grease the top. Cover the bowl with a damp tea towel and a solid cover and set it in a draft-free spot.

5. Depending upon temperature and the specific dough, the rising period may take anywhere from 8 to as much as 40 hours. Warm temperatures—actually anything over about 70 degrees—promote more rapid fermentation but also may increase sourness in the bread, since bacteria that produce a sour flavor thrive in warmer doughs. So it's better to keep it on the cool side. Cool room temperature is generally fine. Even if it hasn't risen, turn the dough out and knead it briefly every 6 to 8 hours; at the same time, redampen the towel covering the bowl. The fragrance and feel of the dough will gradually alter: it will have a sweet-and-

slightly-sour smell and it will spread out and begin to rise—though probably not as dramatically and evenly as a commercially yeasted or sourdough dough.

6. Turn the dough out and knead it briefly. Cover it for a few minutes, until it relaxes again. Then shape a loaf and press it into a greased pan; the dough should fill about two-thirds of the pan's volume. You could make a freestanding loaf, but this is a soft dough and the support provided by a sided container results in a better-shaped bread.

7. Lightly grease the top of the loaf and cover it with a damp towel or, to avoid the dough sticking to the towel, put the pan into a large plastic bag and trap air inside when you twist it closed, forming a big bubble around the pan. Set aside until the dough rises to the top of the pan. This may take from 2 to 6 hours at room temperature. To speed up rising, set the panned dough in a warmer location, such as inside a gas oven with a pilot light. Be sure the temperature isn't hot enough to kill the yeast, that is, over about 120 degrees. In a warm spot, the dough will probably rise in 30 minutes to an hour.

8. Once the dough has risen, slash the top of the loaf and place it in a cold oven. Set the oven to 300 degrees. By heating the oven with the loaf already in it, you'll give the bread an extra boost. Bake 1½ hours or until the bread is well browned and slips out of the pan readily. The bread should sound distinctly hollow when removed from the pan and thumped on the bottom.

9. Set the baked loaf on a rack and cool it thoroughly before slicing or storing. Keep the bread in a covered container or wrapped in clean, dry tea towels in a cool, dry location. If it begins to dry out, steam slices briefly.

VARIATIONS

To vary the flavor and texture of the bread, you can replace some of the ingredients with others and/or add ingredients. For instance, substitute another flour for a small proportion, 10 to 20 percent, of the whole wheat. Maintain at least 80 percent whole wheat bread flour, though, to ensure the dough strength necessary for rising. Cooked whole grains and soaked cracked grains provide textural interest as well as flavor.

Chopped raw or cooked vegetables such as onions or carrots, fruit chunks or purées, minced fresh or crushed dried herbs, spices, dried fruits, seeds, and nuts also contribute to a bread's personality.

Explore the following recipes, then devise your own.

MISO BREAD
ᴡᴡᴡ

Miso takes the place of salt in this natural-rise bread and gives it a special, unique flavor. I usually use hatcho miso (see page 240), but try other kinds; they will subtly alter the taste of the bread. Be sure to use unpasteurized miso, since it has active enzymes which assist the fermentation and rising of the dough. This loaf is superbly moist and slices thinly.

YIELD: 1 large loaf

PREPARATION TIME: 30 to 40 minutes for the dough; 8 or more hours for rising; 1½ hours to bake

> 2 *tablespoons unpasteurized miso*
> 2½ *cups warm spring water*
> 2 *tablespoons corn or sesame oil*
> 6 *to* 6½ *cups whole wheat bread flour*

In a large bowl, whisk the miso and ¼ cup of the warm water to a smooth paste. Whisk in the remaining water and the oil. Gradually stir in enough of the flour to form a dough.

Follow steps 2 to 9 on page 101.

BARLEYCORN BREAD
ᴡᴡᴡ

John Barleycorn is only present in this bread as a by-prod-uct of the fermentation of the dough, but the wonderfully nutty flavor of roasted barley flour and cornmeal pervades the finished loaf. This is a light, even-textured bread.

YIELD: 1 large loaf

PREPARATION TIME: About 1 hour for the dough; 8 hours or more for rising; 1½ hours to bake

> 2 *tablespoons sesame oil*

> ½ *cup barley flour*
> ½ *cup cornmeal*
> 3 *cups spring water*
> 2 *teaspoons sea salt*
> 5½ *to* 6 *cups whole wheat bread flour*

Heat 1 tablespoon of the oil in a heavy-bottomed skillet over low heat. Stir in the barley flour and cornmeal and cook, stirring often, until the grains are lightly roasted and fragrant; transfer to a large bowl.

Heat the water to boiling, add the salt, and gradually whisk with the roasted flours to form a smooth batter. Whisk in the remaining tablespoon of oil. Gradually stir in enough of the wheat flour to form a dough.

Follow steps 2 to 9 on page 101.

NATURAL-RISE GRITS BREAD
ᴡᴡᴡ

This fine loaf has the wonderful depth of flavor that only its key ingredient—time—can bestow. Grits add a subtle crunch.

YIELD: 2 medium-sized loaves

PREPARATION TIME: 30 to 60 minutes for the dough; 12 or more hours for rising; 1½ hours to bake

> 3 *cups spring water*
> 2 *teaspoons sea salt*
> ¼ *cup soy grits*
> 2 *tablespoons corn oil*
> 8 *to* 9 *cups whole wheat bread flour*

Heat the water to boiling, add the salt, and pour over the grits in a large bowl. Cover and cool to lukewarm.

Stir in the oil and gradually add enough of the flour to form a dough.

Follow steps 2 to 9 on page 101.

NOTES

- Substitute corn, barley, or rice grits, cracked wheat or rye, or steel-cut oats for the soy grits.

- Brush the loaves with an egg wash and sprinkle on sesame seeds just before baking.

NATURAL-RISE OAT BREAD
ᴡᴡᴡ

Oats give this bread an especially sweet, rich taste and a pleasantly chewy texture.

YIELD: 1 large loaf

PREPARATION TIME: 1 hour for the dough; 8 or more hours for rising; 1½ to 2 hours to bake

> *3 cups spring water*
> *1 cup rolled oats*
> *2 teaspoons sea salt*
> *2 tablespoons sesame oil*
> *5 to 6 cups whole wheat bread flour*

Heat the water to boiling and pour it over the oats and salt in a large bowl. Cover and set aside until lukewarm.

Stir the oil into the oats. Gradually stir in enough of the flour to form a dough.

Follow steps 2 to 9 on page 101.

NOTES

- Substitute rolled wheat, rye, or barley for the oats.

NATURAL-RISE SPROUT BREAD
▾▾▾

Sprouts may accelerate the rising of this moist, flavorful bread. Begin sprouting ¼ cup wheat berries about three days ahead of time; the sprouts should be about the same length as the wheat berries when you make the dough.

YIELD: 1 large loaf

PREPARATION TIME: 30 to 40 minutes for the dough; 8 or more hours for rising; 1½ hours to bake

> *2½ cups spring water*
> *1½ teaspoons sea salt*
> *2 tablespoons sesame or corn oil*
> *6 cups whole wheat bread flour*
> *2 cups wheat sprouts, coarsely chopped (see page 242)*

Heat the water and cool to lukewarm.

In a large bowl, stir together the water, salt, and oil. Gradually stir in 2½ cups of the flour to form a thick batter. Stir in the sprouts. Gradually stir in enough of the remaining flour to form a dough.

Follow steps 2 to 9 on page 101.

NOTES

- Try sprouting rye or triticale berries or whole barley and substitute them for part or all of the wheat sprouts. You can also use sprouted lentils.

STEAMED BROWN BREAD
▾▾▾

Boston Brown Bread is a steamed bread traditionally made with a mixture of cornmeal and rye and wheat flours, sweetened with molasses, and leavened with baking soda and/or baking powder. In the Northeastern grocery stores of my childhood, cans of brown bread were stacked on the same shelf as the baked beans, with which it was commonly served. Steamed breads are especially moist and digestible, and this compact, even-textured, raisin-studded variation-on-a-classic is no exception. Slice it razor thin and serve it warmed, toasted, plain, spread, or with beans! For the steaming arrangement, you'll need a fairly deep, straight-sided container for the bread that will fit inside a large pot or a canning kettle. I use a deep, ovenproof, ceramic bowl. You can also use a couple of smaller containers, such as wide-mouthed, pint-sized canning jars or cans (without lead-soldered seams).

YIELD: 1 loaf

PREPARATION TIME: 30 to 40 minutes for the dough; 8 or more hours for rising; 3 hours to steam (or 1 hour to pressure-steam)

> *1 cup cornmeal*
> *1 cup rye flour*
> *1½ to 1¾ cups whole wheat bread flour*
> *1 teaspoon sea salt*
> *1½ cups spring water*
> *½ cup raisins*

Sift the cornmeal, rye flour, 1 cup of the wheat flour, and salt into a medium-sized bowl and make a well in the center. Warm the water and pour it into the dry mixture. Stir until a dough forms.

Follow steps 2 to 5 on page 101.

When the dough has risen, knead in the raisins. Cover the dough and let rest for several minutes.

Shape and pan the dough; the container should be about two-thirds full. Cover and set aside to rise.

Cover the container with a lid or with waxed paper, baking parchment, or heavy muslin tied on with string. Set it on a rack in a deep pot and add boiling water halfway up the sides of the container. Cover the pot and steam the bread for 3 hours, adding more water if necessary. Or steam it in a pressure cooker for 1 hour. For small containers steam 1½ hours or pressure-steam for 30 minutes.

Cool the bread in the container on a rack briefly; remove it from the pan to finish cooling.

NOTES

- Omit the raisins if you prefer a less sweet bread.

CIDER-RICE BREAD
▾▾▾

Apple cider works wonders as a booster in this subtly sweet and chewy natural-rise bread, which strikes an excellent balance between hearty and light. Be sure to get unpasteurized cider without preservatives so that it will ferment rather than spoil. Once the rice/cider sponge is ready, the bread-making process is similar in methods and time requirements to that for making a basic yeasted whole wheat bread using the sponge technique.

YIELD: 2 loaves

PREPARATION TIME: 8 to 12 hours for the rice; 2½ hours for sponge and dough; 5 to 6 hours for rising; 1½ hours to bake

> *1 cup short- or medium-grain brown rice*
> *2 cups spring water*
> *2 cups apple cider (unpasteurized, with no preservatives)*
> *7 to 8 cups whole wheat bread flour*
> *2 teaspoons sea salt*
> *2 tablespoons corn oil*

Combine the rice and water in a medium-sized saucepan and bring to a boil. Stir once, cover tightly, turn the heat to very low, and cook 40 minutes. Turn off the heat and leave the pot covered for an hour or more—until the rice has cooled to lukewarm. Transfer to a large bowl. Add the cider and cover. Leave for several hours or overnight—until obviously bubbly and active.

Beat in 2 cups of the flour to form a thick batter. Cover and set aside for about 2 hours or until a sponge develops.

Stir the salt and oil into the sponge. Gradually stir in enough of the remaining flour to form a dough.

Turn the dough out onto a lightly floured surface, cover, and let rest for several minutes. Knead until the dough is smooth and elastic, adding more flour as necessary to keep the dough from sticking.

Form the dough into a ball and put it in a lightly greased bowl. Cover and set in a draft-free spot for about 2 hours, or until the dough has risen and a finger pressed into it leaves a depression. Turn the dough out

and knead it briefly. Return it to the bowl and set aside for about 2 hours, until the dough has risen again.

Shape and pan the dough. Cover and set aside until the dough has risen to the top of the pans. Slash the tops of the loaves. Bake at 300 degrees for about 1½ hours—until the loaves are well browned, firm, and sound distinctly hollow when removed from the pans and tapped on the bottom.

Cool the bread thoroughly before slicing or storing it.

NOTES

- The rice/cider mixture becomes active more quickly if the cider has already begun to turn from sweet to hard.

- Small wineries sometimes sell unpasteurized grape juice that doesn't contain any preservatives; substitute this for the apple cider.

- This dough is great for rolls; bake 3- to 4-ounce rolls for about 45 minutes.

NATURAL-RISE RYE BERRY BREAD
▾▾▾

Like CIDER-RICE BREAD, this bread relies on fermented apple cider to boost its rising, and the methods and time requirements for making it resemble those for a basic yeasted whole wheat bread—once the rye/cider sponge has developed. Rye berries contribute their unique rugged flavor. Use part of the dough to make rolls or terrific bagels!

YIELD: 3 loaves

PREPARATION TIME: 12 to 24 hours for the rye berries; 2 to 12 hours for sponge and dough; 5 to 6 hours for rising; 1½ hours to bake

> *1½ cups rye berries*
> *4 cups spring water*
> *3 cups apple cider (unpasteurized, no preservatives)*
> *8 to 9 cups whole wheat bread flour*
> *¼ cup blackstrap molasses*
> *¼ cup corn oil*
> *1 tablespoon sea salt*
> *1 tablespoon fennel seeds*
> *1 tablespoon caraway seeds*

Heat the water to boiling and pour it over the rye berries in a saucepan. Cover and soak for at least an hour. Uncover and bring to a boil. Cover, turn the heat to very low, and cook about an hour—until the rye is tender and the water absorbed. Cool in the pot.

Transfer the rye berries to a large bowl, add the cider, cover, and soak 12 to 24 hours, until the mixture is bubbly and active—the length of this period depends on the sweetness/hardness of the cider to begin with.

Stir in enough of the flour to form a thick batter. Cover and set in a draft-free spot for several hours, until the batter develops into a sponge.

Stir the molasses, oil, salt, and fennel and caraway seeds into the sponge. Gradually stir in enough of the remaining flour to form a dough.

Turn the dough out onto a lightly floured surface, cover, and let rest for several minutes. Knead thoroughly, adding flour as necessary to keep the dough from sticking.

Form the dough into a ball and put it in a lightly greased bowl. Cover and set in a draft-free spot for about 2 hours or until the dough has risen and does not spring back when pressed. Turn the dough out and knead it briefly, then return it to the bowl for about 2 hours, until it has risen again.

Shape and pan the dough. Cover the loaves and set them aside until the dough rises to the top of the pans.

Slash the tops of the loaves. Bake at 300 degrees for 1½ hours or until the loaves are well browned, firm, and sound hollow when removed from the pans and tapped on the bottom.

Cool the bread thoroughly before slicing or storing it.

NOTES

- Substitute wheat berries or whole oats for the rye berries and omit the molasses, fennel, and caraway.

RICE KAYU BREAD
▼▼▼

Kayu is a Japanese grain porridge that is traditionally cooked to a soft, creamy consistency. I prefer the texture of relatively firm grains of rice in this bread, but adjust the amount of liquid to suit your own taste. Slice this loaf thinly and savor its complex flavors.

YIELD: 1 large loaf

PREPARATION TIME: 24 hours or so for the rice; 30 to 40 minutes for the dough; 6 to 12 hours for rising; 1½ hours to bake

> 1 cup short- or medium-grain brown rice
> 2½ to 3 cups spring water
> 1½ teaspoons sea salt
> 2 tablespoons corn or sesame oil
> 5 to 6 cups whole wheat bread flour

Combine the rice and 2 cups of the water in a medium-sized saucepan and bring to a boil. Turn the heat to low,

cover the pot tightly, and cook 40 minutes. Leave the lid in place and cool the rice. Transfer to a large bowl, cover, and leave at room temperature for about 24 hours or until it smells slightly sour.

Warm the remaining ½ to 1 cup water and add enough of it to the rice to achieve a thick, porridgelike consistency. Stir in the salt and oil. Gradually stir in enough of the flour to form a dough.

Turn the dough out onto a lightly floured surface, cover, and let rest for several minutes. Knead thoroughly, adding flour as necessary to keep the dough from sticking. Cover the dough and let it rest until relaxed.

Shape and pan the dough—this doesn't rise in the bowl before shaping. Slash the top of the loaf and enclose it in a large plastic bag tied to form a big bubble. Set aside for 6 to 12 hours—until the dough has risen in the pan.

Place the loaf in a cold oven and set the oven to 300 degrees. Bake 1½ hours or until the bread is well browned and firm and sounds distinctly hollow when removed from the pan and tapped on the bottom.

Cool the bread thoroughly before slicing or storing it.

NOTES

- For *MILLET KAYU BREAD*, substitute 1 cup millet for the rice.

- Substitute 3 to 4 cups leftover rice or millet—or a combination of cooked grains—and omit the cooking water. You can also add leftover vegetables and even salad; blend these with a bit of liquid (or leftover soup) and mix with the grain(s).

BARLEY KAYU BREAD
▼▼▼

Barley does it again—this bread is exceptionally sweet and moist!

YIELD: 1 large loaf

PREPARATION TIME: 24 hours or so for the barley; 30 to 40 minutes for the dough; 6 to 12 hours for rising; 1½ hours to bake

> 2¾ to 3 cups spring water
> ¾ cup whole barley
> 1½ teaspoons sea salt
> 2 tablespoons sesame or corn oil
> 5 to 6 cups whole wheat bread flour

Heat 2¼ cups water to boiling and pour it over the barley in a medium-sized saucepan. Soak for an hour or longer. Bring just to a boil, reduce the heat, cover loosely, and cook until tender. Add additional water if necessary. Cool the barley to lukewarm. Transfer to a large bowl, cover, and leave at room temperature for about 24 hours or until the barley smells slightly sour.

Warm any remaining water and add it to the barley as necessary to achieve a thick, porridgelike consistency. Stir in the salt and oil. Gradually stir in enough of the flour to form a dough.

Turn the dough out onto a lightly floured surface, cover, and let rest for several minutes. Knead thoroughly, adding flour as necessary to keep the dough from sticking. Cover the dough and let rest until relaxed.

Shape and pan the dough. Slash the top of the loaf and put it inside a large plastic bag tied to form a bubble. Set aside for 6 to 12 hours, until the dough has risen to the top of the pan.

Put the pan into a cold oven and set it to 300 degrees. Bake 1½ hours or until the bread is well browned, has firm sides, and sounds distinctly hollow when removed from the pan and tapped on the bottom.

Cool the bread thoroughly before slicing or storing it.

BASIC AMASAKE BREAD
▾▾▾

This bread is sweet-tasting and fine-grained. The technique for making it is similar to that for RICE KAYU BREAD, page 105, except that this one starts off with a sponge. This recipe is a prototype for the next several breads.

YIELD: 1 large loaf

PREPARATION TIME: 2 to 3 hours for sponge and dough; several hours or overnight for rising; 1½ hours to bake

> *1 cup AMASAKE (see box)*
> *2 cups spring water*
> *7 cups whole wheat bread flour*
> *2 teaspoons sea salt*
> *2 tablespoons sesame or corn oil*

1. In a large bowl, stir together the amasake and water. Stir in 3 cups of the flour to form a batter. Cover and set aside for 2 or more hours, until a sponge develops.

2. Stir in the salt and oil. Gradually stir in enough of the remaining flour to form a dough.

3. Turn the dough out onto a lightly floured surface, cover, and let rest for a few minutes. Knead thoroughly, adding flour as necessary to keep the dough from sticking; it will stay a bit tacky. Cover the dough and let rest for several minutes.

4. Shape and pan the dough. Slash the top of the loaf. Cover the pan with a large pot or put it into a large

---

Amasake

AMASAKE, which means "sweet sake" in Japanese, is prepared by combining freshly cooked rice—or another grain—with a cultured rice called *koji* and setting it in a warm spot for 12 or so hours. During this time, enzymes in the koji break down the complex carbohydrates in the grain into simple sugars, rendering them sweet-tasting and easily digestible. This rice-pudding-like mixture can be blended with water or fruit to make smoothie-type beverages; it is also an ingredient in some nondairy ice creams. I use amasake in a number of the recipes that follow; it boosts rising and adds sweetness to these breads. You may find ready-made amasake in natural foods markets and mail order catalogs; look for koji there too. If do you purchase amasake, be sure that it has active enzymes for effective leavening.

> *1 cup short-grain brown rice*
> *2¾ cups water*
> *1 cup rice koji*

Combine the rice and water in a large saucepan and bring to a boil. Cover tightly, reduce the heat to very low, and cook 1 hour. Leave the lid in place and cool the rice to lukewarm. Thoroughly stir in the koji. Transfer to a glass or ceramic container and compact the mixture with a wooden spoon or spatula. Cover with a lid or plate and place in a warm spot, such as in a gas oven with just the pilot on or on a high shelf. Leave about 12 hours—until obviously active and bubbly when stirred.

Store amasake in a clean, tightly covered quart jar in the refrigerator; it will keep 3 to 4 weeks.

---

plastic bag, gathered and tied to form a big bubble—you want to keep the dough from drying out but prevent anything from sticking to its surface. Leave it several hours or overnight, until the dough has risen to the top of the pan.

5. Place the pan in a cold oven. Set the oven to 300 degrees and bake the bread for 1½ hours or until it is well browned, the sides are firm, and the loaf sounds distinctly hollow when removed from the pan and tapped on the bottom.

6. Cool the bread thoroughly before slicing or storing it.

NOTES
- For *AMASAKE-RAISIN BREAD*, knead a cup of raisins into the dough before shaping.

AMASAKE-RICE BREAD
‍‍‍▾▾▾

This bread tastes similar to AMASAKE BREAD (page 106-7), but cooked rice adds texture.

YIELD: 1 large loaf

PREPARATION TIME: 12 to 24 hours for the rice and dough; 6 to 12 hours for rising; 1½ hours to bake

> 1 cup short- or medium-grain brown rice
> 2 cups spring water
> 1 cup AMASAKE (page 106)
> 1½ teaspoons sea salt
> 2 tablespoons sesame or corn oil
> 5 cups whole wheat bread flour

Rinse the rice, combine with the water in a saucepan, and bring to a boil. Give a quick stir, cover tightly, reduce the heat to very low, and cook 40 minutes. Leave the lid in place and cool the rice to lukewarm.

In a large bowl, thoroughly stir together the rice and amasake. Cover and set in a draft-free spot for 12 to 24 hours, until active and bubbly, particularly when stirred.

Stir in the salt and oil. Gradually stir in enough of the flour to form a dough.

Follow steps 3 to 6 on page 101.

AMASAKE-MILLET BREAD
▾▾▾

This bread amazed me the first time I made it—it is subtly sweet and light, somehow summery.

YIELD: 1 large loaf

PREPARATION TIME: 12 to 24 hours for the millet and dough; 6 to 12 hours for rising; 1½ hours to bake

> 1 cup millet
> 2 cups spring water
> 1 cup AMASAKE (page 106)
> 1½ teaspoons sea salt
> 2 tablespoons sesame or corn oil
> 5 to 5½ cups whole wheat bread flour

Rinse the millet. Heat the water to boiling and pour it over the millet in a medium-sized saucepan. Bring back to a boil, stir once, and cover tightly. Turn the heat to

very low and cook 30 minutes. Leave the pot lid in place and cool the millet to lukewarm.

Transfer the millet to a large bowl and thoroughly mix in the amasake. Cover and set in a draft-free spot for 12 to 24 hours—until sweet-smelling and bubbly when stirred.

Stir in the salt and oil. Gradually stir in enough of the flour to form a dough.

Follow steps 3 to 6 on page 101.

AMASAKE-BARLEY BREAD
▾▾▾

This is a great bread—full of chewy nubs of barley and wonderfully complex flavors. Whole barley has an incomparable flavor and texture; if you can't find it, look for barley that has been minimally pearled.

YIELD: 1 large loaf

PREPARATION TIME: Several hours or overnight to soak and cook barley; 12 to 24 hours for fermentation and dough; 6 to 12 hours for rising; 1½ hours to bake

> ⅔ cup whole barley
> 2⅔ cups spring water
> 1 cup AMASAKE (page 106)
> 2 teaspoons sea salt
> 2 tablespoons sesame or corn oil
> 5 cups whole wheat bread flour

Rinse the barley. Heat the water to boiling and pour it over the barley in a medium-sized saucepan. Cover and soak for several hours or overnight. Bring just to a boil, reduce the heat to very low, cover loosely, and cook 50 to 60 minutes—until the barley is tender and the water has been absorbed. Cover and cool to lukewarm.

Transfer the barley to a large bowl and thoroughly stir in the amasake. Cover and leave at room temperature for 12 to 24 hours—until bubbly, particularly when stirred.

Stir in the salt and oil. Gradually stir in enough of the flour to form a dough.

Follow steps 3 to 6 on page 101.

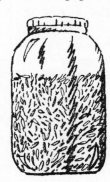

AMASAKE-OAT BREAD
▼▼▼

The chewy sweetness of whole oats and amasake team up to make this a superb bread.

YIELD: 1 large loaf

PREPARATION TIME: Several hours or overnight for oats; 12 to 24 hours for fermentation and dough; 6 to 12 hours for rising; 1½ hours to bake

> ¾ cup whole oats
> 2¼ cups spring water
> 1 cup *Amasake* (page 106)
> 1½ teaspoons sea salt
> 2 tablespoons sesame oil
> 5 cups whole wheat bread flour

Rinse the oats. Heat the water to boiling and pour it over the oats in a medium-sized saucepan. Cover and soak for several hours or overnight. Bring to a boil, then cover and reduce the heat to very low. Cook 40 to 60 minutes—until the oats are tender and the water has been absorbed. Leave covered and cool to lukewarm.

Transfer the oats to a large bowl and stir in the amasake. Cover and leave at room temperature for 12 to 24 hours—until bubbly, particularly when stirred.

Stir in the salt and oil. Gradually stir in enough of the flour to form a dough.

Follow steps 3 to 6 on page 101.

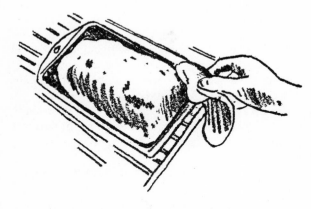

AMASAKE CORN BREAD
▼▼▼

This natural-rise corn bread requires some time but little of your energy or attention. It is a sweet, moist companion to beans and soups and is good sliced and toasted for breakfast, too.

YIELD: 1 8-inch square or 9-inch round bread

PREPARATION TIME: About 1 hour to prepare; several hours or overnight to ferment; 1½ to 2 hours to bake

> 2 cups spring water
> 2 cups cornmeal
> ⅔ cup *Amasake* (page 106)
> 1 cup whole wheat pastry flour
> 1 teaspoon sea salt
> 1 tablespoon corn oil

Heat the water to boiling and stir with the cornmeal in a medium-sized bowl to form a smooth batter; cool to lukewarm. Stir in the amasake and flour. Cover and set in a draft-free spot for several hours or overnight, until bubbly.

Beat in the salt and oil. Spread the batter evenly in a well-greased 8-inch square or 9-inch round pan. Put the pan into a cold oven and set the oven to 300 degrees. Bake 1½ hours or until a tester inserted in the center comes out clean—the bread will brown and shrink slightly from the sides of the pan. Turn the bread onto a rack to cool.

AMASAKE MUFFINS
▼▼▼

Amasake both sweetens and leavens these moist, chewy muffins. This recipe provides basic ingredient proportions and describes a technique for making natural-rise muffins; vary the grains and/or include additional sweetener, dried fruits, or lightly toasted seeds or chopped nuts to modify the flavor and texture. This particular version is good with both sweet and savory spreads.

YIELD: 6 large muffins

PREPARATION TIME: Several hours to prepare and ferment the batter; 80 to 90 minutes to bake

> 1 cup spring water
> 1 cup rolled oats
> 1 cup *Amasake* (page 106)
> 1 cup whole wheat pastry flour
> ½ teaspoon sea salt
> 2 tablespoons sesame or sunflower oil

Boil the water and pour it over the oats in a medium-sized bowl. Set aside for about an hour, until cooled to lukewarm. Stir in the amasake. Thoroughly stir in the flour to form a batter. Cover and leave several hours or overnight—until it becomes somewhat bubbly and rises in the bowl.

Beat in the salt and oil. Distribute the batter equally among well-greased muffin tins; fill each cup just about to the top for large muffins that will rise well above the top of the pan. Place the muffin tin in a cold oven and set the oven to 300 degrees. Bake 80 to 90 minutes. Test by inserting a tester in the center of a muffin. Cool about 30 minutes before serving.

NOTES

- If you substitute flour (for instance, a cup of oat flour) for the rolled oats, omit the grain-soaking step. Simply mix the amasake, a cup of warm water, and the 2 cups of flour together to form the batter; cracked or rolled grains need the extra softening that soaking provides.

MIXED GRAIN WAFFLES
▾▾▾

The flavors mingle and mellow and the grains soften as this batter rests. In the morning, it becomes light, crisp waffles. Serve them with maple syrup or PEAR BUTTER (page 135).

YIELD: 4 waffles—2 to 4 servings

PREPARATION TIME: 10 minutes to mix; several hours or overnight to sit; 4 to 5 minutes to bake each batch

$1/3$ *cup whole wheat pastry flour*
$1/3$ *cup rye flour*
$1/3$ *cup barley flour*
$1/3$ *cup oat flour*
$1/3$ *cup cornmeal*
$1/2$ *teaspoon sea salt*
$1 2/3$ *cups soy milk, scalded*
1 *tablespoon sesame or sunflower oil*

In a medium-sized mixing bowl, sift together the flours and salt. Gradually whisk in the milk to form a batter. Cover and set aside for several hours or overnight. Add the oil and whisk well.

Heat a waffle iron according to its directions—my cast-iron one is ready when water dropped on the surface sizzles immediately. Lightly grease the grids—remember, a mixture of half sesame or sunflower oil and half liquid soy lecithin works especially well to prevent sticking. Ladle in batter and close the iron. Bake according to the directions for your waffle iron—about 2 minutes per side for a stove-top cast-iron one.

Serve the waffles immediately or place them directly on the rack in a low oven to keep warm.

NOTES

- Substitute spring water or vegetable or noodle stock for the soy milk; for extra nutrients, add a tablespoon of soy flour to the dry mixture and add an extra tablespoon of liquid to correct the consistency.

CHAPTER 8

Flat Breads

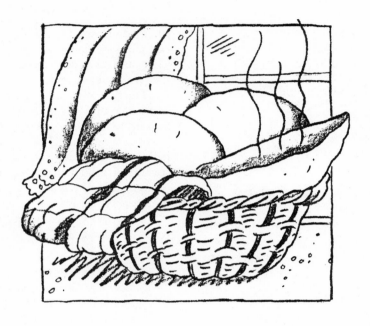

AS SOON AS WE ENTERED, the irresistible aroma of fresh corn tortillas overwhelmed us. In the same instant, a loud, accusing voice bellowed, "What do you think you're doing here?!" "Here" was a small Mexican restaurant that I had been wanting to try, and the unexpected outcry immediately aroused in me simultaneous sensations of free-floating guilt, bewilderment, and amusement. But something in the tone seemed to discourage all six of us from laughing. We focused on an imposing aproned woman across the room. She was standing in an open kitchen, separated from the dining area by a waist-high counter. At once, we knew that this must be the illustrious "Señora," whose reputation for eccentricity was apparently well founded. Somehow, we convinced her to let us stay and eat, even though we hadn't called ahead. Before the meal was finished, she had offered to sell us the restaurant, including recipes for dishes which she had cooked for the president of Mexico. To this day, I associate corn tortillas with this singular personality.

Most cuisines feature a flat bread of some sort, tortillas being the predominant bread in Mexico. Some of the French make crêpes, others make *socca*, a crêpe-like chickpea flour bread. *Dosas*, *chapatis*, and *parathas* prevail in different parts of India. Mandarin pancakes and scallion bread are products of China. The Japanese call their thick, meal-sized griddlecakes *okonomiyaki*. Pita is now almost as popular in the United States as in its original home, the Middle East; Lebanese wrapper bread is another Middle Eastern flat bread. Crackers of various types are found throughout the world. Johnnycakes are probably more American than apple pie, and they vary from thick patties to lacy rounds.

Although they all end up flat, a few of these breads do some rising or puffing along the way. Pita and Lebanese wrapper bread are made from yeasted doughs and rise in the early stages of their development, which makes the dough stronger and enhances its flavor. Pita puffs up in the oven as a result of steam inside the dough, not from the yeast, and falls flat as it cools. Some crackers use leavenings but end up flat since they are rolled thinly and baked quickly.

Most flat breads, however, are unleavened. They are made from either kneaded doughs or beaten batters and are often cooked on the stovetop. Though unleavened flat breads may be cooked immediately after mixing, they benefit in flavor, texture, and probably nutrition from a rest period between mixing and baking. The extra time allows the grains to absorb the liquid, which tenderizes them and releases their full flavors. Some fermentation may also take place, making the grains easier to digest and assimilate.

Flat breads don't rely much on gluten development to achieve their shape, so they provide creative bakers with opportunities to use other flours besides wheat. Kneaded flat breads require some high-gluten flour for adhesiveness, but up to about half of the flour in these doughs can be low in gluten. Batter-based flat breads, such as crêpes, don't need any wheat gluten at all.

CRÊPES

Crêpes are very thin pancakes prepared from a batter consisting of flour, liquid, salt, egg, and sometimes a little oil. Traditional paper-thin French crêpes are made with either wheat flour or buckwheat flour. The ingredients are vigorously blended by hand or machine and then left to sit for 30 minutes, preferably longer. Resting the batter before cooking allows the particles of flour to soak up the liquid and become soft and spongy, resulting in light, tender crêpes. I make crêpe batter in the evening to cook the following morning; I mix it in the morning if I plan on crêpes for dinner.

Every crêpe maker has a favorite pan. Classic French crêpe pans are made from relatively thin steel and are flat bottomed with low, sloping sides. I use a small griddle with a slight lip. A lightweight pan is advantageous, since you will need to manipulate it with one hand. For especially efficient crêpe making, work with two pans at once. Cook the second side of one crêpe in one pan as you start a new one in the other pan.

The following recipes produce fine, delicate crêpes but are nontraditional in that they go easy on the eggs, may substitute other liquids for milk, and call for a variety of whole grain flours. See chapter 12 for crêpe fillings, or invent your own.

WHEAT CRÊPES
▾▾▾

Use the directions for these delicate French pancakes as a prototype for the crêpe recipes that follow.

YIELD: 12 6-inch crêpes

PREPARATION TIME: About 1 hour, plus a minimum of 30 minutes to rest the batter

> 1 cup whole wheat pastry flour
> Pinch of sea salt (optional)

> 1 egg
> 1½ cups milk or soy milk
> 1 tablespoon vegetable oil

To prepare the batter by hand, sift the flour and salt into a bowl; whisk the egg, liquid, and oil in another bowl; then vigorously whisk everything together. To make the batter in a blender, blend the egg and, with the machine still running, add the salt and then gradually add flour for as long as it is absorbed. Add some of the liquid and continue to add the remaining flour and liquid alternately. Finally, add the oil and blend until thoroughly smooth. Strain the batter if any lumps remain, pour it into a deep bowl or pitcher, and cover. Rest the batter for 30 minutes to several hours—in the refrigerator if for more than a brief period.

Heat your crêpe pan over medium-high heat. Be sure the pan is hot before you begin cooking. Test it by sprinkling a few drops of water on the surface; they should splutter and sizzle and evaporate immediately. Grease the pan lightly.

To begin cooking, give the batter a stir; with one hand, pour some batter into the center of the pan from a ladle, pitcher, or large spoon. With the other hand, immediately lift, tilt, and rotate the pan to spread the batter. Quickly return any excess to the batter container and place the pan back on the burner. The amount of batter needed for each crêpe will depend on the size of your pan, but it will probably be about 2 to 4 tablespoons. The batter should spread out readily to less than ⅛ inch thick. If the batter seems too thick, thin with additional liquid, whisking in a small amount at a time. Sometimes it takes a little while to achieve the right batter consistency, amount of batter per crêpe, and pan heat. You'll probably want to make a couple of test crêpes initially.

Crêpes cook quickly and are ready to turn in as little as 30 seconds, when the edges begin to curl and the underside has browned. Slide a slim spatula under the crêpe to loosen it from the pan and flip it over. Cook the second side briefly; this side will be speckled rather than evenly browned when it is done. Lightly grease the pan again if the crêpes seem to be sticking at all. To keep crêpes soft for easy rolling, stack them on a plate and cover with an inverted bowl.

Crêpes store quite well. Separate them with waxed paper to keep them from sticking together. They will keep for a day or two in the refrigerator, longer in the freezer. Wrap well for freezing, perhaps in meal-sized packages. Thaw crêpes in a covered container in a 300-degree oven for about 10 minutes.

NOTES
- Substitute oat, rye, or barley flour for the wheat flour.

BUCKWHEAT CRÊPES
✦✦✦

These crêpes are fully as thin as wheat ones, but the hearty flavor and dark color of buckwheat flour give them a somewhat rustic quality. If you want to tone down the buckwheat, use part whole wheat pastry flour.

YIELD: 12 6-inch crêpes

PREPARATION TIME: About 1 hour, plus a minimum of 30 minutes to rest the batter

> 1 cup buckwheat flour
> ¼ teaspoon sea salt
> 1 egg
> 1½ cups water
> 1 tablespoon vegetable oil

Whisk or blend the ingredients together to form a smooth batter. Cover and set aside for 30 minutes to several hours or overnight.

Lightly grease a crêpe pan which you have preheated over medium-high heat. Add batter and lift and rotate the pan immediately to spread it out evenly, about ⅛ inch thick. Turn the crêpe when the bottom is golden and the edges begin to curl. Cook briefly on the second side. Stack and cover crêpes to keep them warm. **(For detailed instructions, refer to the directions for WHEAT CRÊPES on page 111.)**

CORN CRÊPES
✦✦✦

These crêpes are Mexican in mood yet more delicate than tortillas. Wrap them around REFRITOS (page 136) or GUACAMOLE (page 135) and top them with a salsa (pages 143, 146).

YIELD: 12 6-inch crêpes

PREPARATION TIME: About 1 hour, plus a minimum of 30 minutes to rest the batter

> ⅔ cup cornmeal
> ⅓ cup whole wheat pastry flour
> ¼ teaspoon sea salt
> 1 egg
> 1¼ cups water or stock
> 1 tablespoon corn oil

Sift together the cornmeal, flour, and salt, then whisk or blend with the other ingredients to form a smooth batter. Cover and set aside for 30 minutes to several hours or overnight.

Heat a crêpe pan over medium-high heat and grease it lightly. Add batter and immediately lift and rotate the pan to spread it out evenly, about ⅛ inch thick. Turn the crêpe when the bottom is golden and the edges begin to curl. Cook the second side briefly. Stack and cover the crêpes to keep them warm.

(For detailed instructions, refer to the directions for WHEAT CRÊPES on page 111.)

LEMON CRÊPES
✦✦✦

For a refreshing dessert, fold these into quarters and spoon LEMON GLAZE (see box) on top. Or roll them around lemon sorbet or a fruit filling, such as that for CRISS-CROSS COFFEE CAKE (page 182).

YIELD: 12 6-inch crêpes

PREPARATION TIME: About 1 hour, plus a minimum of 30 minutes to rest the batter

---

LEMON GLAZE
✦✦✦

Dress up any cake with this tangy topping; I like it on GINGERBREAD (page 228-29), CARROT CAKE (page 229), or TEASECAKE (page 230-31). It's also good as a sauce for dessert crêpes.

> 6 tablespoons plus 1 teaspoon unsweetened apple juice
> 1 teaspoon kuzu powder
> 2 tablespoons lemon juice
> 1 tablespoon maple syrup or mild-flavored honey

In a small bowl, combine 1 teaspoon apple juice and the kuzu; set aside for several minutes, until the kuzu is thoroughly dissolved.

In a small saucepan, stir together the lemon juice, syrup, and remaining 6 tablespoons of apple juice. Heat just to a simmer and stir in the dissolved kuzu. Reduce the heat and cook, stirring, until the mixture has thickened.

Cool before spreading on a cake.

NOTES
- For ORANGE GLAZE, omit the lemon juice, substitute orange juice for all or part of the apple juice, and add finely grated orange zest to taste.

1 *cup whole wheat pastry flour*
Pinch of sea salt
Grated zest of 1 lemon
1 *egg*
1 *tablespoon Sucanat, mild-flavored honey, or*
maple syrup
1½ *cups milk or soy milk*
1 *tablespoon light vegetable oil*

Whisk or blend the ingredients together to form a smooth batter. Cover and set aside for 30 minutes to several hours or overnight.

Lightly grease a crêpe pan which you have preheated over medium-high heat. Add batter and lift and rotate the pan immediately to spread it out evenly, about ⅛ inch thick. Turn the crêpe when the bottom is golden and the edges begin to curl. Cook briefly on the second side. Stack and cover crêpes to keep them warm.

(For detailed instructions, refer to the directions for *WHEAT CRÊPES* **on page 111.)**

CAROB CRÊPES

Carob crêpes are definitely for dessert. Drizzle a little carob syrup or maple syrup over them or roll them around ice cream or dairyless frozen desserts or fresh fruit—peaches are good. You can also use them for CAROB-ALMOND CRÊPES *(see box).*

YIELD: 12 6-inch crêpes

PREPARATION TIME: About 1 hour, plus a minimum of 30 minutes to rest the batter

¼ *cup roasted carob powder*
¾ *cup whole wheat pastry flour*
Pinch of sea salt
1 *egg*
1½ *cups milk or soy milk*
1 *tablespoon mild-flavored honey, maple syrup, or*
Sucanat
1 *tablespoon light vegetable oil*

Whisk or blend the ingredients together to form a smooth batter. Cover and set aside for 30 minutes to several hours or overnight.

Lightly grease a crêpe pan which you have preheated over medium-high heat. Add batter and lift and rotate the pan immediately to spread it out evenly, about ⅛ inch thick. Turn the crêpe when the bottom is golden and the edges begin to curl. Cook briefly on the second side. Stack and cover crêpes to keep them warm.

(For detailed instructions, refer to the directions for *WHEAT CRÊPES* **on page 111.)**

CAROB-ALMOND CRÊPES

Carob crêpes rolled around a carob-almond mousse-like filling makes for a rich dessert. Make the filling enough ahead of time to thoroughly chill it. You can also make the crêpes in advance. Garnish with chopped toasted almonds and/or a drizzle of carob syrup.

1 *cup unsweetened apple juice*
¼ *cup roasted carob powder*
3 *tablespoons mild-flavored honey*
3 *tablespoons tahini*
2 *teaspoons pure vanilla extract*
2 *tablespoons amaretto liqueur*
1 *pound tofu*
1 *tablespoon sesame oil*
¼ *teaspoon sea salt*
1 *dozen* CAROB CRÊPES

Heat the apple juice in the top of a small double boiler. Sift the carob powder if it is lumpy, then whisk it into the juice. Cover and cook over barely boiling water for several minutes, until the mixture is a thoroughly smooth syrup. Whisk in the honey and tahini. Cover and cook briefly. Whisk in the vanilla and amaretto and remove from the heat.

In a blender or food processor fitted with the metal blade, blend the tofu. While the machine is still running, add the oil, salt, and carob mixture and blend until smooth. Chill thoroughly to set.

Fill the crêpes with the mixture and roll them up or fold them. Serve immediately.

NOTES
▪ This is also a good filling for *ORANGE CRÊPES*; substitute Grand Marnier or another orange-flavored liqueur for the amaretto.

ORANGE CRÊPES
▼▼▼

Serve these for dessert with ORANGE GLAZE (see box) or filled with fresh berries or other fruits.

YIELD: 12 6-inch crepes

PREPARATION TIME: About 1 hour, plus a minimum of 30 minutes to rest the batter

> 1 *orange*
> *About 1 cup unsweetened apple juice*
> 1 *cup whole wheat pastry flour*
> *Pinch of sea salt*
> 2 *eggs*
> 1 *tablespoon orange-flavored liqueur, such as Grand Marnier or Cointreau*
> 1 *tablespoon light vegetable oil*

Grate the zest of the orange. Juice the orange and add apple juice to equal 1¼ cups.

Whisk or blend the zest and juice with the other ingredients to form a smooth batter. Cover and set aside for 30 minutes to several hours or overnight.

Lightly grease a crêpe pan which you have preheated over medium-high heat. Add batter and lift and rotate the pan immediately to spread it out evenly, about ⅛ inch thick. Turn the crêpe when the bottom is golden and the edges begin to curl. Cook briefly on the second side. Stack and cover crêpes to keep them warm.

(For detailed instructions, refer to the directions for *WHEAT CRÊPES* on page 111.)

Tortillas

Tortillas are Mexican flat breads made with finely ground cornmeal or wheat flour. In northern regions of Mexico, tortillas are typically prepared solely from wheat flour. All-corn tortillas are prevalent elsewhere. I sometimes make nontraditional tortillas with a combination of cornmeal and wheat flour.

You might ask, why make tortillas—corn or wheat—when they are now so easy to buy ready-made? The answer is simple: freshly made tortillas really do taste better than prepared ones. Also, with the right ingredients and equipment, tortilla making isn't much of a chore, particularly when a team is working at it—one person flattening the tortillas and another cooking them. If you are working alone, prepare all the tortillas before beginning to cook. Stack them between pieces of waxed paper to prevent them from sticking together or drying out.

The most traditional corn tortillas are made with masa, a specially prepared corn dough. In this process, dried corn is simmered in a lime solution to soften the hard hulls so that it can be ground to a smooth consistency; increased availability of the B vitamin niacin is an added benefit. For centuries in Mexico, masa was deftly patted by hand into thin rounds and toasted on griddles called *comales*. Now it is more often rolled and cut mechanically and baked on conveyor belts in large factories.

Making homemade masa is more of a production than most of us would want to undertake on a regular basis—or maybe even ever. If you're intrigued by the challenge, you can purchase whole corn and lime from some mail order sources and natural foods stores. If tortillas are produced commercially in your community and you'd like to try working with masa, you might inquire about purchasing some fresh masa. Use it up the day you get it, though, since it doesn't keep well in a raw form even when refrigerated or frozen, and tortillas made with old masa will be heavy.

Masa harina, dried masa in a flour form, is the best alternative to fresh masa for an adhesive tortilla dough, and you can keep this product on hand. Mixed with warm water and seasoned with a bit of salt, masa harina almost instantly becomes a manageable dough. When I lived in Tennessee, I was delighted to find masa harina prepared from organically grown blue corn, which I used to make lavender tortillas. They created quite a color show when combined with black or brown refried beans, chartreuse guacamole, and bright red salsa or tomatoes! Blue cornmeal is now quite readily available from Arrowhead Mills and other distributors, but so far blue masa harina is nowhere to be found in Texas, where I now live. However, Quaker Oats Company's masa harina from yellow corn is on almost every grocery store shelf and is an acceptable second choice.

I've made my share of corn tortillas from cornmeal. If the cornmeal—of whatever color—is particularly finely ground, it's not difficult to achieve a workable dough, but the uncooked tortillas are very fragile compared to those made with masa or masa harina doughs, and the finished product is coarser and not as flexible for rolling. Fresh cornmeal tortillas do have a good flavor, though.

A tortilla press greatly simplifies the flattening process for all-corn doughs. This handy, inexpensive device, usually made of cast aluminum or cast iron, consists of two hinged disks and an attached handle for

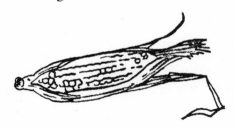

applying pressure. To use it, lay a piece of waxed paper or sheet of thin reusable plastic long enough to double over on the bottom disk, position a smooth ball of dough about the size of a walnut in the center, fold the waxed paper or plastic over the ball, lower the top disk, pull the handle over it, and push down. The ball of dough inside the press will instantly spread out into a thin 6-inch round. Lift up the dough and carefully pull the paper or plastic off one side; with this exposed side resting on your palm, peel the paper or plastic off the other side, and cook the tortilla.

Without a press, you will need to roll out tortillas by hand between pieces of waxed paper. Position the ball of dough in the center of the paper and press down on it with the bottom of a pie plate, then use a rolling pin to finish flattening it into a thin circle about 6 inches across. Needless to say, this method is much more tedious and time-consuming than using a press.

Tortilla doughs composed of all or mostly wheat flour are too glutenous to flatten with a press. Roll them out as thin as possible with a rolling pin on a lightly floured surface. You may rest these doughs as little as 30 minutes before rolling, but leaving them longer improves handling, flavor, and probably digestibility too.

Cook tortillas on a hot, well-seasoned but ungreased griddle or heavy skillet just until they are barely toasted, turning them once. As they are done, stack them in a bowl or basket lined with a tea towel or large cloth napkin and tuck another over the top to retain their warmth.

All tortillas are at their best as soon as they are cooked, though you may reheat them. Lay individual tortillas on a hot griddle for a few moments on each side, steam them briefly, or wrap and heat them in a low to moderate oven for a few minutes until warm. You can keep cooked tortillas in the refrigerator for several days; they also freeze well. Reheat as above.

Tortillas of all kinds are used in combination with other foods in numerous ways, from crisp chips for dipping to rolled or folded stuffed packages. See chapter 11 for recipes for filled tortillas.

CORN TORTILLAS
▼▼▼

Though you may not want to tackle them on a daily basis, homemade corn tortillas aren't really much of a production if you use a masa harina dough and a tortilla press. This activity can even be part of a party. You can make the dough and keep it at room temperature for several hours. Along with wheat tortillas, these are the basic breads of Mexico, and they are used in various ways in Mexican cuisine—see chapter 11 for some of them.

YIELD: 8 6-inch tortillas

PREPARATION TIME: About 15 minutes, plus 30 minutes to rest the dough

> 1½ *cups masa harina*
> ½ *teaspoon sea salt (optional)*
> ⅔ *to* ¾ *cup water*

In a medium-sized bowl, add water to the masa harina and salt to form a soft dough. It should be moist but not sticky. Knead until smooth, adjusting the consistency with more water or masa if necessary until it is puttylike. When you flatten a small ball of it into a thin round with your fingers, it shouldn't crack around the edge; if it does, knead in a little more water. Place the dough in a covered bowl and let it rest at least 30 minutes.

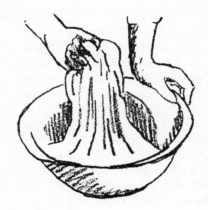

Divide the dough into 8 equal balls and cover. Press or roll out the tortillas as described on page 114-15. If you prepare them all before you begin to cook, don't peel off the waxed paper or plastic until just before you cook each tortilla.

Heat an ungreased griddle until water dripped on it sizzles. Cook a tortilla for about 30 seconds on one side, turn, and cook 30 seconds. Turn it twice more, again cooking 30 seconds on each side. The tortilla may puff up during cooking—especially if you press down on the center with your fingers or a tea towel; it will deflate when removed from the heat. Immediately wrap the cooked tortilla in a tea towel. Cook the remaining tortillas, stacking and wrapping them as they are done. Serve them warm.

NOTES

- Substitute finely ground cornmeal for the masa harina. This dough will be rather fragile. To facilitate handling, use waxed paper rather than plastic. After flattening the tortilla, peel the paper off one side, and lay the tortilla, paper side up, on the griddle, then carefully remove the second piece of paper.

WHOLE WHEAT TORTILLAS

In Mexico, wheat flour tortillas are generally made with white flour and lard. Whole wheat flour gives these a full, nutty flavor and, along with vegetable oil, contributes to a better nutritional profile. Use them for Mexican dishes such as BURRITOS (page 162-63) and FAJITAS (page 163).

YIELD: 6 10-inch tortillas

PREPARATION TIME: About an hour, plus a minimum of 30 minutes to rest the dough

> ½ cup whole wheat bread flour
> ½ cup whole wheat pastry flour
> ¼ teaspoon sea salt
> 1½ teaspoons sesame, corn, or other vegetable oil
> ½ cup hot spring water

In a small bowl, stir together the flours and salt. Drizzle in the oil and, using a fork or your fingers, evenly distribute it throughout the flour. Add the water and stir to form a dough. Turn the dough out onto a lightly floured surface and cover it with a tea towel. Wash the bowl and lightly grease it.

Thoroughly knead the dough, lightly sprinkling either bread or pastry flour on the kneading surface only as necessary to keep the dough from sticking. When the dough is smooth and resilient, form it into a ball, return it to the bowl, cover with a damp towel and plate, and set aside for at least 30 minutes but preferably several hours or overnight. It will keep for several days refrigerated.

Divide the dough into 6 equal pieces, form each one into a ball, and cover with a damp towel. Using flour as necessary to keep the dough from sticking, roll each ball as thin as possible into a circle about 10 inches across. Stack the tortillas between waxed paper and cover.

Heat a griddle until water dripped on it sizzles immediately. Lay a tortilla on the griddle and cook 20 seconds, until the bottom is slightly browned and bubbles appear on the surface. Turn and cook 15 to 20 seconds more. It should still be soft and pliable. Immediately wrap the tortilla in a tea towel and cover with an inverted bowl. Cook and wrap the remaining tortillas in the same manner. Serve warm.

NOTES
- For *SESAME-WHEAT TORTILLAS*, omit the oil and add 2 tablespoons of ground roasted sesame seeds to the dough. These have an irresistible aroma and flavor.

CORN-WHEAT TORTILLAS

These combination tortillas have a subtle corn flavor and the flexibility and larger size of wheat tortillas. This dough, too, can be made ahead of time.

YIELD: 6 10-inch tortillas

PREPARATION TIME: About an hour, plus a minimum of 30 minutes to rest the dough

> ½ cup cornmeal (blue, yellow, or white)
> 1 tablespoon sesame, corn, or other vegetable oil
> ½ cup spring water
> ¼ teaspoon sea salt
> ½ cup whole wheat bread flour

In a small bowl, thoroughly mix the cornmeal and oil. Heat the water to boiling, add the salt, and pour over the cornmeal. Wait a few minutes until the cornmeal has absorbed the water and has cooled to lukewarm.

Stir in the flour to form a dough. Turn the dough out onto a lightly floured surface. Wash the bowl and lightly grease it. Thoroughly knead the dough, lightly sprinkling flour under it only as necessary to keep it from sticking. When it is smooth and resilient, form it into a ball and place it in the bowl. Cover with a damp towel and plate and set aside for at least 30 minutes, but preferably for several hours or overnight.

Divide the dough into 6 equal pieces, form them into balls, and cover. On a lightly floured surface, roll each ball into a 10-inch circle. Stack between waxed paper and cover.

Cook tortillas on a hot griddle for about 20 seconds on each side, until lightly browned but still soft and pliable. Wrap in a tea towel and serve warm.

OKARA TORTILLAS

If you make your own soy milk or tofu, you're undoubtedly always looking for ways to use okara, the high-fiber, protein-rich soybean pulp residue from both of these projects. It provides both nutrients and moisture in this tortilla variation. You will have about 1 packed cup or more of okara left after making about 2 pounds of tofu or 8 cups of soy milk. You may also be able to purchase okara at local soy dairies and Oriental groceries. These tortillas have a slightly coarser texture than plain flour tortillas.

YIELD: 8 10-inch tortillas

PREPARATION TIME: About an hour, plus a minimum of 30 minutes to rest the dough

> ½ cup okara
> 1 tablespoon corn oil
> ½ cup masa harina or cornmeal
> ½ teaspoon sea salt
> 2 tablespoons water or vegetable stock
> 1 cup whole wheat bread flour

In a medium-sized bowl, mix together the okara, oil, masa harina, salt, and liquid. Add flour to form a soft dough. Turn the dough out onto a lightly floured surface and knead until smooth and elastic. Form the dough into a ball, place it in an oiled bowl, cover, and let rest at least 30 minutes, preferably several hours or overnight.

Cut the dough into 8 equal parts and form them into balls. Flatten each one on a lightly floured surface and, with a rolling pin, roll it into a thin 10-inch circle. Stack tortillas between pieces of waxed paper and cover with a damp tea towel.

Heat a griddle until water dripped on it sizzles immediately. Cook the tortillas one at a time for about 1 minute on each side—just until they are lightly browned. Keep them warm and soft by wrapping them in a towel immediately after cooking.

Chapatis and Parathas

Wheat is grown in the northern part of India, and much of the grain consumed in that region of the country is eaten as bread. *Chapatis* are unleavened Indian flat breads made from a kneaded dough and cooked on a griddle. They are usually made with finely ground wheat flour, but you may mix in small amounts of other flours or some ground seeds to vary the taste and texture. Freshly ground flour noticeably enhances the flavor of these breads. Resting the dough before rolling and cooking also improves the flavor and handling and likely the chapatis' nutritive value, too.

Unless you are working with someone else, roll out the whole batch of chapatis before you begin cooking them, since cooking will demand your undivided attention. You may also finger-press chapatis into thicker rounds. Of course, these will take longer to cook than thin ones. During cold upstate New York winters, my friend Jonathan cooks exceptional finger-pressed chapatis on top of his wood stove.

Bubbles often form in chapatis when they contact a hot griddle and, like pita, the steam often causes these breads to puff up completely. The steam assists in thorough cooking and contributes to lightness. As you'll see in the recipe for chapatis, certain techniques encourage this ballooning effect. Even chapatis that puff up end up thin and flat, since they collapse as they cool.

Parathas are a variation on chapatis, prepared by rolling layers of oil or *ghee* (clarified butter) into the dough before it is rolled out for a final time. The layers separate somewhat upon cooking, producing a light, though still essentially flat bread. Parathas may also be stuffed with various fillings, such as spicy vegetable mixtures.

Chapatis and parathas are traditionally served with meals and are often torn into pieces as they are used to scoop up vegetable and meat preparations. I sometimes roll whole chapatis or parathas around fillings, too.

CHAPATIS
▼▼▼

In India, chapatis are commonly served with spicy curries, dals, and vegetable dishes. They are excellent vehicles for all kinds of spreads and fillings, but they're also delicious "nekked"—as we say in Texas.

YIELD: 12 7-inch chapatis

PREPARATION TIME: About 1 hour, plus a minimum of 30 minutes to rest the dough

> ¾ cup whole wheat bread flour
> ¾ cup whole wheat pastry flour
> ⅜ teaspoon sea salt
> ¾ cup warm spring water

Sift the flours and salt into a small mixing bowl and make a well in the center. Pour in the water and stir until a dough forms. Turn the dough out and cover with a tea towel. While the dough rests briefly, wash the bowl and grease it lightly.

Thoroughly knead the dough, lightly sprinkling flour under it only if necessary to keep it from sticking. After 10 to 15 minutes, when the dough is smooth and springy, form it into a ball. Place it in the bowl, cover with a damp towel and plate, and set aside for at least 30 minutes but preferably several hours or overnight. Refrigerated, it will keep for several days.

Divide the dough into 12 equal pieces, form into balls, and cover. Using flour as necessary to prevent sticking, roll each ball into a thin circle about 7 inches in diameter. Stack, between pieces of waxed paper, and cover.

Heat a griddle until water sizzles immediately when dropped on the surface. Lay a chapati on the griddle and cook 30 to 40 seconds—until the edges begin to curl up and the bottom is slightly browned. Turn it over. With a clean, dry tea towel, pot holder, or oven mitt, lightly press down on the surface of the chapati as it is cooking to encourage air pockets to form—it may puff up completely. If it doesn't puff, hold it over a gas flame briefly with tongs or, if you have an electric stove, set the chapati on a wire rack over the burner coil. This should all be done quickly so that the chapati stays soft and flexible rather than becoming brittle and crisp. Don't worry if the chapatis never puff—they'll still taste good.

Immediately wrap cooked chapatis in a towel and cover with an inverted bowl. Serve warm.

NOTES

- Store chapatis in the refrigerator for several days, or freeze them—separated by waxed paper and well wrapped—for longer storage. To reheat, cook briefly on each side on a hot griddle, or wrap and heat for several minutes in a 350-degree oven.

- The flour combination in this recipe provides a good balance between dough strength and a tender texture. Chapatis made with all bread flour have a tougher texture than these; those prepared with all pastry flour lack the strength to withstand thin rolling.

- Substitute oat, rye, millet, barley, or rice flour for all or part of the whole wheat pastry flour. For dough strength, always use about half whole wheat bread flour.

- Substitute lightly toasted ground sunflower seeds for about 2 tablespoons pastry flour. Sesame seeds or poppy seeds are also good.

PARATHAS
▼▼▼

Like chapatis, parathas are griddle breads that double as eating utensils for the delicious, spicy dishes characteristic of Northern Indian cuisine. Paratha dough often contains ghee or oil and layers of ghee or oil are also rolled into it, making parathas richer and lighter than chapatis. Parathas are sometimes filled before they are cooked (see box). Ghee is clarified butter; to prepare it, refer to page 239.

YIELD: 12 7-inch parathas

PREPARATION TIME: 50 to 60 minutes, plus a minimum of 30 minutes to rest the dough

> ¾ cup whole wheat bread flour
> ¾ cup whole wheat pastry flour
> ⅜ teaspoon sea salt
> 1 tablespoon ghee or sesame oil, plus extra for rolling into the dough
> ¾ cup warm spring water

Sift the flours and salt into a small mixing bowl. Drizzle in the 1 tablespoon of ghee or oil and thoroughly mix it in with a fork or your fingers. Make a well in the center. Pour in the water and stir until a dough forms. Turn the dough out and cover with a tea towel. While the dough rests briefly, wash the bowl and grease it lightly.

Thoroughly knead the dough, lightly sprinkling flour under it only if necessary to keep it from sticking. After 10 to 15 minutes, when the dough is smooth and springy, form it into a ball. Place it in the bowl, cover with a damp towel and plate, and set aside for at least 30 minutes but preferably several hours or overnight. Refrigerated, it will keep for several days.

Divide the dough into 12 equal pieces, form into balls, and cover. Using flour as necessary to prevent sticking, roll each ball into a thin circle about 7 inches in diameter. Lightly brush it with ghee or oil. Fold it in half, brush with ghee or oil, and then fold in half again. Roll this wedge back into a circle of the original size. Repeat this process two or three times more. Stack between pieces of waxed paper and cover with a damp tea towel.

Heat a griddle until water sizzles immediately when dropped on it. Cook a paratha for about a minute—until the bottom begins to brown. Brush a little ghee or oil on the top. Turn and cook the second side. Brush the top of the paratha lightly with ghee or oil and turn it again if it doesn't seem quite done—parathas take slightly longer to cook than chapatis. The breads will probably puff up to some degree as they cook.

Stack cooked parathas on a plate, and cover with an inverted bowl. Serve warm.

NOTES
- Reheat by cooking briefly on each side on an ungreased griddle or skillet.

Pita

This traditional Middle Eastern pocket bread caught the American fancy over a decade ago and continues to occupy a firm niche in our casual cuisine. There's something appealing about a hollow, stuffable bread. Pita is great for sandwiches—they're less messy to handle

CAULIFLOWER-STUFFED PARATHAS
▼▼▼

To make this recipe, begin by preparing the dough for parathas—in advance if possible. The filling may also be made ahead of time, though the flavor is best when it's fresh. Unlike regular parathas, the dough for stuffed ones is not layered; it is simply rolled, filled, and rolled out again—thicker than regular parathas. Since stuffed parathas end up relatively flat, they too are often used to scoop up dals and other savory mixtures. They are also good accompaniments for soups and salads. Use the spicy potato filling for dosas (page 124) as an alternative stuffing.

> 1 tablespoon ghee or sesame oil, plus extra for brushing the parathas
> 2 green onions, finely chopped
> 1 clove garlic, pressed or minced
> 1 teaspoon minced fresh ginger root Freshly ground black pepper, to taste
> ½ teaspoon ground cumin
> ⅛ teaspoon each ground coriander, cardamom, cloves, cinnamon, turmeric, and cayenne
> 1 cup finely chopped cauliflower (4 ounces)
> 2 tablespoons vegetable stock or water Sea salt, to taste
> PARATHAS dough

To make the filling, heat the 1 tablespoon ghee or oil in a medium-sized skillet over moderate heat and sauté the onion, garlic, and ginger briefly. Stir in the spices and cook, stirring, for a minute or two. Add the cauliflower and sauté for a few minutes. Add the liquid, cover, and cook for about 5 minutes, stirring occasionally, until the cauliflower is tender. Remove the lid and cook away any extra liquid. Add salt to taste and set aside to cool.

Divide the dough into 6 equal pieces and roll each one into a ball. On a lightly floured surface, roll or press each ball into a 4-inch circle. Brush the middle with a bit of ghee or oil and spoon about 1½ tablespoons of filling on top. Draw the edges of the dough around the filling and pinch them firmly together to enclose it. Cover with a damp tea towel.

On a lightly floured surface, gently roll the stuffed parathas into 6-inch circles—a bit of the filling may ooze out here and there but try to minimize this. Stack them on a lightly floured baking sheet, separated by waxed paper, and cover.

Heat a griddle until it is hot, and grease it lightly. Cook each paratha for 2 to 3 minutes—its surface will be heaving and perhaps puffing a bit. Pressing the surface lightly with a spatula encourages puffing. When the bread has lightly browned, turn it and cook another minute. Lightly brush the surface with ghee or oil, turn it again, and cook for about 15 seconds. Brush with ghee or oil, turn it once again, and cook briefly. Serve the parathas immediately or cover to keep them warm.

NOTES
- Reheat stuffed parathas, loosely covered, in a moderate oven for several minutes.

than sliced bread sandwiches, and they can be stuffed with a seemingly endless variety of fillings. You can open one end of a whole pita, cut it in half to make two symmetrical pockets, or slice it open into two thin circular breads which can each be rolled around a filling or used as a base for toppings. Wedges of pita are also good with dips.

To make pita, you need a strong, well-developed dough. Use the recipes that follow or any plain yeasted dough or sourdough from chapters 5 and 6, which should work well, too. Next time you're making a basic bread, you can use part of the dough for pita. Just pre-

pare the dough up to the point of shaping. As with any other yeasted bread, the bowl rises for pita stretch and strengthen the gluten in the dough. This prepares pita dough well for the puffing that occurs during baking as a result of steam expanding inside of it.

When you roll the dough out, do it gently and evenly. Place the dough circles on baking sheets dusted with cornmeal, cover, and let rest for 30 minutes. I put two breads on each baking sheet and bake one sheet at a time. Set the timer for 30 minutes after you have rolled the first ovenload of breads; by the time you've finished rolling the other breads, the first ones will be ready to bake. Keep all the breads covered so that they won't dry out.

Preheat the oven so that it is hot when the first breads are ready to go in. Gently shake the sheet to be sure that the dough isn't sticking. If the dough circles don't slide freely, lift them carefully and sprinkle more cornmeal underneath. If the pita are stuck to the sheet, they may tear as they puff up or may not puff up at all.

Baking pita makes me glad for the window in my oven door. I can sit in front of it and cheer them on. Be sure that the oven heats back up to 500 degrees before you put in each tray of breads, and use the lowest rack. An immediate blast of bottom heat is important for instigating steam within the dough. Pita actually cooks from the inside out. What you're aiming for is thoroughly baked breads that are still soft, not crisp.

Look for filling ideas in Chapter 11: Filled Flat Breads.

AMALTHEA'S PITA

When we were naming our baking business, the cornucopia kept coming to mind as a positive, bounteous symbol. Though this term and its image had been overworked commercially to the point of banality, it still held an appeal for us. So we researched its origins and learned that, according to Greek legend, the cornucopia or horn of plenty had belonged to Amalthea, a goat—or nymph—who had nurtured the infant god Zeus when he was hidden in a cave on the isle of Crete. Zeus's father, Cronus, the king of the Titans, had received a prophecy that one of his children would wrest his power and had swallowed each of Zeus's older brothers and sisters immediately after birth. When Zeus was born, his mother presented Cronus with a swaddled stone and whisked the baby away to Crete, where Amalthea broke off one of her horns and used its inexhaustible, overflowing riches to nourish his growth. We chose Amalthea as the name for our business as a symbol of nurturance.

This is the recipe we used for the pita we sold with the Amalthea label. We rolled out so many breads on a baking day that we often suffered from "pita elbow," but the wonderful breads were worth the discomfort. These are strong, flavorful, and dependable.

YIELD: 6 8-inch breads

PREPARATION TIME: 45 minutes to prepare; 3 to 5 hours for rising; 5 minutes to bake each tray

> ½ teaspoon active dry yeast
> 1 cup lukewarm spring water
> 2½ cups whole wheat bread flour
> 1 teaspoon sea salt
> 1 tablespoon vegetable oil or olive oil
> 1 tablespoon soy flour

In a medium-sized bowl, sprinkle the yeast over the water, and add a teaspoon of wheat flour. Cover and set in a warm spot for 5 to 10 minutes to proof. Stir in 1 cup of the wheat flour to form a batter. Cover and set aside for about 30 minutes or until a sponge develops.

Stir the salt, oil, and soy flour into the sponge. Add the remaining wheat flour, ½ cup at a time, stirring well after each addition, until the dough pulls away from the sides of the bowl and balls up in the center. Turn the dough out onto a lightly floured surface, cover, and let rest for a few minutes.

Thoroughly knead the dough, adding flour only as necessary to keep it from sticking. When the dough is smooth and elastic, form it into a ball and place it in a lightly greased bowl. Cover and set in a draft-free spot for 1 to 2 hours or until the dough has risen and does not rebound when pressed with a finger.

Turn the dough out and knead briefly. Return it to the bowl, cover, and set aside to rise for another 1 to 2 hours or until it does not spring back when pressed.

Divide the dough into 6 equal balls. Cover and let rest 30 minutes. On a lightly floured surface, use a rolling pin to roll each ball into an 8-inch circle slightly less than ¼ inch thick. Arrange on baking sheets lightly dusted with cornmeal. Cover and set aside for 30 minutes.

Move a rack to the lowest position (leaving lots of space above it) and preheat the oven to 500 degrees. Before baking, make sure that the dough circles are not sticking to the baking sheet; if they are, sprinkle more cornmeal underneath. Cross your fingers and bake the bread for 5 minutes. The breads should puff up like balloons and be lightly browned. Do not open the oven door to peek before the 5 minutes is up, and be sure the oven has reheated to 500 degrees before putting in another sheet. If a bread doesn't puff, it will still taste good but won't have a pocket to fill.

Line a bowl with a dry tea towel and wrap the baked breads as soon as you remove them from the oven. Serve warm. Thoroughly cool the breads before storing.

NOTES
- You can omit the soy flour.

- To reheat, wrap breads in foil or place them in a covered baking dish and warm them in a 350-degree oven for just a few minutes, so that they heat through but don't become dry and crisp.

- Pita freezes well; place waxed paper between breads so they will not stick together (then you can take them out one at a time) and wrap well.

meal or rice flour underneath. Bake one sheet at a time, 5 minutes each, and be sure the temperature has returned to 500 degrees before putting in each sheet. Do not open the oven door during baking. The breads should puff up completely and lightly brown.

Wrap the baked breads in a tea towel as you take them out of the oven. Serve warm. Cool breads thoroughly before storing.

SOURDOUGH PITA

▼▼▼

This is a sourdough version of pita; it has a similar texture but a slightly tangy taste. Use this just as you do regular yeasted pita for dips and fillings. I think it goes particularly well with Indian dishes, such as LENTIL DAL (page 136-37) and INDIAN EGGPLANT (page 134-35).

YIELD: 6 8-inch breads

PREPARATION TIME: 2½ to 3½ hours for sponge and dough; 4 to 5 hours for rising; 5 minutes to bake each tray of bread

> 1 cup spring water
> ½ cup sourdough starter
> 3 cups whole wheat bread flour
> 1 teaspoon sea salt
> 1 tablespoon corn, sesame, or olive oil

In a medium-sized mixing bowl, stir together the water, starter, and 1½ cups of the flour to form a batter. Cover and set aside for 2 to 3 hours, until a sponge develops.

Stir in the salt and oil. Add enough of the remaining flour, ½ cup at a time, stirring well after each addition, to form a dough. Turn it out onto a lightly floured surface, cover, and let rest while you wash the bowl.

Thoroughly knead the dough until smooth and elastic, adding flour only as necessary to keep it from sticking. Form the dough into a ball. Lightly grease the bowl and put the dough inside. Cover and set aside for about 2 hours or until the dough has risen and does not rebound when pressed. Turn the dough out and knead it briefly. Return it to the bowl for a second rise.

Divide the dough into 6 equal balls. Cover and let rest for 30 minutes. On a lightly floured surface, roll each ball into an 8-inch circle with a rolling pin. Arrange these on baking sheets lightly dusted with cornmeal or rice flour; I put two breads on each sheet. Cover and let rest for 30 minutes.

Move a rack to the lowest position (leaving lots of space above it) and preheat the oven to 500 degrees. Before baking, check to be sure that the breads are not sticking to the sheet; if they are, sprinkle more corn-

LEBANESE WRAPPER BREAD

▼▼▼

This is lavosh—large, thin, flexible Middle Eastern flat breads, made from a strong, yeasted wheat dough. They're used for scooping or wrapping up vegetable or bean dips, salads, or kebabs. You can bake it either on a sheet in a hot oven or on top of the stove—either draped over an inverted wok or on a griddle if the breads are small enough to fit. As with pita, the yeast in this dough contributes to its flavor and texture; the bread doesn't rise when baked.

YIELD: 6 12-inch breads

PREPARATION TIME: About 1½ hours to prepare and roll out the dough; 2½ to 4½ hours for rising; 30 to 40 seconds to bake each bread

> ¼ teaspoon active dry yeast
> ½ cup lukewarm spring water
> 1¼ to 1½ cups whole wheat bread flour
> ½ teaspoon sea salt

In a medium-sized mixing bowl, sprinkle the yeast over the warm water. Sprinkle in a teaspoon of flour, cover, and set in a draft-free spot for a few minutes to proof the yeast. Stir in ½ cup of the flour to form a batter. Cover and set aside for about 30 minutes, until a sponge develops.

Stir in the salt. Add flour, ¼ cup at a time, stirring after each addition, until a dough forms. Turn it out onto a lightly floured surface, cover, and let rest briefly.

Thoroughly knead the dough, lightly sprinkling flour under it only as necessary to keep it from sticking. When the dough is smooth and resilient, form it into a ball. Place it in a clean, lightly greased bowl, cover, and set aside for 1 to 2 hours, until the dough has risen and does not rebound when pressed with a finger.

Turn the dough out and knead it a few times. Return it to the bowl, cover, and set aside for another 1 to 2 hours, until it has risen again and does not spring back when pressed.

Cut the dough into 6 equal pieces and roll each one into a ball. Set the balls on a lightly floured surface, cover, and let rest for 30 minutes.

On a lightly floured surface, with a rolling pin, roll each ball into a 12-inch circle. Stack, separated by waxed paper, and cover with a damp tea towel.

Preheat the oven to 500 degrees. Bake on an ungreased pan for 15 to 20 seconds on each side. Alternatively, use a hot griddle or inverted wok on top of the stove. In any case, work quickly so that the breads stay soft and flexible.

As each bread is done, fold it in quarters, wrap in a clean, dry tea towel, and cover with an inverted tray or bowl. Serve warm.

NOTES

- Refrigerate or freeze the breads when they have cooled thoroughly. Wrap and reheat in a 350-degree oven for several minutes.

TEMPEH SHISH KEBABS IN LEBANESE WRAPPER BREAD
▾▾▾

These shish kebabs are especially for warm weather, when fresh herbs and summery vegetables are plentiful and you can cook outdoors. When it's inclement, grill the kebabs in the broiler in the kitchen, roll them up in the warm flat breads, and just pretend you're on a picnic.

> 8 *large mushrooms*
> 1 *large bell pepper, cut into 1-inch squares*
> 1 *cup water*
> 1 *tablespoon olive oil, plus extra for brushing the eggplant*
> 1 *4-ounce cake tempeh*
> 1 *small eggplant*
> 2 *tablespoons mellow barley miso*
> ¼ *cup lemon juice*
> 6 *tablespoons tahini*
> *Freshly ground black pepper—several grindings*
> 2 *tablespoons minced fresh basil leaves*
> 2 *tablespoons minced fresh parsley leaves*
> 8 *cherry tomatoes*
> 4 *LEBANESE WRAPPER BREADS (page 121-22)*
> 2 *green onions, finely chopped*

Steam the mushrooms and peppers briefly, using about 1 cup water, and reserve the steaming water.

Heat the 1 tablespoon oil in a small skillet over moderate heat. Add the tempeh and brown both sides. Add ¼ cup of the reserved steaming water and cover tightly. Steam until the liquid has cooked away. Cut the tempeh into 8 squares.

Cut the eggplant crosswise into 1-inch slices; salt them lightly and layer in a colander; place a plate and a weight of some kind on top. Press at least 30 minutes, then rinse and pat dry. Lightly brush both sides of slices with olive oil and arrange on a baking sheet. Broil, turning once, until just tender—or bake at 350 degrees for 10 to 15 minutes, until tender. Cut into 1-inch cubes.

In a medium-sized bowl, whisk the miso, lemon juice, and tahini. Whisk in ⅔ cup of the steaming water to form a smooth sauce. Grind in black pepper and whisk in the basil and parsley. Fold in the mushrooms and the bell pepper, tempeh, and eggplant pieces. Marinate 20 to 30 minutes or longer.

Arrange the marinated items and cherry tomatoes on skewers. Grill or broil, turning and basting the kebabs several times, until they are browned. Simmer extra marinade briefly, until it thickens somewhat.

Wrap the breads in foil and warm briefly over the grill or in a moderate oven. Fill with the cooked kebabs, garnish with some of the thickened marinade and green onions, and roll or fold. Serve immediately.

NOTES

- If you use Oriental eggplant, it isn't necessary to salt and press; simply slice, brush with oil, and broil or bake.

- Substitute 1-inch chunks of lightly steamed zucchini or another summer squash, or boiled or steamed small new potatoes or peeled whole onions for the eggplant.

- Substitute 8 ounces tofu for the tempeh and omit the tablespoon of olive oil. Press the tofu well, cut it into 8 cubes, steam briefly, and marinate with the vegetables before grilling.

- Add 1 to 2 cloves pressed or minced garlic to the marinade.

- Substitute other fresh herbs, such as dill or tarragon, for the basil and/or parsley.

JOHNNYCAKES
▼▼▼

As it hits the hot griddle, this thin batter immediately spreads out into delicate lacy rounds, which are crisp, lightly browned, and decidedly corn-flavored when they're done. The fresher the cornmeal, the better the flavor will be. Serve these for breakfast, drizzled with maple syrup, or top them with REFRITOS (page 136), TOFU SOUR CREAM (page 148), salsa (pages 143 or 146), and chopped fresh cilantro for lunch or supper.

YIELD: About 2 dozen 3-inch pancakes

PREPARATION TIME: 30 to 40 minutes, plus a minimum of 30 minutes to rest the batter

> 1⅔ cups spring water
> ¼ teaspoon sea salt
> 1 cup cornmeal
> 2 teaspoons corn, sesame, or sunflower oil

Heat 1 cup of the water to boiling, add the salt, and pour over the cornmeal in a medium-sized bowl. Whisk vigorously until the mixture is smooth, then whisk in the remaining ⅔ cup water to form a loose batter. Cover and set aside for 30 minutes to several hours or overnight.

Heat a griddle until water sprinkled on it sizzles immediately, then grease it lightly. Whisk the oil into the batter. Ladle out about a tablespoon of batter for each pancake. Cook until the top surface appears dry. Carefully run a metal spatula under the pancakes, flip them over, and cook several minutes more, until they are quite crisp.

Serve johnnycakes hot off the griddle or cover them with an inverted bowl to keep them warm.

SOCCA
▼▼▼

Socca, a crêpe-like flat bread made from chickpea flour, is a specialty of Nice, in southern France, where it is sold as a snack in the marketplace and by vendors on the street. Traditionally, socca is baked in large, shallow copper pans in wood-fired ovens; lacking both of those, I improvise with my blackened steel pizza pan and home oven. Chickpea flour and olive oil give socca a wonderfully robust flavor. I grind chickpeas in my grain mill; the flour is also sometimes available in ethnic markets and natural foods stores. Serve socca as an hors d'oeuvre or with SALADE COMPOSÉE (page 214-15) or a hearty Provençal soup or vegetable stew and a fine red wine.

YIELD: 1 12-inch socca—2 to 4 servings

PREPARATION TIME: 40 to 45 minutes

> ⅔ cup chickpea flour
> ¼ teaspoon sea salt
> ⅔ cup spring water
> 1 tablespoon olive oil, plus extra for the pan
> Freshly ground black pepper—several grindings

Sift the flour and salt into a medium-sized bowl. Gradually whisk in the water to form a batter. Whisk in the oil and pepper. Cover and set aside for 30 minutes or so—the batter will thicken somewhat upon standing as the flour absorbs the water.

Preheat the oven to 450 degrees. Liberally grease a 12-inch pizza pan with olive oil. Give the batter a stir and pour it onto the pan—it should spread out to about ⅛ inch thickness. Bake for 5 minutes, until the top is well set and beginning to brown—it will have a crêpe-like consistency. Brush the top lightly with olive oil and bake a minute or two longer, but watch it closely!

Serve the socca hot from the oven cut into wedges or strips and with extra pepper ground on top.

NOTES

- You can also prepare the batter in a blender or food processor.

DOSAS
▼▼▼

Dosas are South Indian pancakes made from a grain or grain and legume batter which is usually fermented. The most traditional recipes call for soaking uncooked whole grains and beans for several hours or overnight, then blending them with sufficient water to form a thin batter. You can also make dosa batter with flour and water or another liquid, as I have here. For the lightest dosas, ferment the batter before cooking. Like crêpes, dosas are cooked on a hot, lightly oiled griddle on top of the stove. They are slightly thicker, moister, and more porous than crêpes, and they take longer to cook. Though usually served for breakfast in India, dosas are delicious for brunch, lunch, or supper too. They are often folded over a spicy vegetable filling, in which case they are called masala dosas, masala meaning spicy (see box). Dals and chutneys are other good accompaniments.

YIELD: 8 6-inch dosas

PREPARATION TIME: Several hours or overnight to ferment the batter; 30 minutes to cook

> 1 cup rice flour
> 1½ to 1¾ cups soy milk
> ¼ teaspoon sea salt

In a medium-sized bowl, whisk the flour with 1½ cups of the soy milk. Whisk in the salt. Cover and set aside for several hours or overnight, until the batter has fermented—it should smell slightly tangy and appear bubbly when you stir it. If it is not readily pourable, thin the batter with additional soy milk.

Heat a griddle until water dances on the surface

▪▪▪▪▪▪▪▪▪▪▪▪▪▪▪▪▪▪▪▪▪▪▪▪▪▪▪▪▪▪▪▪▪▪▪▪▪

MASALA DOSAS
▾▾▾

A piquant potato mixture such as this one is traditional for filling dosas in southern India. Prepare the dosa batter ahead of time and then have the filling ready before you cook the dosas. Serve the dosas immediately after you fill them.

> 2 *medium-sized potatoes (12 ounces)*
> 1 *tablespoon sesame oil or ghee*
> 1 *teaspoon black mustard seed*
> 1½ *cups finely chopped onion*
> 1 *small hot pepper, seeds and membranes removed, finely chopped*
> ½ *teaspoon ground cumin*
> ½ *teaspoon turmeric*
> 1½ *teaspoons finely minced ginger root*
> 1 *tablespoon grated coconut*
> ½ *cup potato cooking water*
> ½ *teaspoon sea salt*
> 1½ *teaspoons lemon juice*
> 8 *Dosas*

Boil the potatoes in water to cover until they are just tender. Drain, reserving the cooking water. When the potatoes are cool enough to handle, dice them, and set aside.

Heat the oil in a medium-sized skillet over moderate heat. Add the mustard seed and cook, stirring, until it browns. Add the onion and continue to cook, stirring often, until it is just tender. Stir in the minced pepper and sauté for several minutes. Add the cumin, turmeric, ginger root, and coconut, and sauté briefly. Stir in the potatoes, the ½ cup potato water, and salt. Cover the pan and cook, stirring frequently, for several minutes, until the liquid is absorbed. Mash the potatoes somewhat with a fork. Stir in the lemon juice.

Prepare the dosas, then spoon on filling and fold them over. Serve immediately.

NOTES
- This filling is also good with chapatis, parathas, and other flat breads.

▪▪▪▪▪▪▪▪▪▪▪▪▪▪▪▪▪▪▪▪▪▪▪▪▪▪▪▪▪▪▪▪▪▪▪▪▪

and grease it lightly. Stir the batter and ladle or pour about ¼ cup on the griddle. Immediately spread it out as thin as you can with the back of a wooden spoon. The batter will bubble as soon as it hits the griddle, but wait until the underside is golden brown and the surface appears dry before carefully turning it over with a thin-bladed spatula. Cook the second side for a shorter time.

Serve dosas immediately or keep them in a warm oven until you are ready. Although dosas are best when freshly made, leftovers may be refrigerated and reheated in a low to moderate oven or in a steamer. You can also keep extra batter in the refrigerator or freezer.

NOTES
- Substitute other flours, such as whole wheat pastry, barley, or oat flour, for the rice flour.
- Substitute water for the soy milk.

MANDARIN PANCAKES
▾▾▾

These thin, tortilla-like pancakes originated in northern China, where wheat is an important crop. A mandarin was a high-ranking official in imperial China; the application of the term to these pancakes identifies them as aristocratic fare. My use of whole wheat flour might seem to undermine their refined image, but these pancakes are still exceedingly thin and they are more flavorful than their white flour counterparts. Though the pancakes are almost translucent, their delicate appearance is deceptive, since they are sturdy enough to securely hold a stir-fried filling. They are usually associated with Peking duck and mu-shu pork, but they are excellent with stir-fried vegetables too (see box).

YIELD: 12 6-inch pancakes

PREPARATION TIME: About an hour, plus a minimum of 30 minutes to rest the dough

> ⅓ *cup whole wheat pastry flour*
> ⅔ *cup whole wheat bread flour*
> ½ *cup spring water, boiling*
> *Sesame oil*

Mix the flours in a small bowl and make a well in the center. Pour in the boiling water and stir to form a soft dough. Turn the dough out onto a lightly floured surface, cover, and rest for a few minutes.

Thoroughly knead the dough, adding flour only as necessary to keep it from sticking. After 10 to 15 minutes, when the dough is smooth and springy, form it into a ball, and place it in a lightly greased bowl. Set aside, covered, for at least 30 minutes but preferably several hours or overnight.

FILLED MANDARIN PANCAKES
▼▼▼

Vary the vegetables in this filling to suit your taste and what you have on hand; bean sprouts, snowpeas, julienned green beans, turnips, and other kinds of mushrooms are all possible substitutions. If you plan on serving this dish in the evening, soak the dried mushrooms early in the day. You can also substitute fresh shiitake mushrooms for the dried ones; use a mild vegetable stock in the recipe in place of the mushroom soaking water. Make the pancakes ahead of time and steam them briefly as you're cooking the filling just before serving. Since mandarin pancakes are eaten out of hand, make the stir-fry rather dry.

> 1 cup water
> 6 small dried shiitake mushrooms
> ½ teaspoon roasted sesame oil
> 2 tablespoons tamari
> 1 tablespoon HOT SHERRY (page 240)
> 8 ounces tofu, well pressed and cut into small strips
> 1 teaspoon kuzu powder
> 2 tablespoons sesame oil
> 2 eggs, beaten
> ⅔ cup carrot cut into 1-inch julienne
> ⅔ cup daikon cut into 1-inch julienne
> ¼ cup finely chopped green onions
> 1 teaspoon pressed or minced garlic
> 1 teaspoon minced fresh ginger root
> 2 cups finely sliced Chinese cabbage or bok choy
> 12 MANDARIN PANCAKES

Heat the water to boiling and pour it over the mushrooms in a small bowl. Soak the mushrooms for several hours, until the caps are completely softened; the stems will stay hard. Drain, reserving the stock. Cut off the tough stems and slice the caps into thin slivers—you should have about ¼ cup—and set aside.

In a small bowl, whisk together the roasted sesame oil, 1 tablespoon of the tamari, and hot sherry. Add the tofu pieces and stir gently. Marinate for 30 minutes or so, stirring occasionally.

Combine the kuzu, 1 teaspoon of the mushroom stock, and the remaining tamari; set aside until the kuzu has thoroughly dissolved.

Heat a wok over moderately high heat and add 1 tablespoon of the sesame oil. Pour in the beaten egg and cook it, lifting the edge with a spatula as necessary to allow the uncooked portion to run underneath. As soon as the egg has set, fold it into thirds, transfer it from the pan to a cutting board, and cut it into thin strips.

Heat the wok and add the remaining tablespoon of oil. Sauté the carrot and daikon strips, stirring constantly, until almost tender. Toss in the green onion, garlic, ginger, and slivered mushrooms, and continue to cook, stirring, for several minutes. Add the cabbage and sauté briefly. Add ⅜ cup of the shiitake stock and the tofu in its marinade. Cover and steam briefly, until the tofu is hot and soft. Add the egg strips and the kuzu mixture, and cook, stirring, until the liquid thickens.

Wrap the pancakes in a damp towel and steam for a few minutes to reheat them. Serve immediately alongside the filling, having people fill and roll up their own and eat them out of hand.

On an unfloured surface, roll the dough with your palms into a 12-inch log. Cut it into 12 1-inch pieces and press each piece into a 2-inch circle. Brush one side of each round lightly with sesame oil. Press the oiled sides of two rounds together. Pair the remaining rounds in the same way, and let them rest briefly, covered.

On a lightly floured surface, roll each pair of rounds with a rolling pin into a 6- to 7-inch circle. Stack them, separated by pieces of waxed paper to keep them from sticking together, and cover.

Heat a griddle until water dropped on it sizzles immediately. Place one double pancake on the griddle and cook briefly, just until the underside begins to brown. Turn and cook the second side briefly—the pancake should still be soft and flexible. Remove and carefully pull the two thin pancakes apart. Place them on a plate with another plate inverted on top. Cook the remaining pancakes in the same manner. Serve warm.

NOTES

• To reheat, steam the pancakes for a few minutes.

• These pancakes freeze well. Insert waxed paper between them before freezing. Thaw before reheating.

JAPANESE VEGETABLE PANCAKES
▼▼▼

Thick griddlecakes, called okonomiyaki, *are a favorite fast food in Japan. Try these all-vegetable ones, brushed with a spicy sauce and sprinkled with various garnishes, for a quick, nourishing meal at home. Delicate, paperlike* nori *is a seaweed that is perhaps most widely known for its use in making sushi rolls.*

YIELD: 2 to 4 servings

PREPARATION TIME: About 30 minutes to prepare; 5 to 10 minutes to cook

> 1 cup whole wheat pastry flour
> ½ teaspoon sea salt
> 1 cup soy milk (or vegetable stock or water)
> 2 eggs
> 4 shiitake mushrooms, thinly sliced
> 2 green onions, finely chopped
> 1 small carrot, grated
> 1 small turnip or daikon, grated
> 1 cup thinly sliced Chinese cabbage or bok choy
> 1 cup finely chopped spinach or other greens
> 1 tablespoon hatcho miso
> 2 tablespoons tahini
> 2 tablespoons vegetable stock or water
> ¼ teaspoon roasted sesame oil
> ¼ teaspoon umeboshi vinegar
> Pickled ginger
> Nori, toasted and torn or cut into thin strips
> Fresh cilantro leaves, coarsely chopped

Sift the flour and salt into a medium-sized mixing bowl. Whisk in the 1 cup soy milk or other liquid. Thoroughly whisk in the eggs. Fold in the mushrooms, onions, carrot, turnip or daikon, cabbage, and spinach.

Preheat a griddle until water dropped on the surface sizzles immediately and lightly grease the surface. Stir the batter, ladle it onto the griddle, and spread it evenly—okonomiyaki are usually made quite large and about ½ inch thick. Cook for 4 to 5 minutes—until the underside has browned. Turn and cook several minutes more; these pancakes take longer to cook through than thinner ones.

Meanwhile, whisk together the miso, tahini, the 2 tablespoons stock or water, roasted sesame oil, and vinegar. Turn the pancakes back to the first side and spread on the sauce. Serve immediately, garnished with the ginger, nori, and cilantro.

NOTES
- Substitute dried shiitake mushrooms. Pour boiling water over them to cover and soak several hours, until they are fully reconstituted. Drain and use the soaking water as part of the liquid in the batter. Cut off tough stems and discard before slicing.

- To make slightly lighter pancakes, sift ½ teaspoon baking powder with the flour and salt.

- Small cubes of tofu (pressed and marinated or not) or strips of cooked tempeh are good additions to the batter; fold them in with the vegetables.

CHINESE SCALLION BREAD
▼▼▼

Chopped scallions are rolled right into these delicious flat breads. They are sold by street vendors in China, where they are a popular snack food. They make tasty companions to soups as well.

YIELD: 2 10-inch breads

PREPARATION TIME: About 45 minutes, plus a minimum of 30 minutes to rest the dough

> ⅔ cup whole wheat bread flour
> ⅔ cup whole wheat pastry flour
> ⅔ cup spring water
> 5 teaspoons regular sesame oil
> 1 teaspoon roasted sesame oil
> ½ teaspoon sea salt
> ½ cup finely chopped green onions

Sift the bread and pastry flours into a medium-sized mixing bowl and make a well in the center. Heat the water to boiling, pour it into the well, and stir to form a dough. Turn out onto a lightly floured surface, cover, and rest briefly.

Thoroughly knead the dough, dusting the surface with flour only as necessary to keep the dough from sticking. When it is smooth and springy, place the dough in a clean, lightly greased bowl, cover, and set aside for at least 30 minutes but preferably several hours or even overnight.

Divide the dough in half and form each piece into a ball. With a rolling pin on a lightly floured surface, roll one of the balls into a 12-inch circle. Brush 1 teaspoon regular sesame oil and ½ teaspoon roasted sesame oil over the surface. Evenly sprinkle on ¼ teaspoon salt, then half the green onions. Tightly roll the dough into a long cylinder and pinch the ends closed. Firmly coil it, snail-like, into a circle, tucking the outer end underneath.

On a lightly floured surface, gently roll the coil into a 10-inch circle, periodically turning the dough to keep it from sticking. Place the round on a baking sheet lightly dusted with flour and loosely cover it with a tea towel.

Prepare the second ball of dough in the same manner.

Heat a griddle or large skillet until water sizzles when dropped on the surface. Add 1½ teaspoons regular sesame oil and tilt the pan to evenly grease the surface. Cook one of the breads 1 to 2 minutes on each side, until lightly browned in spots. Add the remaining 1½ teaspoons oil and cook the other bread.

Cut the breads into wedges and serve hot.

NOTES
- Refrigerate or freeze leftovers. Reheat in a 450-degree oven for several minutes.

Crackers

Just as with fine homemade bread, one taste of fresh homemade crackers is likely to spoil your appetite for the commercial product for good! Oh, no—not another requisite baking project, you might think. Crackers are generally simple, rather unexacting flat breads. Matzohs, for instance, are nothing more than flour and water. Homemade crackers are fresher and less expensive than store-bought ones—even when you take the preparation time into account.

Many crackers are made without leavens, and even those that are leavened with baking powder or baking soda or with yeast remain fundamentally flat, so you don't have to be particularly concerned about rising. Crispness rather than rise is a cracker's signature characteristic.

You may make specific doughs for crackers, but perhaps the easiest approach to cracker making is to treat it as an extension of bread making. When you make a yeasted, sourdough, or natural-rise bread dough or tortilla or chapati dough, reserve a portion of it. Just a small piece of dough goes a long way when you're making crackers.

A pasta machine doubles as an excellent cracker roller. Or use a rolling pin and roll the dough out ⅛ inch thick or less, as evenly as possible. Roll it out on a lightly greased surface or directly on a greased baking sheet. Roll some seeds on top of a plain dough for an extra special crunch.

Cut out crackers with a sharp knife or use biscuit or cookie cutters for fancier shapes. Prick the surface with a fork to prevent the formation of air bubbles.

Bake crackers immediately in a 350-degree oven. Most take 10 to 15 minutes to become lightly browned and crisp. Doughs containing cooked grains might take slightly longer, and these bake through better at a slightly lower temperature. Keep a close eye on baking crackers since they can burn easily.

Cool crackers thoroughly before storing. To maintain crispness, keep them in a tightly closed tin or other well-sealed container. They should stay fresh for a couple of weeks. To re-crisp crackers, place them on a baking sheet in a low oven for a few minutes.

I like to use grainy doughs for crackers, such as those for yeasted or sourdough cracked wheat or steel-cut oat breads. *CIDER-RICE BREAD*, *NATURAL-RISE RYE BERRY BREAD*, and *NATURAL-RISE GRITS BREAD* are good natural-rise doughs to use. *SPROUTED WHEAT BREAD*, *TOFU-HERB BREAD*, and all rye doughs make delicious crackers, and *SESAME-WHEAT BREAD* crackers are outstanding!

GRAHAM CRACKERS
▼▼▼

These slightly sweet whole wheat crackers are a classic American "comfort food." They assuaged our anxieties in kindergarten and still help us get through sleepless nights. Homemade grahams are especially fresh and crisp, and they don't have to be square.

YIELD: About 2 dozen crackers

PREPARATION TIME: 40 minutes to prepare; 10 to 15 minutes to bake

> ¼ cup milk or soy milk
> 1 teaspoon lemon juice or vinegar
> ¼ cup sunflower oil
> ¼ cup honey or maple syrup
> 2 cups sifted whole wheat pastry flour
> ½ teaspoon baking soda
> ½ teaspoon baking powder
> ¼ teaspoon sea salt

Combine the milk and lemon juice and set aside for a few minutes to curdle. In a small bowl, whisk the oil and honey. Whisk in the curdled milk.

In a medium-sized bowl, sift the sifted flour, baking soda, baking powder, and salt. Make a well in the center and pour in the liquid mixture. Stir gently until the dough pulls away from the sides of the bowl and balls up in the center.

Preheat the oven to 350 degrees. Lightly grease baking sheets or line them with baking parchment.

Using a rolling pin on a lightly greased or lightly floured surface, roll the dough out about ⅛ inch thick. Cut out traditional squares or other shapes—I like to use cookie cutters. Arrange them on the prepared sheets and prick the dough with a fork. Bake in the preheated oven 10 to 15 minutes, until lightly browned.

Transfer the crackers to racks and cool thoroughly before storing in a tightly closed tin. They will keep well for several weeks.

NOTES
- Substitute ¼ cup buttermilk or beaten yogurt for the milk or soy milk and omit the lemon juice.

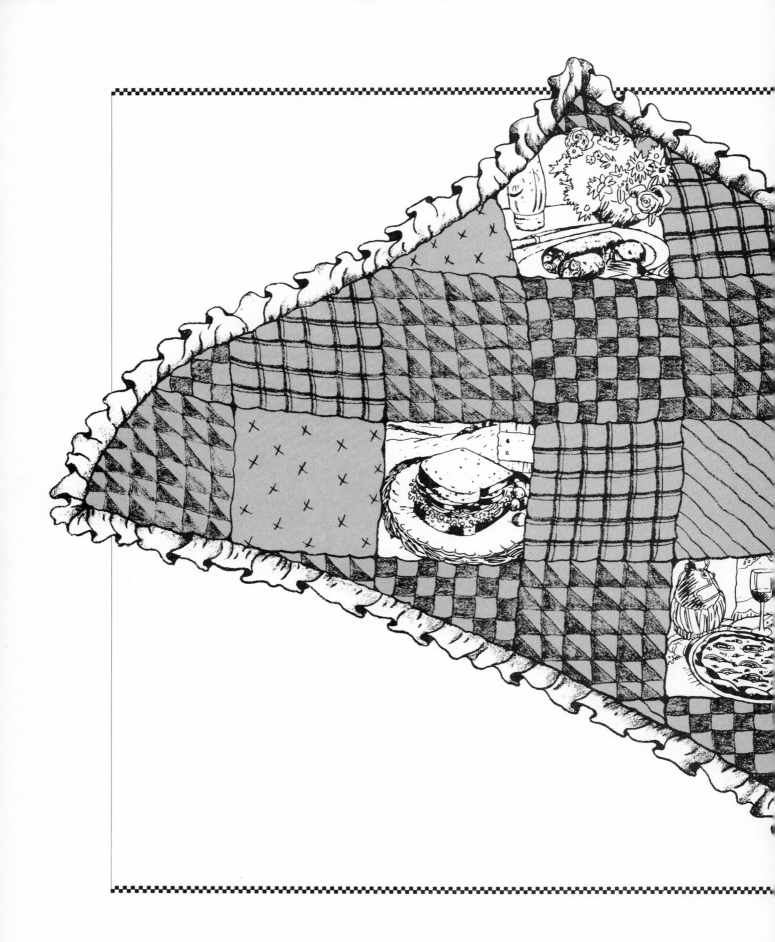

GETTING INTO BREAD:
BAKING/COOKING
COLLABORATIONS

THE DISHES ARE DONE and the kitchen is cleaned up. Freshly baked bread rests on racks on the table, cool now but still fragrant. I cut off a piece and, with undivided attention, savor every bite, catching every nuance in flavor and texture. What greater pleasure than fresh bread all by itself?

Yet, as good as fresh breads are on their own, I think of them, and all grain actually, as the foundation for meals. When planning a meal, I start with a grain, often bread, and go from there. So, when I make bread, I'm already thinking about how it will fit into a meal plan.

You can start with baked breads and serve them topped with spreads or made into sandwiches—pocket breads just beg to be filled; flat breads seem designed to be rolled or wrapped around something or other. Bread dough can be made into pizzas, bread-crusted tarts, main dish turnovers, or sweet or savory spiral-filled loaves or buns.

Besides sparking my interest and challenging my ingenuity, I find that basing meals on breads is extremely efficient. The bread that gets eaten this way is legitimately part of a healthy daily meal plan. Although all of the recipes in this book produce highly nutritious bread, you can enhance their nutritional worth even further by combining them with other foods.

Leftovers—cooked grains, baked sweet potatoes or squash, extra carrots, or applesauce; a sourdough starter that needs exercising; or simply a craving for a certain grain may dictate the particular bread I decide to make at a given time. If cilantro is abundant in my garden, I know I'll be whipping up some tortillas or chapatis to go with Mexican and/or Indian dishes. Pita is a particular favorite of mine in summer for impromptu picnics, with Middle Eastern salads and dips or stuffed. On leisurely weekend mornings, I may make popovers, muffins, pancakes, or scones. I can assure you that this kind of integrative planning becomes habitual; you won't even be able to turn it off after awhile.

Since we're shifting gears now from baking to cooking, we'll be working with some new ingredients:

When I specify "a large clove of **garlic**" in recipes, I mean a *large* clove—one that will fill a teaspoon when pressed or minced.

Several recipes call for peeled fresh **tomatoes**. The easiest way to peel tomatoes is to put them into boiling water very briefly, then immediately plunge them into cold water; the skins will slip off readily.

Roasted sweet and hot **peppers** also will appear. To roast a pepper, hold it on a fork over a gas flame or put it under the broiler and turn it periodically so that it is evenly charred. Put it in a covered bowl until cool enough to handle. Peel off the skin, then cut it open and remove the seeds and membranes.

We've already used **tofu** in some of the breads, but some recipes will call for pressing it. To do this, sandwich a square of tofu between two folded paper towels or tea towels on a tray or plate and place a moderately heavy object on top. I have a square stone paperweight that is just right for one piece of tofu, and I find that putting the tofu and weight inside of one of those small plastic baskets that berries or cherry tomatoes come in keeps the arrangement stable. Lots of things work as weights, including a container of water; whatever you use, it should gradually compress the tofu, not squash it. If you're pressing several pieces of tofu at once, place them on a baking sheet and put a second sheet on top with a weight on top of that, or arrange the tofu in a colander and cover it with a towel, plate, and weight.

Moving on to cooking will also require some other tools:

In addition to an adequate collection of **pots** and **pans**, you'll need a **cutting board** and some good quality **knives** in assorted sizes. Except for those with serrated edges, keep your knives well sharpened; dull blades are not only frustratingly ineffective, they are also accidents waiting to happen.

A **toaster oven** is a versatile appliance that I use every day. Besides toasting or warming breads, it toasts nuts and bakes and broils vegetables and sandwiches using a minimum of energy.

A **flame tamer**—a hollow round metal plate for positioning between a stove burner and pan—buffers the heat and spreads it evenly over the bottom of a pan. These are great for minding simmering sauces or anything else that is prone to burning.

If I had to single out the most useful kitchen tool to appear on the scene in recent years, I would undoubtedly choose a **salad spinner**. This simple apparatus saves me a lot of time and paper towels every day by quickly and effectively drying fresh herbs and greens.

Spreads and sauces are a good way to start integrating bread into your cooking, and we'll focus on them next. They may be used as toppings and fillings for the sandwiches, filled flat breads, and filled doughs in the chapters that follow. Leftovers of all kinds of things that are insufficient on their own to constitute a significant part of a meal have new potential when viewed as ingredients for these combination items. We'll finish up this part with some ideas for using a baker's ultimate leftover—leftover bread.

CHAPTER 9

▾▾▾▾▾▾▾▾▾▾▾▾▾▾▾▾▾▾▾▾▾▾▾▾▾▾▾▾▾▾▾

Spreads and Sauces and Such

THERE'S OFTEN A FINE line between spreads and sauces, and frequently they stand in for one another with the greatest of ease. Sometimes the only difference between a spread and a sauce is consistency; for instance, tahini-miso spread thinned with a bit of orange juice readily becomes tahini-miso sauce. Spreads and sauces alike play multiple culinary roles: organizing flavors, harmonizing textures, and adding accents in taste and appearance to specific dishes and also to meals as a whole. I like to think of them as "accessories" for food in the same way that scarves, belts, shoes, handbags, and hats tie together and perk up wardrobes.

A repertoire of spreads, sauces, and condiments is an asset for cooking in general, but it is especially important for the collaborative dishes we're about to undertake. Aside from breads, these are some of the basic raw materials you'll need to create a broad variety of bread-based dishes—whether a simple sandwich or a flamboyant pizza. No doubt, like me, you'll find yourself coming back to these versatile recipes again and again for both old and new applications. There's a lot of variety here, even though these tasty, nutritious combinations are all vegetarian and nondairy. They are based on beans, tofu, nuts, seeds, vegetables, and fruits. Herbs, spices, citrus zest, garlic, ginger root, and hot peppers add extra pizzazz. Some of them, such as hummus, baba, refritos, guacamole, salsas, pesto, and dal, are borrowed from other cultures and adapted to my own particular taste and ingredient preferences. Others, such as tofu spreads and sauces, pesto variations, and bean and vegetable pâtés, derive more from sheer invention, though they, too, often reflect cultural influences. A few basics—fruit and nut butters, baked garlic, tomato sauces, and hollandaise—round out the selection.

Though many spreads and sauces have a particular ethnic bent or are customarily linked with particular breads or bread-based dishes in some other way, there are no hard and fast rules for combining. Let your senses be your guide; trust your instincts. Add your own favorite spreads and sauces to this collection and update it as you discover new ones.

When I was very young, my favorite sandwich was made with peanut butter, jelly, and Marshmallow Fluff; during my kindergarten year, I ate that particular trio every day for lunch. Now that I'm an advocate of a balanced diet and, moreover, now that I know about the tremendous variety of spreads and sauces that can be experienced in one short lifetime—smooth, chunky, sweet, savory, spicy, herby, it especially seems a shame that I devoted a whole year to such a boring combination. But I'm sure that I have more than made up for lost time in the years since.

TAHINI-MISO SPREAD
▼▼▼

This rich-tasting, creamy sesame spread is good on all kinds of breads, from quick to flat. It goes well with a variety of flavors, both sweet and savory. I like it on muffins for breakfast or combined with vegetables or fruits in sandwiches for lunch (see BLONDIE'S DAGWOOD, *page 151-52). This spread is quick to make as needed; refrigerated, it will also keep well.*

YIELD: About ⅓ cup

PREPARATION TIME: 10 minutes

> ¼ cup unsalted tahini
> 1 to 2 teaspoons mellow barley miso, to taste
> Freshly grated orange zest, to taste

In a small bowl, thoroughly whisk together the tahini and miso. Add the zest, to taste. Thin, if desired, by mixing in fruit juice, stock, or water. Serve the spread immediately or cover it tightly and store it in the refrigerator.

NOTES

▪ Roasting the tahini first gives the spread an even richer flavor. Stir it in a pan over low heat for several minutes until it becomes a bit darker in color and wonderfully fragrant; cool before mixing in the miso.

▪ Substitute lemon zest or minced fresh herbs, such as dill, basil, tarragon, chives, or parsley, for the orange zest.

PEANUT BUTTER-BANANA SPREAD
▼▼▼

I'm still a peanut butter fan—though now I can do without the Fluff and even the jam. Mashed banana moistens this spread and gives it a natural sweetness. Substitute other fruits in season; try strawberries, raspberries, peaches, nectarines, or apple sauce or pear sauce. Miso seasons the mixture and makes it more digestible. This is good on all kinds of breads. I often spread it on toast for a quick breakfast or lunch.

YIELD: 1 or 2 servings

PREPARATION TIME: 10 minutes

> 1 tablespoon unsalted peanut butter
> About ¼ cup mashed banana
> ½ to 1 teaspoon mellow barley miso

In a small bowl, thoroughly mash together the peanut butter and banana; thoroughly mix in the miso to taste.

CURRIED TOFU SPREAD
▼▼▼

Tofu has a fantastic capacity to absorb flavors. Here, seasoned with curry spices, it assumes an Indian character. You can make this spicy spread a bit ahead of time so that the flavors have a chance to mingle. It goes well with lots of breads; I particularly like it on grainy ones, such as cracked wheat, oat, or rice breads, or stuffed into pita. Combine it with thinly sliced tomatoes or apples and crisp lettuce for a terrific sandwich.

YIELD: Enough for 2 to 4 sandwiches

PREPARATION TIME: 30 minutes

> ¼ teaspoon each ground turmeric, cumin, coriander, and chili powder
> ⅛ teaspoon each ground cloves, cardamom, cinnamon, and cayenne
> 1 tablespoon sesame oil
> 1 clove garlic, pressed or minced
> 1 teaspoon finely grated fresh ginger root
> 1 small carrot, finely chopped or grated
> ¼ teaspoon kelp powder (optional)
> 8 ounces tofu, pressed
> 2 green onions, finely chopped
> ¼ cup loosely packed fresh parsley, finely chopped
> 3 tablespoons lightly toasted, finely chopped almonds
> 1 teaspoon lemon juice
> 3 to 4 tablespoons TOFU MAYONNAISE (page 141) or another mayonnaise
> Sea salt

With a mortar and pestle or spice grinder, combine the turmeric, cumin, coriander, chili powder, cloves, cardamom, cinnamon, and cayenne.

Heat the oil in a small skillet. Briefly sauté the garlic and ginger. Stir in the spice mixture, carrot, and kelp powder and continue to cook, stirring, for a couple of minutes. Remove from the heat.

In a medium-sized bowl, using a large fork, mash the tofu well; add the sauté, green onions, parsley, almonds, lemon juice, and 3 tablespoons mayonnaise and mix thoroughly. Add more mayonnaise if necessary to achieve the desired consistency. Season with sea salt to taste.

Serve at room temperature or chilled.

NOTES

- Substitute roasted peanuts for the almonds.

HERBED TOFU-ALMOND SPREAD
▗▖▗▖▗▖

Mustard greens give this spread a pleasant spiciness—or you can substitute other greens or vegetables, such as finely chopped watercress, arugula, celery, bell pepper, or radish, for all or part of them. Refrigerated, this spread will keep well for a couple of days; the flavor may even improve. Serve it on thinly sliced bread, rolled up in flat breads, or stuffed into pita. Garnish with fresh sprouts or tomatoes if they are in season.

YIELD: Enough for 4 to 6 sandwiches

PREPARATION TIME: About 30 minutes

> 1 pound tofu, pressed
> 2 cloves garlic, pressed or minced
> 2 to 3 teaspoons each minced fresh basil, tarragon, and dill weed
> 1 teaspoon dry mustard
> ¼ teaspoon celery seed
> ½ teaspoon kelp powder
> 2 large green onions, finely chopped
> 1 small carrot, grated
> ¼ cup finely chopped fresh parsley
> ½ cup finely chopped tender mustard greens
> ½ cup lightly toasted almonds, finely chopped
> 6 to 8 tablespoons TOFU MAYONNAISE (page 141) or other mayonnaise
> 1 teaspoon mellow rice or mellow barley miso
> Sea salt

In a medium-sized bowl, mash the tofu well. Add the garlic and minced herbs and mix. With a mortar and pestle or a spice grinder, grind the mustard and celery seed; add this, the kelp powder, green onions, carrot, parsley, greens, and almonds and mix thoroughly.

In a small bowl, whisk together 6 tablespoons of mayonnaise and the miso. Add this to the tofu mixture and stir thoroughly. If necessary, add more mayonnaise, a tablespoon at a time, until the spread is a desirable consistency. Season with salt, to taste.

NOTES

- When fresh basil, tarragon, and dill are unavailable, substitute dried herbs; use about 1 teaspoon of each dried herb and grind them with the mustard and celery seed.

TOFU-SESAME SPREAD
▗▖▗▖▗▖

Sesame seeds are present in three different forms in this tasty, nourishing blend. Spread it on thin slices of bread or in pita and layer thin tomato and/or crisp radish slices, lettuce or other dark greens, and sprouts on top; or serve it as a dip with crunchy raw vegetables or bread sticks.

YIELD: Enough for 4 sandwiches

PREPARATION TIME: 25 minutes

> 12 ounces tofu, pressed
> 1 tablespoon lemon juice
> ½ teaspoon roasted sesame oil
> ¼ teaspoon umeboshi plum paste
> ¼ cup tahini
> 1 clove garlic, pressed or minced
> 1 tablespoon hatcho miso
> 3 green onions, finely chopped
> ¼ cup fresh parsley, finely chopped
> 2 to 4 tablespoons toasted sesame seeds

In a medium-sized bowl or in a food processor, mash or blend the tofu well. Add the lemon juice, roasted sesame oil, umeboshi plum paste, tahini, garlic, and miso and combine thoroughly. Mix in the green onions and parsley. Add sesame seeds to taste. Thin, if desired, by adding vegetable stock or water.

NOTES

- Substitute finely chopped chives or Chinese chives for all—or part—of the green onions.

- Substitute lightly toasted, finely chopped sunflower seeds or walnuts for the sesame seeds.

ROASTED GARLIC
▗▖▗▖▗▖

The first time I tasted a whole roasted onion, I was surprised by the sweet succulence I discovered beneath the charred outer layers. The mellowness of roasted garlic is similarly amazing. Enjoy this rich, nutty-tasting spread on bread, or purée it for a pizza topping.

YIELD: 4 to 8 servings

PREPARATION TIME: About 1 hour

>   *4 large whole heads firm fresh garlic*
> *¼ teaspoon sea salt*
>   *Water*
> *2 tablespoons olive oil*

Peel off the parchmentlike skin down to the layer adjacent to the cloves. Place the peeled garlic in a small pot and add the salt and water to cover. Bring to a boil and simmer for about a minute. Remove the garlic, reserving the water.

Arrange the garlic in an oiled baking dish and drizzle the oil over it. Bake at 350 degrees for about an hour, basting the bulbs several times with the reserved liquid, until the cloves are exceedingly soft when pierced.

Spoon the liquid in the pan over the bulbs and serve them whole, instructing diners to separate the cloves and squeeze them to extract the creamy spread inside.

NOTES

- Grind a bit of fresh pepper or sprinkle a bit of minced fresh or crushed dried herbs, such as thyme or rosemary, over the garlic bulbs before baking.

- I like to substitute elephant garlic for the smaller varieties; leave the bulbs intact or separate them into cloves. Allow extra baking time.

- To prepare a purée, put the roasted cloves through a food mill to remove the skins and mash the garlic.

BABA
▼▼▼

Baba Ganouj, Baba Ghanoush, Baba Ghanoosh . . . I just call this scrumptious Middle Eastern eggplant purée "Baba." Serve it as a dip for raw vegetables, as a spread for pita (page 120-21) or other breads, or use it in a sandwich. Refrigerated, this will keep for a couple of days.

YIELD: About 1½ cups

PREPARATION TIME: 30 to 50 minutes to bake the eggplant; 20 minutes thereafter

> *1 medium-sized eggplant*
> *1 large clove garlic, pressed or minced*
> *5 teaspoons lemon juice*
> *5 tablespoons tahini*
> *2 teaspoons hatcho miso*
> *¼ cup fresh parsley, finely chopped*

Pierce the eggplant in several places with a fork; place it on a baking sheet in a 450-degree oven; bake 30 to 50 minutes, until it appears wrinkled and is very soft.

Set aside to cool.

In a medium-sized bowl, whisk together the garlic, lemon juice, tahini, and miso to form a smooth paste. (Or use a blender or a food processor fitted with the metal blade.)

When the eggplant is cool enough to handle, cut it in half and scoop out the pulp. Add these eggplant "innards" to the garlic-tahini mixture and thoroughly mash or blend the two together. Stir in the parsley.

Serve at room temperature or chilled. Spread it in a smooth layer on the bottom and around the sides of a shallow bowl, and drizzle with a bit of olive oil if you wish.

INDIAN EGGPLANT
▼▼▼

Green tomatoes add a hint of tartness to this delicious eggplant dish. It can be a spread, dip, or filling for flat breads. Serve it for lunch or dinner along with some fresh, warm CHAPATIS (page 117-18) or PARATHAS (page 117-18) and perhaps a dal (page 136-37) or Indian salad (page 216-17). This will keep in the refrigerator for a couple of days.

YIELD: About 4 cups

PREPARATION TIME: About 1 hour

> *1½ pounds eggplant*
> *¾ teaspoon fennel seeds*
> *1 teaspoon ground coriander*
> *½ teaspoon each chili powder, turmeric, and ground cumin*
> *1 tablespoon sesame oil or ghee*
> *1 large onion, finely chopped*
> *2 medium-sized green tomatoes, finely chopped*
> *¾ teaspoon sea salt*
> *1 tablespoon chopped fresh cilantro leaves*

Pierce the eggplant with a fork; place it on a baking sheet in a 450-degree oven. Bake 30 to 50 minutes, until it appears wrinkled and is very soft. Set aside until it is cool enough to handle, then cut it open, scrape the pulp into a bowl, and mash it thoroughly.

Toast the fennel seeds in a dry skillet. Grind them to a coarse consistency in a mortar or spice grinder. Add the coriander, chili powder, turmeric, and cumin and grind again.

Heat the oil or ghee in a skillet over moderate heat and sauté the onion for a few minutes. Add the tomatoes and continue to sauté until both vegetables are tender. Stir in the spice mixture and cook, stirring, for a couple of minutes. Stir in the salt and eggplant, reduce the heat, and cook for several minutes, stirring occasionally, until the excess liquid has cooked away. Garnish with the cilantro.

NOTES

- If you substitute ripe tomatoes, add a teaspoon of lemon juice at the end of the cooking.

- If you like things hot, remove the seeds and membranes from a small chili pepper, mince it, and add part of it—or all of it—along with the eggplant.

GUACAMOLE
▾▾▾

Well-ripened avocados have a smooth, creamy texture and a full, rich, nutty flavor. Many recipes for this traditional Mexican purée call for tomato, onion, garlic, chilies, or other spices, but I think it's best at its simplest—with just a touch of lime, black pepper, and salt, and a light sprinkling of chopped fresh cilantro leaves. Serve it with soft or crisp tortillas or raw vegetable chunks, or use it as a sandwich spread or salad topping. The flavor, texture, and color of guacamole are best when it is fresh; if you must wait to serve it, keep it tightly covered.

YIELD: About 1 cup

PREPARATION TIME: 10 minutes

> *1 medium-sized ripe avocado, peeled and pitted*
> *1 to 1½ teaspoons lime juice*
> *Freshly ground black pepper, to taste*
> *Sea salt, to taste*
> *2 tablespoons coarsely chopped fresh cilantro leaves*

In a small, shallow bowl, mash the avocado pulp with a fork to the consistency of a coarse paste. Stir in lime juice to taste. Season to taste with pepper and salt. Garnish with the cilantro and serve immediately.

NOTES

- The two most commonly available avocados are the dark, bumpy-skinned Hass from California, and the brighter green, smooth-skinned Fuerte from Florida. I prefer the Hass since they tend to be richer-tasting than the sometimes watery Florida ones, although I've had some avocados from Florida that were excellent too.

PEAR BUTTER
▾▾▾

When I moved to Texas, I discovered Kieffer pears, which are crisp yet juicy when they are ripe. I don't really care for them as an eating pear, but they make the most wonderful pear sauce and pear butter, projects I look forward to every autumn. You can substitute other kinds of pears; you may need to adjust the cooking time, since most kinds take less time to soften.

YIELD: 2½ to 3 pints, depending on how thick you make it

PREPARATION TIME: 30 minutes to prepare; several hours to cook it down

> *5 pounds of pears (Kieffer, Comice, Bartlett, Seckel, Anjou, Bosc, etc.)*

Quarter the pears lengthwise and remove the seeds and cores. Cut into chunks and put them into a 6-quart heavy-bottomed pot. Cover and set on a flame tamer over low to moderate heat. Cook, stirring occasionally, until the fruit is soft, 2 to 3 hours for Kieffer pears. Put the fruit through a food mill or force it through a strainer to remove the skins. Return the sauce to the pot, partially cover, and cook until it reaches the consistency you desire.

Pour the hot mixture into sterilized canning jars, leaving about ¼ inch of head space; screw on sterilized lids and process in a boiling water bath for 10 minutes. Store the sealed jars in a cool, dry cupboard or pantry.

If you do not seal the jars, store them in the refrigerator or freezer after they have cooled. Unopened, they will keep for several weeks refrigerated and up to a year frozen.

NOTES

- Add ground allspice, cinnamon, and nutmeg, to taste.

- For *LEMON-GINGER PEAR BUTTER*, stir 1 teaspoon lemon zest and 1 teaspoon finely grated fresh ginger root or 1 teaspoon ground ginger into the sauce after you have milled it.

- For *PEAR SAUCE*, do not cook the milled fruit to a thick consistency.

- Make plain or spiced *APPLE SAUCE* or *APPLE BUTTER* by the same method. Firm-fleshed, tart apples, such as Pippins, Northern Spies, Crispins, and Granny Smiths, make especially flavorful apple sauce and apple butter. Use one variety or a combination.

- For *PEACH BUTTER*, remove the skins before pitting and cutting up the fruit by dipping the peaches briefly in boiling water and then plunging them into cold water. The skin should slip off readily. Proceed with the recipe. This fruit butter, too, is good plain or spiced.

REFRITOS
ˇˇˇ

Refried beans are a staple in Latin America—and in my house. Serve them simply with greens, rice, and corn or wheat tortillas (page 115-16) or use them as a key component of other dishes, such as MEXICAN PIZZA (page 167), BEAN BURRITOS (page 162-63), TOWERING TOSTADAS (page 160-61), and TORTILLA FLATS (page 161). Refried beans are traditionally cooked in lard; using olive oil lowers the cholesterol in these and they are tremendously tasty. They will keep several days refrigerated, or you can freeze them.

YIELD: About 6 cups

PREPARATION TIME: 35 minutes

 3 *tablespoons olive oil*
 2 *medium-sized onions, finely chopped*
 2 *medium-sized bell peppers, finely chopped*
   Freshly ground black pepper—several grindings
 2 *teaspoons ground cumin*
 1/2 *teaspoon ground coriander*
 5 *cups cooked red beans—pinto, kidney, anasazi, aduki—or black turtle beans (see page 238)*
 1/2 *to 1 cup bean stock*
 2 *tablespoons hatcho miso, or to taste*
 1 *tablespoon lemon juice*

Heat the oil in a large skillet over medium heat. Sauté

the onion until it is almost tender. Add the bell pepper, black pepper, cumin, and coriander, and continue to sauté until the vegetables are tender. Add two-thirds of the cooked beans to the sauté, stir, and reduce the heat to low.

Add a few tablespoons of bean stock to the remaining beans and mash them to a paste. Stir the mashed beans into the sauté mixture. Cover and cook over low heat, stirring occasionally, for 15 to 20 minutes, until the beans are hot and the flavors are integrated.

Thoroughly mix the miso with 2 tablespoons of the bean stock. Stir this mixture into the hot beans. Mix in the lemon juice. If the bean mixture is too thick, stir in additional stock, a tablespoon at a time.

LENTIL DAL
ˇˇˇ

These are delicately spiced refried beans, Indian style. Serve them with basmati rice and flat breads such as CHAPATIS (page 117-18), PARATHAS (page 117-18), or SOURDOUGH PITA (page 121). This is also a delicious topping or filling for DOSAS (page 123-24).

YIELD: About 3 cups

PREPARATION TIME: 1 to 1½ hours

 1 *cup red lentils*
 1 *2-inch piece kombu, optional*
 3 *cups water*
 1 *teaspoon turmeric*
 1½ *teaspoons cumin seed*
 1 *teaspoon ground coriander*
 1/4 *teaspoon ground cardamom*
 1/8 *teaspoon each ground cinnamon, cloves, and cayenne*
 1 *tablespoon sesame oil or ghee*
 1 *small onion, finely chopped*
   Freshly ground black pepper—several grindings
 1½ *tablespoons lemon juice*
 1½ *tablespoons mellow barley miso*
 1/2 *cup fresh cilantro leaves, coarsely chopped*

Sort through the lentils and pick out any foreign matter. Rinse the lentils under cool water. Place them and the kombu in a 1½- to 2-quart saucepan. Add the water and bring it to a boil over moderate heat. Skim off the foam that forms on the surface. Reduce the heat to low and stir in the turmeric. Loosely cover the pot and cook, stirring occasionally, for 45 to 60 minutes, until the lentils are tender—they will separate into a thick layer on the bottom and a soupy layer on top. Turn off the heat and cover tightly.

Heat a heavy-bottomed skillet over moderate heat and roast the cumin seeds for several minutes, stirring or agitating the pan often to prevent them from burning. Grind the seeds to a coarse consistency in a mortar or spice grinder; add the coriander, cardamom, cinnamon, cloves, and cayenne and grind again.

Heat the oil in a skillet over moderate heat. Sauté the onion until it is tender. Add the black pepper and the spice mixture and cook briefly, stirring constantly to keep the spices from burning. Stir in the cooked lentils. Turn the heat to low and cover the pan. Cook for several minutes, until the mixture is hot and the flavors are blended.

Whisk together the lemon juice and miso to form a smooth paste. Stir this into the lentil mixture. If it is too thick, thin with several tablespoons of water, vegetable stock, or coconut milk. Serve warm, garnished with the cilantro.

NOTES

- Substitute yellow split peas or green lentils for the red lentils.

- Substitute a bit of finely minced hot pepper (seeds and membrane removed) for the cayenne; sauté it with the onion briefly before you add the spices.

- If fresh cilantro is not available, garnish the dal with a tablespoon or two of chopped fresh mint leaves.

CURRIED CHICKPEAS
▼▼▼

Serve this spicy chickpea dish as a dip or filling for Indian flat breads, such as **CHAPATIS** *(page 117-18) or* **PARATHAS** *(page 117-18) or* **DOSAS** *(page 123-24)—for brunch, lunch, or dinner. It will keep for several days in the refrigerator.*

YIELD: About 3 cups

PREPARATION TIME: 30 to 40 minutes

- *½ teaspoon cumin seeds*
- *½ teaspoon turmeric*
- *1 teaspoon ground coriander*
- *⅛ teaspoon each ground cloves, cardamom, cinnamon, and cayenne*
- *1 tablespoon sesame oil or ghee*
- *1 medium-sized onion, finely chopped*
- *1 large clove garlic, pressed or minced*
- *1 teaspoon finely grated or minced fresh ginger root*
  Freshly ground black pepper—several grindings
- *1 medium-sized ripe tomato, chopped*
- *2 cups cooked chickpeas (see page 238)*
- *¼ cup chickpea stock*
- *1 tablespoon lemon juice*

- *1 tablespoon hatcho miso*
- *½ cup fresh cilantro leaves, coarsely chopped*

Heat a heavy-bottomed skillet over moderate heat and roast the cumin seeds for several minutes, stirring or agitating the pan often to prevent them from burning. Grind them to a coarse powder in a mortar or spice grinder. Add the turmeric, coriander, cloves, cardamom, cinnamon, and cayenne and grind again.

Heat the oil in a medium-sized skillet over moderate heat and sauté the onion for several minutes. Stir in the garlic and ginger and continue to sauté until the onion is just tender. Grind in the black pepper, add the spice mixture, and cook briefly, stirring constantly. Stir in the tomato, chickpeas, and stock and bring the mixture just to a simmer. Cover and turn the heat to low. Cook for 10 to 15 minutes, until the tomato is soft and the flavors have blended. Whisk together the lemon juice and miso and stir it into the chickpeas.

Serve warm, garnished with the cilantro.

NOTES

- Substitute a small hot pepper for the cayenne. Remove the seeds and membranes, mince, and add to the sauté along with the garlic and ginger.

- If you don't have chickpea stock, substitute vegetable stock or water.

HUMMUS
▼▼▼

Hardly "ho-hummus," a term coined by my friend Darcee to describe uninspired versions of this Lebanese chickpea spread or dip, this one is a pert and lively blend. Serve it with warm pita (page 120-21) or other flat breads, or with crisp raw vegetables. Refrigerated, hummus will keep for several days, or you can freeze it.

YIELD: About 1½ cups

PREPARATION TIME: 15 minutes

- *¼ cup tahini*
- *2 tablespoons lemon juice*
- *2 cloves garlic, pressed or minced*
- *2 teaspoons hatcho miso*
- *3 tablespoons chickpea stock*
- *1 cup cooked, drained chickpeas (see page 238)*
- *¼ cup fresh parsley*

In a food processor fitted with the metal blade or in a blender, thoroughly blend the tahini, lemon juice, garlic, miso, and stock to a smooth paste. Add the chickpeas and blend well. Blend in the parsley. If necessary, blend in additional stock, a tablespoon at a time, until it is the consistency you desire. Add a touch more miso and/or lemon juice if needed.

WHITE BEAN SPREAD
▼▼▼

Serve this light, refreshing dip or spread with pita (page 120-21) or other flat breads or with crisp raw vegetables and briny black olives.

YIELD: About 1½ cups

PREPARATION TIME: 15 minutes

>   2 small cloves garlic, pressed or minced
>   3 tablespoons bean stock
>   2 tablespoons lemon juice
> 2½ teaspoons mellow barley miso
>   ¼ cup tahini
>   ¼ cup fresh mint leaves
>   1 cup cooked navy beans (see page 238)

In a blender or in a food processor fitted with the metal blade, combine the garlic, stock, lemon juice, miso, and tahini and blend until thoroughly smooth. Blend in the mint. Add the beans and blend until smooth. To thin, blend in an additional tablespoon or two of bean stock. Garnish the spread with minced mint leaves or parsley, if desired.

This will keep for several days in the refrigerator; freeze it for longer storage.

MEDITERRANEAN BEAN SPREAD
▼▼▼

I used to stop at a Middle Eastern restaurant on the road between Northampton and Amherst, Massachusetts, and often ordered an unusual red bean purée, along with more familiar hummus and baba. This is my version of that wonderful concoction. I usually serve this dip or spread with large folded circles of LEBANESE WRAPPER BREAD (page 121-22), as the restaurant did, but it goes well with other flat breads and raw vegetables too.

YIELD: About 1½ cups

PREPARATION TIME: 25 minutes

>   1 tablespoon olive oil
>   1 small onion, chopped
>   1 large clove garlic, pressed or minced
>   Several grindings black pepper
>   ¼ teaspoon fresh thyme leaves, minced
>   Pinch of cinnamon
>   2 teaspoons lemon juice
>   1 tablespoon hatcho miso
>   2 tablespoons tahini
>   3 tablespoons bean stock
>   1 cup cooked red beans—anasazi, pinto, aduki, kidney, etc. (see page 238)
>   2 tablespoons minced fresh parsley

Heat the oil in a small skillet over moderate heat and sauté the onion for several minutes. Add the garlic and continue to sauté until the onion appears translucent and is tender. Add the pepper, thyme, and cinnamon and cook briefly.

Transfer to a blender or food processor fitted with the metal blade. Add the lemon juice, miso, tahini, and stock and blend until smooth. Add the beans and blend thoroughly. Thin with additional bean stock if necessary.

Serve at room temperature or chilled. Garnish with the parsley.

This will keep in the refrigerator for several days, or you can freeze it.

ANASAZI BEAN SPREAD
▼▼▼

Anasazi means "ancient ones" in the Navajo Indian language, and anasazi beans are in fact the ancestors of pinto beans. This spread or dip combines the special sweetness of these beans, the mild heat of a poblano pepper, and the delightful poignancy of fresh cilantro in a rich, appealing blend. You can substitute other red beans, such as pinto beans or kidney beans, for the anasazi beans.

YIELD: About 1½ cups

PREPARATION TIME: 20 to 30 minutes

>   1 small poblano pepper
>   1 tablespoon olive oil
>   1 small onion, chopped
>   1 clove garlic, pressed or minced
>   1 teaspoon ground cumin
> 2½ teaspoons hatcho miso
>   2 teaspoons lemon juice
>   3 tablespoons anasazi bean stock
>   1 cup cooked anasazi beans (see page 238)
>   ½ cup fresh cilantro leaves

Roast and peel the pepper as described on page 130.

Heat the olive oil in a small skillet over moderate heat; sauté the onion for several minutes. Add the garlic and continue to sauté until the onion is tender and appears translucent. Stir in the cumin and cook briefly—just a couple of minutes. Transfer the contents to a blender or a food processor fitted with the metal blade. Add the miso, lemon juice, and bean stock, and blend briefly. Add the beans and blend until the mixture is smooth. If it seems too thick, blend in a tablespoon or two more bean stock. Add ¼ of the pepper and blend. Taste and blend in more of the pepper to taste. Blend in the cilantro.

NOTES

- You may substitute another variety of hot pepper for the poblano. Follow the roasting procedure or mince the pepper (after removing the seeds and membrane) and add part or all of it to the sauté. Peppers (even those of the same variety) vary considerably in hotness, and I prefer to control the hotness of the spread by the roast-and-add-it-gradually method above.

MUSHROOM PÂTÉ
▼▼▼

Serve this delectable spread as an appetizer or as part of a light meal. I especially relish it with rye or pumpernickel breads.

YIELD: 6 or more servings

PREPARATION TIME: 30 minutes to prepare; 1½ hours to bake

   1 teaspoon kuzu powder
1½ tablespoons Marsala
   2 tablespoons unsalted soy margarine, butter, or vegetable oil
   1 small onion, chopped
  ¼ cup chopped celery
   8 ounces mushrooms, sliced
  ⅛ teaspoon each dried basil, oregano, and rosemary
    Freshly ground black pepper—several grindings
  ½ teaspoon kelp powder
  ¼ cup chopped fresh parsley
   8 ounces tofu
   1 tablespoon mellow rice or mellow barley miso
   1 tablespoon lemon juice, or more to taste
  ½ cup lightly toasted walnuts
  ½ cup bread crumbs

Combine the kuzu and Marsala and set aside until the kuzu has thoroughly dissolved.

Heat the margarine in a medium-sized skillet over moderate heat; add the onion and sauté until it becomes translucent. Stir in the celery, mushrooms, dried herbs, pepper, and kelp powder and continue to sauté until the celery is just tender. Stir in the parsley and remove from the heat.

In a blender or a food processor fitted with the metal blade, blend the tofu until it is smooth. Add the miso and lemon juice and blend well. Add the walnuts,

bread crumbs, dissolved kuzu, and the sauté. Blend thoroughly. Taste and adjust seasonings.

Grease an 8 × 4-inch loaf pan. Line it with waxed paper and grease the paper. Pour the mixture into the pan and spread it evenly. Bake in a preheated 325-degree oven for 1½ hours. Remove from the oven and allow to cool on a rack for 30 minutes or so. Carefully invert the pâté onto a plate, and gently peel off the paper.

Serve warm or chilled.

NOTES

- If available, substitute ¼ to ½ teaspoon minced fresh herbs for each of the dried ones.

- For a zestier version, substitute a large pinch of cayenne for the black pepper.

LENTIL PÂTÉ
▼▼▼

This rich-tasting pâté is good warm or chilled, spread on thin slices of bread or toast. Serve it as an appetizer or with a SALADE COMPOSÉE (page 214-15) for a light but luxurious meal.

YIELD: A lot!—a full 8-inch springform pan

PREPARATION TIME: 30 minutes to prepare; 1 hour to bake

   1 tablespoon olive oil
   1 medium-sized onion, finely chopped
   2 cloves garlic, pressed or minced
   1 medium-sized bell pepper, finely chopped
    Freshly ground black pepper—several grindings
   1 teaspoon ground cumin
    Pinch of cinnamon
  ½ teaspoon minced fresh thyme leaves
   1 tablespoon minced fresh basil leaves
   1 teaspoon minced fresh oregano leaves
   4 ounces tofu, mashed
   3 cups cooked green lentils (see page 238)
   2 tablespoons lemon juice
   2 tablespoons mellow barley miso
  ½ cup fresh parsley, finely chopped
  ½ cup toasted fine bread crumbs
  ¼ cup lightly toasted pine nuts

In a medium-sized skillet over moderate heat, heat the oil; sauté the onion until it appears translucent. Stir in the garlic and bell pepper and continue to sauté until the pepper is just tender. Add the black pepper, cumin, cinnamon, thyme, basil, and oregano and sauté briefly. Stir in the tofu and remove the skillet from the heat.

Put the lentils and sauté into a food processor fitted

with the metal blade. Mix together the lemon juice and miso to form a smooth paste and add it to the processor; blend until thoroughly combined. Add the parsley, bread crumbs, and pine nuts and blend briefly.

Grease the bottom and sides of an 8-inch springform pan. Trace around the bottom of the pan on a double thickness of waxed paper. Cut out the two circles and grease one side of each; fit one paper circle, greased side up, in the bottom of the pan; spread the thick mixture evenly in the pan; place the second circle of paper, greased side down, on top, and cover the pan with an ovenproof plate.

Bake in a preheated 375-degree oven for 1 hour. Remove the plate and place the pan on a cooling rack for at least 30 minutes.

Peel off the waxed paper on the top, invert the pâté onto a plate, and peel off the bottom piece of waxed paper.

Serve warm or chilled. This will keep in the refrigerator for several days.

NOTES
- Substitute half as much dried herbs for the fresh ones; crush them just before cooking.

NEAPOLITAN PÂTÉ
▾▾▾

When I was a child, we sometimes had Neapolitan ice cream for special occasions. It was in brick form with three different colored layers and flavors and was sliced vertically so that every serving had some of each. This tripledecker, tricolor spread looks something like that special ice cream, but it is composed of individually seasoned carrot, spinach, and cauliflower layers. Though a bit of a production to assemble, it is a triumph in flavor and appearance. Serve it for lunch or as an appetizer, at room temperature or chilled, with thin slices of bread or toast—I especially like it with natural-rise breads.

YIELD: 4 generous meal-sized portions or more smaller servings

PREPARATION TIME: An hour or so to prepare; 45 minutes to bake

- 1½ *teaspoons kuzu powder*
- 1½ *teaspoons dry vermouth*
- 12 *ounces tofu*
- 1 *teaspoon or more sea salt*
- 3 *tablespoons lemon juice*
- 3 *tablespoons sunflower oil or other vegetable oil*
- 2 *tablespoons tahini*
- 2 *tablespoons sesame oil*
- 1 *large onion, finely chopped*
- 3 *large cloves garlic, pressed or minced*

- *Freshly ground black pepper—several grindings*
- ¾ *teaspoon kelp powder*
- 6 *ounces (1½ cups) carrot, thinly sliced*
- ½ *teaspoon ground dried tarragon (or pericon), or 1 teaspoon minced fresh*
- ⅔ *cup water*
- 8 *ounces (8 cups, loosely packed) fresh spinach leaves, finely chopped*
- ¼ *teaspoon freshly grated nutmeg*
- 6 *ounces (1½ cups) cauliflower, thinly sliced*
- ½ *teaspoon ground dried dill weed, or 1 teaspoon minced fresh*

Combine the kuzu and vermouth; set aside for several minutes, until the kuzu is thoroughly dissolved.

Grease the bottom and sides of a 1-quart soufflé dish. Fit a circle of waxed paper into the bottom and a strip around the inside and grease them.

In a food processor fitted with the metal blade or a blender, blend the tofu. While the machine is running, add ¾ teaspoon salt, the lemon juice, sunflower oil, and tahini. Blend until the mixture is thoroughly smooth. Blend in the dissolved kuzu. Transfer the mixture to a 2-cup measure; set the unwashed processor aside.

Heat 1 tablespoon sesame oil in a medium-sized skillet over moderate heat. Sauté the onion and garlic until the onion is just tender; grind in the pepper, stir in the kelp powder, and continue to cook, stirring, for a minute or two. Remove two-thirds of the sauté to a bowl.

Add 1 teaspoon sesame oil, the carrot, and the tarragon to the onions in the skillet. Sauté briefly over moderate heat. Add ¼ cup water, tightly cover the pan, and reduce the heat to low. Steam for several minutes, until the carrot is tender. Transfer the sauté to the processor and blend. Add one-third of the tofu mixture (½ to ¾ cup) and blend well. Add a bit of salt, to taste. Evenly spread the carrot purée in the bottom of the prepared dish.

Add half the remaining sautéed onions, 1 teaspoon sesame oil, and the spinach and nutmeg to the skillet. Sauté briefly over moderate heat. Add 2 tablespoons water, cover, reduce the heat, and steam briefly, until the spinach is tender but still bright green. Transfer to the processor (well scraped of the carrot purée) and blend. Add another third of the tofu mixture and blend well. Season with salt to taste. Carefully spread the spinach purée evenly over the carrot layer.

Add the cauliflower, 1 teaspoon sesame oil, remaining onions, and the dill to the skillet and sauté briefly. Add ¼ cup water, cover, and steam until the cauliflower is tender. Blend in the processor. Add the remaining tofu mixture and blend well. Add salt to taste. Spread on top of the spinach layer.

Bake in a preheated 300-degree oven 45 to 50 minutes, until a knife inserted in the center comes out clean. Cool the pâté thoroughly in the dish before inverting it onto a plate and peeling off the waxed paper.

TOFU MAYONNAISE
❦❦❦

This mayonnaise is lighter and less caloric than conventional ones, but you can use it in the same ways—as a sandwich spread or as an ingredient in other spreads, as a dressing for potato and egg salads, and so on. It also makes an ideal dip for artichokes. It is eggless, so it is virtually cholesterol-free.

YIELD: About ½ cup

PREPARATION TIME: 10 minutes

> 4 ounces tofu
> 1 tablespoon lemon juice
> 1 tablespoon cider vinegar
> 1 tablespoon olive oil
> 1 tablespoon light vegetable oil (safflower, sunflower, canola, etc.)
> Freshly ground black pepper—several grindings
> ¼ teaspoon ground mustard
> ¼ teaspoon sea salt

Combine all the ingredients in a blender or in a food processor fitted with the metal blade and blend until thoroughly smooth.

This will keep for several days in a covered container in the refrigerator.

NOTES

- For a slightly different texture and flavor, substitute tahini for the olive oil.

- Blend in a small amount of a crushed dried or a minced fresh herb, such as dill, tarragon, or basil. Fresh parsley is another good addition.

SOYSAGE
❦❦❦

This spicy vegetarian loaf is good warm or cold. Slice it up and serve it in sandwiches with your favorite condiments and lettuce, tomato, and sprouts. It is also delicious when lightly pan-fried, and, sautéed with vegetables, it makes a savory filling for CORNISH PASTIES (page 175) or for SICILIAN PIZZA ROLL (page 181-82). This is a good way to use up okara, the nutritious soybean pulp that is leftover from making soy milk and tofu.

YIELD: 1 loaf

PREPARATION TIME: 15 minutes to mix; 1½ hours to steam

> 2 cups fresh okara
> 1 cup whole wheat bread flour
> ¼ cup nutritional yeast flakes
> ½ cup sesame oil
> ½ cup water or vegetable stock
> 1 teaspoon sea salt
> 2 teaspoons dry mustard
> ¼ teaspoon cayenne
> 4 cloves garlic, pressed or minced
> 1 small onion, finely chopped
> 2 tablespoons tamari
> 1 teaspoon fennel seed
> ½ cup uncooked cracked wheat

Thoroughly mix together all of the ingredients—a food processor fitted with a metal blade works well, but, to retain some texture, first blend together everything but the fennel seed and cracked wheat and add these two items last, mixing just enough to distribute them evenly.

Grease a heatproof container that is large enough to accommodate some expansion—I use a small, deep stainless steel bowl. Pour in the mixture and spread it evenly. Cover with greased waxed paper and then with a lid or plate.

Place the container in a steamer or on a rack over boiling water in a deep pot. Cover and steam for 1½ hours.

Turn the loaf out onto a wire rack and cool thoroughly before slicing.

PRESTO—PESTO!
❦❦❦

Pesto has become almost as basic as tomato sauce these days. It is an easy way to an elegant meal in almost minutes. It might coat pasta one evening and top PESTO PIZZA (page 166-67) the following day. It is a crowning touch to beans, new potatoes, and summer squash that have been tossed with a bit of olive oil and seasoned with freshly ground black pepper. Try it on baked potatoes or use it as a sandwich spread or a sauce for stuffed pita (see POCO PESTO POCKETS, page 155-56). The pleasantly piquant aroma of fresh basil is synonymous with summer for me, and that's when I crave this sauce and make it often. You can also freeze it for use throughout the year, though I think it's at its best as soon as it is made. There are many varieties of basil; experiment with lemon, anise, Thai, cinnamon, and others as well as standard Italian basils in your pesto. This is a nondairy version of pesto, but few would guess it; dark barley miso provides the rich saltiness of aged hard cheese. Use a salad spinner to most effectively dry the basil and parsley.

YIELD: About 1½ cups—enough for 4 generous servings of pasta

PREPARATION TIME: 20 minutes

> 7½ to 8 cups loosely packed fresh basil leaves (7½ ounces)
> 1 cup loosely packed fresh parsley
> 1 tablespoon lemon juice
> 3 cloves garlic
> 5 teaspoons dark barley miso
> ½ cup olive oil
> ⅔ cup lightly toasted pine nuts or walnuts
> 2 to 4 tablespoons vegetable stock or pasta cooking water

In a food processor fitted with the metal blade or in a blender, combine the basil, parsley, lemon juice, garlic, miso, and oil and blend thoroughly. Add the nuts and blend again. Blend in the stock, a tablespoon at a time, until the sauce reaches a desirable consistency. Taste and add more miso if necessary.

NOTES

- Flat Italian parsley is especially good in this sauce.

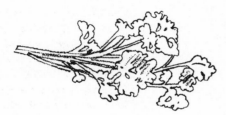

TOFU PESTO
▰▰▰

A choice of pestos is the spice of life for basil lovers. This nouvelle formula is smooth and light, nondairy, and high in protein too. Use it as you would PRESTO—PESTO! *(page 141-42). Again, use a salad spinner to most effectively dry the basil and parsley.*

YIELD: Enough for 2 servings of pasta or 1 pizza

PREPARATION TIME: 20 minutes

> 1 small tomato, chopped
> 1 large clove garlic, chopped
> 2½ to 3 cups loosely packed fresh basil leaves
> ½ cup loosely packed fresh parsley
>   Freshly ground black pepper—several grindings
> 4 ounces tofu
> 2 tablespoons lemon juice
> 3 tablespoons olive oil
> ⅓ cup lightly toasted pine nuts or walnuts
> ½ teaspoon sea salt, or to taste

In a food processor fitted with the metal blade or in a blender, thoroughly blend the tomato and garlic. With the processor or blender running, gradually add the basil and parsley. Add the pepper, tofu, lemon juice, and oil and blend until the mixture is smooth. Add the nuts and blend well. Add sea salt to taste.

NOTES

- Substitute miso, to taste, for the salt.

WATERCRESS PESTO
▰▰▰

In Tennessee, I had a friend who would bring me a large bucket of beautiful fresh watercress every time he came to visit in the spring. This splendid variation on basil pesto resulted from those gifts. Substitute it at will for PRESTO—PESTO! *(page 141-42) or* TOFU PESTO *(page 142). Different misos subtly change the flavor of the sauce; try light and dark ones and decide which you like the best.*

YIELD: About 1½ cups—enough for 1 pound of pasta or 2 pizzas

PREPARATION TIME: 15 minutes

> 8 cups loosely packed watercress, leaves and fine stems (8 ounces)
> 1 cup loosely packed fresh parsley
> 1 tablespoon lemon juice
> 2 large cloves garlic
> ¼ cup olive oil
> ½ cup lightly toasted walnuts or almonds
> 1 tablespoon dark or light miso, or to taste

In a food processor fitted with the metal blade or in a blender, combine the watercress, parsley, lemon juice, garlic, olive oil, and nuts. Blend until the mixture is smooth. Blend in miso to taste. If the sauce is too thick, blend in several tablespoons of vegetable stock or pasta cooking water.

NOTES

- Substitute about ¼ cup (½ ounce) minced fresh dill weed for the parsley.

TEX-MEX PESTO
▰▰▰

This is a regional variation on the ever popular pesto sauce. It is made more like traditional pesto—chopped rather than blended. I serve this sauce on pasta, on pizzas, or in sandwiches. For a special pasta dish, arrange whole wheat spaghettini on a bed of finely chopped mild greens, top with this sauce, and garnish with lightly steamed sweet green peas or sugar snap peas and diced avocado that you have tossed with lime juice.

YIELD: About ¾ cup—enough for 2 servings of pasta or 1 pizza

PREPARATION TIME: 25 minutes

    1 teaspoon finely minced garlic
    1 tablespoon lime juice
    2 tablespoons olive oil
    1/8 teaspoon sea salt, or to taste
    2 cups loosely packed fresh cilantro leaves, finely chopped
    1/4 cup finely minced green onion
    1/2 cup lightly toasted pecans, finely chopped

Combine all of the ingredients in a bowl. Mix well with a long-tined fork.

EMILIO'S SALSA VERDE
▀▄▀▄

This isn't Emilio's recipe, but he gave me the idea of combining green tomatoes and tomatillos in salsa verde. Serve it as a dip or sauce. Refrigerated, this will keep for several days.

YIELD: About 2 cups

PREPARATION TIME: About 30 minutes

    2 small poblano peppers
    1 tablespoon olive oil
    1 small onion, minced
    1 clove garlic, pressed or minced
    1/2 pound green tomatoes, chopped
    1/2 pound tomatillos, chopped
    1/4 teaspoon sea salt
    1/4 cup fresh cilantro leaves

Roast and peel the peppers as described on page 130. Set aside.

    Heat the oil in a medium-sized skillet over moderate heat. Sauté the onion and garlic for several minutes, until the onion appears translucent and is almost tender. Stir in the tomatoes and tomatillos and continue to cook, stirring occasionally, for several minutes, until they are just tender. Stir in the salt.

    Put the sauté in a food processor fitted with the metal blade or in a blender. Add the cilantro and 1 of the roasted peppers. Pulse the mixture briefly, so that it maintains a chunky texture. Taste the salsa for hotness and if it is not hot enough add part or all of the remaining pepper, to taste; pulse again briefly.

AVOCADO SALSA CRUDA
▀▄▀▄

This uncooked sauce is a perky mixture of flavors and textures. It is rather fragile, so serve it as soon as possible. Scoop it up with any kind of tortillas (pages 114-17), or

try it with MEXICAN BEAN BURGERS *(page 154),* BEAN BURRITOS *(page 162-63), or* TOWERING TOSTADAS *(page 160-61).*

YIELD: 2 to 3 cups

PREPARATION TIME: About 15 minutes

    2 teaspoons minced green onions or shallots
    1 small chili pepper (seeds and membranes removed), minced
    1 large ripe avocado, peeled and cut into small cubes
    2 tablespoons lime juice
    1 large tomato, cut into small cubes
    1/4 teaspoon kelp powder
    1/4 cup coarsely chopped fresh cilantro leaves

Stir the ingredients together and serve immediately.

PICO DE GALLO
▀▄▀▄

A pico de gallo—literally translated "rooster's beak"—is a Mexican salad or relish of raw vegetables or fruits chopped to a chunky consistency, probably named for the traditional way of eating it by picking up pieces with the fingers as a rooster pecks kernels of grain. This one, redolent of fresh cilantro, is the customary sauce for FAJITAS *(page 163), but it is a suitable condiment for other Mexican-style dishes as well. It is best when freshly made.*

YIELD: 2 to 2½ cups

PREPARATION TIME: 25 minutes

    1 clove garlic, finely minced
    1 medium-sized mild onion, finely chopped
    1 medium-sized tomato, finely chopped
    1/2 to 1 small serrano pepper, finely minced
    1 generous cup loosely packed fresh cilantro leaves, finely chopped
    1/4 to 1/2 teaspoon sea salt, to taste

Combine all of the ingredients in a medium-sized bowl, adjusting the amount of hot pepper and salt to taste.

    Serve immediately.

ROASTED RED PEPPER SAUCE
▀▄▀▄

This is a delightful, vibrant reddish-orange topping for pasta or pizza or a spread for sandwiches. Any sweet red pepper will work, but especially look for dark red, thick-skinned, fleshy pimientos in your market at the end of summer; these are the sweetest. These peppers have long been familiar as the stuffings for green olives; now they're becoming increasingly available fresh. Pericon is a Texas substitute for tarragon, since it can tolerate the heat; the flavors of the two herbs are similar, though pericon tends to be somewhat stronger.

YIELD: Enough for 2 servings of pasta, a large pizza, or 2 to 4 sandwiches

PREPARATION TIME: 40 minutes

> 8 medium-sized red peppers
> 1 tablespoon olive oil
> 1 teaspoon lemon juice
> ¼ teaspoon kelp powder
> ¼ teaspoon sea salt
> 1 tablespoon minced fresh basil leaves
> 1 tablespoon minced fresh tarragon leaves (or pericon), to taste

Roast and peel the peppers as described on page 130. Place them in a blender or in a food processor fitted with the metal blade; add the remaining ingredients and blend the mixture to a coarse purée.

Serve immediately. This will keep for several days in the refrigerator and can also be frozen.

ITALIAN GREEN SAUCE
⬩⬩⬩

Outstanding in color and flavor, this bright green sauce makes an excellent topping for pasta and pizza (page 165-66) and can also serve as a sandwich spread or a dip. This is at its best and brightest when freshly made. Cover any that is left over tightly, refrigerate, and use it up within a couple of days.

YIELD: 1 to 1½ cups

PREPARATION TIME: 25 minutes

> 1 tablespoon olive oil
> 1 small onion, finely chopped
> 1 large clove garlic, pressed or minced
> Freshly ground black pepper—several grindings
> ¼ teaspoon freshly grated nutmeg
> ¾ teaspoon dried basil or ¼ cup fresh basil leaves, minced

> ½ teaspoon dried tarragon or 1 tablespoon fresh tarragon leaves, minced
> ¼ teaspoon kelp powder
> 4 to 5 cups loosely packed fresh spinach leaves (4 to 5 ounces)
> ½ cup loosely packed fresh parsley
> 4 ounces tofu
> 1 tablespoon lemon juice
> 1 tablespoon light vegetable oil
> 1 tablespoon mellow rice miso

Heat the olive oil in a small skillet over moderate heat and sauté the onion and garlic until the onion is tender. Add the pepper, nutmeg, basil, and tarragon and continue to sauté for a few more minutes. Stir in the kelp powder and remove from the heat.

In a food processor fitted with the metal blade or in a blender, combine the sauté, spinach, parsley, tofu, lemon juice, vegetable oil, and miso; blend until the mixture is smooth. If the sauce is too thick, blend in vegetable stock, a tablespoon at a time.

HEARTY TOMATO SAUCE
⬩⬩⬩

This is a basic sauce with a multitude of uses. I usually make extra and freeze some. For pizza, I like to cook it down to a rather thick consistency. Miso contributes to its rich flavor and digestibility; don't boil the sauce after you've added the miso.

YIELD: About 2 quarts

PREPARATION TIME: 45 minutes to assemble; several hours to cook

> 2 quarts fresh tomatoes (about 4 pounds) or home-canned tomatoes
> 2 tablespoons olive oil
> 1 large onion, finely chopped
> 3 to 6 cloves garlic, pressed or minced
> 1 medium-sized carrot, finely chopped
> 1 medium-sized parsnip, finely chopped
> 1 medium-sized turnip, finely chopped
> 1 large bell pepper, finely chopped
> ½ pound mushrooms, sliced
> Freshly ground black pepper—several grindings
> 2 teaspoons dried basil
> ¾ teaspoon dried oregano
> ¼ teaspoon dried thyme
> 1 teaspoon kelp powder
> ¼ cup dry red wine
> 2 tablespoons finely chopped fresh parsley
> 2 tablespoons hatcho miso

Peel fresh tomatoes as described on page 130. Set them aside.

In a large (5- to 6-quart), heavy-bottomed pot, heat the oil; add the onion, garlic, carrot, parsnip, and turnip and sauté until the onion appears translucent. Add the bell pepper, mushrooms, black pepper, and crushed herbs and continue to sauté for several minutes. Stir in the kelp powder, tomatoes, and wine. Cover the pot and bring the sauce just to a simmer. Partially uncover the pot and allow the sauce to cook at a low simmer, stirring occasionally, until it reaches a desirable consistency. Tomato sauce burns easily, so it's a good idea to place the pot on a flame tamer.

Stir in the parsley. Whisk the miso with several tablespoons of the thickened sauce to form a smooth paste. Thoroughly stir it into the tomato sauce.

NOTES
- Substitute fresh herbs for the dried ones, using at least twice as much of the fresh.

- Substitute 4 1-pound cans of commercially canned tomatoes for the fresh or home-canned ones.

EXPEDITIOUS TOMATO SAUCE
▼▼▼

Keep this quickly prepared tomato sauce on hand for impromptu pizzas. Refrigerated, it will keep well for several days; for longer storage, freeze it.

YIELD: 1 cup—enough for 2 pizzas

PREPARATION TIME: 35 minutes

> 1 tablespoon olive oil
> 1 medium-sized onion, finely chopped
> 1 large clove garlic, pressed or minced
>   Freshly ground black pepper—several grindings
> ½ teaspoon dried basil, or 1 teaspoon minced fresh basil leaves
> ½ teaspoon dried oregano, or 1 teaspoon minced fresh oregano leaves
> 1½ cups chopped fresh tomatoes
> 1 teaspoon hatcho miso
> 1 teaspoon water, vegetable stock, or dry red wine

Heat the olive oil in a medium-sized skillet over moderate heat. Sauté the onion for several minutes, until it appears translucent. Stir in the garlic and continue to sauté until the onion is just tender. Add the pepper and herbs and cook briefly, stirring often. Stir in the tomatoes, cover the pan, and reduce the heat to low; simmer until the tomatoes have juiced and the skins are soft. Remove from the heat.

In a blender or in a food processor fitted with the metal blade, blend the mixture to a coarse purée. Return the purée to the skillet and cook over low heat for several minutes, until it is thick. Whisk together the miso and liquid; stir it into the sauce.

LISA'S TOMATO KETCHUP
▼▼▼

Use some of the summer's tomato bounty to prepare this thick, smooth, spicy condiment; you'll never be satisfied with the commercial stuff again.

YIELD: About 3 pints

PREPARATION TIME: 2 to 3 hours

> 6 pounds (about 24 large) tomatoes
> 1 cup chopped onion
> ½ cup chopped bell pepper, preferably red
> 1½ teaspoons celery seed
> 1 teaspoon mustard seed
> 1 teaspoon whole allspice
> 1 stick cinnamon
> 1 tablespoon sea salt
> 1½ cups apple cider vinegar
> 1 tablespoon paprika
>   Honey

Peel the tomatoes as described on page 130, then chop them. Combine with the onion and pepper in a large pot and cook until soft. Put the mixture through a food mill and return it to the pot. Simmer about an hour, until the volume is reduced by about one-half.

Put the celery seed, mustard seed, allspice, and cinnamon into a cheesecloth bag and add it and the salt to the tomato mixture; cook gently about 25 minutes, stirring frequently. Stir in the vinegar and paprika and cook until thick. Add honey to taste near the end of cooking.

Remove the cheesecloth bag. Pour the boiling hot mixture into sterilized canning jars, leaving about ⅛ inch of head space; screw on sterilized lids and process in a boiling water bath for 10 minutes. If you do not process the ketchup, refrigerate it after it has cooled; it will keep two to three weeks.

BLENDER HOT SAUCE
▼▼▼

This is a simply prepared, cooked, spicy tomato salsa with many uses. Use it for MEXICAN PIZZA (page 167), EMPANADAS DE PICADILLO (page 178), BEAN BURRITOS (page 162-63), or TOFU ENCHILADAS (page 161-62). Serve it as a topping on TOWERING TOSTADAS (page 160-61) or MEXICAN BEAN BURGERS (page 154) or simply as a dip for soft or crisp tortillas (page 114-17). This sauce will keep for a couple of weeks in the refrigerator; it also freezes well.

YIELD: About 2 cups

PREPARATION TIME: 15 minutes to combine; about 1 hour to cook

    1 large onion, cut into chunks
    4 large cloves garlic
    1 jalapeño (approximately 1½ inches long) or
      other hot pepper, seeds and membranes removed
    ½ teaspoon kelp powder
    6 or 7 peeled, medium-sized ripe tomatoes or 1
      1-pound can
    1½ teaspoons hatcho miso

Put the onion, garlic, pepper, and kelp powder into a blender; add half the fresh tomatoes—or half of the canned tomatoes plus the juice. Blend well, until everything is thoroughly pulverized. Pour the mixture into a saucepan. Briefly pulse the remaining tomatoes and add this coarse purée to the saucepan.

Over medium heat, bring the sauce to a simmer. Turn the heat to low and cook, stirring occasionally, until the sauce reduces and thickens—about 1 hour. Cook the sauce on a flame tamer to prevent it from burning.

Mix the miso with a small amount of the hot, thickened sauce. Stir it back into the sauce.

NOTES
- For a spicier sauce, add ¾ teaspoon ground cumin and ¼ teaspoon ground coriander to the first blended mixture.

MOLE SAUCE
▼▼▼

In the Central American Indian language, a stew or its sauce is a "molli," meaning concoction. The Spaniards altered the word to mole, *perhaps an association with the Spanish verb* moler—to grind. *Moles are rich, smooth, subtly seasoned Mexican sauces which typically include ground chilies, herbs, spices, nuts or seeds, tomatoes, and a touch of chocolate. They are usually served with poultry or meats in stewlike preparations, often for festive occasions. This nontraditional version substitutes carob for chocolate. I like it as a sauce for tempeh-filled enchiladas (see box). I often make extra sauce and freeze it, so making another meal of enchiladas is quick and easy. This sauce is also good on pasta and as a topping for an unusual pita sandwich—stuffed with chopped greens, finely sliced onions, tempeh strips, and sliced jicama and avocado sprinkled with lime juice. Mexican oregano refers to a piquant variety of this many-spiced herb which thrives in Mexico and the southwestern United States; substitute another oregano if you can't find it.*

YIELD: About 1⅓ cups

PREPARATION TIME: 45 minutes

    1 3-inch poblano pepper
    2 medium-sized ripe tomatoes
    1 large clove garlic, peeled
    ⅛ teaspoon ground cinnamon
    ⅛ teaspoon ground cloves
    ¼ teaspoon minced fresh Mexican oregano
    ¾ cup vegetable stock or water
    1 tablespoon lightly roasted almonds
    1½ teaspoons roasted carob powder
    1 tablespoon hot water
    ½ teaspoon sea salt, or to taste

Roast and peel the pepper as described on page 130. Set it aside.

In a small ovenproof pan (with sides—to catch the juice) broil the tomatoes and garlic for 20 to 30 minutes, turning them occasionally so they become evenly charred. (I do this in the enamel tray of my toaster oven.) The garlic will be tender and the tomatoes will be very soft and juicy and somewhat blackened.

In a blender or a food processor fitted with the metal blade, combine the prepared pepper and garlic, cinnamon, cloves, and oregano; blend, gradually adding ½ cup of the stock or water, until the mixture is thoroughly smooth. Pour it into a medium-sized skillet and cook over moderate heat, stirring often, for several minutes.

Meanwhile, put the tomatoes and their juice and the almonds in the blender or processor; blend until thoroughly smooth. Add this to the mixture in the skillet and stir.

ENCHILADAS DE MOLE
···

In these enchiladas, the corn tortillas are coated with subtly spiced mole sauce and rolled around juicy tempeh strips and thinly sliced sweet onions.

> 1 to 2 tablespoons sesame or olive oil
> 1 8-ounce cake tempeh
> ½ cup vegetable stock or water
> 1 teaspoon tamari
> 6 CORN TORTILLAS (page 115)
> 1⅓ cups MOLE SAUCE
> 1 medium-sized sweet onion, thinly sliced

Heat 1 tablespoon of the oil in a medium-sized skillet over moderate heat. Add the tempeh and brown on both sides, adding more oil as needed. Pour in the stock, cover tightly, and cook until the skillet is almost dry. Add the tamari, turn the tempeh to coat it, and cook away the remaining liquid. Cut the tempeh into thin strips.

If the tortillas are not freshly made and still warm and pliable, wrap them in a tea towel, steam briefly, and then leave them in the covered steamer off the heat for several minutes. Or wrap and heat them in a moderate oven for several minutes.

Spread a thin layer of the sauce on the tortillas, lay tempeh strips and onion slices down the middle, and roll them up. Arrange on plates, top with the remaining sauce, and serve immediately.

In a small bowl, whisk the carob and 1 tablespoon hot water until the carob is thoroughly dissolved. Stir this, the remaining stock or water, and the salt into the pepper-tomato mixture. Cook over very low heat, stirring occasionally, about 20 minutes, until the sauce has thickened somewhat and the flavors have mingled. The sauce should be rather thin; if it is too thick, add a little water or vegetable stock, taste, and add a pinch of salt if necessary.

NOTES

- Poblanos vary in hotness: if yours is relatively mild or if you prefer a hotter sauce, add an additional pepper or two, prepared in the same manner.

- Fresh Anaheim peppers are a reasonable substitute for poblanos. Or use anchos, which are dried red poblanos; stirring often, toast them in a hot pan, remove the seeds and membranes, soak them in hot water to cover for 15 to 20 minutes, and drain before blending.

SPICY PEANUT SAUCE
···

This zesty, rich sauce has myriad applications. Use it as a dip for raw vegetables, a dressing for cooked vegetables and grains, or a topping for INDONESIAN PIZZA *(page 167) or a pita sandwich. Covered tightly and refrigerated, this sauce will keep well for several days; freeze it for longer storage.*

YIELD: About 3 cups

PREPARATION TIME: 30 to 40 minutes

> 2 tablespoons sesame or peanut oil
> 1 large sweet onion, finely chopped
> 2 cloves garlic, pressed or minced
> 1 teaspoon minced ginger root
>   Pinch of cayenne
> 1 cup unsalted peanut butter
> 2 tablespoons lemon juice
> 2 tablespoons tamari
> 3 cups vegetable stock, soy milk, or water
> ½ teaspoon sea salt, or to taste

Heat the oil in a heavy-bottomed saucepan. Sauté the onion until it is browned. Add the garlic, ginger, and cayenne, and continue to cook, stirring frequently. Remove from heat and add the peanut butter, lemon juice, and tamari. Stir in 1 cup of the liquid. Place the pan over low heat and add the remaining liquid. Cook, stirring often, until the sauce is well thickened, about 30 minutes. Season to taste with salt.

NOTES

- Add more cayenne for a hotter sauce.

- Substitute all or part of a minced fresh chili pepper for the cayenne.

- Substitute tahini for up to half of the peanut butter.

- Substitute a mellow miso for the salt: make a paste with the miso and a few tablespoons of sauce, then stir the mixture into the cooked sauce.

SESAME SAUCE
·▾·

This smooth, light sauce has a touch of tartness. It's a perfect topping for NOUVELLE FALAFEL (page 156) and other vegetable-stuffed pitas.

YIELD: ½ cup

PREPARATION TIME: 15 minutes

   1 *tablespoon lemon juice*
  1½ *teaspoons hatcho miso*
   ½ *teaspoon umeboshi plum paste*
   1 *teaspoon roasted sesame oil*
   2 *tablespoons tahini*
 ¼ to ½ *cup chickpea stock*

In a small bowl, whisk together the lemon juice, miso, and umeboshi paste until smooth. Thoroughly whisk in the oil and tahini. Gradually whisk in the stock until the mixture reaches the consistency you desire.

NOTES
- Substitute vegetable stock, another bean stock, or water for the chickpea stock.

MELLOW MUSTARD SAUCE
·▾·

This sauce is a natural with tempeh, sauerkraut, kasha, and rye bread. Use it to make REUBEN'S PIZZA (page 168-69) or REUBEN'S POCKETS (page 155).

YIELD: About 1¼ cups

PREPARATION TIME: 15 minutes

  2 *teaspoons kuzu powder*
  2 *teaspoons cold vegetable stock or water*
  2 *tablespoons mustard*
 1½ *teaspoons lemon juice*
  1 *tablespoon mellow barley miso*
 ¾ *cup vegetable stock or water*
  2 *tablespoons sauerkraut juice*

Combine the kuzu and 2 teaspoons cold liquid; set aside for a few minutes, until the kuzu is thoroughly dissolved. Whisk in the remaining ingredients. Transfer to a small saucepan and cook over low heat, stirring often, just until the mixture thickens.

GINGER AIOLI
·▾·

I have to credit Café Sport, a wonderful restaurant in Seattle, for the inspiration for this recipe. This sauce is excellent on fish or cooked vegetables, and it can also be used as a dip or a sandwich spread. For best results, have

the ingredients at room temperature. This will keep for up to a week in the refrigerator; the taste may actually improve as the flavors meld.

YIELD: About ⅔ cup

PREPARATION TIME: 15 minutes

  1 *clove garlic, pressed or minced*
  2 *teaspoons finely grated fresh ginger root*
  1 *small egg*
 ½ *cup sesame oil*
 ¼ *teaspoon sea salt*
  2 *teaspoons lemon juice*

In a blender or in a food processor fitted with the metal blade, blend the garlic, ginger, and egg. While the machine is running, *very* slowly dribble in the oil—the mixture should emulsify. Blend in half the salt and half the lemon juice. Taste and adjust the seasonings.

NOTES
- If the mixture does not emulsify, pour it into a bowl. Blend another egg, and with the machine running gradually add the sauce to the egg.

- You may substitute another vegetable oil for part or all of the sesame oil.

TOFU SOUR CREAM
·▾·

This sauce is a very convincing imposter, and it is much lower in fat and cholesterol than the real thing. It tends to thicken somewhat upon standing.

YIELD: About 1 cup

PREPARATION TIME: 15 minutes

  8 *ounces tofu*
 ½ *teaspoon sea salt*
  2 *tablespoons lemon juice*
  2 *tablespoons mild-flavored vegetable oil*
  4 *teaspoons tahini*

In a food processor bowl fitted with a metal blade or in a blender, blend the tofu thoroughly. Add the remaining ingredients and blend until the mixture is thoroughly smooth. Blend in a little water if it is too thick.

HOLLANDAISE À L'ARBERTI
·▾·

Hollandaise sauce is a traditional topping for steamed vegetables such as broccoli and asparagus, and for poached eggs and fish. It's good on sandwiches, too—serve it over open-faced arrangements or vegetable-stuffed pitas. This adaptation, named for the friend who developed it, uses whole eggs rather than egg yolks and less fat than the classic sauce, but is still plenty rich-tasting. It is also practically foolproof to make—just be sure to use gentle heat, whisk constantly, and remove the sauce from the heat as soon as it thickens. This is best served fresh, though you can hold it for several hours in the refrigerator.

YIELD: ¾ to 1 cup

PREPARATION TIME: 15 minutes

   2 *eggs*
  ¼ *cup milk or soy milk*
   2 *tablespoons lemon juice*
  ⅛ *teaspoon sea salt*
     Freshly ground black pepper, to taste

  ¼ *teaspoon minced fresh tarragon leaves, or* ⅛
     teaspoon crushed dried tarragon
   3 *tablespoons unsalted soy margarine or butter*

In the top of a small double boiler, beat together the eggs, milk, lemon juice, salt, pepper, and tarragon. Over barely boiling water, heat the mixture, whisking constantly, until it begins to thicken. Add the margarine or butter and continue to beat until the mixture has almost reached the desired consistency. Remove from the heat and immediately transfer the sauce to another container to arrest its cooking.

Serve warm, at room temperature, or chilled.

NOTES
- Substitute dill for the tarragon.

CHAPTER 10

▼▼▼▼▼▼▼▼▼▼▼■■■□□□□□■■■■▼▼▼▼▼▼▼▼▼▼▼

Sandwiches

IT IS SAID THAT the Fourth Earl of Sandwich, way back in the eighteenth century, ordered his meals served to him in a manner that would allow his perpetual attendance at the gambling table. Someone cleverly solved the problem by putting two slices of bread together with meat or cheese or something else in between. With this compact arrangement in one hand and the other one free, the Earl munched away happily and everyone breathed a great sigh of relief. At the time, no one could possibly have foretold the impact this invention would have on our eating habits; almost 200 years later, we are still imitating his efficient approach to mealtime.

A sandwich can be as plain as one piece of bread topped with a single item or simple spread or as elaborate as the extravagant structures that Dagwood Bumstead builds—and devours—in the middle of the night. Sandwiches may be open-faced, closed, or gaping pita pockets. They are usually hand-held, but they can also be knife-and-fork fare. Though they may be fancy and fussed-over, sandwiches are more often, true to their namesake's spirit, casual meals, assembled on short notice and frequently consumed on the go.

Now, given a broad repertoire of breads and a selection of toppings and fillings, we can begin to put them together. Here, I offer just a few of the countless possible combinations and permutations. Stuffed pitas have become one of the most popular types of sandwiches in recent years. Though these are technically filled flat breads, I'm including them in this chapter since most of us think of them as sandwiches and they almost invariably appear in the sandwich section of menus. I'm also including a variety of vegetarian versions of the all-American sandwich tradition, the burger. These are made with grains and beans or soybean products, making them high-protein yet low cholesterol alternatives. They can be made ahead of time and cooked just before you're ready to eat.

Sandwiches are great user-uppers of the dibs and dabs that accumulate in every kitchen. A tablespoon or two of pesto or another sauce makes a terrific sandwich spread; small amounts of cooked grains and beans, vegetables, and nuts join together to become delicious meatless burgers; the leavings in a salad bowl fill a pita. A blend of flavors created in this way almost always ends up greater than the sum of its parts.

▼▼▼

GRILLED PEANUT BUTTER AND PEAR

When I traveled in Europe for several months, I was surprised to find that I missed—actually, craved—peanut butter. One of my companions took pity on me and obtained a small jar from the PX in Istanbul. Peanut butter never tasted so good! Cut and arrange the fruit carefully and these simple open-faced sandwiches will be works of art.

YIELD: 2 open-faced sandwiches

PREPARATION TIME: 15 minutes

> 2 *tablespoons unsalted peanut butter*
> 1 *teaspoon mellow barley miso*
> 2 *slices bread*
> 1 *medium-large ripe pear*

Put the peanut butter in a small bowl and warm briefly in the oven set on warm. Thoroughly mix in miso, to taste. Lightly toast the bread. Spread the seasoned nut butter evenly on both slices. Quarter and core the pear, and peel it if the skin is thick or tough. Cut thin lengthwise wedges and arrange them over the nut butter. Broil the sandwiches several minutes, until the fruit is very tender. Serve immediately.

NOTES
- Substitute an apple or peach for the pear.

ALMOND BUTTER STRATAWICH

If I had to choose between almond butter and peanut butter, I'd be in a fix. As much as I like the old familiar flavor of peanut butter and rely on its great versatility, it would still have a tough time measuring up to sweet, crunchy almond butter. This is a truly classy spread! It's not an empty pleasure either, since almonds contain 18 percent protein and a significant amount of B vitamins, calcium, iron, potassium, and phosphorus. Almond butter is high

in fiber and contains unsaturated fats, making it low in cholesterol. Now, go out to the garden and pluck a ripe tomato, pick a cucumber, and pinch a few sprigs of dill, and you're halfway to an easygoing summertime lunch. I especially like to use thin slices of a rice or millet bread for these open-faced sandwiches.

YIELD: 2 open-faced sandwiches

PREPARATION TIME: 15 minutes

> 2 *tablespoons unsalted crunchy almond butter*
> 1 *teaspoon mellow barley miso*
> 2 *slices bread*
> *Thinly sliced cucumber and tomato*
> *Minced fresh dill weed*

Put the almond butter in a small bowl in the oven set on warm for a few minutes to soften it. Thoroughly mix in miso, to taste. Spread the almond butter on the bread. Arrange cucumber and tomato slices on top and sprinkle minced dill over all. Serve the sandwiches open-faced.

BLONDIE'S DAGWOOD

Blondie always looks so trim and seems so sensible that I can't imagine her indulging in junk food. I picture her making a sandwich such as this one if she ever joins Dagwood in a nocturnal kitchen foray. I'm partial to thinly sliced natural-rise bread for this sandwich.

YIELD: 1 sandwich

PREPARATION TIME: 15 minutes

> 2 *slices bread*
> *TAHINI-MISO SPREAD (page 132)*
> *Mustard*
> *TOFU MAYONNAISE (page 141) or GINGER AIOLI (page 148)*
> 2 *to 4 ounces tofu or five-spice tofu*
> *Thinly sliced carrot, cucumber, tomato, and turnip or radish*
> *Alfalfa sprouts*
> *Lettuce, spinach, or other dark greens*

To firm up fresh plain tofu, press it well, blanch it briefly, and drain well. (Five-spice tofu is already firm.) Thinly slice the tofu.

Spread one slice of bread with *TAHINI-MISO SPREAD* and the other slice with mustard and *TOFU*

MAYONNAISE or *GINGER AIOLI*. Arrange the tofu slices on top of the *TAHINI-MISO SPREAD*. Add layers of sliced vegetables. Top with sprouts and greens. Perch the second piece of bread on the peak.

Now try to get your mouth around this monster.

T.L.T. FOR TWO
▼▼▼

Tempeh is a traditional Indonesian soy food that is rapidly becoming popular in the United States, especially among vegetarians. Made from whole soybeans—sometimes combined with grains—tempeh is high in protein and free of cholesterol. Because tempeh is a fermented product, it is easy to digest and is rich in B vitamins, including B-12, an important nutrient for vegetarians. Like tofu, tempeh is exceedingly versatile in terms of seasoning and preparation techniques, but its texture is chewier. Tempeh is generally available as flat cakes, sold fresh or frozen in natural foods stores. Here, tempeh replaces bacon in an American institution: bacon, lettuce, and tomato sandwiches.

YIELD: 2 sandwiches

PREPARATION TIME: About 30 minutes to prepare the tempeh; 10 minutes to assemble

    ½ teaspoon fennel seed
    ½ teaspoon cumin seed
    2 cloves garlic, pressed or minced
      Freshly ground black pepper
    1 tablespoon tamari
    ½ cup water
    1 4-ounce cake tempeh, sliced into ¼-inch strips
      Olive oil or sesame oil
    4 slices bread
      TOFU MAYONNAISE (page 141) or other mayonnaise
      Thinly sliced tomato
      Lettuce

Roast the fennel and cumin in an ungreased heavy skillet over moderate heat for several minutes, agitating the pan or stirring the seeds frequently to prevent them from burning. When they are fragrant and crunchy, transfer the seeds to a mortar or grinder and pulverize them to a coarse consistency.

Combine the ground seeds, garlic, pepper, tamari, and water in medium-sized skillet or saucepan; add the tempeh strips and bring just to a boil. Cover and simmer gently about 15 minutes.

Remove the tempeh from the marinade and arrange it on a greased baking sheet. Store any remaining marinade in a tightly closed container in the refrigera-

tor and reuse it another time. Broil the tempeh about 15 minutes, turning it at least once, until it is brown and somewhat crisp.

Toast the bread, if desired, and make the sandwiches.

NOTES
- For even quicker T.L.T.s, look for commercially prepared tempeh "bacon" in the refrigerator or freezer case of natural foods stores.

TOFU BURGERS
▼▼▼

These light burgers are seasoned with herbs and finely chopped vegetables; walnuts and bread crumbs add a subtle crunch. Powdered kuzu, a tasteless, healthful substance prepared by grinding the roots of the kuzu (or kudzu) plant, helps to hold the burgers together. You can substitute egg for the dissolved kuzu if you prefer. Like TEMPEH BURGERS, *tofu burgers are relished by vegetarians and meat-eaters alike. Serve them with crisp lettuce leaves or sprouts, fresh tomato slices, and your other favorite fixings.*

YIELD: 6 burgers

PREPARATION TIME: 25 minutes to prepare; 25 minutes to cook

    1 tablespoon kuzu powder
    1 tablespoon cold vegetable stock or water
    1 tablespoon olive oil
    1 small red onion, finely chopped
    2 large cloves garlic, pressed or minced
    1 small bell pepper, finely chopped
    1 small carrot, grated
      Freshly ground black pepper—several grindings
    2 teaspoons minced fresh basil leaves
    2 tablespoons finely chopped parsley
 1½ pounds tofu, pressed well
    1 tablespoon mellow barley or mellow rice miso
    ¼ cup fine bread crumbs
    ¼ cup lightly toasted, finely chopped walnuts
      Sea salt
    6 whole grain buns

Combine the kuzu and cold liquid; set aside until the kuzu is thoroughly dissolved.

Heat the oil in a medium-sized skillet over moderate heat. Briefly sauté the onion, garlic, bell pepper, carrot, black pepper, and herbs—until the vegetables are just tender; remove from the heat.

In a medium-sized bowl, mash together the tofu and miso until they are thoroughly mashed and mixed.

Add the sauté, crumbs, walnuts, and dissolved kuzu and mix thoroughly. Add salt to taste.

Shape the mixture into 6 patties. Arrange them on an oiled baking sheet. Brush lightly with oil and broil until the tops are well browned—about 10 minutes. Carefully turn the patties over. Broil until they are firm and browned—about 10 minutes longer.

Serve immediately in the buns.

NOTES

- Add other minced fresh herbs, such as oregano, thyme, tarragon, or dill, to the burger mixture, or sauté crushed dried herbs (about half the amount of the fresh ones) along with the vegetables.

- Substitute 1 beaten egg for the dissolved kuzu.

- The burgers may be baked rather than broiled. Arrange them on an oiled baking sheet and bake in a preheated 400-degree oven for 20 to 30 minutes—until browned and firm.

MOROCCAN BURGERS
▼▼▼

A traditional North African grain, couscous is cracked durum wheat which has usually been refined. It is generally precooked and requires only soaking to prepare. You might want to plan ahead next time you're making chickpeas and couscous, so that you have leftovers for these rather exotic-tasting burgers. You can substitute cooked rice or cracked wheat or bulgur for the couscous or 8 ounces of tofu for the chickpeas. Serve the burgers with lettuce, tomatoes, cucumbers, and chopped green onions. SESAME SAUCE (page 148) makes a great topping.

YIELD: 4 burgers

PREPARATION TIME: 30 minutes to prepare; 20 to 30 minutes to bake

> 1 tablespoon olive oil
> 1 medium-sized onion, finely chopped
> 1 large clove garlic, pressed or minced
>   Pinch of cayenne
> 1/2 teaspoon ground coriander
> 1/2 teaspoon turmeric
> 1 1/2 teaspoons ground cumin
> 1/4 cup currants or chopped raisins
> 2 tablespoons chickpea stock
> 1 egg
> 1 tablespoon hatcho miso
> 1 tablespoon lemon juice
> 1 cup cooked chickpeas (see page 238)

COUSCOUS
▼▼▼

Couscous is light and fluffy and quick to prepare. I mix it with a little oil before soaking to keep the individual grains more separate; olive oil imparts a subtle, rich flavor.

> 1 cup couscous
> 1 teaspoon oil
> 1 1/2 cups water or vegetable stock
> 1/2 teaspoon sea salt

In a medium-sized bowl, thoroughly mix together the couscous and oil with a fork or your fingers.

Heat the water or stock to boiling, add the salt, and pour over the couscous. Cover with a plate and set aside for 10 to 15 minutes, until the grain has absorbed all of the liquid.

Fluff with a fork before serving.

> 1 cup cooked couscous (see box)
> 1/4 cup lightly toasted, finely chopped almonds
> 1/4 cup fresh parsley, finely chopped
> 1/3 cup fine bread crumbs
> 4 whole grain buns or pita

Heat the oil in a medium-sized skillet over moderate heat. Add the onion and garlic and sauté until the onion is tender and translucent. Add the cayenne, coriander, turmeric, and cumin and sauté a few more minutes, stirring constantly. Stir in the currants and stock; cover and cook briefly. Remove from the heat.

In a medium-sized bowl, beat the egg. Add the miso and lemon juice and beat until smooth. Add the chickpeas and mash well. Use a food processor to blend the mixture if you prefer. Thoroughly mix in the sauté, couscous, almonds, and parsley.

Shape the mixture into 4 equal balls. Roll them in bread crumbs and flatten into 1/2 inch-thick patties. Arrange them on a lightly greased baking sheet and bake in a preheated 400-degree oven 20 to 30 minutes, until firm and lightly browned. Or broil, turning them once.

Serve immediately in the buns or pita.

NOTES

- For eggless burgers, omit the egg and beat an extra tablespoon of chickpea stock and 1 tablespoon tahini with the miso and lemon juice.

TEMPEH BURGERS

Here, juicy seasoned tempeh becomes vegetarian "hamburger." Even meat-eaters crave these quarter-pounders after just one taste. If time allows, marinate the tempeh for several hours before cooking. Save leftover marinade to use for more burgers or for flavoring stir-fries and noodles.

YIELD: 2 burgers

PREPARATION TIME: Several hours to marinate tempeh; 20 to 30 minutes to prepare sandwiches

> *½ cup tamari*
> *2⅔ tablespoons brown rice vinegar*
> *2 cups vegetable stock or water*
> *1 8-ounce cake of tempeh, cut in half*
> *2 tablespoons sesame oil*
> *2 whole grain buns*

Combine the tamari, vinegar, and 1½ cups of the stock or water in a shallow bowl or small pie plate. Marinate the tempeh in this mixture, refrigerated, for several hours or overnight. If the tempeh isn't covered by the marinade, turn it periodically.

Remove the tempeh from the marinade and drain. Store the remaining marinade in the refrigerator.

Heat 1 tablespoon of the oil in a medium-sized skillet over moderate heat. Brown the tempeh on one side. Add the remaining oil, turn the tempeh, and brown the second side. Add the remaining ½ cup of liquid and tightly cover the pan. Cook until the liquid has disappeared. Remove from the heat.

Serve the tempeh in the buns with your favorite condiments and garnishes.

NOTES

- In a pinch, omit the marinating step and season the tempeh with about a teaspoon of tamari near the end of its steaming.

MEXICAN BEAN BURGERS

Beans and rice are a classic Latin American combination; prepared in this north-of-the-border format, they provide a quick, highly nutritious meal. Serve these burgers warm on whole grain buns (corn or rice breads are especially compatible) topped with a salsa (pages 143, 146) and/or GUACAMOLE (page 135).

YIELD: 4 burgers

PREPARATION TIME: 40 minutes

> *1 tablespoon olive oil*
> *1 small onion, finely chopped*
> *1 clove garlic, pressed or minced*
> *1 small poblano pepper (or another relatively mild pepper), seeds and membranes removed and finely chopped*
> *1 small carrot, grated*
> *1 small turnip, grated*
> *1 teaspoon ground cumin*
> *½ teaspoon ground coriander*
> *1 egg*
> *1 tablespoon hatcho miso*
> *¼ teaspoon sea salt*
> *1½ cups cooked pinto, anasazi, or black beans (see page 238)*
> *1½ cups cooked brown rice (see page 13-14)*
> *¼ cup lightly toasted almonds, finely ground*
> *¼ to ½ cup toasted fine bread crumbs*
> *4 buns*

Heat the oil in a medium-sized skillet over moderate heat. Add the onion and garlic and sauté until the onion appears translucent. Stir in the pepper, carrot, and turnip and sauté until these vegetables are just tender. Add the cumin and coriander and cook briefly, stirring. Remove from the heat.

In a medium-sized bowl, whisk the egg, miso, and salt. Mash in the beans. Mix in the rice, almonds, and the sauté to form a moist but firm mixture.

Shape the mixture into 4 equal balls and roll them in the crumbs. Flatten the balls into thick patties and arrange them on an oiled baking sheet. Bake in a preheated 400-degree oven for 20 to 30 minutes, until they are browned and crisp on the outside. Or broil, turning them once.

Serve immediately on the buns.

CURRIED LENTIL BURGERS

I often use leftovers from an Indian dinner as the basis for these burgers. Basmati rice is particularly good in them. Spread some GINGER AIOLI (page 148) on the buns.

YIELD: 4 burgers

PREPARATION TIME: 25 minutes to prepare; 20 to 30 minutes to bake

1 tablespoon sesame oil
2 green onions, finely chopped
1 clove garlic, pressed or minced
1 teaspoon minced fresh ginger root
¼ cup finely chopped carrot
  Freshly ground black pepper—several grindings
½ teaspoon ground cumin
1½ teaspoons mellow barley miso
1½ teaspoons lemon juice
1 cup LENTIL DAL (page 136-37)
2 tablespoons raisins
1½ cups cooked rice (see page 13-14)
¼ cup lightly toasted cashew pieces, finely chopped
⅓ to ½ cup toasted fine bread crumbs
4 whole grain buns

Heat the oil in a small skillet over moderate heat. Add the onion, garlic, ginger, and carrot and sauté for several minutes, until the carrot and onion are just tender. Add the pepper and cumin and cook, stirring, for a minute or two. Remove from the heat.

In a medium-sized bowl, whisk together the miso and lemon juice to form a smooth paste. Stir in the dal, raisins, rice, cashews, and the sauté to form a thick yet moist mixture. If it seems too moist—probably due to the consistency of the dal—add more rice or stir in some bread crumbs; taste and adjust the seasoning, if necessary, by adding a bit more miso and lemon juice.

Shape the mixture into 4 equal balls. Roll them in the crumbs until they are thoroughly coated. Flatten into thick patties and place them on an oiled baking sheet. Bake in a preheated 400-degree oven for 20 to 30 minutes, until they are browned and crisp on the outside—they will still be moist inside. Or broil, turning them once.

Serve immediately on the buns.

REUBEN'S POCKETS
▾▾▾

No matter how stuffed you are, you'll long for more of these bulging pockets. Somehow tempeh, mustard, and sauerkraut just seem to belong together. Serve with dill pickles.

YIELD: 2 sandwiches

PREPARATION TIME: About 30 minutes

1 to 2 tablespoons vegetable oil
1 8-ounce cake tempeh
½ cup vegetable stock or water
½ recipe MELLOW MUSTARD SAUCE (page 148), uncooked
2 pita (page 120 or 121)
12 lettuce leaves or other tender greens

4 green onions or shallots, finely chopped
2 cups well-drained sauerkraut

Heat 1 tablespoon of the oil in a medium-sized skillet over moderate heat. Brown the tempeh on one side. Turn and brown the second side, adding more oil if necessary. Pour in the stock and cover the pan tightly. Cook until the liquid has been absorbed, turning the tempeh once or twice. Remove from the heat and cut the tempeh lengthwise into three strips and then crosswise into thin strips. Add the mustard sauce to the skillet and cook over low heat, stirring often, until the sauce thickens. Remove from the heat.

To warm the pita, wrap them in foil and place in a 300-degree oven for a few minutes. Cut each pita in half to form two pockets. Line each of the pockets with 3 lettuce leaves—one along the bottom and one along each side. Spoon the tempeh into the pockets, sprinkle in some chopped onions, and tuck in some sauerkraut. Serve immediately, 2 pockets to each diner.

NOTES

- Try different kinds of stock to vary the flavor. Mushroom stock and beet stock are both delicious!

- For out-of-pocket Reubens, top slices of a rye or pumpernickel bread with lettuce leaves, sauced tempeh, minced green onions, and sauerkraut; serve the sandwiches open-faced or closed.

POCO PESTO POCKETS
▾▾▾

For its fans, there are never too many ways to consume pesto; here it enhances pita stuffed with a combination of fresh and cooked summer vegetables. The pungent dark green called arugula is an especially effective foil to the sweetness of the basil. This sandwich provides a good way to use up small amounts of leftover pesto sauce and vegetables.

YIELD: 1 sandwich

PREPARATION TIME: 25 minutes

1 pita (page 120-21)
¼ cup pesto (page 141-43)
1 to 2 cups torn spinach leaves or chopped arugula
¼ cup sliced, lightly steamed zucchini or other summer squash
¼ cup lightly blanched or steamed sugar snap peas or green beans
¼ cup cooked, sliced potatoes
1 medium tomato, diced
2 tablespoons minced fresh parsley

To warm the pita, wrap it in foil and place in a 300-degree oven for a few minutes. Cut the pita in half to form 2 pockets. Spread half the pesto in each pocket, add the greens and vegetables, and sprinkle parsley on top.

NOTES

- Substitute *WATERCRESS PESTO* (page 142) for the basil pesto.

- Substitute *TEX-MEX PESTO* (page 142-43) for the pesto and fill the pita with torn greens, steamed or blanched peas or beans, and diced tomatoes and avocado. Sprinkle minced parsley on top.

- Substitute *ITALIAN GREEN SAUCE* (page 144) for the pesto and fill the pita with torn greens, diced tomatoes, and chopped toasted almonds.

NOUVELLE FALAFEL
▾▾▾

Traditional falafel, Middle Eastern chickpea croquettes, contain eggs and are deep-fried. In this lighter, baked version, tofu replaces the egg. Tuck these crisp, spicy little chickpea balls into pita along with chopped tomatoes and cucumbers; drizzle SESAME SAUCE (page 148) on top.

YIELD: 2 sandwiches

PREPARATION TIME: 40 minutes

1 tablespoon sesame oil
1 small onion, finely chopped
2 large cloves garlic, pressed or minced
Pinch of cayenne, to taste
1½ teaspoons ground cumin
½ teaspoon ground coriander
½ teaspoon kelp powder
2 ounces tofu
1½ cups cooked chickpeas (see page 238)
2 tablespoons lightly toasted sesame seeds
1 tablespoon hatcho miso
1 tablespoon lemon juice
½ cup fresh parsley
2 pita (page 120-21)
1 medium-sized tomato, chopped
1 medium-sized cucumber, chopped
SESAME SAUCE (page 148)

Heat the oil in a small skillet over moderate heat. Add the onion and garlic and sauté until the onion is tender and translucent. Stir in the cayenne, cumin, coriander, and kelp powder and cook briefly, stirring. Remove from the heat.

In a food processor fitted with the metal blade, blend the sauté, tofu, chickpeas, and sesame seeds. Blend in the miso and lemon juice. Add the parsley and blend briefly.

Shape the mixture into 8 equal balls and arrange them on a lightly greased baking sheet. Bake in a preheated 375-degree oven for 20 to 30 minutes—until lightly browned.

To warm the pita, wrap them in foil and place in a 300-degree oven for a few minutes. Cut each pita in half to form 2 pockets. Divide the falafel among the pita, add the chopped raw vegetables, and top with the sauce.

NOTES

- For coarser-textured falafel, mash the tofu and chickpeas in a medium-sized mixing bowl using a fork. Thoroughly mix in the sauté, sesame seeds, miso and lemon juice. Mince the parsley and add it to the mixture.

- For crunchier falafel, roll the balls in fine bread crumbs before baking.

CHAPTER 11

Filled Flat Breads

FLAT BREADS ARE NATURAL holders of other foods, and we usually think of them as stuffed or rolled or folded around a filling. As we discussed in Chapter 8: Flat Breads, people in southern India typically fold pancakes called *dosas* over spicy vegetable and bean mixtures (page 124) and northern Chinese roll their mandarin pancakes around stir-fried mixtures (page 125). Mexicans have specific names for the various ways that they roll or fold corn and wheat tortillas around fillings. In France and everywhere else, crêpes are almost always served filled. Middle Easterners have long wrapped shish kebabs in large thin flat breads called *lavosh* and packed small chickpea croquettes known as *falafel* into pita. In this country, pitas are so customarily stuffed that they have become a sandwich category. In fact, filled flat breads of all types are so close to sandwiches in concept that it's often difficult to identify where one category ends and the other begins.

Even when flat breads are served plain, they are usually intended to be edible "plates" for toppings or consumable "utensils" for dips and sauces. Hummus, baba, and other Middle Eastern dips and salads are tra-

ditionally scooped up with wedges of pita or torn pieces of lavosh. Northern Indians dispense with silverware and use chapatis and parathas to pick up morsels of other foods. Mexicans layer toppings on crisp corn tortillas and shovel up bites of salsa and guacamole with soft tortillas or tortilla chips.

Many flat breads are linked with particular fillings, mainly because of culinary traditions, but I see no reason why flat breads and fillings can't be mixed and matched in our more cosmopolitan setting. Fill wheat tortillas with hummus or Mediterranean bean spread, crêpes with curried potatoes, chapatis with refritos and salsa, or mandarin pancakes with almond butter and sliced bananas. As a matter of course these days, pita already gets stuffed with anything and everything.

The flat bread/filling combinations that follow provide examples of various formats, some fairly traditional, others rather more innovative, but all within my own basic guidelines—light on fats and dairy products. In many of them, I use tofu or tempeh as the protein source. Preparation times given do not include time needed to prepare the flat breads.

Filled Crêpes

Provincetown was just waking up for the season when we arrived in early June. One of the new merchants there to try her hand at an undoubtedly frenetic and hopefully lucrative summer was Genevieve, a Frenchwoman. She was setting up a small crêpe café. Her primary piece of equipment was a large freestanding griddle imported from France. She poured on the thin batter, distributed it quickly and evenly with a wooden spreader, and peeled off large, perfect pancakes. She arranged cheeses, vegetables, or whatever a patron requested from her daily selection of fillings in the center of each crêpe and folded it into a neat, golden brown package. I was impressed with Genevieve's deft crêpe-making skills and admired the sense of adventure which had led her to attempt a summer business on Cape Cod. Her dream, she confided, was to open a wild foods restaurant, supplied with the edible treasures of her foraging. I've often wondered if she ever managed to fulfill this passion. If she has, I'm sure the menu includes an ever-changing choice of unusual filled crêpes.

Filled crêpes are fine light fare for any time of the day or night. A seasoned tomato-and-egg-filled crêpe makes a light yet satisfying breakfast. A bit heartier, crêpes stuffed with sautéed mushrooms, herbed spinach, or ratatouille (page 209-10) are just right for lunch or supper. Crêpes with sweet fillings are great for dessert or late night snacks. Some are doused with brandy or liqueurs and become flaming wonders.

In France, buckwheat crêpes usually enclose savory main dish fillings and wheat ones are generally wrapped around sweet dessert fillings. Neighborhood crêperies are appealing, lively establishments, offering numerous delectable choices in both categories, served with several kinds of *cidre*—apple cider—which is what the French traditionally consume with crêpes. Even in their native territory, crêpes are filled with almost any imaginable, palatable combination of meat, fish, poultry, cheese, vegetables, fruits, or sauces. They're a great way to use up leftovers in an organized, somewhat "classy" way. You can ignore French custom and fill wheat crêpes with main dish fillings—or buckwheat crêpes with sweet ones.

Crêpe dishes are ideal for entertaining, since the crêpes can be prepared ahead of time, as can most fillings. They can then be quickly assembled and reheated just before serving. Keep crêpes on hand in the freezer, and you'll have the makings of an elegant meal even on short notice.

Always serve crêpes with the evenly browned side (the one that was cooked first) on the outside. Though they're usually rolled around the filling, crêpes can also be simply folded over it or folded into a package around it. For an impressive dessert or main dish, stack crêpes flat, layer cake style, with a sweet or savory filling spread between them. Cut this "crêpe cake" into wedges to serve.

A few of my favorite recipes for filled crêpes follow.

HERBED SPINACH CRÊPES
▼▼▼

Here, crêpes are rolled around a creamy herbed spinach and tofu stuffing. You can make the filling ahead of time. Serve these plain or garnish them with a drizzle of tomato sauce (page 144-45), ROASTED RED PEPPER SAUCE (page 143-44), HOLLANDAISE À L'ARBERTI (page 148-49), or even pesto (page 141-42).

YIELD: 2 servings (6 filled crêpes)

PREPARATION TIME: 30 minutes

  8 *ounces tofu*
 1/2 *teaspoon sea salt*
  2 *tablespoons lemon juice*
  2 *tablespoons light vegetable oil*
  4 *teaspoons tahini*
 1 1/2 *teaspoons mellow rice miso*
  1 *tablespoon olive oil*
  1 *medium-sized onion, finely chopped*
  1 *large clove garlic, pressed or minced*
   Freshly ground black pepper—several grindings
 1/2 *teaspoon freshly grated nutmeg*
  1 *teaspoon dried tarragon*
  1 *teaspoon dried dill weed*
  8 *cups fresh spinach leaves (8 ounces), chopped*
 1/2 *teaspoon kelp powder*
 1/4 *cup parsley, finely chopped*
 1/4 *cup lightly toasted fine bread crumbs*
  6 *BUCKWHEAT CRÊPES (page 112) or*
   WHEAT CRÊPES (page 111)

In a food processor fitted with the metal blade or a blender, blend the tofu. With the processor running, add the salt, lemon juice, vegetable oil, tahini, and miso. Blend until thoroughly smooth, and set aside.

Heat the olive oil in a medium-sized skillet over moderate heat. Sauté the onion and garlic until the onion is tender and translucent. Add the pepper, nutmeg, tarragon, dill, spinach, kelp powder, and parsley, and sauté briefly.

Add the sauté and crumbs to the tofu mixture. Blend briefly—just long enough to combine the ingredients, because you want to maintain some texture.

Fill the crêpes with the mixture and roll them up. Serve warm.

NOTES
- Substitute 2 to 3 teaspoons each fresh tarragon and fresh dill weed for the dried herbs.
- Substitute 4 ounces sliced fresh mushrooms for 4 ounces of the spinach.

Mushroom-Stuffed Crêpes
▚▚▚

Buckwheat crêpes especially complement this filling. I've combined tofu with the mushrooms for extra protein; you can substitute tempeh for the tofu or simply double the mushrooms. You can make this filling ahead of time, but be sure to warm it over low heat so as not to destroy beneficial enzymes in the miso in the sauce.

YIELD: 2 servings (6 filled crêpes)

PREPARATION TIME: 30 to 40 minutes

   3 tablespoons unsalted margarine or butter
   1 medium-sized onion, finely chopped
   2 cloves garlic, pressed or minced
   1 teaspoon dried basil
   1 teaspoon dried tarragon
  1/2 teaspoon dried marjoram
    Freshly ground black pepper—several grindings
  1/2 pound fresh mushrooms, sliced
   8 ounces tofu, well pressed and sliced into small strips
   3 tablespoons whole wheat pastry flour
  3/4 cup milk or soy milk
   1 tablespoon mellow rice or mellow barley miso
  1/4 cup fresh parsley, minced
   6 BUCKWHEAT CRÊPES (page 112) or WHEAT CRÊPES (page 111)

Heat 1 tablespoon of the margarine or butter in a skillet over moderate heat and sauté the onion and garlic until the onion is tender and translucent. Crush the herbs and add them, along with the pepper and mushrooms, and continue to sauté for several minutes. Stir in the tofu and cook briefly. Cover and remove from the heat.

In a small skillet, melt the remaining 2 tablespoons margarine or butter over low heat. Whisking constantly, sprinkle in the flour to make a smooth roux and cook for several minutes to brown the flour. Whisking constantly, slowly pour in the milk or soy milk. Cook, whisking, until the mixture thickens. Remove from the heat and thoroughly whisk in the miso.

Stir the sauce and parsley into the sauté.

Fill the crêpes with the mixture and roll them up or fold them. Serve warm.

NOTES
- Substitute minced fresh basil, tarragon, and marjoram; use about double the amount of the dried herbs.
- If you substitute tempeh for the tofu, brown a 4-ounce cake of it on both sides in vegetable oil, then add 1/4 cup of vegetable stock or water, cover tightly, and steam until the liquid has disappeared. Cut the tempeh into thin strips and add it to the sauté.

Sweet Potato-Apple-Onion Crêpes
▚▚▚

Delicate spicing enhances the natural sweetness of the sweet potato, apple, and onion in this filling. Garnish the crêpes with chopped toasted almonds or pecans and a dollop of sour cream, yogurt, or TOFU SOUR CREAM (page 148). You can make the filling ahead of time. It's also good in omelets; this is enough for two large ones.

YIELD: 2 generous servings (6 filled crêpes)

PREPARATION TIME: About 30 minutes

   1 tablespoon sesame oil
   1 medium-sized sweet onion, finely chopped
   1 large apple, peeled, cored, and finely diced
   1 large sweet potato, peeled and finely diced
    Freshly ground black pepper—several grindings
  1/4 teaspoon ground allspice
  1/4 teaspoon freshly grated nutmeg
  1/8 teaspoon ground cinnamon
  1/8 teaspoon ground cloves
   6 tablespoons unsweetened apple juice or vegetable stock
  1/2 teaspoon sea salt, or to taste
   6 WHEAT CRÊPES (page 112) or BUCKWHEAT CRÊPES (page 111)

Heat the oil in a medium-sized skillet over moderate heat and sauté the onion for several minutes. Stir in the apple and continue to sauté. Add the sweet potato and sauté briefly. Add the pepper and spices and cook briefly, stirring constantly. Add the liquid, cover, reduce the heat to low, and cook until the sweet potato is tender. Season with salt and mash slightly.

Fill the crêpes and serve immediately.

CRÊPE CAKE

This is an attractive-looking dish. You can make it in no time at all if you have the crêpes, sweet potato, and fruit sauce already made. If possible, make it ahead of time, since the flavor is even better after reheating. Substitute other main dish fillings, such as those in the preceding recipes. For dessert, spread a fruit butter or jam between the crêpes.

YIELD: 2 to 4 servings

PREPARATION TIME: 20 minutes to assemble; 30 minutes to bake

> 2 *cups mashed baked sweet potato*
> ¼ *teaspoon sea salt, or to taste*
> 16 *6-inch* BUCKWHEAT CRÊPES *(page 112) or* WHEAT CRÊPES *(page 111)*
> ½ *cup lightly toasted, finely chopped pecans*
> ¼ *cup unsweetened apple sauce or pear sauce (see page 136)*

Season the sweet potatoes with the salt.

Lightly grease an 8-inch pie pan or other oven-proof dish. Place a crêpe in the pan and spread 2 tablespoons of the sweet potato on the surface. Sprinkle about 1½ teaspoons of pecans on the sweet potato. Place another crêpe on top and add another layer of sweet potato and pecans. Continue alternating layers of crêpes and filling, ending with a crêpe. Trim the edges of the cake if they appear uneven. Spread the fruit sauce on top and sprinkle the remaining pecans over all.

Bake in a preheated 350-degree oven for 30 minutes. Serve warm, cut into wedges.

Filled Tortillas

Tortillas—both corn and wheat—are used extensively in Mexican cuisine, and they are prepared in a variety of traditional ways, some of which have become fixtures on the American fast food scene. Most Americans think of tacos as crispy corn tortillas that have been fried, folded, and stuffed with ground beef, beans, shredded lettuce, chopped tomatoes, and grated cheese, but in Mexico a taco is any type of tortilla folded or rolled around any type of filling, and the tortillas can be soft, slightly fried, or fried crisp, though the soft ones are most common. Tostadas are flat, crisp corn tortillas piled with an assortment of toppings. Enchiladas are also made with corn tortillas; the soft tortillas are coated with a sauce, rolled around a filling, and usually heated in the oven. Burritos are made with soft flour tortillas; one end is often tucked up inside to permit eating out of hand without leakage. Tex-Mex *fajitas* ("sashes" in Spanish) are actually burrito variations. Their name comes from their traditional filling—thin strips of grilled skirt steak resembling sashes; now, sashlike strips of anything qualify as fajita fillings.

Except for enchiladas, these filled tortillas are generally eaten out of hand, and fall into the category of *antojitos*, or snack foods, often sold—and eaten—on the street in Mexico. They are great appetizers—you can make miniature versions to serve as hors d'oeuvres. They are also perfectly acceptable main dishes, if served in sufficient quantity. Use Mexican-style fillings or substitute less conventional ones, as I have in some cases here.

TOWERING TOSTADAS

Several layers of classic Mexican ingredients top the crisp corn tortilla of this tostada, but possibilities for toppings are practically endless; exercise your imagination and use your leftovers to come up with new combinations.

YIELD: 2 to 4 servings

PREPARATION TIME: 20 to 30 minutes

> 4 CORN TORTILLAS *(page 115)*
> *Corn or sesame oil*
> 2 *cups warmed* REFRITOS *(page 136)*
> ¼ *cup finely chopped green onions*
> 2 *cups finely chopped lettuce or other tender greens*
> 1 *cup* GUACAMOLE *(page 135)*
> ½ *cup* BLENDER HOT SAUCE *(page 146) or* EMILIO'S SALSA VERDE *(page 143), plus extra for passing*

Coarsely chopped fresh cilantro leaves
Lightly toasted chopped almonds
Sour cream or TOFU SOUR CREAM *(page 148)*

Brush both sides of each tortilla lightly with oil. Place them on a baking sheet and bake several minutes in a preheated 350-degree oven until crisp—watch that they don't burn!

For each tostada, spread ½ cup of beans on a tortilla and then evenly distribute the green onion, lettuce, guacamole, salsa, cilantro, and almonds, in that order. Top with the sour cream.

Serve immediately, with additional salsa for those who want more.

NOTES

- Instead of baking the tortillas, you can crisp them by frying in about an inch of hot oil (380 degrees) for about 30 seconds on each side; drain on paper towels.

- Substitute *AVOCADO SALSA CRUDA* (page 143) for the guacamole and salsa.

TORTILLA FLATS

Here's a good way to use up leftover rice and beans in a new guise. Serve these Mexican-style "sandwiches" with sautéed greens or a tossed green salad for a complete meal. You can make these with any corn tortillas; I especially like to use blue corn ones.

YIELD: 2 servings

PREPARATION TIME: About 30 minutes

      4 *ounces tofu*
    ¼ *teaspoon sea salt*
      1 *tablespoon lemon juice*
      1 *tablespoon light vegetable oil*
      2 *teaspoons tahini*
      2 *tablespoons water*
    1½ *cups cooked rice (see page 13-14)*
      2 *tablespoons finely chopped green onions*
      4 CORN TORTILLAS *(page 115)*
         Corn or sesame oil
      1 *cup* REFRITOS *(page 136)*
      1 *cup loosely packed fresh cilantro leaves, coarsely chopped*
    ½ *cup* EMILIO'S SALSA VERDE *(page 143)*

Preheat the oven to 350 degrees.

In a blender, combine the tofu, salt, lemon juice, vegetable oil, tahini, and water. Blend until thoroughly smooth and set aside.

Toss the rice and green onions together.

Lightly brush one side of two tortillas with corn or sesame oil; place them on a baking sheet, oiled side down. Spread each with half the refried beans, then with half the rice mixture. Sprinkle on ¼ cup of the chopped cilantro and top each stack with a second tortilla and spread on about 2 tablespoons of salsa.

Bake for 5 to 10 minutes, until the tortillas soften and the stacks are heated through. Remove the stacks to serving plates and garnish with the tofu mixture and the remaining salsa and cilantro. Serve immediately.

TOFU ENCHILADAS

These sauced, seasoned tofu-filled corn tortillas are a light alternative to cheese-laden enchiladas. If the tortillas are freshly made and have been kept wrapped in a tea towel, they will still be soft and flexible. If the tortillas aren't freshly made, soften them by wrapping them in a tea towel, steaming for about a minute, and then leaving them in the covered steamer off the heat for about 15 minutes. Or wrap and heat them in a moderate oven for several minutes—just until they are soft and pliable. Still another way to soften tortillas for enchiladas is to "wilt" them in hot oil: slip one into a skillet of hot oil, turn it over immediately, and remove it with tongs just as it softens; drain wilted tortillas on absorbent paper before filling them. Serve the enchiladas with an avocado salad or sautéed greens.

YIELD: 2 generous servings (6 enchiladas)

PREPARATION TIME: About 40 minutes

      1 *tablespoon sesame oil*
      1 *medium-sized onion, finely chopped*
      2 *cloves garlic, pressed or minced*
    ¼ *cup finely chopped or grated carrot*
    ¼ *cup finely chopped or grated turnip*
    ½ *teaspoon dried Mexican oregano*
    ½ *teaspoon ground coriander*
    1½ *teaspoons ground cumin*
      1 *teaspoon chili powder*
    12 *ounces tofu, well mashed*
    1½ *tablespoons lemon juice*
    1½ *tablespoons mellow barley miso*
      6 CORN TORTILLAS *(page 115)*
         EMILIO'S SALSA VERDE *(page 143)*
    ¼ *to* ½ *cup fresh cilantro leaves, coarsely chopped*

Heat the oil in a medium-sized skillet over moderate heat and sauté the onion, garlic, carrot, and turnip until tender. Grind together the oregano, coriander, cumin, and chili powder, and stir the mixture into the sauté.

Stir in the tofu, cover the pan, turn the heat to low, and cook for several minutes, until the mixture is heated through and the flavors are well blended. Whisk the lemon juice and miso to a smooth paste and stir it in. Remove from the heat.

Soften the tortillas and lightly spread them with salsa. Spoon in the filling and roll them up. Arrange on plates and top with more salsa and the cilantro. Serve immediately. If you must wait to serve the filled enchiladas, hold them in a covered casserole in a warm oven; garnish with the cilantro just before serving.

NOTES

- Mexican oregano is one of many species of oregano throughout the world; if you don't have it, substitute another zesty-flavored variety.

- Substitute a red salsa, such as *BLENDER HOT SAUCE* (page 146), for the salsa verde.

SCRAMBLED POTATO TACOS
▾▾▾

Warm, soft tortillas folded over a spicy potato filling are a favorite breakfast item in central Texas. They are usually made with wheat tortillas, but corn tortillas are good, too. Tofu reduces the cholesterol in this version, but you can substitute eggs. Serve the tacos with REFRITOS *(page 136) and a salsa (pages 143,146)—if you can take the heat!*

YIELD: 2 servings

PREPARATION TIME: About 45 minutes

    1 poblano pepper
    1 large potato (½ pound), cut into small cubes
    1 tablespoon sesame oil
    1 medium-sized onion, finely chopped
    2 large cloves garlic, pressed or minced
    ½ teaspoon ground coriander
    1½ teaspoons ground cumin
    4 ounces tofu, cut into small cubes

    1 tablespoon lemon juice
    ½ teaspoon sea salt, or to taste
    2 WHEAT TORTILLAS (page 116) or 4 CORN TORTILLAS (page 115)

Roast and peel the pepper as described on page 130. Chop fine and set aside.

Simmer the potato cubes in water until they are just tender; drain and save the water for bread, soup stock, and other uses.

Heat the oil in a medium-sized skillet over moderate heat and sauté the onion and garlic until the onion is just tender. Stir in the coriander and cumin and cook briefly, stirring constantly. Add 1 tablespoon of the chopped pepper and the tofu and cook, stirring, for several minutes, until the tofu is hot and soft. Stir in the cooked potato, lemon juice, and ½ teaspoon salt. Lower the heat, cover, and heat the mixture for several minutes, stirring occasionally. Taste and add more chopped poblano pepper or salt if necessary.

Warm the tortillas by wrapping them in a tea towel and steaming briefly, wrapping them in foil and heating in a moderate oven for several minutes, or laying them on a hot griddle briefly, turning once. Take care that they do not stiffen, but stay soft and pliable. Fill and fold or roll the tortillas. Serve immediately.

NOTES

- Chopped *SOYSAGE* (page 141) is a good addition to the filling; add it along with the peppers and tofu.

- Omit the tofu and scramble in 2 beaten eggs after you have added the potato and seasonings.

BEAN BURRITOS
▾▾▾

Some of the best bean burritos I ever tasted were from a pushcart on the main street in Amherst, Massachusetts. The cart had some kind of a warming device for large flour tortillas and refried beans and a cooler for crisp greens, guacamole, and shredded cheese, and the vendor assembled steaming, fresh, custom-made burritos right on the spot. You can quickly put together your own burritos at home if you have some basic ingredients on hand—perhaps the leftovers from a Mexican dinner.

YIELD: 2 servings

PREPARATION TIME: 15 to 20 minutes

    2 WHOLE WHEAT TORTILLAS (page 116)
    2 cups REFRITOS (page 136)
    2 cups finely shredded greens
    ½ cup GUACAMOLE (page 135)

½ cup EMILIO'S SALSA VERDE (page 143) or BLENDER HOT SAUCE (page 146)
¼ cup fresh cilantro leaves, coarsely chopped

Warm the tortillas by laying them on a hot griddle for a few moments on each side, wrapping them in a tea towel and steaming them briefly, or wrapping them in foil and heating in a low to moderate oven briefly. Reheat the refried beans.

Spread half the beans along the middle of the upper two-thirds of each tortilla; then evenly distribute the greens, guacamole, salsa, and cilantro, in that order.

Fold up the bottom third of the tortilla and fold in the sides, leaving the top open. Serve the burritos—to be eaten out of hand—immediately.

NOTES

- Substitute *CORN-WHEAT TORTILLAS* (page 116) or *OKARA TORTILLAS* (page 116-17) for the all-wheat tortillas.

- Substitute 1 cup *AVOCADO SALSA CRUDA* (page 143) for the guacamole and salsa.

- Of course, you may also add a sprinkling of a grated cheese, such as Monterey jack or mild cheddar; add 2 or more tablespoons per burrito, depending on tastes.

- Chopped roasted almonds and finely chopped green onions are other tasty additions.

TEMPEH FAJITAS
▀▀▀

Thin strips of cooked marinated tempeh are excellent vegetarian stand-ins for the traditional skirt steak "sashes" in this latest trend in Mexican cuisine.

YIELD: 2 generous servings

PREPARATION TIME: About 30 minutes, not including marinating the tempeh

>   *2 cloves garlic, pressed or minced*
>   *⅓ cup lime juice*
>   *1 8-ounce cake tempeh*
>   *1 to 2 tablespoons olive oil*
>   *½ cup vegetable stock or water*
>   *1 teaspoon tamari*
>   *2 to 4 WHOLE WHEAT TORTILLAS (page 116)*
>   *PICO DE GALLO (page 143)*

Whisk together the garlic and lime juice and pour it over the tempeh in a flat dish. Cover and marinate in the refrigerator for several hours, occasionally turning the tempeh.

Heat 1 tablespoon oil in a medium-sized skillet over moderate heat. Remove the tempeh from the marinade and brown it on both sides, adding more oil if necessary. Add the stock and cover the pan tightly. Steam until the pan is almost dry. Add the tamari and turn the tempeh to coat it. Cover and cook away the remaining liquid. Cut the cooked tempeh into thin strips.

Warm the tortillas by laying them on a hot griddle briefly on each side, wrapping them in a tea towel and steaming briefly, or wrapping in foil and heating them in a moderate oven for several minutes. Arrange the tempeh strips down the middle of the tortillas, spoon some pico de gallo over the tempeh, and fold or roll up the tortillas.

Serve immediately with additional pico de gallo.

NOTES

- Substitute *CORN-WHEAT TORTILLAS* (page 116) or *OKARA TORTILLAS* (page 116-17) for the all-wheat ones.

STUFFED CHAPATIS
▀▀▀

Use chapatis as wrappers rather than as pincers for this Indian version of Mexican burritos. Serve INDIAN CUCUMBER-TOMATO SALAD (page 216) or INDIAN COLESLAW (page 217) on the side.

YIELD: 2 servings

PREPARATION TIME: 15 to 20 minutes

>   *2 CHAPATIS (page 117-18)*
>   *2 cups LENTIL DAL (page 136-37)*
>   *2 green onions, finely chopped*
>   *2 tablespoons raisins (Monukka raisins are particularly good)*
>   *1 banana, sliced*
>   *¼ cup lightly toasted cashew pieces*

Wrap the chapatis and warm them in a moderate oven for a few minutes. Warm the dal.

Spread half the dal down the center of the upper two-thirds of each chapati. Evenly distribute the onions, raisins, banana slices, and cashews on top. Fold the unfilled end of the chapati up and fold the sides in, leaving the top open.

Serve immediately—to be eaten out of hand.

NOTES

- Substitute *CURRIED CHICKPEAS* (page 137) for the dal.

- There's a lot of room for other substitutions or additions here: consider chopped fresh cilantro or mint leaves; almonds, hazelnuts, or sesame seeds; other fruits. Work with what you have on hand.

CHAPTER 12

Filled Doughs

IT SEEMS THAT ALMOST every culture has at least one traditional dish that combines a yeasted dough and a filling in some way; pizza is undoubtedly the most familiar example of this concept to us in the United States. But Italians have turnovers and spiral filled doughs too, as do a lot of other cuisines. Steamed buns are another filled dough—from China. In each case, the filling is either spread on top of the dough or else the dough is folded over or rolled around the filling, sealing it inside. I borrow these basic formats for my own dough and filling combinations and make pizzas, savory bread-crusted tarts, turnovers, and spiral filled loaves or rolls, coffee cakes, and steamed buns. These are the kinds of things I think about making when I am making bread, since the dough is already available. My fillings are often reinterpretations of traditional ethnic fillings.

Besides being convenient to make when you're making bread, most filled doughs are even more suitable than most sandwiches for picking up and munching out of hand without a mess, so they're excellent for parties, picnics, ballgames, or lunchboxes.

The following recipes document some of my explorations with doughs, toppings, and fillings. Hopefully, these will give you some ideas for your own original combinations. Use what you especially like and/or have on hand when you are baking and realize it is time for a meal. A turnover filling may be as easy as a simple stir-fry or a combination of grated cheese or nut butter and sliced vegetables or fruits. Surprisingly small quantities of sauce and toppings suffice for a pizza. Filled doughs might even provide a solution to the little bits of leftovers that you have qualms about throwing out but know in the back of your mind you are merely saving to discard tomorrow. Think before you toss: today's trash might be a key element of tomorrow's delightful, innovative dinner. Though some filled doughs require rather extensive planning and effort, others don't take much forethought or prep work at all.

Preparation times in particular recipes do assume that you have bread dough and certain sauces on hand. If you want a lot of extra dough, you'll need to increase bread recipes; for my small family, I generally just use part of a regular bread recipe for a filled item and make the rest into loaves or rolls. Doughs should have at least one bowl rise, but for flavor and strength, I recommend two full rises. If the dough is ready before the filling is, form the dough into a ball, place it in a covered bowl, and refrigerate it.

Pizzas

Until quite recently, pizza almost always consisted of a white wheat crust smeared with tomato sauce, covered with melted cheese, mostly mozzarella, and topped with a scattering of predictable items—sliced onions, bell peppers, mushrooms, pepperoni, sausage, or anchovies. Occasionally someone got creative and included something different, such as olives, broccoli florets, eggplant, or zucchini slices. But, basically, pizza was pizza. Then nouvelle cuisine came along and gave pizza a make-over. Now you can get a whole wheat or sourdough crust, and it can be paper-thin or thick and puffy by design. Pesto, ratatouille, sun-dried tomatoes, and garlic confit are just some of the contemporary replacements for tomato sauce. Every cheese imaginable stands in for the mozzarella—or there may be no cheese at all. And the most unusual and exotic items and combinations thereof serve as toppings—artichoke hearts, wild mushrooms, caviar, capers, chicken, chilies, duck, smoked salmon, prosciutto, pineapple, clams, shrimp, ad infinitum. Plain old pizza has not completely disappeared, but the word no longer depicts a dish; now it describes an adaptable culinary concept.

Just the other day, I heard on the radio that one of the large American pizza chains, expanding into the international market, is tuning into cultural diversity; they are still pushing pizza, but toppings will be regional, such as raw fish in Japan and chopped egg in France. Ironically, this broadened American definition of pizza has probably brought it closer to its actual roots. I imagine that, in Italy, this bread-based pie originated as a convenient means to a meal in bakeries or in homes where bread was in the making, and regional circumstance determined the particular constellation of ingredients—tomato sauce, cheese, and so on—that came to characterize it.

Purists might be appalled at the present eclectic state of pizza and claim that traditional dishes should be made true to their original form or not at all. But I don't believe for a minute that, at any point in time, if an Italian baker had some unconventional ingredients in his larder on a baking day, he would have hesitated to slap them onto a piece of dough and call it a pizza. When I worked in my baking business for 12- to 18-hour stretches, I appeased my hunger with various combinations of the available dough, cheese, peanut butter and other spreads, and assorted sliced fruits and vegetables.

Think of pizza as a format, a dough base which becomes a three-dimensional collage of colors, textures, and flavors with the addition of sauces and various toppings. The character of the dough you begin with may point you in a particular direction. For instance, a corn-wheat crust may suggest a Mexican, New Mexican, or northern Italian theme; a rice-wheat dough might lead to a Mexican, Indian, Indonesian, or Chinese pizza; a rye, pumpernickel, or buckwheat dough seems to attract onions, cabbage, mushrooms, sauerkraut; a sweet dough topped with a fruit sauce and nuts becomes a dessert or breakfast pizza. You can even make a pizza with a split personality: for instance, spread pesto sauce on one half and tomato or roasted red pepper sauce on the other half and vary the toppings on each side. There really are few limits on how far the pizza format can be extended. The key to pizza-making fun is to throw out your stereotypes; let your good taste and creative intuition be your guide. For convenience, you might want to freeze sauces in pizza-sized portions.

The first pizza recipe is a basic one, closest to the conventional notion, but even it has a lot of built-in flexibility. The recipes that follow it are really all variations, though not what you're likely to find at your local pizza parlor—yet. For a terrific crisp crust, I recommend blackened steel pizza pans or baking tiles or stones, and by all means use a very hot oven. The most effective way I've found to cut pizza is with a razor-sharp Chinese cleaver directly on a wooden cutting board.

BASIC PIZZA
▼▼▼

Here's a classic pizza—well, not quite, since it's cheeseless and has a tofu topping—but you can still use this recipe as a touchstone as you brainstorm new combinations. Pizza is one of the simplest meals to make on a bread-making day. Italian-type doughs are traditional, but any dough is a possibility—just set aside a piece of dough whenever you make bread. This recipe is a guide and exceedingly variable, depending on individual tastes and available ingredients: add minced fresh herbs—basil, thyme, oregano, parsley, rosemary; substitute other vegetables—briefly steam or blanch those that don't cook as quickly as these; include sliced olives, nuts, grated or shredded cheeses. It's your show. The pizza recipes that follow this one provide examples of other combinations.

YIELD: 1 pizza—2 generous servings

PREPARATION TIME: 30 to 40 minutes to prepare; 10 minutes to bake

> 4 *ounces tofu, pressed and blanched*
> 2 *teaspoons lemon juice*
> 2 *teaspoons olive oil, plus a bit for the pan and dough*
> 1 *teaspoon minced garlic*
>   *Black pepper or minced dried hot red pepper flakes, to taste*
> 12 *ounces bread dough*
>   *Cornmeal*
> ½ *cup tomato sauce (page 144-45)*
> 1 *small onion, sliced crosswise into thin rings*
> 1 *medium-sized bell pepper, sliced crosswise into thin rings*
> 1 *cup thinly sliced mushrooms*

Cut the tofu into small cubes or strips. In a small bowl, whisk the lemon juice, 2 teaspoons olive oil, garlic, and pepper. Stir in the tofu pieces and set aside to marinate.

Preheat the oven to 500 degrees. Lightly grease a 14- to 15-inch pizza pan with olive oil and dust it with cornmeal.

On a lightly greased surface, roll the dough into a 13-inch circle. Brush the dough lightly with olive oil, then transfer it to the prepared pan. Crimp the edge to form a slight lip. Spread tomato sauce evenly over the dough. Arrange the onion, bell pepper, and mushroom slices over the sauce. Distribute the tofu (including remaining marinade) on top.

Bake on a low rack in the preheated oven 10 minutes, or until the bottom is brown and crisp. Slide the pizza onto a cutting board and cut it into wedges. Serve immediately.

NOTES

- Substitute 4 ounces tempeh for the tofu. Cook it before marinating: brown each side in olive oil over moderate heat, add ¼ cup of stock or water to the pan, cover tightly, steam until the liquid has almost disappeared, add a bit of shoyu for seasoning, and cook away the remaining liquid.

- Substitute ROASTED RED PEPPER SAUCE (page 143-44) for the tomato sauce.

- Sauté the vegetable toppings briefly in olive oil before arranging them on the sauce.

PESTO PIZZA
▼▼▼

Some bread dough, leftover pesto, a few toppings, and wow—what a meal! I usually choose an Italian or French dough for this one.

YIELD: 1 pizza—2 generous servings

PREPARATION TIME: About 30 minutes to prepare; 10 minutes to bake

> 2 *teaspoons lemon juice*
> 2 *teaspoons olive oil, plus extra for the pan and dough*
> 1 *clove garlic, pressed or minced*
>   *Freshly ground black pepper—several grindings*
> 4 *ounces tofu, pressed and blanched*
> 12 *ounces bread dough*
>   *Cornmeal*
> ½ *cup pesto (page 141-43)*
> 2 *medium-sized tomatoes, thinly sliced*
> 2 *tablespoons minced fresh parsley leaves*
> ¼ *cup pine nuts or chopped walnuts*

In a small bowl, whisk the lemon juice, 2 teaspoons olive oil, garlic, and pepper. Cube or crumble the tofu and stir it into the mixture in the bowl. Set aside to marinate, stirring occasionally.

Preheat the oven to 500 degrees. Lightly grease a 14- to 15-inch pizza pan with olive oil and dust it with cornmeal.

On a lightly greased surface, roll the dough into a 13-inch circle. Brush the dough lightly with olive oil, then transfer it to the prepared pan. Crimp the edge to form a slight lip. Spread pesto over the dough and arrange tomato slices on top. Toss the parsley, nuts, and marinated tofu together and distribute this mixture, including any remaining marinade, over the tomatoes.

Bake on a low rack in the preheated oven for 10 minutes, or until the bottom is brown and crisp. Slide the pizza onto a cutting board and cut it into wedges. Serve immediately.

NOTES

- Substitute *WATERCRESS PESTO* (page 142) for the basil pesto.

MEXICAN PIZZA
▼▼▼

Rice or cornmeal doughs are especially appropriate for this pizza.

YIELD: 1 pizza—2 generous servings

PREPARATION TIME: 10 to 15 minutes to prepare; 10 minutes to bake

>   12 ounces bread dough
>   Sesame or olive oil
>   Cornmeal
>   1 cup REFRITOS (page 136)
>   ¼ cup salsa (page 143, 146), plus extra for garnish
>   1 medium-sized ripe avocado
>   1 tablespoon lime juice
>   ¼ cup coarsely chopped fresh cilantro leaves

Preheat the oven to 500 degrees. Lightly grease a 14- to 15-inch pizza pan with oil and dust it with cornmeal.

On a lightly greased surface, roll the dough into a 13-inch circle. Brush the dough lightly with oil, then transfer it to the prepared pan. Crimp the edge to form a slight lip. Spread the beans over the dough. Spread the salsa on the beans.

Bake on a low rack in the preheated oven for 10 minutes, or until the bottom is brown and crisp. While the pizza is baking, peel and thinly slice the avocado into lengthwise strips. Sprinkle lime juice over the avocado and fold gently with a rubber spatula to coat the avocado with juice.

Slide the baked pizza onto a cutting board. Decoratively arrange the avocado slices on top and sprinkle chopped cilantro over all. Cut the pizza into wedges and serve immediately. Pass additional salsa for diners to add at their own discretion.

INDONESIAN PIZZA
▼▼▼

Arrange an Indonesian salad on top of a rice dough crust!

YIELD: 1 pizza—2 generous servings

PREPARATION TIME: 30 to 40 minutes to prepare; 10 minutes to bake

>   1½ teaspoons tamari
>   ½ teaspoon brown rice vinegar
>   ¼ cup plus 1½ tablespoons vegetable stock or water
>   1 4-ounce cake tempeh
>   1 tablespoon sesame or peanut oil, plus a bit for the pan and dough
>   12 ounces bread dough
>   Cornmeal or rice flour
>   1 cup SPICY PEANUT SAUCE (page 147)
>   ¼ cup sliced green onions
>   1 cup finely sliced Chinese cabbage
>   ½ cup thinly sliced carrots, lightly steamed
>   2 cups broccoli florets, lightly steamed

Whisk together the tamari, brown rice vinegar, and 1½ tablespoons stock. Add the tempeh and marinate (refrigerated) for 30 minutes to several hours or overnight. Drain, reserving any remaining marinade.

Heat 1 tablespoon oil in a small skillet over moderate heat. Brown the tempeh on both sides. Add ¼ cup stock and cover the pan tightly. Steam until the liquid is almost gone. Add the marinade and steam until the pan is dry. Cut the tempeh into small strips.

Preheat the oven to 500 degrees. Lightly grease a 14- to 15-inch pizza pan with oil and dust it with cornmeal or rice flour.

On a lightly greased surface, roll the dough into a 13-inch circle. Brush the dough lightly with oil, then transfer it to the prepared pan. Crimp the edge to form a slight lip. Spread ½ cup peanut sauce over the dough. Sprinkle on the green onions and chopped cabbage. Distribute the carrots, broccoli, and tempeh pieces evenly. Drizzle the remaining peanut sauce on top.

Bake on a low rack in the preheated oven for 10 minutes, or until the bottom is brown and crisp. Slide the pizza onto a cutting board and cut it into wedges. Serve immediately.

NOTES

- Substitute other raw or steamed vegetables.

PIZZA À LA GRECQUE
▼▼▼

SESAME BREAD (page 65) dough makes a great crust for this Greek-style pizza.

YIELD: 1 pizza—2 generous servings

PREPARATION TIME: About 30 minutes to prepare; 10 minutes to bake

>   2 tablespoons olive oil, plus extra for the pan and dough

1 tablespoon lemon juice
2 tablespoons Calamata olive brine
8 ounces tofu, pressed and briefly blanched
1 small red onion, thinly sliced into rings
1 clove garlic, pressed or minced
1 heaping cup small cauliflower florets (4 ounces), lightly blanched or steamed
4 cups loosely packed fresh spinach leaves (4 ounces), finely chopped
12 ounces bread dough
  Cornmeal
½ cup thick tomato sauce (page 144-45)
10 to 12 Calamata olives, pitted and sliced

In a large bowl, whisk 1 tablespoon of the olive oil with the lemon juice and olive brine. Cut the tofu into small cubes and stir it into the mixture in the bowl. Set aside to marinate, stirring periodically.

Heat 1 tablespoon olive oil in a large skillet over moderate heat. Briefly sauté the onion rings and garlic. Stir in the cauliflower and spinach and remove from the heat. Add to the tofu and toss together.

Preheat the oven to 500 degrees. Lightly grease a 14- to 15-inch pizza pan with olive oil and dust it with cornmeal.

On a lightly greased surface, roll the dough into a 13-inch circle. Brush the dough lightly with olive oil, then transfer it to the prepared pan. Crimp the edge to form a slight lip. Spread tomato sauce over the dough. Scatter on the tofu-vegetable mixture. Sprinkle the olives on top.

Bake on a low rack of the preheated oven for 10 minutes, or until the bottom is brown and crisp. Slide the pizza onto a cutting board and cut it into wedges. Serve immediately.

NOTES

- The cauliflower is optional.

- Substitute ½ to ¾ cup crumbled feta cheese (about 4 ounces) for the tofu. It isn't necessary to marinate the cheese—just combine it with the marinade ingredients and the sauté and mix thoroughly.

PIZZA PRIMAVERA
❦

Use a sourdough or yeasted French or Italian dough for this savory spinach-and-herb-sauced pizza.

YIELD: 1 pizza—2 generous servings

PREPARATION TIME: About 20 minutes to prepare; 10 minutes to bake

12 ounces bread dough
  Olive oil
  Cornmeal
1 cup ITALIAN GREEN SAUCE (page 144)
¼ cup finely chopped fresh parsley leaves
1 large red bell pepper, thinly sliced into rings
¼ cup chopped almonds

Preheat the oven to 500 degrees. Lightly grease a 14- to 15-inch pizza pan with olive oil and dust it with cornmeal.

On a lightly greased surface, roll the dough into a 13-inch circle. Brush the dough lightly with olive oil, then transfer it to the prepared pan. Crimp the edge to form a slight lip. Spread the sauce over the dough and sprinkle on the parsley. Arrange the pepper rings on top and sprinkle the almonds over all.

Bake on a low rack in the preheated oven for 10 minutes, or until the bottom is brown and crisp. Slide the pizza onto a cutting board and cut into wedges. Serve immediately.

REUBEN'S PIZZA
❦

Buckwheat or rye dough is an appealing base for this Old World pizza. Serve it with sautéed greens and dill pickles.

YIELD: 1 pizza—2 generous servings

PREPARATION TIME: 30 minutes to prepare; 10 minutes to bake

2 tablespoons sesame oil, plus extra for the pan and dough
1 8-ounce cake tempeh
½ cup vegetable stock or water
½ recipe MELLOW MUSTARD SAUCE (page 148), uncooked
  Cornmeal
12 ounces bread dough
½ cup finely chopped green onion
1 cup well-drained sauerkraut
½ cup thinly sliced red bell pepper

Heat the 2 tablespoons sesame oil in a medium-sized skillet over moderate heat. Brown the tempeh on both sides. Add the stock and tightly cover the pan. Steam until the pan is dry. Remove the tempeh and slice it into thin, short strips. Return it to the skillet and add the sauce. Cook over low heat, stirring occasionally, until the sauce thickens.

Preheat the oven to 500 degrees. Lightly grease a 14- to 15-inch pizza pan with sesame oil and dust it with cornmeal.

On a lightly greased surface, roll the dough into a 13-inch circle. Brush the dough lightly with sesame oil, then transfer it to the prepared pan. Crimp the edge to form a slight lip. Spread the sauced tempeh over the dough and sprinkle on the onion. Arrange the sauerkraut on top and scatter on the pepper slices.

Bake on a low rack of the preheated oven for 10 minutes, or until the bottom is brown and crisp. Slide the pizza onto a cutting board and cut it into wedges. Serve immediately.

NOTES

- Omit the mustard sauce. Marinate the tempeh in a mixture of 1 tablespoon tamari, 1 teaspoon brown rice vinegar, and 3 tablespoons vegetable stock or water. Drain, reserving the marinade. Brown and steam as above, adding the remaining marinade near the end of cooking. Spread 3 tablespoons prepared coarse mustard on the dough and add the tempeh and other toppings.

BREAKFAST PIZZA
▼▼▼

Once when we were camping, I dreamed that someone came to the door of the tent in the morning and announced: "Here's your breakfast pizza!" The dream was so vivid that I was disappointed when I woke up and there wasn't a pizza for breakfast. A pizza like this one is just what I would have ordered. Serve it for breakfast or any other meal of the day.

YIELD: 1 pizza—2 generous servings

PREPARATION TIME: 30 minutes to prepare; 10 minutes to bake

2 *medium-sized red bell or pimiento peppers*
2 *medium-sized green bell peppers*
3 *eggs*
Freshly ground black pepper—several grindings
1/8 *teaspoon sea salt*
1/4 *cup minced baby shallots, green onions, chives, or garlic chives*
1 *tablespoon minced fresh basil leaves*
1 1/2 *to 2 teaspoons minced fresh tarragon or pericon leaves*
Olive oil

Cornmeal
12 *ounces bread dough*

Roast and peel the peppers as described on page 130. Cut them into thin strips—you should have about 1/2 cup of each kind.

In a medium-sized bowl, whisk the eggs. Whisk in the black pepper, salt, shallots, and herbs.

Preheat the oven to 500 degrees. Lightly grease a 14- to 15-inch pizza pan with olive oil and dust it with cornmeal.

On a lightly greased surface, roll the dough into a 13-inch circle. Brush the dough lightly with olive oil, then transfer it to the prepared pan. Crimp the edge to form a 3/4- to 1-inch lip. Pour the eggs onto the dough and arrange the pepper strips on top.

Bake on a low rack of the preheated oven for 10 minutes, or until the bottom is brown and crisp and the eggs are set. Slide the pizza onto a cutting board and cut it into wedges. Serve immediately.

NOTES

- Vary the herbs in the filling and, instead of or in addition to the pepper strips, lay on thinly sliced tomatoes or lightly sautéed sliced mushrooms or zucchini.

PISSALADIÈRE
▼▼▼

This Provençal pizza originated in Nice. It is traditionally smothered in sweet sautéed onions and decorated with anchovies and ripe olives. Though slightly different, my version preserves the spirit of the original dish.

YIELD: 1 pizza—2 generous servings

PREPARATION TIME: About 30 minutes to prepare; 10 minutes to bake

2 *tablespoons olive oil, plus extra for the pan and dough*
2 *large onions, finely sliced*
1/2 *teaspoon minced fresh thyme leaves*
1/4 *teaspoon minced fresh rosemary leaves*
1/4 *teaspoon kelp powder*
Cornmeal
12 *ounces bread dough*
1/2 *cup tomato sauce (page 144-45)*
10 *to 12 Calamata olives, pitted and cut into slivers*

Heat the 2 tablespoons olive oil in a medium-sized skillet over moderate heat. Sauté the onions for several minutes. Reduce the heat to low and continue to cook, stirring occasionally, until the onions are very tender and lightly browned. Stir in the herbs and kelp powder and cook briefly.

Preheat the oven to 500 degrees. Lightly grease a 14- to 15-inch pizza pan with olive oil and dust it with cornmeal.

On a lightly greased surface, roll the dough into a 13-inch circle. Brush the dough lightly with olive oil, then transfer it to the prepared pan. Crimp the edge to form a slight lip. Spread tomato sauce over the dough, spread the onions on top, and sprinkle on the olives.

Bake on a low rack in the preheated oven for 10 minutes, or until the bottom is brown and crisp. Slide the pizza onto a cutting board and cut it into wedges. Serve immediately.

PRONTO PIZZA
▾▾▾

When you don't have yeasted bread dough but yearn for pizza, this biscuit crust may be quicker—and tastier—than sending out. Check the other pizza recipes for topping combinations or create a new one from sundries in your refrigerator and pantry. The tenderest biscuits are made with pastry flour; the pastry-bread flour blend in this recipe provides an effective balance between tenderness and dough strength.

YIELD: 1 pizza—2 generous servings

PREPARATION TIME: 15 to 20 minutes to prepare; 10 to 15 minutes to bake

- ¼ cup olive oil, plus extra for the pan and dough
  Cornmeal
- ½ cup thick tomato sauce (page 144-45) or another sauce, such as pesto (page 141-43) or ROASTED RED PEPPER SAUCE (page 143-44)
  Vegetables or other toppings
- ½ cup milk or soy milk
- 1½ teaspoons lemon juice or vinegar
- ¾ cup whole wheat bread flour
- ¾ cup whole wheat pastry flour
- ¼ teaspoon sea salt
- ½ teaspoon baking soda
- 1 teaspoon baking powder

Preheat the oven to 450 degrees. Lightly grease a 14-inch pizza pan with olive oil and dust it with cornmeal. Prepare and assemble all toppings.

Combine the milk and lemon juice and set aside to curdle.

Sift together the flours. Measure out 1½ cups and set the remainder aside for kneading. Sift the 1½ cups flour, salt, baking soda, and baking powder into a medium-sized bowl. Make a well in the center of the dry ingredients.

Whisk the ¼ cup olive oil into the curdled milk and pour into the dry mixture. Stir gently with a fork until a soft dough forms. Turn out onto a lightly floured surface and knead briefly—15 to 20 times—just until smooth. Form the dough into a ball.

On a lightly floured surface, roll the dough out into a 12- to 13-inch circle, about ¼ inch thick. Lightly brush the dough with olive oil and transfer to the prepared pan. Crimp the edge of the dough to form a slight lip. Spread sauce evenly over the dough and arrange the toppings.

Bake immediately in the preheated oven for 10 to 15 minutes, until the bottom is brown and crisp. Slide the pizza onto a cutting board, cut it with a cleaver, and serve it pronto!

NOTES

- Omit the lemon juice and baking soda and increase the baking powder to 1½ teaspoons, or substitute ½ cup buttermilk or yogurt for the milk or soy milk.

FRUIT SAUCE PIZZA
▾▾▾

Serve this sweet pizza as an unusual dessert, breakfast, or brunch dish. For the dough, I like to use SWEET BREAD (page 66), APPLE OR PEAR SAUCE BREAD (page 70), or squash or sweet potato or egg doughs (pages 67, 69, 89). Plump the raisins ahead of time by steaming them or soaking them for 30 minutes or so.

YIELD: 1 pizza—2 generous servings

PREPARATION TIME: 10 to 15 minutes to assemble; 10 minutes to bake

- ¼ cup raisins
- 1 tablespoon unsalted soy margarine or butter, melted, plus extra for the pan
  Cornmeal
- 12 ounces bread dough
- 1 cup apple sauce or pear sauce (see page 136)
- ¼ cup lightly toasted slivered almonds

Steam the raisins or soak them in boiling water to cover for about 30 minutes and drain them well.

Preheat the oven to 500 degrees. Lightly grease a 14- to 15-inch pizza pan with margarine or butter and dust it with cornmeal.

On a lightly greased surface, roll the dough into a 13-inch circle. Brush the dough lightly with 1 tablespoon melted margarine or butter, then transfer it to the prepared pan. Crimp the edge to form a slight lip. Spread the fruit sauce over the dough and sprinkle the raisins and nuts on top.

Bake on a low rack in the preheated oven for 10 minutes, or until the bottom is brown and crisp. Slide the pizza onto a cutting board and cut it into wedges. Serve warm or cooled.

APPLICIOUS PIZZA
▼▼▼

Save some dough from a batch of bread and make this attractive fruit-topped pizza for breakfast, brunch, or dessert. APPLE OR PEAR SAUCE BREAD *(page 70) dough is especially good for the crust.*

YIELD: 1 9-inch pizza—4 dessert-sized wedges

PREPARATION TIME: About 1 hour to prepare; 30 minutes to bake

> 2 large Pippin apples
> 2 tablespoons lemon juice
> 2 tablespoons maple syrup
> 1 tablespoon unsalted soy margarine or butter, melted, plus extra for the pan
> Cornmeal
> 8 ounces bread dough

Peel and quarter the apples. Core each quarter and cut into thin lengthwise slices less than ¼ inch at their thickest part. As you cut the slices, mix them with the lemon juice in a bowl. Drizzle in the maple syrup and mix gently. Cover and set aside for about 45 minutes.

Lightly grease a pizza pan with margarine or butter and dust it with cornmeal. Preheat the oven to 375 degrees.

On a lightly greased surface, roll the dough into a 9½-inch circle. Brush the dough lightly with the tablespoon of melted margarine or butter and transfer it to the pan. Decoratively crimp the edge to form a ½-inch lip. Beginning at the outside edge, arrange apple slices, slightly overlapping one another, so that they spiral into the center and cover the entire surface of the dough. Reserve the apple marinade.

Bake the pizza 30 minutes—until the crust is crisp and the apples are tender. Meanwhile, heat the remaining apple marinade just to the boiling point, and simmer until it is reduced to a somewhat thickened glaze.

Brush this over the apples as soon as the pizza is done. Serve warm or at room temperature.

NOTES
- Substitute another variety of apple or use pears, peaches, or nectarines.

DEEP-DISH BROCCOLI-MUSHROOM PIZZA
▼▼▼

I first had deep-dish pizza in a little pizzeria called Bella Casa in Cambridge, Massachusetts. The crisp bread shell was loaded with succulent plump mushrooms, fresh broccoli florets, and walnuts, and topped with melted cheese. Here is a good cheeseless version.

YIELD: 1 10-inch pizza—2 to 4 servings

PREPARATION TIME: About 45 minutes, including baking

> 8 ounces tofu, pressed
> 2 teaspoons tamari
> 1 tablespoon olive oil, plus extra for the pan and dough
> 1 packed teaspoon minced garlic
> 8 ounces mushrooms, whole or sliced in half lengthwise
> 4 cups broccoli florets and diagonally sliced stems (8 ounces)
> 2 tablespoons dry white wine
> 8 ounces bread dough
> ½ cup thick tomato sauce (page 144-45)
> ½ cup lightly toasted, coarsely chopped walnuts

Cut the tofu into ½-inch cubes. Combine with the tamari and marinate, stirring occasionally.

Heat the 1 tablespoon oil in a medium-sized skillet over moderate heat. Add the garlic and cook briefly, stirring constantly. Stir in the mushrooms and broccoli and sauté briefly. Add the marinated tofu and wine. Cover and steam very briefly, just until the broccoli turns bright green and the tofu is soft. Uncover and quickly cook away any liquid. Set aside to cool.

Preheat the oven to 450 degrees. On a lightly greased surface, roll the dough into an 11-inch circle. Lightly brush the dough with olive oil and transfer it to a greased 10-inch pie plate. Crimp the edge of the dough just below the rim of the pan. Spread the tomato sauce on the dough. Sprinkle the walnuts over the sauce and spoon the sauté on top.

Bake the pizza 15 minutes, until the crust is crisp. Cut and serve immediately.

NOTES
- This recipe is ripe for substitutions: replace the marinated tofu with cooked tempeh, substitute cauliflower for the broccoli—put your imagination to work!

Bread-Crusted Tarts

Savory tarts have long been one of my favorite main dishes for dinner parties, since they can be made before guests arrive, are attractive, easy to serve, and leftovers keep well. Several years ago, I began making them with bread dough crusts rather than pastry crusts on days when I was already making bread, and I eliminated half the work in the process. Plus, I've found that the new bread-crusted versions have just as much appeal. They are less rich than the pastry-crusted originals, but this seems to be to their advantage in these health-conscious times. Many classic main dish tart fillings, notably quiches, are loaded with eggs, cream, and cheese as it is; the extra fat in a pastry crust is gilding the lily, as my mother was wont to say. Of course, you can cut down on richness in fillings too. Tofu sour cream, for instance, reduces fat and cholesterol without sacrificing a creamy texture, and it also performs the binding function usually accomplished with eggs. Look back through your recipe file and retrieve your favorite tart fillings; you may want to alter them for a better nutritional profile.

When you're making bread and plan to make a tart, simply save out a piece of dough after it has risen at least once, preferably twice, in the bowl. If you're not ready to put the tart together, form the dough into a ball and put it in a covered bowl in the refrigerator. As the recipes describe, you'll shape the dough just as you would a pastry dough. Bread-crusted tarts are best when doughs and fillings are mutually enhancing: for example, rye doughs go especially well with things like onions, cabbage, mushrooms, and sour cream.

Cut bread-crusted tarts into large wedges for main dish servings or into small pieces for hors d'oeuvres or snacks. They can be made in square or rectangular pans as well as round ones.

PIZZA RUSTICA
▼▼▼

Pizza means "pie" in Italian, and this one, with a deep, rich filling, is more like a pie as we know it. Like the other bread dough–crusted tarts to follow, this can also be made in a pastry crust. I like to serve it by candlelight with a crisp salad and a robust wine. Try a French or Italian dough for the crust.

YIELD: 1 9-inch tart—4 to 6 servings

PREPARATION TIME: 30 to 40 minutes to prepare; 30 minutes to bake

- 1 tablespoon kuzu powder
- 1 tablespoon Marsala
- 1 pound tofu, well pressed
- ³⁄₄ teaspoon sea salt
- 2¹⁄₂ tablespoons lemon juice
- 3 tablespoons light vegetable oil
- 2 tablespoons olive oil, plus extra for the pan and dough
- 1 medium-sized onion, finely chopped
- 2 cloves garlic, pressed or minced
  Freshly ground black pepper—several grindings
- 1 teaspoon dried basil, or 1 to 2 tablespoons minced fresh leaves
- ¹⁄₂ teaspoon kelp powder
- ¹⁄₄ to ¹⁄₂ pound mushrooms, sliced
- ¹⁄₄ to ¹⁄₂ cup fresh parsley, minced
- 1 cup tomato sauce (page 144-45)
- 8 ounces bread dough
- ¹⁄₂ cup lightly toasted, coarsely chopped walnuts
- 1 large bell pepper, seeded and sliced into thin rings

Combine the kuzu and Marsala and set aside until the kuzu has dissolved.

In a blender or a food processor fitted with the metal blade, blend the tofu. Add the salt, lemon juice, and vegetable oil and blend until thoroughly smooth. Set aside.

Heat the 2 tablespoons olive oil in a medium-sized skillet over moderate heat. Add the onion and sauté for several minutes. Add the garlic and sauté until the onion is just tender. Grind in the black pepper and add the basil, kelp powder, and mushrooms. Cook briefly, stirring often, until the mushrooms no longer appear dry. Stir in the parsley and tomato sauce and bring just to a simmer. Add the dissolved kuzu and cook, stirring, until the mixture thickens. Cool.

Preheat the oven to 350 degrees. On a lightly greased surface, roll the dough into a 10-inch circle. Brush the dough lightly with olive oil. Grease a 9-inch pie plate and fit the dough into it, fluting the edge. Sprinkle half the walnuts on the bottom. Spread on half the tofu mixture. Spread on half the tomato-vegetable sauce. Arrange half the pepper rings on top. Repeat these four layers, ending with the remaining pepper rings decorating the top of the pie.

Bake the pie 30 minutes. Cool in the pan briefly. Cut into wedges and serve.

CABBAGE KUCHEN
▰▰▰

Kuchen, German for cake, is traditionally made with yeasted bread dough rather than pastry dough. This filling goes well with many different doughs, but I especially like it with ryes.

YIELD: 1 9-inch tart—4 to 6 servings

PREPARATION TIME: 30 to 40 minutes to prepare; 30 minutes to bake

>   1   teaspoon caraway seeds
>   ½   teaspoon dried dill weed
>   3   tablespoons light vegetable oil, plus extra for the pan and dough
>   1   medium-sized onion, finely chopped
>   4   to 5 cups finely chopped cabbage
>   ½   teaspoon kelp powder
>   ½   to ¾ teaspoon sea salt
>   8   ounces tofu
>   2   tablespoons lemon juice
>   4   teaspoons tahini
>   8   ounces bread dough
>   1   teaspoon poppy seeds

In a heavy-bottomed, medium-sized skillet over moderate heat, toast the caraway seeds, stirring often to prevent them from burning. Grind to a coarse consistency with a mortar and pestle or spice grinder. Add the dill and grind again. Set aside.

Heat 1 tablespoon of the oil in the skillet over moderate heat. Sauté the onion for several minutes, until it appears translucent and is barely tender. Stir in the cabbage and cook a few minutes, stirring often. Stir in the ground herbs and kelp powder and sauté briefly. Remove from the heat and add a pinch of salt. Transfer to a medium-sized bowl and set aside to cool somewhat.

In a blender or a food processor fitted with the metal blade, blend the tofu. With the machine running, add ½ teaspoon salt, the lemon juice, remaining 2 tablespoons oil, and the tahini. Blend until thoroughly smooth. Fold this mixture together with the sauté.

Preheat the oven to 350 degrees. On a lightly greased surface, roll the dough into a 10-inch circle. Lightly brush the dough with oil and transfer it to a greased 9-inch pie plate. Flute the edge just below the rim of the pan. Spread in the filling and sprinkle the poppy seeds on top.

Bake 30 minutes, until the crust is crisp and the filling is set—the point of a sharp knife inserted into the center should come out clean. Cool in the pan briefly. Cut into wedges and serve warm.

NOTES

- Substitute 1 teaspoon minced fresh dill weed for the dried dill weed.

- Omit the poppy seeds and lightly sprinkle paprika on top of the filling.

- Fit the dough into an 8-inch square pan rather than the pie plate.

- To make *ONION KUCHEN*, follow the recipe with these changes: substitute 1 teaspoon cumin seeds for the caraway and omit the dill; omit the cabbage and increase the onions to 1 pound (weighed after paring and peeling), but slice them thinly rather than chopping them; add freshly ground black pepper; and stir in 1 tablespoon whole wheat pastry flour along with the kelp powder.

SPINACH TART
▰▰▰

A creamy, herbed spinach mixture fills this savory bread dough tart. Crustless, the filling is a delicious pâté.

YIELD: 1 9-inch tart—4 to 6 servings

PREPARATION TIME: 30 to 40 minutes to prepare; 30 minutes to bake

>   8   ounces tofu
>   ½   teaspoon sea salt, plus more to taste
>   2   tablespoons lemon juice
>   2   tablespoons light vegetable oil
>   4   teaspoons tahini
>   1   tablespoon olive oil, plus extra for the pan and dough
>   1   medium-sized onion, finely chopped, or ½ cup minced green onions or shallots
>   1   clove garlic, pressed or minced

Freshly ground black pepper—several grindings
¼ teaspoon freshly grated nutmeg
1 tablespoon minced fresh dill weed, or 1½ teaspoons dried
1 teaspoon minced fresh tarragon or pericon, or ½ teaspoon dried
8 cups loosely packed fresh spinach leaves (8 ounces), finely chopped
½ teaspoon kelp powder
¼ cup fresh parsley, minced
8 ounces bread dough

In a food processor fitted with the metal blade, blend the tofu. Add the salt, lemon juice, vegetable oil, and tahini and blend until thoroughly smooth. Set the processor aside.

Heat the 1 tablespoon olive oil in a medium-sized skillet over moderate heat. Sauté the onion a few minutes. Add the garlic and sauté until the onion is tender. Stir in the pepper, nutmeg, dill, tarragon or pericon, spinach, kelp powder, and parsley and cook, stirring, just until the spinach is wilted. Cool briefly, add to the processor, and pulse a couple of times to combine the two mixtures but not purée. Taste and add a pinch of salt if necessary.

Preheat the oven to 350 degrees. On a lightly greased surface, roll the dough into a 10-inch circle. Brush the dough lightly with olive oil. Grease a 9-inch pie plate with olive oil and fit the dough into it, fluting the edge just below the rim of the pan. Spread the filling in the dough crust.

Bake the tart 30 minutes, until the crust is crisp and the filling is set—the point of a sharp knife inserted into the center should come out clean. Cool in the pan briefly. Cut into wedges and serve warm.

NOTES
- Substitute ¼ pound sliced mushrooms for half the spinach; add the mushrooms to the sauté along with the garlic.

HARVEST MOON
▼▼▼

The sight of this brilliant orange main dish tart may set you to howling. Any strong bread dough works well for the crust, though I like ANADAMA BREAD (page 62-63) or an egg dough (page 69 or 89).

YIELD: 1 9-inch tart—4 to 6 servings

PREPARATION TIME: 30 to 40 minutes to prepare; 30 to 40 minutes to bake

1 tablespoon sesame oil, plus extra for the pan and dough

1 large onion, finely chopped
1 large apple, peeled, cored, and finely chopped
Freshly ground black pepper—several grindings
¼ teaspoon freshly grated nutmeg
½ teaspoon dried marjoram
¼ teaspoon dried thyme
⅛ teaspoon dried rosemary
3 medium-sized eggs
2 cups mashed cooked butternut squash
1 tablespoon mellow barley miso
⅓ cup lightly toasted, coarsely chopped pecans
8 ounces bread dough

Heat the 1 tablespoon sesame oil in a medium-sized skillet over moderate heat. Sauté the onion for several minutes, until it appears translucent and is almost tender. Add the apple and sauté until tender. Add the pepper and nutmeg. Grind the dried herbs with a mortar and pestle or spice grinder and add to the sauté. Cook briefly, stirring often.

Blend the eggs in a food processor fitted with the metal blade. Add the squash and miso and blend thoroughly. Add the sauté and pulse briefly, just to combine but not purée. Fold in the pecans.

Preheat the oven to 350 degrees. On a lightly greased surface, roll the dough into a 10-inch circle. Brush the dough lightly with oil. Grease a 9-inch pie plate and fit the dough into it. Decoratively flute the edge. Spread in the filling.

Bake the tart 30 minutes, until the crust is crisp and the filling is set—the point of a sharp knife inserted into the center should come out clean. Cool in the pan briefly. Cut into wedges and serve warm.

NOTES
- Substitute minced fresh herbs for the dried ones; use twice as much.

Turnovers

There's some kind of a turnover or otherwise stuffed, sealed bread in just about every cuisine around the world. Made in much the same way in every case, the differences lie in the particular dough and filling and perhaps the cooking technique. Italians fold over and seal up pizzas and call them *calzone*. Spaniards and Latin Americans stuff yeasted dough or puff or cornmeal pastry with spicy mixtures of onions, peppers, and meat or fish to make *empanadas*. Eastern Europeans enclose seasoned kasha or chopped chicken livers in pastry dough rich with chicken fat. Greeks wrap cheese, spinach, or meat fillings in fine, flaky phyllo dough. Russians fill the pastry or bread dough covers of their *piroshki* with hearty cabbage, chopped egg, or ground meat mixtures. Indian *samosas* are delicately crusted, dough-encased pyramids filled with superbly spiced vegetable fillings. And Cornish pasties, palm-sized baked turnovers traditionally filled with gravy-moistened leftover meat and potatoes and perhaps even a dab of jam in one end for dessert, have long occupied a prominent place in English lunch pails.

Some of these items are baked, some fried or even steamed. I prefer baking to frying, for health reasons and also because it is less involved, with no extra greasy pans to clean up. I generally make turnovers when I'm already making bread and bake them at the same time. So I've adapted some items that are customarily fried—such as Indian samosas or Latin American empanadas—and bake them. I also usually use bread dough rather than specialized doughs for the same reason—bread dough is available and therefore convenient. Just save out what you need for the turnovers after the dough has risen at least once, and preferably twice, in the bowl. I often match up doughs and fillings in terms of cultural considerations as well as flavors and textures, though these criteria always seem to go hand in hand anyway: buckwheat or rye doughs for piroshki, cornmeal doughs for empanadas, and Italian doughs for calzone are a few examples.

Turnovers may vary in size all the way from tiny, bite-size canapés to those large enough for several servings. Shape them to suit your meal plan. An egg wash or other surface treatment makes turnovers especially attractive.

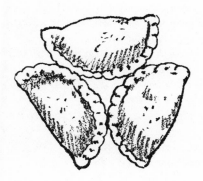

CORNISH PASTIES
▾▾▾

Cornish pasties originated in Cornwall, a southwestern county of Britain, centuries ago. These turnovers have always consisted of some kind of dough—usually pastry dough—filled with diced vegetables and meat when it was available. This vegetarian version has an Italian flair. Soysage goes well with different seasonings; try out different herbs and vegetables for variations. Soy dairies often make a Soysage-like product with their okara; look

for it in the refrigerator or freezer case of natural foods stores if you don't have homemade Soysage on hand.

YIELD: 4 large turnovers—4 servings

PREPARATION TIME: 30 to 40 minutes to prepare; 20 minutes to bake

> 3 *to 4 medium-sized potatoes, cut into small dice (about 2 cups)*
> 2 *tablespoons olive oil, plus extra for the dough*
> 1 *medium-sized red onion, finely chopped*
> 1 *medium-sized carrot, finely sliced*
> 2 *cloves garlic, pressed or minced*
> 1 *cup finely sliced fennel bulb*
> ½ *teaspoon dried basil, crushed*
> 2 *cups sliced fresh mushrooms*
> 8 *ounces* SOYSAGE *(page 141), cut into small dice*
> *Freshly ground black pepper—several grindings*
> ½ *teaspoon kelp powder*
> ¼ *teaspoon sea salt, or to taste*
> ¼ *cup finely chopped fresh parsley*
> 1 *pound bread dough*

Steam or boil the diced potatoes until just tender and set aside.

In a medium-sized skillet, heat 2 tablespoons olive oil over moderate heat and sauté the onion and carrot. When the carrot is almost tender, add the garlic, fennel, and basil and sauté briefly. Stir in the mushrooms, Soysage, pepper, kelp powder, and potatoes and cook, stirring, until the mushrooms are done. Add the salt and parsley and remove from the heat.

Divide the dough into 4 equal pieces. Roll into balls, cover with a damp tea towel, and leave them for a few minutes, until the dough has relaxed.

On a lightly greased surface, roll one of the balls into a 9- to 10-inch circle. Transfer the dough to a lightly greased or parchment-lined baking sheet. Brush the dough lightly with olive oil, leaving a 1-inch border around the edge. Spoon ¼ of the filling onto the dough, fold in half, and firmly crimp the edges together to seal in the filling. Make the other turnovers in the same manner. Cover with a damp tea towel.

Preheat the oven to 400 degrees. Brush the turnovers lightly with olive oil and prick with a fork in two or three places to allow steam to escape as they bake. Bake 20 minutes, until browned and crusty. Cool briefly on a rack and serve warm.

NOTES

- If fresh fennel is unavailable, substitute ½ to 1 teaspoon dried fennel weed or seeds and perhaps 1 cup finely sliced celery for texture.

- In season, substitute minced fresh basil; use at least twice as much fresh as dried.

INDIAN TURNOVERS
▼▼▼

Indian samosas are deep-fried turnovers prepared from a pastry dough and spicy vegetable filling. Here is a less fatty, baked, bread dough version. I like to use a cracked wheat dough for these.

YIELD: 4 large turnovers—4 servings

PREPARATION TIME: 30 to 40 minutes to prepare; 20 minutes to bake

> 1 *large potato*
> 2 *tablespoons ghee or sesame oil*
> 1/2 *teaspoon black mustard seeds*
> 1 *medium-sized onion, finely chopped*
> 2 *cloves garlic, pressed or minced*
> 1 *teaspoon minced fresh ginger root*
> 1 *medium-sized carrot, thinly sliced*
> 1 *cup sliced mushrooms*
> 3/4 *teaspoon ground cumin*
> 1/4 *teaspoon ground coriander*
> 1/8 to 1/4 *teaspoon cayenne, to taste*
> 1 *cup shelled green peas or sugar snap peas*
> 1 *teaspoon lemon juice*
> 1/2 *teaspoon sea salt*
> 1/2 *cup* TOFU SOUR CREAM *(page 148) or yogurt*
> 1 *pound bread dough*

Cut the potato into quarters and simmer in water to cover until tender. Drain thoroughly and, when cool enough to handle, dice into 1/4-inch cubes.

Heat 1 tablespoon of the ghee or oil in a large skillet over moderate heat. Cook the black mustard seeds until they begin to pop. Add the onion, garlic, and ginger and sauté for several minutes, until the onion appears translucent. Stir in the carrot, mushrooms, cumin, coriander, and cayenne and sauté until the carrot is just tender. Stir in the peas, cubed potatoes, lemon juice, and salt and cook briefly, stirring often. Stir in the sour cream or yogurt and remove from the heat.

Divide the dough into 4 equal pieces. Roll into balls, cover with a damp tea towel, and leave them for a few minutes, until the dough has relaxed.

On a lightly greased surface, roll one of the balls into a 9- to 10-inch circle. Transfer the dough to a lightly greased or parchment-lined baking sheet. Brush the dough lightly with ghee or oil, leaving a 1-inch border around the edge. Spoon 1/4 of the filling onto the dough, fold in half, and firmly crimp the edges together to seal in the filling. Make the other turnovers in the same manner. Cover with a damp tea towel.

Preheat the oven to 400 degrees. Brush the turnovers lightly with ghee or oil and prick with a fork in two or three places to allow steam to escape as they bake. Bake 20 minutes, until browned and crusty. For a softer top crust, brush the turnovers lightly with ghee or oil again as soon as you remove them from the oven. Cool briefly on a rack and serve warm.

NOTES
- Instead of ghee or oil, brush the turnovers with an egg wash and sprinkle with poppy or sesame seeds before baking.

PIROSHKI
▼▼▼

When I studied Russian in high school, our enthusiastic teacher gave all of us Russian names and introduced us to traditional foods and folk dancing as well as the language. This is where I learned to make piroshki, baked turnovers that are typically made with a rich pastry dough stuffed with chopped meat or hard-boiled egg and vegetables. I still make piroshki, but now I use bread dough to encase a hearty tempeh-and-vegetable filling. Rye doughs are particularly good for the crust.

YIELD: 4 large turnovers—4 servings

PREPARATION TIME: About 45 minutes to prepare; 20 minutes to bake

> 1 *teaspoon kuzu powder*
> 1 *teaspoon cold vegetable stock or water*
> 1 *teaspoon caraway seeds*
> 1 *teaspoon dried dill weed, or 2 to 3 teaspoons minced fresh*
> 3 to 4 *tablespoons sesame oil*
> 1 *8-ounce cake tempeh*
> 1/2 *cup plus 2 tablespoons vegetable stock or water*
> 1 *large onion, chopped*
> 1 *small carrot, finely diced*
> 1 *small turnip, finely diced*
> 2 *cups sliced mushrooms*
> 2 *cups finely chopped cabbage*
> *Freshly ground black pepper—several generous grindings*
> 1/2 *teaspoon kelp powder*
> 2 *tablespoons mellow barley miso*
> 1 *pound bread dough*
> 1 *tablespoon beaten egg mixed with a bit of water*
> *Poppy seeds*

Combine the kuzu and teaspoon of cold liquid and set aside until the kuzu has thoroughly dissolved.

In a heavy-bottomed skillet over moderate heat, toast the caraway seeds, agitating the pan frequently to keep the seeds from scorching. Grind together with the dill with a mortar and pestle or spice grinder.

Heat 1 to 2 tablespoons of the oil in a large skillet over moderate heat. Brown the tempeh on both sides. Add the ½ cup stock and tightly cover the pan. Steam, turning the tempeh occasionally, until the liquid has cooked away. Remove the tempeh from the pan and cut it into narrow lengthwise strips and then crosswise into small pieces.

Heat the remaining 2 tablespoons oil in the skillet over moderate heat and sauté the onion, carrot, and turnip until just tender. Stir in the mushrooms, cabbage, pepper, ground herbs, and kelp powder. Cook several minutes, stirring often. Stir in the tempeh and cook briefly over low heat. Whisk the miso and remaining 2 tablespoons liquid with the dissolved kuzu until smooth. Stir into the sauté and cook briefly.

Divide the dough into 4 equal pieces. Roll into balls, cover with a damp tea towel, and leave them for a few minutes, until the dough has relaxed.

On a lightly greased surface, roll one of the balls into a 9- to 10-inch circle. Transfer the dough to a lightly greased or parchment-lined baking sheet. Brush the dough lightly with oil, leaving a 1-inch border around the edge. Spoon ¼ of the filling onto the dough, fold in half, and firmly crimp the edges together to seal in the filling. Make the other turnovers in the same manner. Cover with a damp tea towel.

Preheat the oven to 400 degrees. Brush the turnovers with the egg wash and sprinkle on poppy seeds. Prick with a fork in two or three places to allow steam to escape as they bake. Bake 20 minutes, until browned and crusty. Cool briefly on a rack and serve warm.

KASHA KNISHES
▾▾▾

These Eastern European baked or fried specialties traditionally consist of a nonyeasted dough and a potato, chicken liver, or kasha filling. In this variation, a crisp bread crust encloses a moist kasha, tofu, and vegetable mixture. Rye doughs especially complement this filling, and doughs containing winter squash or sweet potato provide other good flavor combinations. Serve the knishes with sauerkraut and dill pickles.

YIELD: 4 large turnovers—4 servings

PREPARATION TIME: 45 minutes to prepare; 30 minutes to bake

 1 *teaspoon kuzu powder*
 1 *teaspoon cold vegetable stock or water*
 2 *tablespoons sesame oil, plus extra for the dough*
 1 *medium-sized onion, finely chopped*
 2 *cloves garlic, pressed or minced*
 ¼ *cup finely diced carrot*
 ¼ *cup finely diced turnip*
 1½ *cups sliced mushrooms (4 ounces)*
 2 *cups loosely packed finely chopped kale*
 Freshly ground black pepper—several liberal grindings
 ½ *teaspoon kelp powder*
 ¾ *teaspoon dried dill, crushed, or 1½ teaspoons or more fresh*
 4 *ounces tofu, mashed*
 2 *cups cooked kasha (see page 13-14)*
 1 *tablespoon hatcho miso*
 1 *tablespoon tahini*
 1 *tablespoon tamari*
 2 *tablespoons vegetable stock or water*
 2 *tablespoons minced fresh parsley leaves*
 1 *pound bread dough*
 1 *tablespoon beaten egg mixed with a bit of water*
 Poppy seeds

Combine the kuzu and cold liquid and set aside until the kuzu is thoroughly dissolved.

Heat 2 tablespoons of the oil in a large skillet over moderate heat. Sauté the onion, garlic, carrot, and turnip until almost tender. Stir in the mushrooms and kale and sauté for several minutes. Add the pepper, kelp powder, dill, and tofu and cook while stirring, briefly. Stir in the kasha, cover the pan, and turn the heat to low.

Add the miso, tahini, tamari, and 2 tablespoons liquid to the dissolved kuzu and whisk until smooth. Thoroughly stir into the skillet mixture. Remove from the heat and mix in the parsley. Cool somewhat.

Divide the dough into 4 equal pieces. Roll into balls, cover with a damp tea towel, and leave them for a few minutes, until the dough has relaxed.

On a lightly greased surface, roll one of the balls into a 9- to 10-inch circle. Transfer the dough to a lightly greased or parchment-lined baking sheet. Brush the dough lightly with oil, leaving a 1-inch border around the edge. Spoon ¼ of the filling onto the dough, fold in half, and firmly crimp the edges together to seal in the filling. Make the other turnovers in the same manner. Cover with a damp tea towel.

Preheat the oven to 400 degrees. Brush the turnovers with the egg wash and sprinkle on poppy seeds. Prick with a fork in two or three places to allow steam to escape as they bake. Bake 20 minutes, until browned and crusty. Cool briefly on a rack and serve warm.

NOTES
- Try substituting other vegetables, such as parsnip, sweet potato, or cabbage, in the same proportions.

EMPANADAS DE PICADILLO
◥◥◥

Empanadas are the Spanish and Latin American versions of turnovers. In Spain, they are usually made with a yeasted dough and are baked. New World empanadas are commonly made with pastry doughs and are deep-fried. Picadillo, a spicy filling for empanadas, is traditionally prepared with shredded meat, but tempeh is an ideal substitute. A corn-wheat dough is an especially good complement to this filling. You can also use the filling to fill any kind of tortillas (see page 114-17) or CORN CRÊPES *(page 112).*

YIELD: 4 large turnovers—4 servings

PREPARATION TIME: 45 to 50 minutes to prepare; 20 minutes to bake

> 3 to 4 tablespoons olive oil
> 1 8-ounce cake tempeh
> 1 medium-sized onion, finely chopped
> 1 medium-sized bell pepper, finely chopped
> 3 medium-sized potatoes, cut into thin slivers
> 2½ teaspoons ground cumin
> ½ teaspoon cinnamon
> ½ teaspoon ground cloves
> ⅓ cup raisins
> ¼ cup plus 1 tablespoon tequila
> ½ cup BLENDER HOT SAUCE (page 146)
> 1 tablespoon barley miso
> ½ cup fresh parsley, finely chopped
> Sea salt, to taste
> 1 pound bread dough

In a large skillet, heat 1 to 2 tablespoons of the oil over moderate heat. Brown the tempeh on both sides. Remove it from the skillet and cut into small strips.

In the same skillet, heat 1 to 2 tablespoons oil. Sauté the onion until it begins to appear translucent. Add the bell pepper and potatoes and sauté until almost tender. Add the cumin, cinnamon, and cloves and sauté briefly. Stir in the tempeh, raisins, ¼ cup tequila, and the hot sauce. Cover and cook over low heat for a few minutes—until the mixture is hot and the pepper and potato are tender.

Combine the miso and remaining tablespoon tequila and mix to a smooth paste. Stir this and the parsley into the tempeh mixture. Taste and season with salt.

Divide the dough into 4 equal pieces. Roll into balls, cover with a damp tea towel, and leave them for a few minutes, until the dough has relaxed.

On a lightly greased surface, roll one of the balls into a 9- to 10-inch circle. Transfer the dough to a lightly greased or parchment-lined baking sheet. Brush the dough lightly with olive oil, leaving a 1-inch border around the edge. Spoon ¼ of the filling onto the dough, fold in half, and firmly crimp the edges together to seal in the filling. Make the other turnovers in the same manner. Cover with a damp tea towel.

Preheat the oven to 400 degrees. Brush the turnovers lightly with olive oil and prick with a fork in two or three places to allow steam to escape as they bake. Bake 20 minutes, until browned and crusty. Cool briefly on a rack and serve warm.

NOTES
- Add ¼ cup lightly toasted slivered almonds to the filling; stir them in after it has cooked.

- If you don't have prepared hot sauce, add a pinch of cayenne to the sauté along with the other spices and add ½ cup chopped tomato.

CALZONE
◥◥◥

Elba's Italian Kitchen was perched at the top of the steepest hill in Ithaca. On Sunday evenings, they offered calzone—large pizza turnovers—filled with the chef's choice of ingredients, usually a delectable combination of spinach, onions, herbs, and soft cheeses. The original Elba's spirit lives on in these crusty, creamy, yet dairyless mushroom-stuffed crescents. You need a sturdy dough for this one: try yeasted or sourdough Italian or French.

YIELD: 2 large turnovers—2 servings

PREPARATION TIME: 45 minutes to prepare; 30 minutes to bake

> 8 ounces tofu
> ½ teaspoon sea salt
> 2 tablespoons lemon juice
> 2 tablespoons light vegetable oil
> 4 teaspoons tahini
> 2 to 3 tablespoons olive oil
> 1 large onion, finely chopped
> 2 cloves garlic, pressed or minced
> ½ pound mushrooms, sliced
> Freshly ground black pepper—several grindings
> ¼ teaspoon minced fresh rosemary leaves
> ½ teaspoon minced fresh thyme leaves
> ¼ teaspoon kelp powder
> Pinch of sea salt, to taste
> 8 ounces bread dough
> Cornmeal

In a blender or a food processor fitted with the metal blade, blend the tofu. With the machine running, add the salt, lemon juice, vegetable oil, and tahini. Blend until thoroughly smooth.

Heat 2 tablespoons of the olive oil in a large skillet over moderate heat. Sauté the onion for several minutes. Add the garlic and sauté until the onion is just tender. Stir in the mushrooms, pepper, herbs, and kelp powder and cook, stirring often, just until the mushrooms no longer appear dry. Cool somewhat. Fold together the tofu and sauté mixtures. Season with salt to taste.

Divide the dough in half. Roll into balls, cover with a damp tea towel, and leave them for several minutes, until the dough has relaxed.

On a lightly greased surface, roll one of the balls into a 9- to 10-inch circle. Grease a baking sheet or pizza pan with olive oil and dust it with cornmeal. Transfer the dough to the pan. Brush the dough lightly with olive oil, leaving a 1-inch border around the edge. Spoon half of the filling onto the dough, fold it in half, and firmly crimp the edges together to seal in the filling. Make the other turnover in the same manner. Cover with a damp tea towel.

Preheat the oven to 400 degrees. Spray the turnovers with water to produce an especially crisp crust. Prick with a fork in two or three places to allow steam to escape as they bake. Bake 20 minutes, until browned and crusty. Cool briefly on a rack and serve warm.

NOTES
- Use the spinach mixture on page 173-74 or the greens mixture on page 179 as alternate fillings.

- I recently learned that calzone means "pants leg." Roll the dough into rectangles and prepare log-shaped calzone if you prefer.

GREENS CROUSTADE
▼▼▼

Croustades are traditionally hollowed out baked loaves of bread stuffed with meat or vegetables. Here, the dough bakes along with the filling, actually making this more of a turnover-in-the-round. The filling is an embellished version of one of my favorite side dishes—sautéed greens and garlic. Mediterranean in concept, it is a subtly sweet combination. Use a basic wheat, cracked wheat, or Italian dough.

YIELD: 4 servings

PREPARATION TIME: About 45 minutes to prepare; 20 to 30 minutes to bake

   2 tablespoons olive oil, plus extra for the dough
   1 large sweet onion, finely chopped
   4 cloves garlic, pressed or minced
  ¼ cup pine nuts
  ¼ cup currants
   8 cups loosely packed kale (8 ounces), finely chopped

    Freshly ground black pepper—several grindings
  ½ *teaspoon kelp powder*
  ½ *cup fresh parsley, finely chopped*
   1 *tablespoon mellow rice or mellow barley miso*
   2 *tablespoons red wine*
   1 *pound bread dough*
    Cornmeal
   1 *tablespoon beaten egg mixed with a bit of water*

Heat 2 tablespoons of the oil in a large, heavy-bottomed skillet over moderate heat. Sauté the onion until tender and translucent. Add the garlic and pine nuts and continue to sauté until the nuts are lightly browned. Stir in the currants, kale, pepper, kelp powder, and parsley and sauté until the greens are just tender. Mix together the miso and wine to form a smooth paste and stir it into the sauté. Remove from the heat.

Divide the dough in half and form each piece into a ball. Cover and leave for a few minutes, until the dough has relaxed.

On a lightly greased surface, roll one of the balls into a 12- to 13-inch circle. Transfer it to a lightly greased, cornmeal dusted pizza pan. Brush the dough lightly with olive oil, leaving a 1-inch border around the edge. Evenly spread the filling over the greased portion of the dough. Roll the other ball out to the same size and place it on top. Firmly crimp the edges together to seal in the filling. Cover with a damp tea towel.

Preheat the oven to 400 degrees. Prick the top of the croustade in several places with a fork and brush it with egg wash. Bake 20 to 30 minutes, until browned and crusty. Cool briefly on a rack. Transfer to a cutting board and cut into wedges with a cleaver. Serve warm.

NOTES
- Substitute finely sliced leeks (the white part) for the onion.

- Substitute spinach, chard, or other dark greens for the kale.

- Instead of pine nuts, use ¼ cup finely chopped almonds.

- If the currants are hard, soak them in boiling water to cover and drain well. You can use the soaking water instead of wine to dilute the miso.

Spiral Filled Doughs

Another way to fill a dough is to flatten it out, spread on a filling, and roll it up. You can either leave the filled roll in loaf form or cut it into slices and bake them as separate buns. Cinnamon rolls are a classic example of the latter format. Loaves or buns filled with savory ingredients will work just as well as sweet ones, and they make unusual main dishes or partners for soups and salads.

As with other filled doughs, the dough for these should have two bowl rises before it is shaped. It is then set aside to rise one more time before baking. Match up doughs and fillings that have compatible flavors. In general, fillings made with fruits and vegetables need to be cooked first, and they shouldn't be too liquid or contain large chunks. Fruit and nut butters, chopped nuts, seeds, dried fruits, minced herbs, and grated cheese are all good possibilities for other filling ingredients.

CINNAMON SWIRL
▼▼▼

In moments, you can transform a plain loaf of bread into a spicy spiraled bread! Use a basic yeasted or sourdough bread dough (pages 46, 86, 87), GOLDEN HARVEST BREAD (page 67), GOLDEN SOURDOUGH BREAD (page 88-89), or a sweeter dough, such as SWEET BREAD (page 66), DATE-ORANGE BREAD (page 70-71), or APPLE or PEAR SAUCE BREAD (page 70).

YIELD: 1 loaf

PREPARATION TIME: 10 minutes to assemble; about 1 hour to rise; 40 to 50 minutes to bake

> ¾ teaspoon cinnamon
> 2 tablespoons date sugar or Sucanat
> 1½ pounds bread dough
> 1 tablespoon unsalted soy margarine or butter, melted
> ¼ cup raisins
> ½ cup lightly toasted, coarsely chopped pecans

In a small bowl, thoroughly mix the cinnamon and sugar with a fork; set aside.

Roll or press the dough into a 10 × 12-inch rectangle. Brush the dough with the melted margarine or butter, leaving a 1-inch border along one short edge. Evenly sprinkle the cinnamon-sugar over the greased portion of the dough. Sprinkle on the raisins and nuts. Beginning with the side opposite the unfilled edge, roll up the dough and pinch a seam to seal it. Place seam side down in a greased 9 × 5-inch loaf pan. Cover and set aside for about an hour, until the dough has risen and rebounds slowly when pressed. Toward the end of the rising period, preheat the oven to 350 degrees.

Bake for about 50 minutes, until the loaf has browned, the sides are firm, and it sounds distinctly hollow when removed from the pan and tapped on the bottom. Brush with margarine or butter to soften the crust. Cool on a rack. Cut into thick slices to serve.

NOTES
- For juicier raisins, steam them or pour boiling water to cover over them, soak for about 30 minutes, and drain well.

- For a simpler filling, omit the nuts and/or raisins.

- To prepare *CINNAMON BUNS* rather than a loaf: leave one of the longer edges unfilled and roll the dough up toward that edge; cut across the roll to form eight equal pieces; arrange these slices on their cut side in a well-greased baking pan, placing them close enough together so that they will rise up against one another; cover and let them rise until the dough springs back slowly when pressed; bake at 350 degrees for 40 minutes, or until browned and crusty.

- For *FRUIT BUTTER BUNS*, substitute ½ cup *PEAR BUTTER* (page 135) or another fruit butter for the cinnamon-sugar and proceed as for Cinnamon Buns.

STICKY BUNS
▼▼▼

Occasionally on weekend mornings, our family would have sweet rolls or coffee cakes of some sort, and this would start my parents reminiscing about Sunday mornings in Detroit during the war, when my dad would get up early and wait in line at Sanders Bakeshop to buy their famous sticky buns. Their sweet memories were the stimulus for these maple-pecan buns. DATE-ORANGE BREAD (page 70-71) and APPLE or PEAR SAUCE BREAD (page 70) are especially appropriate doughs.

YIELD: 8 large buns

PREPARATION TIME: 1 to 1½ hours to prepare and rise; 40 to 50 minutes to bake

> ¾ cup lightly toasted, finely chopped pecans
> ¼ cup maple syrup
> 1½ pounds bread dough
> 1 tablespoon unsalted soy margarine or butter, melted

Sprinkle ¼ cup of the nuts on the bottom of a well-greased 9- to 10-inch glass or ceramic pie pan or comparable container. Drizzle half the syrup over the nuts.

Roll or press the dough into a 10 × 12-inch rectangle. Brush the dough with the melted margarine or butter, leaving a 1-inch border along one long edge, then brush on the remaining syrup. Sprinkle on the remaining nuts. Roll up the dough, beginning with the filled long edge, and pinch a seam to seal it. Cut the roll into 8 equal slices. Arrange these on their cut side in the pan, placing them close enough together so that they will rise up against one another. Cover and set aside for about an hour, until the dough has risen and rebounds slowly when pressed.

Preheat the oven to 350 degrees and bake for about 40 minutes or until browned and crusty. Run a metal spatula around the edge of the baked buns to loosen them, set a plate upside down on top of the pan, and invert the buns onto the plate, so that the sticky side is on top. Serve warm.

NOTES

- ▪ Substitute honey or rice syrup for the maple syrup and walnuts for the pecans.

NUT BUTTER SPIRAL BUNS
▾▾▾

Adults will be just as enthusiastic as kids about these yummy peanut butter buns. Try BASIC WHOLE WHEAT BREAD (page 48) or SESAME BREAD (page 65) for the dough. Like CINNAMON SWIRL (page 180), you can bake this as a loaf rather than buns.

YIELD: 8 large buns

PREPARATION TIME: About 2 hours to prepare and rise; 45 to 50 minutes to bake

> ¼ cup currants
> 1 cup unsalted chunky peanut butter
> 3 tablespoons mild-flavored honey
> 1 teaspoon finely grated orange zest
> ¼ cup toasted sunflower seeds
> ¼ cup toasted sesame seeds
> 2 tablespoons currant-soaking liquid or orange juice
> 1½ pounds bread dough
> 2 tablespoons unsalted soy margarine or butter, melted

Pour boiling water over the currants and set them aside to soak for about 30 minutes. Drain well, reserving the soaking liquid. If the peanut butter is cold, soften it briefly in a warm oven. Thoroughly mix it with the honey, zest, currants, and sunflower and sesame seeds.

Mix in the 2 tablespoons liquid to achieve a spreadable consistency.

Roll or press the dough into a 10 × 12-inch rectangle. Brush the dough with 1 tablespoon of the melted margarine or butter, leaving a 1-inch border along one long edge. Spread on the peanut butter filling. Roll up the dough toward the unfilled edge and pinch a seam to seal the roll. Cut the roll into 8 equal slices and arrange them on their cut side in a well-greased 9- to 10-inch pie pan. Place them close enough together so that they will rise up against one another. Cover and set aside to rise for about an hour, or until the dough springs back slowly when pressed.

Preheat the oven to 350 degrees and bake for about 40 minutes or until the buns are browned and crusty. Brush with the remaining melted margarine or butter. Cool on a rack. Serve warm.

SICILIAN PIZZA ROLL
▾▾▾

These spiraled pizza slices are perfect for a picnic or buffet supper. Any strong dough works well for this roll, but I especially like to use unsweetened ANADAMA BREAD (page 62–63) or an Italian dough. Borrow the format of this dish and use different main dish fillings. If you don't have homemade SOYSAGE, look for a similar commercial product in the refrigerated or freezer case of natural foods stores.

YIELD: 2 to 4 servings

PREPARATION TIME: 1½ hours to prepare and rise; 40 minutes to bake

> 1 to 2 tablespoons olive oil
> 1 medium-sized red onion, finely sliced
> 2 medium-sized bell peppers, finely sliced
>   Freshly ground black pepper—several grindings
> 1 teaspoon minced fresh oregano, or ½ teaspoon dried
> 1 teaspoon minced fresh basil leaves, or ½ teaspoon dried
> 4 ounces SOYSAGE (page 141), chopped
> ½ cup fresh parsley, finely chopped
>   Cornmeal
> 12 ounces bread dough
> ½ cup thick tomato sauce (page 144–45)

Heat 1 tablespoon of the olive oil in a medium-sized skillet over moderate heat. Sauté the onion for several minutes. Stir in the bell pepper and sauté until the vegetables are almost tender. Add the black pepper, oregano, basil, and Soysage and cook, stirring occasionally, for several minutes. Stir in the parsley. Set aside to cool somewhat.

Lightly grease a baking sheet and dust it with cornmeal. On a lightly greased surface, roll the dough into a 10 × 10-inch square. Brush the dough lightly with olive oil, leaving a 1-inch border along three sides. Spread the tomato sauce on the oiled area. Spread on the filling. Roll up towards the unfilled edge and pinch a seam. Fold in the ends and pinch closed. Place on the baking sheet, seam side down. Cover and let rise for about an hour.

Toward the end of the rising period, preheat the oven to 350 degrees. Brush the top of the loaf lightly with olive oil and slash it in several places. Bake 40 minutes or until it is browned and crisp and sounds hollow when tapped on the bottom. Transfer to a rack and cool to room temperature or slightly warmer. Cut crosswise into 1-inch slices to serve.

CRISSCROSS COFFEE CAKE

Crisscross strips of dough conceal a thick layer of spicy apple filling in this coffee cake. You can make it with a variety of doughs; BEER-RYE (page 63-64) provides an interesting taste combination.

YIELD: 1 coffee cake—3 to 6 servings

PREPARATION TIME: About 1½ hours to prepare and rise; 40 minutes to bake

> 1½ *pounds firm tart apples (Pippins are good)*
> ¼ *teaspoon cinnamon*
> ¼ *teaspoon freshly grated nutmeg*
> ¼ *cup raisins*
> 1 *pound bread dough*
> 2 *tablespoons unsalted soy margarine or butter, melted*

Peel and core the apples and cut them into slices or chunks. In a medium-sized saucepan set on a flame tamer over moderate heat, cook them covered, stirring occasionally, until just tender. Stir in the spices and raisins. Cool.

On a lightly greased surface, roll the dough into a 12 × 15-inch rectangle. Brush the dough with 1 tablespoon of the melted margarine or butter. On the two long sides of the rectangle, make 3¾-inch cuts in the dough at 1-inch intervals. Spread the filling down the center of the dough, leaving 1½ to 2 inches of uncovered dough on all sides. Fold in the short sides first; then, beginning at one end, fold in the strips on the long

sides alternately to form a chevron pattern. Cover and let rise 40 to 50 minutes.

Bake in a preheated 350-degree oven about 40 minutes. Remove to a cooling rack and immediately brush with the remaining tablespoon of melted margarine or butter. Serve warm or at room temperature.

NOTES

- Add lightly toasted, coarsely chopped walnuts or pecans to the filling after it has cooked.

- For a sweeter filling, add 2 tablespoons maple syrup.

- Vary the fruit filling: use part or all pears or peaches (add or substitute allspice or ginger); add ½ to 1 cup fresh or frozen cranberries to the apples and add 2 tablespoons of a mild-flavored honey or maple syrup; add fresh or frozen blueberries to the cooked apples or omit the apples and sprinkle the berries over the dough along with the spices and raisins.

CHINESE STEAMED BUNS

Steamed breads are traditional in the northern region of China, but they are typically made with refined flour. This variation substitutes a whole wheat dough. I steam these buns in a double-tiered bamboo steamer set over boiling water in my wok, but you can use any steamer. Stuffed with a spicy vegetable and tofu filling, these rolls, dipped in a tangy sauce, make an unusual light supper, lunch, or even brunch dish. Serve them with a refreshing miso soup (page 196-97).

YIELD: 6 large buns—3 to 6 servings

PREPARATION TIME: 60 to 90 minutes to prepare and rise; 20 to 25 minutes to steam

> ½ *teaspoon kuzu powder*
> ½ *teaspoon cold water*
> 1 *tablespoon tamari*
> 1 *teaspoon roasted sesame oil*
> 1 *tablespoon HOT SHERRY (page 240)*
> 8 *ounces tofu, well pressed and cut into small cubes*
> 1½ *teaspoons sesame oil*
> 2 *large green onions, finely chopped*
> 1 *clove garlic, pressed or minced*
> 1 *teaspoon minced fresh ginger root*
> 1½ *cups finely sliced bok choy or Chinese cabbage*
> 1½ *pounds BASIC YEASTED WHOLE WHEAT BREAD dough (page 48)—made with sesame oil*

1 tablespoon shoyu
1 teaspoon brown rice vinegar
*5 drops **HOT OIL** (page 239)—or to taste*

Combine the kuzu and water. Set aside until the kuzu is thoroughly dissolved.

In a medium-sized bowl, whisk the tamari, roasted sesame oil, and sherry. Fold in the tofu. Set aside to marinate, stirring occasionally.

Heat a wok or skillet and add the sesame oil. Stir-fry the onions, garlic, and ginger briefly, stirring constantly. Add the bok choy or cabbage and continue stir-frying for a minute or two. With a slotted spoon, remove the tofu from the marinade and add it to the stir-fry. Cook briefly. Turn the heat to low.

Whisk the dissolved kuzu into the reserved marinade and pour it over the stir-fry. Cook, stirring, until the liquid thickens. Transfer the stir-fry to the marinating bowl and set aside to cool.

Cut the dough into 6 equal pieces and form them into balls. Cover and let rest for about 30 minutes. On a lightly greased surface, roll each ball into a 6-inch circle. Cover with a damp towel.

Holding a circle in the palm of one hand, spoon ⅙ of the filling into the center. Pleat the edge of the circle and pinch it firmly shut. Place it, pinched side down, on a lightly floured baking sheet and cover. Repeat with the remaining dough. Let the buns rise 30 to 60 minutes—until just about doubled.

Arrange the buns in a steamer. I place each bun on a square of lightly greased waxed paper or baking parchment. Cover and steam over gently boiling water for 20 to 25 minutes—until the dough is thoroughly cooked.

Whisk together the shoyu, vinegar, and hot oil. Serve in individual bowls as a dipping sauce for the warm buns.

NOTES

- Add a few thinly sliced fresh or soaked dried shiitake mushrooms to the stir-fry.

- The sweet potato-apple-onion filling on page 159 is also a delicious stuffing for these buns.

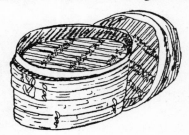

CHAPTER 13

Leftover Bread

ODDS AND ENDS of bread seem to be an inevitable fact of life in baking households. Most enthusiastic bakers don't wait to run out of bread before whipping up another batch, and who wants to eat up all of those scraps of old bread with fresh new ones beckoning? You can always toss it to the birds, but the birds are out of luck when it comes to any over-the-hill bread in my house—I've found too many good ways to use it.

Even though you may have fresher bread in the house by now, variety remains the spice of life, and perhaps the bread from a former baking goes particularly well with the soup you're making for lunch or the dish you're serving for dinner. You can keep surplus breads fresh by freezing them as soon as they've cooled after baking. This is especially effective for small items like rolls, English muffins, bagels, pita, chapatis, and tortillas.

Still, sometimes you'll find yourself with bread that is several days old. First of all, are you absolutely certain that this bread—whatever kind it is—cannot be revived? If it is not too dry, simply reintroducing some

moisture may do the trick. I refresh rolls by spraying them all over with water from an atomizer and placing them directly on the rack of a moderate oven. Voilà! In several minutes they become almost just like their old selves—crisp-crusted and moist and soft inside. You can resuscitate a whole or partial loaf or slices by wrapping them in a damp tea towel and placing them in a covered casserole in a moderate oven for 15 minutes or so, or give the package a brief sauna in your steamer. Steaming is also a good way to revive quick loaves, muffins, and flat breads. Most bread that is past its prime still makes great toast. You can crisp up waffles and crackers by heating them briefly in a moderate oven. Put waffles directly on the rack for all-over crispness.

Even though no longer restorable, truly passé bread is still a valuable resource. Some recipes actually require stale bread: croûtons and French toast are two examples. I always keep both toasted and soft bread crumbs in the freezer. Both have a multiplicity of uses—from breading vegetables, burgers, and croquettes or contributing crunch to the top of stuffed vegetables, casseroles, fruit crisps, or streusel coffee cakes, to becoming, yes, ingredients for pancakes, muffins, and loaves, such as the illustrious black breads of Eastern Europe. Cubed, toasted, and seasoned, dry bread is transformed into flavorful, textural garnishes for soups and salads. Sometimes pieces or cubes of hard bread function as a major salad ingredient, as in Middle Eastern *fattouche* or Italian bread salads. Diced soft bread lends substance to poultry dressings, vegetable stuffings, and bread puddings.

Follow the example of Latin Americans, who never throw a tortilla away. You can easily make them into chips for dips or bases for tostadas. Brush them, whole or cut into wedges, with a little oil and arrange them on a baking sheet in a moderate oven; bake briefly, just until they are crisp. You can also layer aged tortillas in casseroles or cut them into strips for a tortilla soup. The same recycling principle can be applied to almost any bread you make.

I guess you could say that this chapter is more about "getting out of" than "getting into" bread. It looks like we've come full circle, folks. Let the recipes inspire you.

FRENCH TOAST
▾▾▾

Since it isn't as moist and fragile, leftover bread works better than freshly baked bread for French toast; porous yeasted breads are the most effective. Naturally, French bread makes excellent French toast; if it's a baguette, slice the loaf on the diagonal. Other good bread choices are CHALLAH *(page 69),* APPLE OR PEAR SAUCE BREAD *(page 70), and* POPPY SEED BREAD *(page 71). Also, try using* SPICED HONEY BREAD *(page 66-67); omit the spices in the soaking mixture. Serve these crisp, golden slices of French toast with maple syrup or fruit butters, such as* PEAR BUTTER *(page 135). See the notes below for a dairy-free, eggless version with a delicate spiced apple flavor.*

YIELD: 2 generous servings

PREPARATION TIME: 30 to 40 minutes

> Grated zest of 1 lemon
> ½ teaspoon freshly grated nutmeg
> 2 large eggs
> 1 cup milk or soy milk
> 6 slices bread (about ½ inch thick)
> Sesame or sunflower oil

In a medium-sized bowl, combine the zest, nutmeg, and eggs and whisk well. Gradually whisk in the milk. Pour into a shallow pan and arrange the bread slices in it. Soak the bread for about 10 minutes. Carefully turn

CROÛTES AND CROÛTONS
▾▾▾

Croûtes are slices of toasted bread and *croûtons* are cubes. To make croûtes, I brush slices of bread with oil—usually olive oil—arrange them on a baking sheet, and bake them in a low to moderate oven until they are lightly browned and crisp. For croûtons, cut the slices into cubes before baking. Turn slices over and stir cubes occasionally during baking, and remain vigilant, since, like nuts, croûtes and croûtons burn easily. Sometimes I flavor the oil with minced garlic and/or herbs before brushing the bread. To make croûtons from bread that is already cubed, toss the cubes with oil and seasonings in a bowl before baking. You can also toast croûtes or croûtons in an oiled heavy skillet on top of the stove. To make croûtes and croûtons without any oil, simply bake the slices or cubes until they are crisp. If you want to flavor these, mix garlic, herbs, spices, orange or lemon zest, tamari, or whatever, with a small amount of liquid and brush slices or toss cubes with it before baking. To store croûtes or croûtons, cool them thoroughly, wrap them tightly, and put them in the refrigerator or freezer.

Float croûtes in soups or use them as crunchy bases for savory spreads to serve as appetizers or accompaniments for soups or salads. I especially like to spread *BAKED GARLIC* (page 133-34) on olive oil–flavored croûtes. Croûtons add interest to salads and provide a contrast in texture when used as a garnish for hot or cold puréed soups.

the slices over and soak until the egg mixture has been absorbed.

Heat a large skillet or griddle until water dripped onto the surface sizzles. Pour in a small amount of oil and tilt to coat the bottom. Fry the slices until browned and crisp on the bottom. Turn and cook until browned and crisp on the other side. Serve hot.

NOTES

- For a different flavor, substitute 1 teaspoon orange zest for the lemon zest and ¼ teaspoon cinnamon for the nutmeg.

- For *APPLE-CINNAMON FRENCH TOAST*, thoroughly blend 4 ounces of tofu with 1 cup unsweetened apple juice and ¼ teaspoon cinnamon and proceed as with the egg mixture above. If you like, add ¼ teaspoon freshly grated nutmeg. The finely grated zest of 1 orange is another tasty addition; juice the orange and combine the orange juice with apple juice to equal 1 cup.

ITALIAN BREAD SALAD
▪▼▼

Try this terrific Tuscan solution for leftover bread. The cubes of dry bread soften somewhat when they sop up some of the pungent dressing. I like to serve this salad with a hot or cold puréed soup, such as PIMIENTO PURÉE (page 200-01) or LEEK AND BEAN SOUP (page 206), for a light summertime meal. You can prepare the salad a few hours in advance, but cut and add the tomato just before serving to preserve its flavor.

YIELD: 4 servings

PREPARATION TIME: 30 to 40 minutes

   1 cup green beans, diagonally sliced into 1-inch pieces
   1 medium-sized carrot, sliced
   1 medium-sized bell pepper, sliced into thin strips
   1 small red onion, sliced into thin rings
   ½ medium-sized cucumber, seeded if necessary and sliced
   2 cups bread cut into ¾-inch cubes
   4 cups torn dark greens (lettuce, arugula, etc.)
   ¼ cup loosely packed fresh parsley, finely chopped
   ½ cup loosely packed fresh basil leaves, chopped
   1 clove garlic, pressed or minced
   ¼ teaspoon kelp powder
      Freshly ground black pepper—several liberal grindings
   3 tablespoons red wine vinegar
   1 teaspoon dark miso
   3 tablespoons olive oil
   1 large tomato, cubed

Steam or blanch the beans until they are just tender. Combine in a large bowl with the carrot, bell pepper, onion, cucumber, bread cubes, greens, parsley, and basil.

Whisk together the garlic, kelp powder, black pepper, vinegar, and miso. Slowly add the olive oil and whisk constantly to emulsify the mixture. Drizzle over the vegetables and bread and toss thoroughly. If you wish, cover and chill for 20 to 30 minutes or up to several hours.

Add the tomato and toss. Serve immediately.

NOTES

- Substitute an herbed vinegar, such as basil or tarragon vinegar, for the red wine vinegar. If you use basil vinegar, you may wish to decrease the fresh basil or substitute some minced fresh tarragon.

- Substitute sea salt, to taste, for the miso.

- Garnish the salad with freshly grated cheese, such as Romano, Parmesan, or grating ricotta—a solid, mild-flavored white cheese available at some cheese shops and Italian markets.

FATTOUCHE
▪▼▼

This is a good way to use up leftover pita. In Arabic, fattouche means moistened bread. To keep the pita from getting moist to the point of sogginess, though, add it at the very last minute. Include this salad in a buffet or serve it with soup for lunch.

YIELD: 2 to 4 servings

PREPARATION TIME: 30 to 40 minutes

   1 pita (see page 120-21)
   1 clove garlic, pressed or minced
   ¼ teaspoon kelp powder
      Freshly ground black pepper—several grindings
   2 tablespoons lemon juice
   2 tablespoons olive oil
   ¼ cup fresh mint leaves, minced
   ⅛ teaspoon sea salt, or to taste
   4 cups finely shredded lettuce or other greens
   2 green onions, sliced lengthwise and finely chopped
   ½ medium-sized cucumber, sliced
   ½ cup fresh parsley, finely chopped
   1 large tomato, cubed, or about 1 cup whole cherry tomatoes
  10 to 12 Calamata olives

Run a knife around the edge of the pita and separate it into two circles. Place it on a baking sheet in a 350-degree oven and toast until crisp. Break the bread into small pieces and set aside.

In a small bowl, whisk together the garlic, kelp powder, pepper, and lemon juice. Add the olive oil very slowly while whisking constantly to emulsify the mixture. Stir in the mint. Season with salt.

In a large bowl, combine the greens, onions, cucumber, parsley, and tomato. Drizzle in the dressing and toss thoroughly. Add the crumbled pita and toss again. Serve immediately, garnished with olives.

NOTES

- Add about ¼ cup crumbled feta cheese.

BREAD PUDDING

▼▼▼

Transform leftover bread of any kind into a delicately spiced custard for dessert or breakfast. For an especially rich pudding, try making it with leftover brioche or croissants—if you ever have any!

YIELD: 4 to 6 servings

PREPARATION TIME: 20 minutes to assemble; 45 to 55 minutes to bake

> 2 *eggs*
> ¼ *cup mild-flavored honey*
> ⅛ *teaspoon sea salt*
> ¼ *teaspoon cinnamon*
> ½ *teaspoon freshly grated nutmeg*
> 2 *cups milk or soy milk*
> ½ *cup raisins*
> 3 *cups ½-inch bread cubes*

Preheat the oven to 325 degrees. Grease a 9-inch round or 8-inch square ovenproof baking dish.

In a medium-sized bowl, vigorously whisk the eggs. Whisk in the honey, salt, cinnamon, and nutmeg. Gradually whisk in the milk. Stir in the raisins and bread cubes. Pour into the prepared pan and set the pan in a larger pan of hot water. Bake 45 to 55 minutes, or until a knife inserted in the center comes out clean. Serve warm or chilled.

NOTES

- Add about ½ teaspoon finely grated lemon or orange zest to the liquid mixture.

- Substitute maple syrup for the honey.

- For a less sweet pudding, reduce the sweetener to 2 tablespoons.

- Substitute chopped dates for the raisins.

- Serve the pudding topped with lightly toasted chopped nuts.

TORTILLA SOUP

▼▼▼

This soup is sort of an abundantly garnished hot liquid salsa that is enriched with tempeh and garnished with crisp corn tortilla strips.

YIELD: 4 servings

PREPARATION TIME: About 1 hour

> 1 *4-inch poblano pepper*
> 2 *pounds ripe tomatoes*
> 3 *to 4 tablespoons olive oil*
> 1 *8-ounce cake tempeh*
> 3½ *cups vegetable stock or water*
> 2 *medium-sized onions, chopped*
> 4 *cloves garlic, pressed or minced*
> 1 *teaspoon ground cumin*
> 2 *teaspoons sea salt*
> 4 *corn tortillas*
> ½ *cup loosely packed fresh cilantro leaves, coarsely chopped*

Roast and peel the pepper as described on page 130. Transfer to a blender.

In an ovenproof pan (with sides to catch the juice) broil the tomatoes for 20 minutes or so, turning them occasionally to char them on all sides. When soft, blend them and their juice with the pepper.

Heat 1 tablespoon of the oil in a medium-sized heavy-bottomed pot over moderate heat. Brown the tempeh on one side, add a bit more oil, and brown the other side. Add ½ cup of the stock or water and cover the pot. Cook until the liquid disappears. Remove the tempeh and cut into narrow strips.

Heat 2 tablespoons oil (use the tempeh pot) and sauté the onion and garlic until the onion is translucent and almost tender. Stir in the cumin and cook while stirring, briefly. Stir in the tomato/pepper purée, remaining liquid, and salt and bring to a simmer. Cover, reduce the heat, and simmer for 20 to 30 minutes, stirring occasionally, until the flavors are well integrated.

While the soup is simmering, brush both sides of each tortilla lightly with olive oil, cut it into strips about ½ inch wide, and bake in a 350-degree oven for a few minutes, until the underside is golden brown. Turn and brown the second side. Watch them, since they burn easily. Cool slightly, break into halves or thirds, and set aside.

Divide the tempeh strips among four bowls. Ladle in the soup. Sprinkle tortilla strips and cilantro on top, and serve immediately.

NOTES

- For a heartier soup, add a few tablespoons cooked rice to each bowl.

- Another delicious garnish for this soup is sliced ripe avocado.

- Tortilla strips can also be fried in about ¼ inch hot oil; drain on paper towels after cooking. Or add commercial tortilla chips or soft tortilla strips to the soup.

- Poblanos vary considerably in hotness. If this one is very mild or if you prefer spicier foods, sauté a finely chopped jalapeño or serrano pepper along with the onions and garlic. Remove the seeds and membranes of the pepper first, unless you want the soup to be extremely hot!

BREAD CRUMBS
▾▾▾

One way to make bread "good to the last drop" is to make bread crumbs out of it. Any kind of leftover bread, no matter how dry or stale, works, and, of course, whichever kind of bread you use affects the flavor and texture of whatever you use the crumbs for. Whenever I have a few dry slices or crusts hanging around, I make them into crumbs before mold calls first dibs. Unless I have an immediate purpose in mind, I keep the crumbs, soft or toasted, tightly wrapped in the freezer.

Tear or cut the bread into small pieces—approximately ½-inch cubes are fine. Put the small chunks into a blender or a food processor fitted with the metal blade in batches—about one cup in the former, more in the latter—and blend, stopping occasionally to stir around the blade with a chopstick to loosen crumbs that become lodged there. Blend until the crumbs reach the degree of fineness you desire. Either pour them into a bag or container for refrigerator or freezer storage or first spread them evenly on a baking sheet and toast in a 250-degree oven until they are dry and crisp; cool the crumbs thoroughly before wrapping them up.

Use bread crumbs to firm up the consistency and coat the outside of grain and bean burgers and croquettes (pages 152-55) and to provide texture in pâtés (pages 139-41). Dip slices of eggplant first into olive oil and then into crumbs, arrange them on a baking sheet, and bake for 15 to 20 minutes in a moderate oven, until the eggplant is tender. These are good as is or layered in a casserole. For one of my favorite side dishes, dip green tomato slices into crumbs, plain or seasoned with herbs, and fry them in a small amount of olive oil; turn them after the first side is lightly browned and cook until the second side browns and the tomato is fork tender. Sliced vegetables—or tofu—may also be dipped in beaten egg and then coated with crumbs and fried. Mix crumbs with date sugar and spices for a streusel topping (see page 36). You can also use bread crumbs as an ingredient in pancakes, muffins, and breads.

MIGAS
▾▾▾

In Spanish, migas *means "crumbs"—in this case, the last crumbs of leftover tortillas. In this country,* migas *means seasoned scrambled eggs and tortilla strips, and this is a popular item on Southwestern breakfast menus. Serve* EMILIO'S SALSA VERDE *(page 143) or* AVOCADO SALSA CRUDA *(page 143) alongside.* Migas *is a meal in itself, but for an even heartier repast, add* REFRITOS *(page 136), rice, and wheat tortillas (page 116) to the menu.*

YIELD: 2 generous servings

PREPARATION TIME: 30 to 40 minutes

> 1 *poblano pepper*
> 3 *large eggs*
> ¼ *teaspoon sea salt*
> 1 *tablespoon sesame oil*
> 1 *medium-sized onion, chopped*
> 1 *clove garlic, pressed or minced*
> 1 *teaspoon ground cumin*
> 1 *medium-sized tomato, chopped*
> ½ *teaspoon kelp powder*
> 3 *corn tortillas, cut into* ½ × 1½-*inch strips*
> ½ *cup loosely packed fresh cilantro leaves, coarsely chopped*

Roast and peel the pepper as described on page 130. Cut it into thin strips and set aside.

In a small bowl, beat the eggs. Beat in the salt and set aside.

Heat the oil in a medium-sized skillet over moderate heat. Sauté the onion and garlic until the onion is just tender; stir in the cumin and pepper strips and sauté briefly; stir in the tomato and kelp powder and cook briefly. Add the tortilla strips and beaten eggs and cook, stirring, until the eggs are just set. Sprinkle with cilantro and serve immediately.

BREAD CRUMB PANCAKES
▾▾▾

Bread crumbs substitute for part of the flour in these delicate griddlecakes. The character of the crumbs you use for a particular batch will influence its flavor; those I made from a heel of DATE-ORANGE BREAD *(page 70-71) were especially memorable. To save time in the morning, soak the crumbs overnight in the refrigerator and measure the dry ingredients.*

YIELD: About 1 dozen 4-inch pancakes—2 generous servings

PREPARATION TIME: An hour or more to soak the

crumbs; 15 minutes to prepare the batter; 5 minutes to cook

> 1 tablespoon lemon juice
> 1 cup milk or soy milk
> 1 cup soft fine bread crumbs
> 1 tablespoon maple syrup
> 1 tablespoon sunflower or sesame oil
> 1 egg, separated
> ½ cup sifted whole wheat pastry flour
> ¼ teaspoon sea salt
> 1 teaspoon baking soda

Add the lemon juice to the milk and then pour the curdled mixture over the crumbs in a medium-sized bowl. Cover and set in the refrigerator until the crumbs are well soaked.

Whisk the syrup, oil, and egg yolk into the soaked crumbs.

Beat the egg white until stiff but not dry.

Sift together the sifted flour, salt, and baking soda. Gently stir this into the wet mixture—just enough to form a batter. Fold in the beaten egg white.

Drop generous tablespoons of the batter onto a hot, lightly greased griddle. Cook until the tops bubble and appear almost dry. Carefully turn and cook the second side. These pancakes are more fragile than some.

Serve immediately or keep warm in a low oven.

NOTES

- Substitute another sweetener for the syrup or omit it altogether.

- Add the grated zest of a small lemon to the wet ingredients and sift ¼ teaspoon freshly grated nutmeg with the dry ingredients.

SPINACH EN CROÛTE DE PAIN
▾▾▾

Here, a seasoned bread-crumb crust completely encloses a savory spinach filling. You might find something like this in provincial France or Italy. I save stale bread ends, slices, rolls, and so on in a bag in the freezer until I have enough for this unusual dish.

YIELD: 4 to 8 servings

PREPARATION TIME: About 45 minutes to prepare; 1 hour to bake

> 1 pound leftover bread
> 1½ cups water
> 1 egg
> 2 to 3 tablespoons olive oil
> 2 teaspoons pressed or minced garlic
> 2 cups finely chopped onion
> 2 tablespoons minced fresh parsley
> 4 cups loosely packed fresh spinach leaves
>   (4 ounces), finely chopped
> ¼ cup finely chopped green onions
>   Freshly ground black pepper—several liberal
>   grindings
> ¼ teaspoon freshly grated nutmeg
> ¼ teaspoon kelp powder
> 4 ounces tofu, well mashed
> 1 teaspoon lemon juice
> ½ teaspoon sea salt
> ¼ cup lightly toasted, coarsely chopped pine nuts

Make bread crumbs with the leftover bread (see page 188).

Heat the water to boiling and pour it over the crumbs in a medium-sized bowl. Stir with a long-tined fork and cool to lukewarm.

In a small bowl, whisk together the egg and 1 teaspoon of the olive oil. Stir in the garlic, onion, and parsley. Thoroughly stir this mixture into the cooled crumbs and set aside.

Heat 1 tablespoon of the olive oil in a medium-sized skillet over moderate heat. Sauté the spinach and green onions briefly, just until the spinach has wilted. Stir in the pepper, nutmeg, kelp powder, and tofu and cook briefly. Stir in the lemon juice and salt. Remove from the heat and stir in the pine nuts.

Grease a 14-inch pizza pan with olive oil. Spoon half the crumb mixture onto the pan and pat it evenly into a 10-inch circle. Drizzle a little olive oil on top and brush it over the surface. Spread on the filling, leaving a 1-inch border around the edge. Lightly grease a piece of waxed paper and pat the remaining crumb mixture into a 10-inch circle on it. Carefully invert on top of the filling and bottom crust. Peel off the waxed paper and pat the top crust into place. Brush with olive oil. Press around the edge with a fork to seal.

Bake in a preheated 400-degree oven for 20 minutes. Reduce the heat to 350 degrees and bake 30 to 40 minutes longer, until browned and crisp.

Cut into wedges and serve hot or warm. This is good reheated; cover loosely with foil and place in a moderate oven for 20 to 30 minutes.

NOTES

- Substitute other fillings, such as herbed tofu or sautéed mushrooms.

CRUMB BUNS
▀▀▀

This is one of my favorite muffins. Though the basic recipe is terrific, sometimes I vary it—and there are lots of ways to do so; refer to the notes below for some ideas. These muffins stay moist for several days.

YIELD: 10 large muffins

PREPARATION TIME: 30 minutes or so to soak the raisins; 20 to 30 minutes to prepare; 20 minutes to bake

   1½ *cups unsweetened apple juice*
    ½ *cup raisins*
    6 *ounces tofu*
    3 *tablespoons sunflower oil*
    3 *tablespoons maple syrup*
    1 *cup soft bread crumbs*
    2 *cups whole wheat pastry flour*
    ½ *teaspoon sea salt*
    1 *teaspoon baking soda*
    1 *teaspoon baking powder*
    ½ *cup lightly toasted, coarsely chopped pecans*

Heat the apple juice just to boiling, pour it over the raisins, and set aside for about 30 minutes. Drain well, reserving the juice. In a blender or a food processor fitted with the metal blade, blend the tofu, gradually adding the apple juice, until the mixture is thoroughly smooth.

Preheat the oven to 400 degrees. Grease 10 muffin cups.

In a medium-sized bowl, whisk together the oil and syrup. Whisk in the tofu mixture and stir in the raisins and crumbs.

Sift together the flour, salt, baking soda, and baking powder. Add this to the wet ingredients and stir gently—just until a thick batter forms. Fold in the nuts. Immediately spoon the batter into the muffin cups, filling them just to the top. Bake 20 minutes, until browned and a tester inserted in the center comes out clean. Cool the muffins in the pan for a few minutes and then remove to a rack. Serve warm.

NOTES
- Substitute currants or chopped dried dates, apricots, prunes, or figs for the raisins.

- Substitute walnuts, almonds, or hazelnuts for

the pecans. Rub the skins off the hazelnuts after toasting them.

- Add spices, such as cinnamon and/or nutmeg—about ½ teaspoon of each.

- Add the zest of 1 orange or 1 lemon.

- Substitute orange juice for all or part of the apple juice.

RUSTIC RYE BREAD
▀▀▀

Toasted fine crumbs of leftover bread combine with whole grain flours to produce the rich dark color of Eastern European peasant breads. This country rye follows that old tradition. It is moist and hearty, just right with POTATO-LEEK SOUP (page 203-04) or a beet or cabbage soup (pages 199 and 200).

YIELD: 2 loaves

PREPARATION TIME: 1½ to 2 hours for sponge and dough; 5 to 6 hours for rising; 50 minutes to bake

    3 *cups spring water*
    ¾ *teaspoon active dry yeast*
  4½ *to 5 cups whole wheat bread flour*
  1½ *cups toasted fine bread crumbs*
    2 *tablespoons blackstrap molasses*
    2 *teaspoons sea salt*
    2 *tablespoons corn oil*
  1½ *cups whole rye flour*

Heat ¼ cup of the water and cool it to lukewarm. Add the yeast and a teaspoon of wheat flour, cover, and set in a warm spot to proof. Add 1¼ cups of the water and stir in 1½ to 2 cups of the wheat flour to form a thick batter. Cover and set in a draft-free spot for about an hour or until a sponge develops.

Meanwhile, bring the remaining 1½ cups water to a boil and pour it over the crumbs in a large bowl. Add the molasses, salt, and oil. Cover and set aside until lukewarm.

Stir the sponge into the crumb mixture. Add 3 cups wheat flour, a cup at a time, stirring well after each addition. Gradually stir in rye flour until a dough forms, pulling away from the sides of the bowl and balling up in the center. (If you don't add all of the rye flour now, add the remainder later as you knead the dough.) Turn the dough out onto a lightly floured surface, cover, and let rest for a few minutes. Wash the bowl and fill it with hot water.

Thoroughly knead the dough, adding flour only as necessary to keep it from sticking—like other rye doughs, this dough tends to remain a bit tacky. When it is smooth and resilient, form it into a ball.

Dry and lightly grease the bowl. Put in the dough, cover, and set in a draft-free spot for about 2 hours, until it has risen and a finger pressed into it leaves a depression.

Turn the dough out and knead a few times. Form it into a ball and return it to the bowl. Cover and set aside for about 2 hours, until the dough has risen again and does not rebound when pressed.

Divide the dough and shape it into loaves—I usu-

ally make round or oval ones. Cover and set in a draft-free spot for about an hour or until the dough has risen and springs back slowly when pressed.

Slash the loaves and spray them with water or brush on an egg wash and sprinkle on seeds if you wish—I like poppy seeds on this bread. Bake at 350 degrees for 50 minutes or until the loaves have browned, have firm sides, and sound distinctly hollow when removed from the pan and tapped on the bottom.

Cool the bread thoroughly before slicing or storing it.

NOTES

- For an even more robust bread, increase the crumbs and rye flour to 2 cups each and decrease the wheat flour accordingly.

- For a stronger dough, substitute wheat flour for the rye flour.

- Omit the molasses if you prefer.

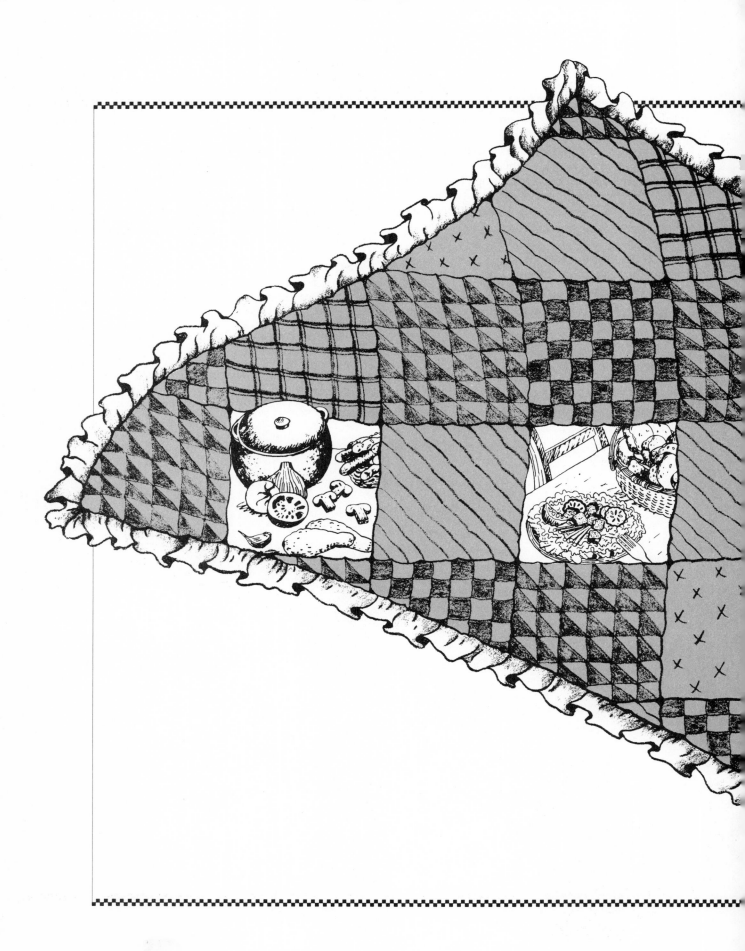

BREADFELLOWS: BREADTIME COMPANIONS

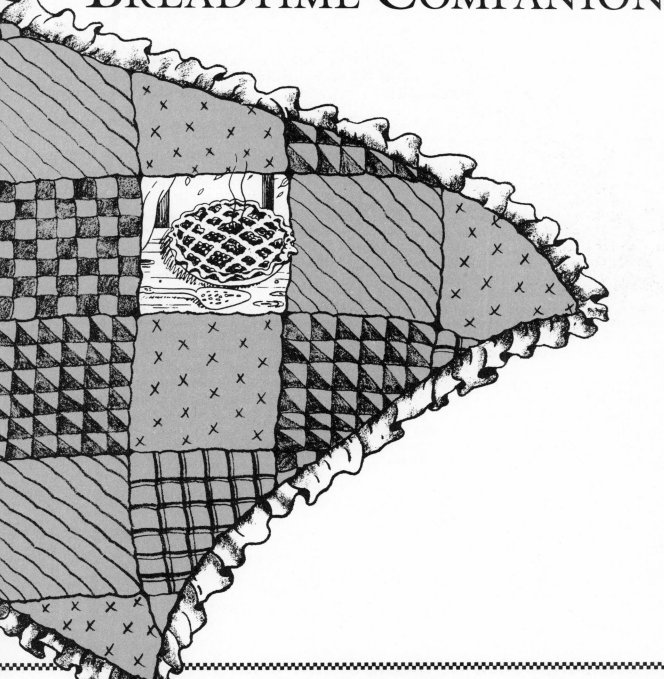

ARLY IN THE MORNING, I crept out into the kitchen as quietly as possible, trying not to wake David, who I knew must have returned in the wee hours from a meeting with his thesis advisor. As I reached out to open the refrigerator, my eye caught a bright pink index card, a new addition to the hodge-podge collage covering the door. "To my favorite breadfellow" was written across the top. Underneath was a sketch of two heads wearing stocking caps, poking out of a comforter made of a loaf of bread, and the invitation "Come on down to Breadfellows for a breadtime snack." I knew this was an acknowledgment of the snack I had left out for David the night before.

"Breadfellows"—he had given a name to my longtime fantasy, a small, genteel bakery-tearoom with lace curtains at the windows, flowers and china on small tables, fresh breads cooling on wrought iron baking racks, the aroma of simmering soups wafting out from the kitchen, and choice baked desserts on display in a glass case. This is the place I'm always looking for when I travel or wishing for when I'm too tired to cook at home—sort of a home away from home serving just the kinds of things that I like to eat in a comfortable atmosphere. I've never found it, but I have come upon parts of it. My imaginary tearoom has developed over the years as a composite of the best features of my favorite bakeries and restaurants—and more.

This is a place to stop by early in the morning for coffee and a roll or muffin to get organized before you head off to work; to meet a friend for a lingering lunch and conversation; to pick up some bread and spreads or sandwiches, stuffed turnovers, salads, and maybe some cold soup for an impromptu picnic; to purchase brioche, croissants, or sweet buns for a weekend breakfast or pies for a holiday dinner. This is an oasis to duck into to gather your thoughts over a cup of tea and a cookie in the midst of a nerve-wracking day or to grab a snack to bolster your energy for your breakneck schedule and tide you over until the next meal. This is where you go at the end of an exhausting day, sink into a chair, and come back to life over a warming soup, a salad, and fresh bread, or go to celebrate an occasion over a pizza or bread-crusted tart, colorful composed salad, and wine. Chances are, you'll find that they've even baked one of your best-loved desserts.

The food at Breadfellows is not super-rich, refined, and meat-based fare. Meals center on the breads from the bakery and include other wholesome, fresh, and seasonal ingredients. The ever-changing menu features the large array of breads in Part Two, combined with the spreads and sauces, and the sandwiches, filled flat breads, and filled doughs that we covered in Part Three. It also teams breads with a wide variety of soups, vegetable stews, and salads and offers baked desserts as a finishing touch. Meals may be ethnic ensembles or more free-form combinations devised by the creative cooks, but whatever they come up with, bread always appears in its best light—in combination with complementary foods. And whether simple or complex, every dish is not only delicious but beautifully presented.

In Part Four then, keeping the broad spectrum of breads and bread-based dishes in mind, let's consider soups and salads that go with them to complete satisfying but light meals. For some helpful tips, you might want to review the introduction to Part Three regarding certain ingredients, techniques, and tools, since these apply to many of the upcoming recipes as well. Finally, I've included recipes for some of those delightful baked desserts that I've always imagined I'd find at Breadfellows. You know—the ones that invite you in for a breadtime snack.

CHAPTER 14

Soups and Vegetable Stews

I CONSIDER MYSELF LUCKY to have experienced soups other than canned ones in my childhood. My mother sometimes made thick pinto bean, lentil, or split pea soups using a leftover ham bone from Sunday dinner. Together with a simple salad and squares of warm corn bread and honey, these hearty soups provided satisfying and inexpensive wintertime suppers for our family. It's this kind of homemade soup experience that I want to keep alive at Breadfellows. There, soups of all kinds are a mainstay of the menu, designed to warm everyone up in cold weather and cool them off when it is hot. And whether a simple broth, a smooth purée, or a chunky mixture that verges on—or is—a stew, a soup invariably tastes best when it is served with a complementary bread; the soups of my childhood wouldn't have been the same without the corn bread. Every day at Breadfellows, the menu features several soups, each one paired with especially compatible breads or bread-based dishes based on flavor, texture, and ethnic themes.

Long, slow simmering suits some soups, such as grain and bean-based ones, and these often taste better after the flavors have mingled for several hours or over-

night. Others, such as miso broths, are ready in a matter of minutes and are at their best as soon as they are made. Each type is a convenience food in its own way: the former can be made ahead of time but served quickly; the latter are quick to prepare.

Soups can be refreshingly chilled or piping hot, and some versatile ones can be enjoyed hot one day and cold the next. Just be sure to serve cold soups thoroughly chilled and hot soups hot. Take care, though, to avoid vigorously boiling any soup. Simmer it gently, so that you don't cook the flavor right out of it. To preserve their flavors, add delicate seasonings such as fresh herbs and fragile dried herbs like dill, tarragon, chervil, parsley, and cilantro to long-simmered soups near the end of cooking.

You'll notice that I season many of my soups with miso of one sort or another. One of the biggest flaws of soups, I find, is a "flat" taste due to improper seasoning. Salt is a flavor enhancer and may correct the situation, but miso adds a certain depth of flavor or rich heartiness to soups as well. Add miso at the end of cooking, and be especially careful not to let the soup boil after adding it or you'll destroy the valuable diges-

195

tive enzymes that miso contains. You can reheat a soup seasoned with miso, just be sure to heat it slowly and gently. A double boiler is a good technique; this is a good way to reheat any soup, whether it contains miso or not.

Making soups is a good way to use up the odds and ends in the refrigerator and pantry or in the garden. Consider all your leftovers—raw or cooked vegetables and fruits, stocks, juices, cooked grains and pasta, sauces, and so on—as potential soup material. For instance, combine leftover stir-fried vegetables, some noodles or rice, and vegetable stock for an especially quick meal; or blend up half a ripe banana, a peach or some strawberries or melon, and the end of a jar of juice and you'll have a fruit soup. In some of the kitchens where I've worked, I've become famous for my "soup kits"—that is, collections of ingredients for soups; this works especially well for leftovers.

A garnish can add a special finishing touch to a soup. Croûtons provide a contrasting texture to a smooth purée, a dollop of sour cream does the same for a chunky soup. Edible flower blossoms and leaves and citrus slices contribute beauty and visual interest. Minced fresh herbs or a sprinkle of a pungent spice add an accent to each serving. But don't forget that complementary bread; it can provide the greatest enhancement of all!

Let's see what is actually simmering on the stove at Breadfellows—or chilling in the cooler. Note that preparation times for soups with dried beans do not include time for cooking the beans. You can also buy many kinds of beans already cooked, though it's a lot more economical to prepare them yourself.

CHILLED CANTALOUPE À L'ORANGE SOUP
▼▼▼

This is a wonderfully refreshing chilled fruit soup that takes minutes to prepare—just what you're looking for in both respects on a sweltering summer day. Serve it with quick loaves or muffins for a light breakfast or lunch, or with something like BREAKFAST PIZZA (page 169) or PESTO PIZZA (page 166-67) for a more substantial meal. Remember to allow time for chilling.

YIELD: 4 servings

PREPARATION TIME: 15 to 20 minutes, plus time for chilling

> 2 *oranges*
> 4 *cups diced cantaloupe*
> 2 *cups unsweetened apple juice*
> *Cinnamon*

Grate ½ to ¾ teaspoon orange zest and juice the oranges.

In a blender or in a food processor fitted with the metal blade, blend the orange juice and cantaloupe. With the machine running, gradually add the apple juice and blend until smooth. Add orange zest to taste. Transfer to another container and chill thoroughly. Serve cold with trace of cinnamon on each serving.

NOTES
- Substitute orange honeydew melon for the cantaloupe.

MISO SOUP
▼▼▼

Some variation on this simple yet satisfying soup is my standby for lunch throughout the year; a bowl of it and a bread and spread see me through the afternoon with flying colors. Miso soup is also good for breakfast or as an appetizer for dinner. To increase the number of servings, simply multiply the ingredients accordingly.

YIELD: 1 serving

PREPARATION TIME: 20 to 30 minutes

> 1 *small strip wakame (about 1-inch square or equivalent), broken into small pieces*
> 1½ *cups vegetable stock or water*
> ½ *teaspoon sesame oil*
> 10 *to 12 thin slices carrot*
> 10 *to 12 thin slices turnip or daikon radish*
> 1 *small green onion, sliced*
> ¼ *to ½ cup thinly sliced Chinese cabbage, bok choy, dark greens (mustard, turnip, kale, etc.), or broccoli florets and sliced stems*
> 1 *to 2 ounces tofu, cubed*
> 1½ *teaspoons dark or light miso, to taste*
> *Umeboshi vinegar, to taste*

Add the wakame to the water or stock and soak for about 15 minutes.

Heat the oil in a small saucepan and sauté the carrot and turnip or daikon a few minutes. Stir in the green onion and remaining vegetables and sauté briefly. Add the wakame and soaking liquid and bring just to a simmer. Simmer gently for about 10 to 15 minutes, until the vegetables are tender; add the tofu near the end of cooking. Remove from the heat.

Whisk the miso and a few spoonfuls of hot soup stock to a smooth paste. Stir this into the soup and add a squirt or two of umeboshi vinegar—to taste. Serve immediately.

NOTES
- Work within this basic framework to vary the soup; you can add almost anything—whatever

you happen to have on hand, or whatever is in season. For instance:

substitute arame or hiziki for the wakame;

sprinkle shredded nori on top after cooking;

simmer a bit of grated fresh ginger root or bonito fish flakes along with the vegetables;

add sliced fresh mushrooms or slivered, soaked shiitake mushrooms—and include the soaking water as part of the liquid;

substitute a few strips of cooked tempeh for the tofu—or omit the tofu altogether;

add cooked rice or noodles;

toss in a few snowpeas near the end of cooking;

vary the kind of miso—longer aged, darker misos are especially appropriate for cold weather, lighter misos for warm days;

add a drop or two of roasted sesame oil;

garnish with minced cilantro or parsley—I have a perennial Japanese parsley called *mitsuba* in my garden that is particularly refreshing.

MADEIRA-MUSHROOM SOUP
▾▾▾

This is a rich, coarse mushroom purée flavored with Madeira, a unique wine that is fortified with brandy and well aged. Remember to soak the dried mushrooms for this soup several hours ahead of time. A chewy buckwheat, triticale, or dark rye bread is a good choice to go with it.

YIELD: 4 servings

PREPARATION TIME: About 45 minutes

½ ounce dried shiitake mushrooms
4 cups boiling water
2 tablespoons olive oil
2 cups finely sliced leeks (2 to 3 large)
1 pound fresh mushrooms, finely sliced
½ cup medium-dry Madeira
5 to 6 tablespoons finely chopped fresh parsley
2 to 3 tablespoons mellow rice or mellow barley miso

Pour the boiling water over the dried mushrooms and soak for several hours. Drain, reserving the stock. Cut off tough stems and cut the caps into thin slivers.

Heat the oil in a large, heavy-bottomed pot over moderate heat and sauté the leeks for several minutes. Stir in the fresh mushrooms and continue to sauté for

several minutes, until they are moist. Add the shiitake mushrooms, wine, 4 tablespoons of the parsley, and the reserved stock. Bring just to a simmer, turn the heat to low, cover loosely, and simmer gently for 20 to 30 minutes, until the vegetables are tender and the flavors are integrated.

Thoroughly whisk 2 tablespoons of the miso with several tablespoons of soup. Stir this into the soup and taste. Add more miso to taste. Remove from the heat. Serve hot, garnished with the remaining parsley.

MUSHROOM-BARLEY SOUP
▾▾▾

Whole grain (or whole) barley gives the best flavor to this soup and also the best nutrition, since the bran layers and germ haven't been pearled away. This is a warming winter soup with sort of an Oriental taste. Different misos subtly vary the flavor. With a simple salad and bread this is a full meal. Try it with SESAME BREAD (page 65), NUT BUTTER BREAD (page 72), or CHINESE SCALLION BREAD (page 126-27).

YIELD: 4 servings

PREPARATION TIME: About 1 hour, not including preparing the barley

2 tablespoons sesame oil
1 large onion, finely chopped
1 tablespoon minced fresh ginger root
3 large cloves garlic, pressed or minced
1 medium-sized carrot, finely chopped
1 medium-sized parsnip, finely chopped
1 small turnip, finely chopped
8 ounces mushrooms, sliced
½ teaspoon kelp powder
1 teaspoon roasted sesame oil
4 cups vegetable stock or water
2 tablespoons miso, or to taste
2 cups cooked barley (see page 13-14)
3 green onions, finely chopped
¼ cup finely chopped fresh parsley
1 cup finely chopped tender mustard greens
8 ounces tofu, pressed and cubed

Heat the sesame oil in a large, heavy-bottomed pot. Sauté the onion until it appears translucent. Add the ginger, garlic, and carrot and sauté briefly. Add the parsnip and turnip and continue to cook, stirring. Add the mushrooms and sauté briefly. Add the kelp powder, roasted sesame oil, and stock or water. Heat to a simmer. Cover and simmer gently for 25 to 30 minutes, until the vegetables are tender.

Whisk several tablespoons of hot soup broth with the miso, and add this to the pot, along with the barley, green onions, parsley, greens, and tofu. Bring the soup just back to a simmer. Taste and add more miso (dissolved in hot broth) if necessary. Serve immediately.

NOTES
- Garnish with additional chopped green onions and parsley or cilantro.

SAUERKRAUT SOUP
▼▼▼

This is a good soup to make when you want something that is hearty but relatively quick to put together. You can also make it ahead of time and reheat it just before serving; when especially pressed for time, I've also enjoyed it cold. Serve it with dill pickles and PUMPERNICKEL-RYE BREAD (page 75-76), PAIN POUR NICOL (page 94), or HEARTY SOURDOUGH BREAD (page 90).

YIELD: 4 servings

PREPARATION TIME: 30 to 40 minutes

> 2 to 3 tablespoons sesame oil
> 1 8-ounce cake of tempeh
> 4½ cups vegetable stock or water
> 1 teaspoon tamari
> 1 large onion, finely chopped
> 8 ounces mushrooms, sliced
> Freshly ground black pepper—several grindings
> 2 cups sauerkraut
> 1 tablespoon finely chopped fresh dill weed
> 1½ cups finely chopped tender mustard greens

Heat 1 tablespoon of the oil in a large pot over moderate heat. Brown the tempeh on both sides, adding more oil if necessary. Add ½ cup of the stock and cover tightly. Steam until the liquid is almost gone. Add the tamari and cook until the pan is dry. Remove the tempeh and cut it into short, thin strips.

Heat 1 tablespoon oil in the tempeh pot. Add the onion and sauté until it is translucent. Add the mushrooms and black pepper and sauté several minutes. Add the remaining 4 cups stock and bring just to a boil. Reduce the heat, cover, and simmer for 15 to 20 minutes.

Stir in the sauerkraut and tempeh, cover, and heat. Serve garnished with the dill and greens.

NOTES
- This soup is easy to vary, depending on what you have on hand: omit the mushrooms and add 2 large cooked, peeled beets cut into small strips or dice; or omit the mushrooms and add 1 medium-sized carrot and 1 medium-sized turnip, each cut into small strips or dice.

RICH ONION SOUP
▼▼▼

This hearty, mellow, oniony soup is standard French bistro fare. Top it with crisp CROÛTES or CROÛTONS (page 185). Serve it with SALADE COMPOSÉE (page 214-15), BOSTON LETTUCE COMPOSÉE (page 215), SPINACH TART (page 173-74), or spinach- or mushroom-stuffed crêpes (page 158-59 and 159).

PREPARATION TIME: About 1 hour

> 1 tablespoon olive oil
> 1 pound onions, finely sliced
> Freshly ground black pepper—several grindings
> ½ teaspoon kelp powder
> 1 tablespoon whole wheat pastry flour
> 4 cups vegetable stock or water
> 1 small bay leaf
> ¼ teaspoon ground sage
> 4 tablespoons dry red wine
> 1 tablespoon mellow barley miso, or to taste

Heat the oil in a large, heavy-bottomed pot over moderate heat. Add the onions and sauté for several minutes. Cover, reduce the heat, and cook the onions for 15 to 20 minutes, stirring occasionally, until they are tender and translucent. Uncover, turn up the heat, and sauté the onions until they brown. Reduce the heat and stir in the pepper, kelp powder, and flour. Cook, stirring, for about 2 minutes to brown the flour. Remove from the heat.

Heat about a cup of the stock or water and, whisking constantly, add it to the onions. Add the remaining liquid, bay leaf, sage, and wine and bring just to a boil. Adjust the heat so that the soup simmers gently and cook for 30 to 40 minutes.

Whisk the miso with several tablespoons of the hot broth to form a smooth paste; thoroughly stir this into the soup. Serve immediately.

NOTES
- Add several strips of soaked chopped wakame to the soup; you can use the soaking water as part of the stock.

- Add a few pieces of diced pressed tofu to each serving.

- Sprinkle grated Parmesan and Swiss cheese on top of croûtes on individual servings and broil briefly.

SOUPE AU PISTOU
▼▼▼

Pistou *is pesto in French, and this heady basil sauce is as popular in southern France as it is in Italy. Here it flavors a summer vegetable soup. Make this when you have lots of fresh basil for pesto (page 141-43). Serve it with garlic-seasoned* CROÛTES *(page 185),* FOCACCIA *(page 89), or a French or Italian bread spread with* ROASTED GARLIC *(page 133-34) or* ROASTED RED PEPPER SAUCE *(page 143-44).*

YIELD: 4 servings

PREPARATION TIME: About 1 hour

    5 cups vegetable stock, bean stock, or water
    1 medium-sized carrot, thinly sliced
    2 medium-sized potatoes, cut into 1/2-inch dice
    3 medium-sized leeks, white and tender inner
       green sections, thinly sliced
       Freshly ground black pepper—several grindings
    1 small bell pepper, cut into 1/2-inch julienne
    1 medium-sized tomato, finely diced
    2 tablespoons toasted fine bread crumbs
    1 cup cooked kidney beans (see page 238)
    1 cup sugar snap peas
  2/3 to 1 cup pesto (see pages 141-43)
    1 tablespoon dark barley miso, or to taste
  1/4 cup fresh parsley, finely chopped

In a large, heavy-bottomed pot, combine the stock or water, carrot, potatoes, leeks, and black pepper and bring just to a boil. Cover, reduce the heat, and simmer for 20 to 30 minutes—until the vegetables are just tender. Add the bell pepper, tomato, bread crumbs, and kidney beans, cover, and simmer for 10 to 15 minutes. Add the peas and simmer just a minute or two. Remove from the heat.

Whisk about a cup of hot soup broth with 2/3 cup pesto and the miso until smooth. Stir this into the soup, taste, and add additional pesto and/or dissolved miso if necessary.

Heat briefly over low heat and serve immediately, garnished with parsley.

NOTES
- Substitute shelled green peas or green beans for the snap peas; beans will take longer to cook—add them with the bell pepper.

- Add about 1 cup sliced zucchini along with the bell pepper.

HEARTY CABBAGE SOUP
▼▼▼

This is a thick, Eastern European–style vegetable soup that's great sustenance in cool weather. Serve it with a robust bread—maybe RUSTIC RYE BREAD *(page 190-91),* BEER-RYE BREAD *(page 63-64), or* SOURDOUGH BRAN BREAD *(page 92-93).*

YIELD: 4 to 6 servings

PREPARATION TIME: About 1 1/2 hours

  1 1/2 teaspoons caraway seeds
      2 tablespoons sesame or olive oil
      1 large onion, finely chopped
      1 medium-sized carrot, sliced
      1 medium-sized apple, cored and chopped
      3 cups finely chopped red or green cabbage
    1/2 pound mushrooms, sliced
         Freshly ground black pepper—several grindings
      2 cups chopped peeled tomatoes (about 3 medium
         tomatoes or a 1-pound can, including the juice)
    1/3 cup raisins
      2 medium-sized potatoes, cut into 1/2-inch dice
      4 cups vegetable stock or water
      1 tablespoon minced fresh dill weed, plus extra for
         garnish
      2 tablespoons lemon juice
      2 tablespoons mellow barley miso
         TOFU SOUR CREAM (page 148), sour cream,
         or yogurt

Roast the caraway seeds in an ungreased, heavy-bottomed skillet over low to moderate heat, shaking the pan or stirring the seeds frequently to prevent their burning. Set aside.

Heat the oil in a large pot over moderate heat and sauté the onion for several minutes, until it appears translucent. Add the carrot, apple, and cabbage and continue to sauté for several more minutes. Stir in the mushrooms, pepper, and caraway and cook briefly, stirring, until the mushrooms appear moist. Stir in the tomatoes, raisins, and potatoes, reduce the heat to low, cover, and cook about 5 minutes. Add the stock or water and bring just to a simmer. Partially cover and adjust the heat so that the soup simmers gently. Cook, stirring occasionally, for 20 to 30 minutes, until the potatoes are tender. Add the dill weed.

Whisk together the lemon juice and miso to form a smooth paste. Stir into the soup and heat briefly. Serve hot, garnished with Tofu Sour Cream, sour cream, or yogurt and a sprinkling of minced fresh dill.

NOTES
- If fresh dill weed is unavailable, substitute 1 1/2 teapoons crushed dried dill weed in the soup and omit the dill for garnish.

VEGETABLE GUMBO
▼▼▼

In central Texas, early autumn is the season for this soup: fresh tomatoes, peppers, and okra are still available at the farmer's market and sweet potatoes are just beginning to come in. Buy small, tender pods of okra. Filé powder is prepared from young sassafras leaves which have been dried and ground; do not boil the soup after adding it or it may become stringy. Serve this zippy Creole blend with a crusty French bread or a corn- or rice-based bread.

YIELD: 4 servings

PREPARATION TIME: 45 to 60 minutes

> 2 *large sweet potatoes, cubed*
> 1 *medium-sized mildly hot pepper (e.g., poblano or Anaheim)*
> 6 *medium-sized tomatoes*
> 2 *tablespoons olive oil*
> 2 *large onions, finely chopped*
> 4 *cloves garlic, pressed or minced*
> 3 *large bell peppers, finely chopped*
>   *Freshly ground black pepper—several grindings*
> ½ *teaspoon ground celery seed*
> ½ *pound okra, cut into ½-inch slices*
> 2 *tablespoons hatcho miso*
> 1 *teaspoon filé powder*

Simmer the sweet potatoes in 2 to 3 cups water until they are tender. Drain, reserving the stock.

Remove the membranes and seeds from the hot pepper and mince it.

Peel the tomatoes as described on page 130 and dice.

Heat the oil in a large, heavy-bottomed pot over moderate heat and sauté the onion and garlic for several minutes. Stir in the bell pepper and hot pepper and continue to sauté. Add the black pepper and celery seed and cook while stirring, briefly. Stir in the tomatoes and 2 cups sweet potato stock and bring just to a simmer. Reduce the heat to low, cover, and cook gently, stirring occasionally, for 20 to 30 minutes, until saucelike.

Add the cooked sweet potatoes and okra and simmer gently for a few minutes, until the okra is just tender.

Whisk the miso and a few tablespoons of sweet potato stock to a smooth paste. Stir into the soup and remove it from the heat. Stir in the filé powder. Serve immediately.

NOTES

- For more control over the spiciness of the soup, roast and peel the hot pepper as described on page 130; mince and add to taste near the end of cooking.

BORSCHT
▼▼▼

Beets give this soup a gorgeous magenta color as well as a wonderfully sweet flavor. The soup is delicious both hot and chilled; either way, garnish it with a dollop of TOFU SOUR CREAM (page 148), sour cream, or yogurt and a sprinkling of fresh dill weed. Serve it with a rye bread and MUSHROOM PÂTÉ (page 139). This soup also goes well with PIROSHKI (page 176), KNISHES (page 177), and CABBAGE KUCHEN (page 173).

YIELD: 4 servings

PREPARATION TIME: About 1 hour

> 4 *large beets with greens*
> 1 *tablespoon olive oil*
> 2 *medium-sized onions, finely chopped*
> 1 *cup chopped carrot*
>   *Freshly ground black pepper—several grindings*
> ½ *teaspoon kelp powder*
> 2 *cups chopped peeled tomatoes (about 3 medium tomatoes or a 1-pound can, including the juice)*
> ¼ *cup raisins*
> 1 *tablespoon minced fresh dill weed, plus extra for garnish*
> ¾ *teaspoon sea salt*
> 1 *tablespoon lemon juice*
> 1 *tablespoon apple cider vinegar*

Cut off the beet greens, rinse and dry them, slice thinly, and set aside. Scrub the beets well, bring just to a boil in about 3 cups water, reduce the heat, and simmer until tender, about 15 to 20 minutes. Drain, reserving the stock, and slip off the skins. Cut the beets into ½-inch dice and set aside.

Heat the oil in a large, heavy-bottomed pot over moderate heat and sauté the onion and carrot for several minutes, until the onions appear translucent. Add the pepper, beet greens, and kelp powder and cook briefly, stirring constantly, just until the greens wilt. Add the tomatoes and raisins, cover, reduce the heat, and simmer gently for about 5 minutes, until the tomatoes are well juiced. Add the beet stock, cover, and simmer 20 to 30 minutes, until the vegetables are all tender.

Stir in the beets, dill, salt, lemon juice, and vinegar and heat briefly. Serve hot or chilled.

PIMIENTO PURÉE
▼▼▼

Make this smooth, red-orange bisque when pimientos— thick-skinned, sweet red peppers—show up in the market, usually in late summer. You can substitute red bell pep-

pers, but pimientos are best. *Serve the soup hot or cold with* CALZONE *(page 178-79),* POCO PESTO POCKETS *(page 155-56), or* SOURDOUGH ITALIAN BREAD *(page 88) and* PESTO PASTA SALAD *(page 218).*

YIELD: 2 generous servings

PREPARATION TIME: 30 to 45 minutes

> 4 *medium-sized pimientos*
> 1 *tablespoon olive oil*
> 1 *medium-sized onion, chopped*
> 2 *cloves garlic, pressed or minced*
>   *Freshly ground black pepper—several grindings*
> 1 *cup cooked navy beans (see page 238)*
> 2 *cups bean and/or vegetable stock*
> 2 *tablespoons lemon juice*
> 2 *tablespoons mellow barley miso*
> 2 *tablespoons finely chopped fresh parsley*

Roast and peel the peppers as described on page 130.

Heat the oil in a small skillet and sauté the onion for several minutes. Add the garlic and sauté until the onion is translucent and tender. Grind in the black pepper and cook briefly. Remove from the heat.

In a blender or in a food processor fitted with the metal blade, combine the peppers, sauté, beans, and about ½ cup of the stock. Blend, gradually adding the remaining stock, until thoroughly smooth.

Transfer to a saucepan and bring just to a simmer over medium heat. Reduce the heat to low.

Whisk the lemon juice and miso to a smooth paste. Thoroughly stir this into the hot soup. Serve immediately or chill the soup first. Garnish with minced parsley.

CASHEW-CARROT SOUP

Bugs Bunny would flip over this piquant vivid orange pu-rée. WHOLE WHEAT RAISIN BREAD *(page 103),* STEAMED BROWN BREAD *(page 103),* POPPYSEED BREAD *(page 71),* SPICED HONEY BREAD *(page 66-67), and* CAULIFLOWER-STUFFED PARATHAS *(page 119) are some good complements.*

YIELD: 4 servings

PREPARATION TIME: About 1 hour

> 1 *tablespoon sesame oil*
> 1 *medium-sized onion, finely chopped*

> 1 *clove garlic, pressed or minced*
> 2 *teaspoons minced fresh ginger root*
> 1 *pound carrots, sliced*
> 4½ *cups mild vegetable stock or water*
> ¾ *cup lightly toasted cashews*
> 1½ *teaspoons lemon juice*
> 4 *teaspoons tamari, or to taste*

Heat the oil in a large, heavy-bottomed pot and sauté the onion for several minutes. Stir in the garlic, ginger, and carrots and continue to cook, stirring often, until the onion appears translucent. Add 3 cups stock or water and bring just to a simmer. Cover, reduce the heat to low, and simmer gently for about 30 minutes, until the carrots are very tender.

Combine the cashews and ¾ cup of stock in a blender. Blend, gradually adding the remaining ¾ cup stock, until smooth. Transfer to another container.

Blend the carrot mixture and then return it to the pot. Stir in the cashew "milk" and lemon juice and heat the soup—but not to boiling! Add tamari to taste. Serve immediately.

TOMATO-GINGER SOUP

Fresh ginger adds pep to this spiced tomato soup; cashew "milk" gives it a rich flavor and a smooth, creamy consistency. Serve it with a rice bread or SESAME BREAD *(page 65) and* CURRIED-TOFU SPREAD *(page 132-33) or with* STUFFED CHAPATIS *(page 163).*

YIELD: 4 servings

PREPARATION TIME: 45 to 60 minutes

> 2 *pounds tomatoes*
> 2 *tablespoons sesame oil*
> 1 *large onion, finely chopped*
> 3 *cloves garlic, pressed or minced*
> 1 *tablespoon minced fresh ginger root*
>   *Freshly ground black pepper—several grindings*
> ½ *teaspoon ground cumin*
> ¼ *teaspoon ground coriander*
> ¼ *teaspoon ground turmeric*
> ½ *cup lightly toasted cashew pieces*
> 2 *cups water*
> 1 *teaspoon sea salt, or to taste*

Peel the tomatoes as described on page 130, then chop.

Heat the oil in a large, heavy-bottomed pot and sauté the onion for several minutes. Stir in the garlic and ginger and continue to sauté for several more minutes, until the onion is just tender. Add the pepper, cumin, coriander, and turmeric and cook, stirring, for a minute or two. Stir in the tomatoes and bring just to a simmer. Reduce the heat, partially cover the pot, and simmer gently for 20 to 30 minutes, until the tomatoes are completely soft.

In a blender, blend the cashews with ½ cup of the water; continue to blend, gradually adding the remaining water, until thoroughly smooth. Transfer the cashew milk to another container.

Add the tomato mixture to the blender. Blend, gradually incorporating the cashew milk. Pour the soup back into the pot and heat it just to a simmer. Season to taste with salt and serve immediately.

NOTES
- Substitute 1 quart home-canned tomatoes or two 1-pound cans.

TOMATO-FENNEL SOUP
▼▼▼

Roasted fennel seeds add a lively licorice taste to this Italian-style tomato soup, and chopped fresh fennel bulb contributes texture. Try it with GREENS CROUSTADE (page 179) or PESTO PIZZA (page 166-67).

YIELD: 4 servings

PREPARATION TIME: 45 to 60 minutes

> 2 *pounds tomatoes*
> 2 *teaspoons fennel seeds*
> 2 *tablespoons olive oil*
> 2 *large red onions, finely chopped*
> 3 *cloves garlic, pressed or minced*
> 1 *cup finely chopped fennel bulb*
> *Freshly ground black pepper—several grindings*
> ½ *teaspoon kelp powder*
> 2 *cups vegetable stock or water*
> 5 *to 6 tablespoons minced fresh parsley*
> 2 *tablespoons hatcho miso*

Peel the tomatoes as described on page 130, then dice.

Roast the fennel seeds in a dry, heavy-bottomed skillet over moderate heat, agitating the pan or stirring the seeds often to keep them from burning. Grind coarsely with a mortar and pestle or spice grinder.

Heat the oil in a heavy-bottomed pot over moderate heat and sauté the onion for several minutes. Stir in the garlic and chopped fennel and continue to cook, stirring often, until the onion appears translucent. Add the pepper and ground fennel seeds and sauté briefly. Stir in the tomatoes and kelp powder, cover, and simmer gently for 5 to 10 minutes. Add the stock or water

and bring back to a simmer. Cover, reduce the heat to low, and simmer for 20 to 30 minutes.

In a blender or a food processor fitted with a metal blade, blend the soup to a coarse purée. Return it to the pot and stir in 4 tablespoons of the parsley.

Thoroughly mix the miso with a few tablespoons of the soup and stir this into the soup. Gently reheat, but do not boil! Serve garnished with a sprinkling of parsley.

NOTES
- Substitute 1 quart of home-canned tomatoes or two 1-pound cans.

GLORIOUS GAZPACHO
▼▼▼

This chilled soup is a terrific blend of summer vegetables and is supremely refreshing in hot weather. Sprinkle some crisp CROÛTONS (page 185) on top of each serving.

YIELD: 4 servings

PREPARATION TIME: 20 to 30 minutes

> 1 *pound tomatoes*
> 2 *small cucumbers*
> 2 *small bell peppers*
> 1 *small carrot*
> 1 *clove garlic*
> 1 *small onion, diced*
> *Freshly ground black pepper—a couple of grindings*
> ½ *teaspoon kelp powder*
> 1½ *tablespoons olive oil*
> 3 *tablespoons lemon juice*
> ½ *cup water*
> 2 *teaspoons hatcho miso*
> 2 *tablespoons minced fresh chives*
> 2 *tablespoons minced fresh parsley*
> 1 *tablespoon minced fresh basil leaves*

Peel the tomatoes as described on page 130 and chop.

Peel the cucumbers if the skin is waxed or tough. Dice one, and finely chop the other. Dice one bell pepper, and finely chop the other. Dice the carrot. Set the finely chopped vegetables aside for garnish.

In a food processor fitted with the metal blade or in a blender, combine the tomatoes, garlic, and onion and blend thoroughly. Add the diced cucumber, bell pepper, and carrot, the black pepper, and the kelp powder, and blend well. With the processor or blender running, add the oil, lemon juice, water, and miso and continue to blend until these ingredients are thoroughly incorporated. Chill well.

Serve cold, garnished with the minced herbs and reserved cucumber and bell pepper.

SOUTHWESTERN SWEET POTATO SOUP

▼▼▼

Savor the subtlety of this carefully balanced blend of flavors. This soup goes well with corn-based breads such as a corn bread, corn tortillas, TRUE GRITS BREAD *(page 74), or* ANADAMA BREAD *(page 62-63).* SPICY BEAN BREAD *(page 68) is also an interesting partner.*

YIELD: 4 servings

PREPARATION TIME: 45 to 60 minutes

    2 medium-sized sweet potatoes, peeled and cubed
 5½ cups water
    2 teaspoons olive oil
    1 large onion, finely chopped
    2 small cloves garlic, pressed or minced
   ½ teaspoon minced serrano pepper (remove
          membranes and seeds first)
   ¼ cup fresh mint leaves (spearmint or a blend)
   ½ to 1 teaspoon sea salt, to taste

In a large pot, simmer the sweet potatoes in the water until tender. Drain, reserving the stock.

Heat the oil in a medium-sized skillet over moderate heat and sauté the onion for several minutes, until it appears translucent. Stir in the garlic and minced pepper and sauté until the onion is tender. Transfer the sauté to a blender or a food processor fitted with the metal blade. Add the sweet potatoes and blend, gradually incorporating the reserved stock. Thoroughly blend in the mint. Season with salt to taste. Return the soup to the pot and heat just to a simmer. Cover and cook gently for 5 to 10 minutes, just to blend the flavors. Serve hot.

SESAME-POTATO SOUP

▼▼▼

The flavors of potato, cumin, sesame, and lemon marry well in this soup, and it goes with a wide range of breads—from ryes to corn breads. Try GOLDEN HARVEST BREAD *(page 67) or* GOLDEN SOURDOUGH BREAD *(page 88-89) for an interesting combination.*

YIELD: 4 servings

PREPARATION TIME: 30 to 40 minutes

    2 teaspoons sesame seeds
    2 teaspoons cumin seeds
    1 tablespoon sesame oil
    1 medium-sized onion, finely chopped
    2 cloves garlic, pressed or minced
        Freshly ground black pepper—several grindings
   ½ teaspoon kelp powder

   ¾ pound potatoes, cut into small dice
    4 cups vegetable stock or water
    1 tablespoon lemon juice
    2 tablespoons tahini
   ¼ teaspoon roasted sesame oil
    1 teaspoon sea salt, or to taste
    2 to 3 tablespoons minced fresh parsley
    2 teaspoons minced garlic chives

Heat an ungreased, heavy-bottomed skillet over moderate heat. Add the sesame seeds and roast them, stirring or agitating the pan often to prevent the seeds from burning. Set the seeds aside.

Add the cumin seeds to the skillet and roast them in the same manner. Grind them to a coarse powder with a mortar and pestle or spice grinder and set aside.

Heat the tablespoon of oil in a heavy-bottomed pot over moderate heat. Add the onion and sauté until it appears translucent. Add the garlic and sauté briefly. Stir in the black pepper, kelp powder, potatoes, and cumin. Add the stock and bring just to a simmer. Reduce the heat, cover, and simmer for about 20 minutes or until the potatoes are very tender.

In a small bowl, whisk the lemon juice, tahini, and roasted sesame oil with a few tablespoons of the soup stock. Stir this mixture into the soup. Stir in 1 teaspoon salt and 2 tablespoons parsley. Heat briefly, but do not boil. Taste and add more salt if necessary.

Serve hot, garnished with the sesame seeds, garlic chives, and a bit more parsley.

POTATO-LEEK SOUP

▼▼▼

Potato-leek soup, known as Vichyssoise when it is served cold, is a classic French soup. It usually contains milk and either heavy cream or sour cream; this nondairy version, which is made with a tofu sour cream substitute, is still "creamy" but with less fat. Serve it either chunky and steaming or puréed and chilled. I like it with rye breads, such as FINNISH RYE *(page 63) or* LIMPA RYE *(page 74-75).*

YIELD: 4 to 6 servings

PREPARATION TIME: 60 to 90 minutes

    3 to 4 large leeks
    1 tablespoon vegetable oil
    2 tablespoons whole wheat pastry flour
    6 cups vegetable stock or water
        Freshly ground black pepper—several grindings
   ½ teaspoon kelp powder
    1 pound potatoes, cut into small dice
    3 to 4 tablespoons mellow barley miso
    1 cup TOFU SOUR CREAM (page 148)
   ½ cup fresh parsley, finely chopped

Slice the leeks thinly, keeping the white part and tender portion of the green separate—you should have about 3 cups of the white and ½ cup of the green.

Heat the oil in a large, heavy-bottomed pot and sauté the white part of the leeks briefly. Reduce the heat, cover, and cook for about 5 minutes—the leeks should be soft but not brown. Gradually sift the flour over the leeks as you stir it in. Cook over moderate heat for several minutes, stirring often. Do not brown the flour. Remove from the heat. Heat 1 cup of the stock and gradually add it to the leeks, stirring constantly to maintain a smooth texture. Stir in 4½ cups stock and add the pepper, kelp powder, leek greens, and potatoes. Bring just to a boil, partially cover, and adjust the heat so that it simmers gently. Cook, stirring occasionally, 45 minutes to an hour, until the vegetables are completely tender.

Whisk the remaining ½ cup stock or water and 3 tablespoons miso to a smooth paste. Stir this into the soup and heat but do not boil it. Taste and add more miso, whisked with a few tablespoons of the soup, if necessary. For a less chunky soup, coarsely blend it after cooking but before adding the miso.

Serve the hot soup immediately, topped with a spoonful or two of Tofu Sour Cream and a sprinkling of chopped parsley. To serve the soup cold, cool it, then blend it along with the Tofu Sour Cream; you may need additional stock to achieve the proper consistency. Chill well. Taste and season with salt if necessary before garnishing and serving.

NOTES
- Minced fresh dill weed or chives are other good garnishes for this soup.

Best Butternut Squash Soup
ᵥᵥᵥ

This soup is based on one that I tasted years ago in a restaurant in Northampton, Massachusetts. It was prepared by Pete, a chef on a round-the-world trek, who had paused there to ply his culinary skills and to earn enough money to continue his journey. His soup was surprisingly light and delicately flavored, more of a broth than the rather thick, creamy squash soups that I was familiar with. I've kept the consistency of his and added finely chopped toasted pecans for a contrast in texture; the sweet flavor of the nuts complements that of the squash too. Bake the squash and prepare the soup stock ahead of time. This goes particularly well with ANADAMA BREAD (page 62-63) and APPLE OR PEAR SAUCE BREAD (page 70).

YIELD: 4 servings

PREPARATION TIME: About 45 minutes, not including squash and stock preparation

   1 *medium-sized butternut squash*
   1 *medium-sized apple*
   6 *cups water*
   2 *tablespoons sesame or other vegetable oil*
   1 *medium-sized sweet onion, finely chopped*
   1 *teaspoon freshly grated nutmeg*
   2 *tablespoons dry sherry*
1½ *teaspoons sea salt, or more to taste*
 ⅓ *cup lightly toasted, finely chopped pecans*

Cut the squash in half lengthwise and place it, cut side down, on a lightly greased baking sheet. Bake at 375 degrees until tender, about 45 minutes. Scoop out the seeds and transfer to a stock pot. Scrape the squash from the skin; add the skin to the pot. Mash the squash and set it aside.

Pare the apple and add the peelings and core to the stock pot, along with the 6 cups water. Bring to a boil and simmer 30 minutes or more, until full-flavored. Strain and measure 5 cups. Chop the apple finely.

Heat the oil in a heavy-bottomed pot over moderate heat and sauté the onion until it is almost tender. Add the apple and nutmeg and continue to sauté until the apple is tender.

Transfer the sauté to a blender or a food processor fitted with the metal blade. Add 1 cup of the squash and blend, gradually adding the reserved stock and additional squash until the soup is the desired consistency; it should be a thin purée. Return to the pot, stir in the sherry and 1½ teaspoons salt, and bring just to a simmer. Reduce the heat, cover loosely, and simmer 20 to 30 minutes, until the flavors are well mingled. Taste and add salt if necessary. Serve hot, generously garnished with the pecans.

A Soup for All Seasons
ᵥᵥᵥ

This nondairy vegetable chowder is almost infinitely variable; substitute vegetables and herbs to match the season. Cut the vegetables into similarly sized pieces, and group vegetables that take about the same length of time to cook and add them to the soup together. The soup goes well with a wide variety of breads—I especially like to serve this particular version with an oat or cracked wheat bread or with TOFU-HERB BREAD (page 68-69).

YIELD: 4 servings

PREPARATION TIME: About 1 hour

2 tablespoons olive oil
1 cup finely sliced leeks
2 cloves garlic, pressed or minced
½ cup sliced carrot
½ cup sliced fennel bulb
½ cup sliced turnip
8 ounces Oriental eggplant, diced
8 ounces mushrooms, sliced
    Freshly ground black pepper—several grindings
1 large potato, diced
2 medium tomatoes, diced
½ teaspoon kelp powder
4 cups mild vegetable stock or water
1 teaspoon minced fresh thyme leaves
1½ teaspoons minced fresh oregano leaves
2 tablespoons finely chopped fresh parsley
3 tablespoons mellow barley miso
2 tablespoons minced green onions or chives

Heat the oil in a large, heavy-bottomed pot over moderate heat and sauté the leeks, garlic, and carrot for several minutes. Stir in the fennel, turnip, and eggplant and continue to sauté for several minutes more. Add the mushrooms and pepper and cook briefly, stirring often. Stir in the potato, tomatoes, kelp powder, and stock. Bring just to a simmer, turn the heat to low, cover, and simmer gently for 20 to 30 minutes, until the vegetables are just tender.

Add the thyme, oregano, and parsley and simmer several minutes more.

Whisk the miso and several tablespoons of the hot broth to a smooth paste. Thoroughly stir this into the soup and remove it from the heat. Serve hot, garnished with a sprinkling of minced green onions or chives.

NOTES

- If you substitute dried herbs (except for delicate ones like tarragon, dill, or chervil), add them to the sauté along with the mushrooms; add delicate dried herbs close to the end of cooking.

- For extra heartiness, add 1 cup cooked navy beans or chickpeas and ¼ cup dry red wine along with the fresh herbs.

MINESTRONE
▼▼▼

Served with bread or rolls, this herby Italian vegetable, bean, and pasta soup makes a meal; try it with SOURDOUGH BERRY BREAD *(page 91). I like to use fusilli or another short cut of pasta, and I cook the pasta separately and combine it with the soup just before serving so that it won't become mushy.*

YIELD: 4 servings

PREPARATION TIME: 1½ to 2 hours

1 tablespoon olive oil
1 large leek, white part only, sliced
3 cloves garlic, pressed or minced
½ cup sliced carrot
½ cup sliced turnip
½ cup sliced fennel bulb
4 ounces mushrooms, sliced
2 cups finely sliced cabbage
    Freshly ground black pepper—several grindings
⅛ teaspoon cinnamon
2 cups chopped peeled tomatoes (about 3 medium tomatoes or a 1-pound can, including liquid)
½ teaspoon kelp powder
¼ cup dry red wine
3 cups bean or vegetable stock
1½ cups cooked chickpeas (see page 238)
¼ teaspoon minced fresh rosemary
1 teaspoon minced fresh oregano
2 tablespoons minced fresh basil
1 tablespoon lemon juice
1 tablespoon hatcho miso
    Sea salt, to taste
4 ounces pasta, cooked al dente
¼ cup minced fresh parsley leaves

Heat the oil in a large, heavy-bottomed pot over moderate heat and sauté the leek and garlic for several minutes. Stir in the carrot, turnip, and fennel and continue to sauté for a few minutes. Add the mushrooms, cabbage, pepper, and cinnamon and sauté briefly, until the mushrooms appear moist. Stir in the tomatoes and kelp powder, cover, reduce the heat, and simmer for about 5 minutes.

Add the wine and stock and bring just to a boil. Reduce the heat, cover, and simmer gently for 20 to 30 minutes, until the vegetables are tender. Stir in the chickpeas, rosemary, oregano, and basil and simmer another 10 minutes.

Whisk together the lemon juice and miso and stir into the soup. Remove soup from the heat, taste, and add salt if necessary.

Divide the pasta among four large bowls and ladle soup on top, or add the pasta to the soup pot if you don't anticipate leftovers. Garnish each serving with minced parsley.

NOTES

- If you don't have fresh herbs, use crushed dried ones—⅛ teaspoon rosemary, ½ teaspoon oregano, 2 teaspoons basil; add them to the sauté.

- Grated Parmesan or Romano cheese is a good additional garnish.

LEEK AND BEAN SOUP

▾▾▾

Cook the beans ahead of time for this light, refreshing, herb-laced purée. Serve it either hot or chilled; float a purple chive flower on each bowl. This is a good accompaniment for PISSALADIÈRE (page 169-70) or SICILIAN PIZZA ROLL (page 181-82). Or simply serve it with YEASTED MUFFINS (page 82) or SPROUTED WHEAT BREAD (page 64) and a salad.

YIELD: 4 servings

PREPARATION TIME: 40 to 50 minutes

 2 tablespoons olive oil
 3 cups chopped leeks (3 to 4 large)
 4 cloves garlic, pressed or minced
   Freshly ground black pepper—several grindings
 ½ teaspoon kelp powder
 2 cups cooked navy beans (see page 238)
 4 cups bean or vegetable stock or water
 1 teaspoon minced fresh thyme leaves
 3 tablespoons minced fresh basil leaves
 ¼ cup minced fresh parsley
 2 tablespoons lemon juice
 2 tablespoons mellow barley miso
 2 tablespoons minced fresh chives

Heat the oil in a large, heavy-bottomed pot over moderate heat and sauté the leeks and garlic for several minutes. Grind in the pepper and add the kelp powder, beans, and stock. Bring just to a simmer, turn the heat to low, cover loosely, and simmer 20 to 30 minutes, until the leeks are tender. Stir in the thyme, basil, and parsley.

In a blender or a food processor fitted with the metal blade, purée the soup to a smooth consistency.

Whisk the lemon juice and miso to a smooth paste and thoroughly stir it into the soup.

To serve the soup hot, heat but do not boil. For cold soup, chill thoroughly. Garnish with a sprinkling of chives.

TEXAS WINTER BEAN AND GREEN SOUP

▾▾▾

The subtly sweet flavors of onions, sweet potatoes, kale, and navy beans marry magnificently in this cool season soup. Serve it with PECAN BREAD (page 65-66), a millet or corn bread, or biscuits.

YIELD: 4 servings

PREPARATION TIME: 60 to 70 minutes

 1 tablespoon olive oil
 1 large onion, finely chopped
 1½ to 2 cups finely diced sweet potatoes
 2 cloves garlic, pressed or minced
 4 cups finely chopped kale
   Freshly ground black pepper—several grindings
 ½ teaspoon kelp powder
 4 cups bean or vegetable stock or water
 2 cups cooked navy beans (see page 238)
 1 teaspoon dried dill weed, crushed
 1 teaspoon dried tarragon (or pericon), crushed
 2 tablespoons lemon juice—or more, to taste
 2 tablespoons mellow barley miso—or more, to taste
 1 to 2 tablespoons minced fresh parsley

Heat the oil in a large, heavy-bottomed pot and sauté the onion and sweet potato for several minutes, until the onion appears translucent. Stir in the garlic, kale, pepper, and kelp powder and continue to cook, stirring often, until the kale wilts. Add the liquid and bring just to a simmer. Stir in the beans, cover, turn the heat to low, and simmer gently for about 20 minutes, until the sweet potatoes are tender. Stir in the dill and tarragon and simmer 5 to 10 minutes longer.

Whisk the lemon juice and miso to a smooth paste. Stir into the soup and turn off the heat. Taste and add more lemon juice and/or miso. Serve hot, garnished with parsley.

INDIAN LENTIL SOUP

▾▾▾

Lentil soups are often rather heavy. This one is light and laced with the unique flavor of fresh cilantro. It's also easy to make, since it mostly involves simmering. I like to serve it hot one day and then chilled the next. Serve it with GINGERY CARROT BREAD (page 69-70), an Indian flat bread—CHAPATIS (page 117-18) or plain or stuffed PARATHAS (page 117-18), spicy potato-filled DOSAS (page 123-24), or with INDIAN TURNOVERS (page 176).

YIELD: 4 generous servings

PREPARATION TIME: About 1½ hours

   1 tablespoon sesame oil
   1 large onion, finely chopped
   4 cloves garlic, pressed or minced
     Freshly ground black pepper—several grindings
 ½ teaspoon kelp powder
   6 cups water
   1 cup red lentils, picked over and rinsed
 ¼ teaspoon ground turmeric
   3 tablespoons lemon juice
   3 tablespoons mellow barley miso
   1 to 1½ cups loosely packed fresh cilantro leaves
   2 tablespoons finely chopped green onions
   2 tablespoons coarsely chopped fresh cilantro leaves

Heat the oil in a large, heavy-bottomed pot over moderate heat and sauté the onion and garlic for several minutes, until the onion is almost tender. Add the pepper and kelp powder and sauté briefly. Add the water, lentils, and turmeric and bring just to a gentle boil. Turn the heat to low, cover the pot loosely, and cook, stirring occasionally, for about an hour, until the onions and lentils are thoroughly soft and tender.

Whisk the lemon juice and miso to a smooth paste.

Using a blender or a food processor fitted with the metal blade, purée the soup. Blend in the lemon-miso mixture and cilantro to taste. If you are going to serve the soup hot, return it to the pot and heat it gently but do not boil. Or, cool the soup, chill, and serve it cold. In either case, garnish with green onions and chopped cilantro.

ORIENTAL NOODLE SOUP
▼▼▼

This is a rich broth crowded with vegetables and thin buckwheat noodles. It is warming in the winter yet light-weight enough to be refreshing in the summer. CHINESE SCALLION BREAD (page 126-27) is a good accompaniment. Soak the dried mushrooms several hours ahead of time.

YIELD: 4 servings

PREPARATION TIME: 30 to 40 minutes

 ¼ cup dried shiitake mushrooms
   1 cup boiling water
   1 teaspoon roasted sesame oil
   2 tablespoons plus 1 teaspoon tamari
   2 tablespoons sake
 10 ounces tofu, well pressed and diced
   1 tablespoon sesame oil
   1 small carrot, sliced
   1 medium-sized onion, thinly sliced
   1 large clove garlic, pressed or minced
   1 teaspoon minced fresh ginger root
   1 medium-sized turnip, sliced
 ½ cup sliced daikon
   2 cups sliced bok choy or Chinese cabbage
   2 to 3 cups finely chopped greens (turnip, mustard, etc.)
   3 cups vegetable stock or water
   3 ounces soba noodles
 ½ teaspoon hot chili oil
 1½ teaspoons umeboshi vinegar
   1 sheet toasted nori, cut into slivers

In a small bowl, pour the boiling water over the mushrooms, cover, and soak until the mushrooms are soft. Drain and reserve the soaking water. Cut off tough stems and cut the caps into thin slivers.

In another bowl, whisk together the roasted sesame oil, 2 tablespoons tamari, and sake. Gently fold in the tofu and marinate for at least 30 minutes, stirring occasionally.

Meanwhile, heat a wok or large, heavy-bottomed skillet over moderately high heat. Add the sesame oil and carrot. Cook, stirring constantly, until the carrot is barely tender. Add the onion, garlic, and ginger and continue cooking and stirring. Stir in the turnip and daikon and, when they are just tender, add the bok choy or Chinese cabbage and the mushroom slivers and stir-fry briefly. Stir in the greens and turn off the heat.

Heat the 3 cups stock or water to boiling in a large saucepan. Add the noodles and stir to separate. Bring the water back to a slow boil, loosely cover the pot, and cook the noodles until they are just tender. Drain, reserving the cooking water.

Put the noodles back in the empty pot, add the hot chili oil, and stir gently with chopsticks to coat them. Add the cooked vegetables, tofu and marinade, shiitake stock, noodle cooking water, remaining teaspoon of tamari, and umeboshi vinegar. Bring just to a simmer and serve immediately, garnished with the nori.

NOTES

• If you don't have hot chili oil or prefer a less spicy flavor, substitute roasted sesame oil.

• When the soup has reached a simmer, stir in a beaten egg.

• For an easy version of this soup, nicknamed "soupy noodles" at my house, add vegetable stock or noodle cooking water and perhaps an egg (after the mixture has heated) to leftover stir-fried noodles and vegetables, add hot oil, tamari and umeboshi vinegar to taste, and sprinkle toasted nori on top; this is a great breakfast dish!

SWEET ROOT CURRY
▾▾▾

This is a mildly hot curried vegetable stew. If you want it spicier, add more hot pepper; including the seeds and membrane will fire it up too. Serve this curry with rice, seasonal fruit slices, and CHAPATIS *(page 117-18) or* PARATHAS *(page 117-18). Cut the root vegetables about the same size—for aesthetic purposes and so that they will cook through in about the same amount of time.*

YIELD: 4 generous servings

PREPARATION TIME: About 1 hour

    4 *whole cloves*
    1 *teaspoon each cumin seed, ground coriander, and turmeric*
  1/2 *teaspoon grated nutmeg*
  1/4 *teaspoon each ground cinnamon, allspice, and cardamom*
  1/8 *teaspoon fenugreek*
    1 *pound tomatoes*
    3 *tablespoons vegetable oil or ghee*
    2 *medium-sized onions, finely chopped*
    4 *large cloves garlic, pressed or minced*
    2 *tablespoons minced fresh ginger root*
    1 *small hot chili pepper (seeds and membranes removed), minced*
  1/2 *cup raisins*
  1/2 *cup fresh coconut milk (or vegetable stock, unsweetened apple juice, or water)*
1 1/2 *cups vegetable stock, water, or part apple juice*
    2 *medium-sized carrots, sliced*
    2 *medium-sized parsnips, sliced*
    2 *medium-sized sweet potatoes, diced*
    1 *large turnip, diced*
    1 *tablespoon hatcho miso*
    1 *to 2 tablespoons lemon juice, to taste*
      Sea salt, to taste
  1/2 *cup lightly toasted, grated fresh coconut*
  1/2 *cup lightly toasted chopped almonds*

With a mortar and pestle or spice grinder, grind together the cloves, cumin, coriander, turmeric, nutmeg, cinnamon, allspice, cardamom, and fenugreek.

Peel the tomatoes as described on page 130; chop.

Heat the oil or ghee in a large, heavy-bottomed pot and sauté the onion over moderate heat until it appears translucent. Add the garlic, ginger, chili pepper, and

ground spices and cook briefly, stirring constantly to prevent the spices from burning. Add the tomatoes, raisins, coconut milk, and stock; cover and bring to a simmer. Lower the heat and simmer about 15 minutes. Stir in the carrot pieces, cover, and simmer 5 to 10 minutes. Add the parsnip, sweet potato, and turnip pieces, cover, and simmer until the vegetables are just tender and the sauce is slightly thickened.

Thoroughly whisk together the miso and several tablespoons of sauce and stir this into the stew. Add lemon juice and sea salt to taste.

Serve garnished with the coconut and almonds.

NOTES
- Substitute 1/4 to 1/2 teaspoon ground red pepper for the chili pepper.

- Substitute 1 pint of home-canned tomatoes or a 1-pound can for the fresh ones.

SESAME-VEGETABLE STEW
▾▾▾

A creamy sesame sauce envelopes tender tofu cubes and chunks of vegetables in this rich, warming winter stew. Cut the root vegetables into pieces of about the same size. Serve the stew with a simple tossed green salad and NUT BUTTER BREAD *(page 72) or a rice, oat, barley, or millet bread.*

YIELD: 4 servings

PREPARATION TIME: 45 to 60 minutes

    2 *tablespoons sesame oil*
    1 *medium-sized onion, chopped*
    3 *cloves garlic, pressed or minced*
  10 *to 12 medium-sized mushrooms, halved or quartered*
  1/4 *teaspoon cayenne*
    3 *cups vegetable stock or water*
    1 *medium-sized carrot, cut into thick slices*
    1 *medium-sized parsnip, cut into thick slices*
    1 *medium-sized turnip, diced*
    1 *medium-sized sweet potato, diced*
    1 *tablespoon kuzu powder*
    2 *teaspoons cold stock or water*
    2 *teaspoons tamari*
    2 *tablespoons mellow rice miso*
  1/2 *cup tahini*
    1 *pound tofu, well pressed, blanched, and cubed*
  1/2 *teaspoon sea salt, or to taste*
    1 *large green onion, finely chopped*
  1/4 *cup fresh parsley, finely chopped*

Heat the oil in a large, heavy-bottomed pot over moderate heat and sauté the onion and garlic for several minutes, until the onion appears translucent. Stir in the mushrooms and cayenne and continue to sauté briefly. Add the stock or water, cover, and bring to a simmer. Add the carrot, parsnip, turnip, and sweet potato pieces and simmer, covered, until just tender.

Meanwhile, combine the kuzu, 2 teaspoons cold stock or water, and 1 teaspoon of the tamari and set aside until the kuzu has thoroughly dissolved.

When the vegetables are tender, remove about a cup of hot broth and whisk with the remaining teaspoon tamari and the miso. Thoroughly whisk in the tahini. Stir into the stew.

While stirring, add the kuzu mixture to the stew and continue to stir gently as the broth thickens. Stir in the tofu and season with sea salt to taste.

Serve immediately, garnished with the chopped green onion and parsley.

NOTES

- Substitute the white portion of a leek for the onion, and other root vegetables, such as daikon or rutabaga, in the same proportions for the carrot, parsnip, turnip, and/or sweet potato.

- For a subtler spiciness, omit the cayenne and add freshly ground black pepper, to taste.

CHILI
▾▾▾

Here is my version of this hot and hearty bean and vegetable stew. I like to include more than one kind of beans; you can cook beans that cook in the same amount of time together. Serve the chili with a rice bread, corn bread, or warm tortillas.

YIELD: 4 servings

PREPARATION TIME: About 1 hour

- 2 *tablespoons olive oil*
- 2 *medium-sized onions, finely chopped*
- 2 *cloves garlic, pressed or minced*
- 1 *stalk celery, finely sliced*
- 2 *bell peppers, finely chopped*
- 1 *medium-sized carrot, finely diced*
- 1 *medium-sized turnip, finely diced*
- 1 *medium-sized rutabaga or parsnip, finely diced*
- 1 *small hot pepper, minced*
- 2 *teaspoons ground cumin*

- ½ *teaspoon ground coriander*
- 1 *teaspoon chili powder*
- ⅛ *teaspoon cinnamon*
- ½ *teaspoon kelp powder*
- 1 *cup chopped tomatoes (1 to 2 medium)*
- 1 *cup bean or vegetable stock*
- 3 *cups cooked pinto, kidney, aduki, or black beans—or a combination (see page 238)*
- 1½ *tablespoons dark miso*
- 1½ *tablespoons lemon juice*
- ¼ *cup fresh cilantro or parsley, chopped*

Heat the oil in a large, heavy-bottomed pot over moderate heat and sauté the onion and garlic until the onion is almost tender. Add the celery, bell pepper, carrot, turnip, and rutabaga or parsnip and continue to sauté for several minutes. Add the hot pepper, cumin, coriander, chili powder, and cinnamon and sauté briefly. Stir in the kelp powder, tomatoes, and stock, cover, and bring just to a boil. Reduce the heat and simmer gently, until the root vegetables are just tender. Add the beans, cover, and bring to a simmer again.

Whisk the miso and lemon juice to a smooth paste and thoroughly stir it into the stew. Heat briefly but not to boiling.

Serve hot, garnished with the cilantro or parsley.

NOTES

- Substitute ¼ teaspoon cayenne (or more to taste) for the hot pepper, or omit and add several grindings of black pepper to the sauté and serve ***BLENDER HOT SAUCE*** (page 146) along with the chili, for diners to add to taste.

RATATOUILLE
▾▾▾

The third time the ratatouille arrived at our table minus its essence, eggplant, it was definitely time for a serious inquiry. The proper, white-coated waiter, whom we later came to know as an expert bookbinder, responded immediately to a beckoning hand. "Well," he explained while carefully straightening the pressed white towel draped over one rigidly bent forearm, "we used to include eggplant, but we decided it was just too difficult to work with." Ratatouille is a Mediterranean vegetable stew that appears with some variations throughout the countries of that region. It definitely contains eggplant, plus zucchini, tomatoes, peppers, onions, garlic, olive oil, and various seasonings. Sometimes potatoes and green beans also show up in this dish. It is sometimes baked in the oven, sometimes simmered slowly over very low heat on top of the stove; I generally do a bit of each, though if you don't want to turn on the oven, just simmer the stew gently on a burner. It tastes best if it is made ahead of time. Serve it hot or chilled with a crusty bread or rolls, or try it with Spoonbread *(page 46). This is also a good pizza topping or crêpe filling.*

YIELD: 4 servings

PREPARATION TIME: About 1½ hours

> 1 *medium-sized eggplant (1 pound)*
> 2 *tablespoons olive oil*
> 1 *medium-sized zucchini, cut into ½-inch dice*
> 2 *medium-sized sweet onions, chopped*
> 3 *to 4 cloves garlic, pressed or minced*
> 2 *medium-sized bell peppers, cut into ½-inch squares*
> *Freshly ground black pepper—several grindings*
> 1½ *to 2 pounds tomatoes, diced (3 to 4 cups)*
> 1 *bay leaf*
> ½ *teaspoon kelp powder*
> 1 *teaspoon minced fresh oregano leaves*
> 1 *teaspoon minced fresh thyme leaves*
> 1 *tablespoon minced fresh basil leaves*
> ¼ *cup finely chopped fresh parsley*
> 2 *tablespoons hatcho miso*
> ⅔ *cup lightly toasted, coarsely chopped walnuts*

Cut the eggplant into ½-inch slices and layer them in a colander, sprinkling salt between each layer. Top with a weight of some kind and press for about 30 minutes. Rinse and pat dry and cut into ½-inch cubes.

Heat 1 tablespoon of the oil in a large skillet over moderate heat and sauté the eggplant and zucchini for 5 to 10 minutes.

Heat the remaining oil in a large, ovenproof, heavy-bottomed pot over moderate heat and sauté the onion and garlic for several minutes, until the onion appears translucent. Add the bell pepper and black pepper and continue to sauté for several minutes. Add the tomatoes, bay leaf, and kelp powder and bring to a simmer. Reduce the heat, cover, and cook 10 to 15 minutes, until somewhat saucy.

Stir in the eggplant and zucchini, cover tightly, and bake in a 350-degree oven for about 20 minutes. Add the oregano, thyme, basil, and parsley and continue to bake, about 10 to 15 minutes longer. The vegetables should be tender but not mushy.

Whisk several tablespoons of the hot liquid with the miso and stir it into the stew.

Serve hot or cold, garnished with the walnuts. If you reheat the stew, take care not to boil it.

NOTES

- If you use Oriental eggplants, you don't have to salt and press them before dicing.

North African Vegetable Stew
▾▾▾

The best time to make this exotically spiced dish is in early fall, when summer vegetables—tomatoes, peppers, eggplant, and zucchini—are still available, yet winter squashes are starting to appear in the market too. Serve it with French bread or pita. Cook the chickpeas ahead of time.

YIELD: 4 servings

PREPARATION TIME: About 1 hour

> 1 *medium-sized eggplant (1 pound)*
> 2 *tablespoons olive oil*
> 1 *medium-sized onion, chopped*
> 2 *large cloves garlic, pressed or minced*
> 1 *medium-sized carrot, sliced*
> 1 *small butternut squash, diced*
> 1 *medium-sized bell pepper, cut into squares*
> 1 *small zucchini, sliced*
> *Pinch of cayenne*
> *Freshly ground black pepper—several grindings*
> ¼ *teaspoon ground cinnamon*
> 1 *teaspoon ground cumin*
> ½ *teaspoon turmeric*
> ¼ *cup raisins*
> 1 *large tomato, diced*
> 1 *cup chickpea or vegetable stock or water*
> 2 *cups cooked chickpeas (see page 238)*
> 2 *teaspoons mellow barley miso*
> 1 *tablespoon lemon juice*
> ¼ *cup lightly toasted, coarsely chopped almonds*
> ¼ *cup fresh parsley, finely chopped*

Cut the eggplant into ½ inch slices and layer them in a

colander, sprinkling salt between each layer. Put a weight on top and press for about 30 minutes. Rinse and pat dry and cut into cubes.

Heat the oil in a heavy-bottomed pot over moderate heat and sauté the onion and garlic until the onion appears translucent. Add the carrot and squash and continue to sauté for several minutes. Stir in the eggplant and cook, stirring, for several minutes. Add the bell pepper and zucchini and sauté briefly. Stir in the cayenne, black pepper, cinnamon, cumin, and turmeric and cook for a minute or two, stirring constantly. Add the raisins, tomato, and stock and bring just to a simmer. Cover, reduce the heat to low, and simmer 20 to 30 minutes, until the vegetables are all tender. Stir in the chickpeas. Add additional stock if the stew is too dry.

Whisk the miso and lemon juice to a smooth paste and stir it into the stew. This is good made ahead of time, but do not boil when reheating. Serve garnished with the almonds and parsley.

NOTES
- If you use Oriental eggplants, you don't have to salt and press them before dicing.

CHAPTER 15

Salads and Dressings

LIKE SOUPS, A WIDE VARIETY of salads figure prominently in the wholesome light meals at Breadfellows, my imaginary bakery-tearoom. Some, such as grain-, bean-, or noodle-based salads and chef's salads, along with a compatible bread and maybe a spread, are truly meals in themselves. Other less substantial salads play more of a supporting role—forming coordinated trios with soups and breads or serving as colorful, crunchy accompaniments to bread-based dishes such as stuffed crêpes, turnovers, pizzas, and the like. Salads can also be sandwich fillings; they are especially good for stuffing into pita or rolling up in other flat breads. Bread can even be a salad ingredient, as in Italian Bread Salad and Fattouche in Chapter 13: Leftover Bread; other salads have croûtons or tortilla chips sprinkled on top.

One salad you won't find at Breadfellows is the classic American "green salad" consisting of lots of pale iceberg lettuce, limp cucumber slices, and insipid pink tomato wedges. You will find green salads, but they contain all kinds and colors of lettuces as well as a host of other greens—spinach, watercress, endive, arugula, mustard, and curly cress, to name just a few. Cucumbers and tomatoes may be there too, but only if they are in season and juicy and flavorful. When they aren't, expect to see something else that is—maybe finely slivered cabbages or fennel bulb, sliced radishes, or grated carrot or beets. Minced fresh herbs and various garnishes—some olives, toasted nuts or seeds, or edible flowers—further expand a green salad's personality.

Salads of all types offer creative cooks innumerable opportunities for transforming random parts into meaningful wholes. A salad artist works from an almost boundless palette, though the result may be a simple masterpiece, as too many colors and flavors and textures in one salad can begin to cancel one another out if overdone. Salads can easily come about from thinning the garden or sorting out the contents of the refrigerator, but most salad enthusiasts also take pleasure in cruising open-air markets, local farmers' markets and produce stands, and even the supermarket produce section for special seasonal ingredients. I'm fortunate to live in a place that has some locally grown produce almost all year round. If you don't, look for the best of what is available at any given time.

The manner in which ingredients are cut for a salad

will shape its character. Delicate, thin slices achieve a different effect than bite-size chunks. Also, with some salads, there's a choice in presentation: the ingredients can be either tossed all together in a bowl or artfully arranged on a plate or platter; both salad styles can be appealing if prepared with care and flair.

One kind of salad that I've learned to be wary of when available in restaurants is fresh fruit salad. Too often, it shows up carelessly cut and messy looking, and even the ones that appear beautiful sometimes contain unripe, tasteless fruits or over-the-hill, off-flavored ones. Not so at Breadfellows, where fruit salads are both attractive and delicious combinations of seasonal fruits. Perhaps topped with a dollop of yogurt and a sprinkling of chopped dried fruit and nuts and served with a muffin, scone, or sweet roll, a properly prepared fresh fruit salad makes a fine breakfast or light lunch. Fresh fruit salad is also wonderful with pancakes and waffles.

So what are Breadfellows' fruit salad secrets? To prepare grapefruits and oranges: peel the fruit with a sharp knife, including all of the inner white rind; cut into the fruit on both sides of each of the membranous partitions—your goal being to remove the fruit while leaving the membranes intact; then squeeze the juice over the fruit slices. Prepare these fruits first so that you can mix apple, peach, and pear slices with the citrus juice as you cut them to keep them from discoloring. Be sure that every fruit you include is at its peak of ripeness—melons are a common crunchy culprit. Always add fragile berries and banana slices just before serving.

Finally, whatever kind of salad you make, don't drown it in dressing. Dressings add savor and also, in varying degree, bind ingredients together. Some, such as mild vinaigrettes, exert a subtle, highlighting effect on the taste of salad components. Others, like basil dressing, are more assertive and tend to dominate delicate flavors.

Now let's see which salads and dressings are on the Breadfellows menu today—and what roles they are playing in meals.

GREEK WATERCRESS SALAD
▼▼▼

Watercress is such a unique and special spicy green; whenever it's in season, I make this salad for lunch or a light supper. Serve it with warm pita or SESAME BREAD (page 65).

YIELD: 4 servings

PREPARATION TIME: About 30 minutes

    8 ounces tofu, when pressed
    2 tablespoons lemon juice or red wine vinegar
    2 tablespoons olive oil
    2 tablespoons vegetable stock or water
  1/2 teaspoon dry mustard
     Freshly ground black pepper—several grindings
  1/4 teaspoon kelp powder
  1/4 teaspoon sea salt
    1 bunch (about 4 ounces or 6 cups) fresh watercress, coarsely chopped
    2 green onions, finely chopped
  1/2 cup fresh parsley, finely chopped
    1 medium-sized carrot, grated
    4 red radishes, thinly sliced
     Calamata or other Greek olives

Press the tofu well—or wrap it in a square of cheesecloth or muslin and squeeze until it is quite dry.

In a medium-sized bowl, whisk together the lemon juice or vinegar, oil, stock, mustard, pepper, kelp powder, and salt. Crumble the tofu into the bowl, stir, and marinate for a few minutes or longer.

Add the watercress, green onions, and parsley and toss well.

Serve garnished with the grated carrot, sliced radishes, and olives.

NOTES

- When watercress is not available, substitute fresh spinach leaves, lettuces, or other tender greens, such as arugula.

- Add minced fresh herbs—try basil and oregano or marjoram.

- Sliced or grated cooked beets are another good garnish for this salad.

ORIENTAL SPINACH SALAD
▼▼▼

You can prepare this salad several hours ahead of time and toss it together just before serving. Use tender spinach leaves for this. Try it with SESAME TORTILLAS (page 116), NUT BUTTER BREAD (page 72), or a rice bread. You can also stuff the salad into pita for sandwiches.

YIELD: 4 servings

PREPARATION TIME: 30 to 40 minutes

> 2 cloves garlic, pressed or minced
> 1 tablespoon minced fresh ginger root
> 1/8 teaspoon ground red pepper
> 1/4 teaspoon ground star anise
> 2 tablespoons rice wine
> 2 tablespoons roasted sesame oil
> 3 to 4 tablespoons tamari, to taste
> 1 pound tofu, well pressed
> 6 to 8 cups fresh spinach leaves, well washed and dried
> 3 green onions, finely chopped

In a large bowl, whisk together the garlic, ginger, red pepper, star anise, rice wine, and roasted sesame oil. Add tamari to taste and whisk thoroughly.

Blanch the tofu briefly, drain well, and cut into small cubes or strips. Add to the bowl and mix gently. Marinate 30 minutes to several hours (refrigerated), stirring occasionally.

Tear the spinach into bite-sized pieces and add to the bowl along with the onion. Toss everything together and serve.

SALADE COMPOSÉE
▼▼▼

The composed salads I was served in France several years ago remain vivid in my mind. One restaurant in particular, called Le Lutin de la Rivière, definitely had artists in the kitchen. The atmosphere was delightfully capricious, with a little horn sounding from the kitchen when orders were ready and a large, gentle black dog— "le propriétaire," as we came to refer to him—stretched out by the front door.

Their *salades composées* differed every day but were always masterpieces of flavor and design. For instance, one evening, a bed of tender Boston-type lettuce was covered with an aesthetic arrangement of sliced crisp fennel and cucumber, ripe red tomato wedges, grated carrot and beets, finely slivered green and red cabbage, and scrumptious little black olives. The dressing was a do-it-yourself affair: small cruets of oil and vinegar, some mustard, and a pepper grinder provided the resources for a custom-made mixture. Another evening, crisp broccoli florets, crunchy strands of sea palm (a kind of seaweed), cantaloupe chunks, and sliced raw mushrooms were artfully arranged on torn lettuce leaves. This time the salad was topped with a mild curry-flavored dressing. Both salads were served with fresh naturally-leavened rye bread.

Since returning home, I have followed the French example when preparing salads for appetizers, lunches, or other light meals by arranging seasonal ingredients with an eye to pattern and color in addition to taste and texture. Composed salads may be intended for individuals or for a couple or group to share, antipasto-style. They may consist of entirely raw ingredients or include lightly cooked ones. For a main course assortment, I often include protein items too, such as marinated beans or tofu or tempeh.

Of course there is seasonal overlap, but here are some suggestions for composed salads around the year:

- For spring, a variegated green combination of asparagus spears and sugar snap peas or snow-peas, green onions or leeks, watercress sprigs, tender young spinach and lettuce leaves, and radishes for an accent of color

- For summer, the palette explodes into vibrant color with beans, zucchini and yellow squash, tomatoes, okra, cucumber, arugula, pimiento and bell peppers, and green and red lettuces

- For fall, include broccoli and cauliflower, brussels sprouts, rosy and golden turnips, Chinese cabbage or bok choy, and perhaps sweet potato

- For winter, look to earthy beets and carrots, green and red cabbage, potatoes, mushrooms, various sprouts, thinly sliced dark greens, and maybe avocado

You can provide the components for a simple vinaigrette (oil, lemon wedges, vinegar, mustard, fresh pepper) or prepare a dressing to match the mood and ingredients of the particular salad. Refer to the dressing recipes at the end of this chapter for some alternatives.

BOSTON LETTUCE COMPOSÉE
▰▰▰

A composed salad can also be made with a single ingredient beautifully arranged. I first enjoyed this simple yet elegant salad one evening at a restaurant in Montreal. Initially, the delicate design of the salad seemed too lovely to disrupt, but one taste of the lemony vinaigrette dispelled my awe. This work of art is meant to be eaten with the fingers. Serve it with filled crêpes or bread-crusted vegetable tarts.

YIELD: 2 servings

PREPARATION TIME: 20 to 30 minutes

> 2 *small, shapely heads of Boston or buttercrunch lettuce*
> 2 *teaspoons prepared mustard*
> ¼ *teaspoon kelp powder*
> *Freshly ground black pepper—several grindings*
> 2 *tablespoons lemon juice*
> 2 *tablespoons mild vegetable stock or water*
> 2 *tablespoons sunflower oil*
> *Minced fresh herbs (dill, tarragon, basil, etc.), to taste*

Carefully disassemble the lettuce heads and wash and dry the leaves, then arrange the leaves of each head in a separate bowl so that the head appears to be intact.

Whisk together the mustard, kelp powder, pepper, lemon juice, and stock or water. Drizzle in the oil while whisking constantly to emulsify the mixture. Whisk in the herbs. Divide this dressing between two small bowls.

Serve each "head" of lettuce with a bowl of dressing alongside for dipping the lettuce leaves.

NOTES
- Substitute another light vegetable oil or olive oil for the sunflower oil.

MEXICALI SALAD
▰▰▰

This colorful layered salad is a quickly prepared, Mexican-style one-dish meal that is perfect for warm weather. Garnish it with PICKLED OKRA *(page 222-23).*

YIELD: 2 generous servings

PREPARATION TIME: 20 to 30 minutes

> 4 CORN TORTILLAS *(page 115)*
> *Corn oil*
> 4 *to 6 cups torn crisp lettuce leaves (or other dark greens)*
> 2 *cups finely sliced cabbage*
> ¼ *cup finely chopped green onion*
> 2 *cups* REFRITOS *(page 136)*
> 1 *medium-sized avocado*
> 1 *tablespoon lime juice*
> ½ *cup red or green salsa (see page 143)*
> ¼ *cup fresh cilantro leaves, coarsely chopped*

Preheat the oven to 350 degrees. Lightly brush both sides of the tortillas with corn oil and arrange them on a baking sheet. Bake, turning once, until they are lightly browned and crisp—watch them, this won't take long!

Divide the lettuce between two large plates. Scatter on the cabbage and sprinkle the onion over that. Spoon the beans over the vegetables. Dice the avocado, toss with the lime juice, and arrange on top of the greens and beans. Drizzle on the salsa and then sprinkle on the cilantro. Break the tortillas into pieces and scatter them over all.

NOTES
- Include other seasonal vegetables—grated carrots, sliced zucchini, bell pepper slivers, tomato wedges, or corn kernels.

- Garnish with a grated mild cheese such as Monterey jack.

TEMPEHTATION SALAD
▰▰▰

This is a chef's salad for tempeh lovers and is open to broad interpretation. Serve it all year, using the freshest seasonal vegetables you can find; drizzle a complementary dressing on top. SPROUTED WHEAT BREAD *(page 64) or a cracked wheat bread goes well with this version.*

YIELD: 2 generous servings

PREPARATION TIME: 30 to 40 minutes

> 1 *cup green beans, diagonally sliced about 1 inch long*
> 1 *large bell pepper*

1 tablespoon olive oil
1 4-ounce cake tempeh
¼ cup vegetable stock or water
½ teaspoon tamari
4 cups torn romaine, ruby, or leaf lettuce
2 cups chopped arugula
½ medium-sized cucumber, thinly sliced
¼ cup thinly sliced radish
1 small carrot, thinly sliced
6 medium-sized mushrooms, quartered
12 whole cherry tomatoes or 1 large tomato cut into wedges
2 tablespoons finely chopped fresh basil leaves
¼ cup minced fresh parsley
½ cup SESAME-LEMON DRESSING (page 223-24) or VINAIGRETTE (page 223)
Garlic-flavored CROÛTONS (page 185)
Black olives

Blanch the beans until just tender.

Roast and peel the pepper as described on page 130; cut it into strips.

Heat the oil in a small skillet over moderate heat and brown the tempeh on both sides, adding a bit more oil if necessary to keep it from sticking. Add the stock or water and tightly cover the pan. Cook until the liquid has almost disappeared. Add the tamari and cook until the pan is just dry. Cut the tempeh into small strips, cubes, or triangles.

Arrange the greens on two dinner plates. Scatter the prepared vegetables, tempeh, and herbs over the greens—or arrange them in a more organized fashion. Top with the dressing and garnish with croûtons and olives.

NOTES

▪ Spinach, tender mustard or turnip greens, lightly steamed broccoli or cauliflower, sugar snap peas, snow peas, turnips, daikon or other radishes, bok choy, Chinese cabbage, green onions or shallots, garlic chives, thinly sliced green or red cabbage, sliced zucchini or other summer squashes, lightly steamed or pickled okra, and plain or pickled beets are other potential components.

INDIAN CUCUMBER-TOMATO SALAD
▼▼▼

There are probably as many ways to make this refreshing salad as there are Indian—and non-Indian—cooks. I wait to add the last three ingredients until just before serving, since tomatoes lose flavor rapidly as soon as they are cut, salt quickly draws liquid out of other ingredients,

and cilantro wilts readily. I like this with CHAPATIS (page 117-18) and LENTIL DAL (page 136-37) or CURRIED CHICKPEAS (page 137) or INDIAN TURNOVERS (page 176).

YIELD: 2 to 4 servings

PREPARATION TIME: 15 to 20 minutes

½ cup finely diced peeled and seeded cucumber
2 tablespoons minced green onion
1 tablespoon lemon juice
Freshly ground black pepper—several grindings
¼ teaspoon sea salt
2 tablespoons coarsely chopped fresh cilantro leaves
1 cup finely diced tomato

Stir together the cucumber, onion, lemon juice, and pepper. Just before serving, stir in the salt, cilantro, and tomatoes.

NOTES

▪ For a more biting combination, add ½ teaspoon minced chili pepper and/or a minced garlic clove.

▪ Add some roasted ground cumin seed to taste.

DILLED BEET AND POTATO SALAD
▼▼▼

This salad is not only sweet and delicious, it's also a magnificent color! Serve it on fresh lettuce leaves and garnish with finely grated carrot, cucumber slices, and cherry tomatoes or tomato wedges. Cooked beets are as easy to peel as tomatoes; simmer them until tender in water to cover, cover with cold water, and slip off the skins. Have this for lunch or a light supper with a rye, bran, or buckwheat bread—or BUCKWHEAT MUFFINS (page 39). You can make the salad ahead of time.

YIELD: 2 to 4 servings

PREPARATION TIME: 20 to 30 minutes, not including cooking and cooling the beets

3 large beets, cooked, peeled, and cut into ½-inch
   dice (about 1½ cups)
3 medium-sized potatoes, cooked and cut into ½-
   inch dice (about 1½ cups)
3 green onions, finely chopped
1 tablespoon finely chopped fresh dill weed, or 1½
   teaspoons dried dill weed
¼ teaspoon kelp powder
½ cup TOFU MAYONNAISE (page 141) or other
   mayonnaise
2 teaspoons mellow rice miso
   Sea salt, to taste

In a medium-sized bowl, gently mix together the beets,
potatoes, green onions, dill, and kelp powder.

Whisk together the mayonnaise and miso until
smooth. Fold with the vegetables—and marvel at the
magenta color! Taste and add a bit of salt if necessary.

Serve at room temperature or chilled.

NOTES

- Substitute minced chives for the green onions.

- Minced fresh mint leaves are an interesting addition to this salad; add them to taste.

INDIAN COLESLAW
▼▼▼

*The spirited flavor and crunchy texture of this cabbage-
carrot salad pleasantly complements other Indian dishes.
Try it with SOURDOUGH PITA (page 121) and IN-
DIAN EGGPLANT (page 134-35). You could also serve it
with MASALA DOSAS (page 124) or CAULIFLOWER-
STUFFED PARATHAS (page 119).*

YIELD: 2 to 4 servings

PREPARATION TIME: 15 to 20 minutes

1 teaspoon finely grated fresh ginger root
1 tablespoon lemon juice
   Freshly ground black pepper—several grindings
1 tablespoon sesame oil
   Sea salt, to taste
1½ cups finely sliced Chinese cabbage or bok choy
1 cup grated carrot
2 tablespoons lightly toasted, coarsely chopped
   cashews

In a medium-sized mixing bowl, whisk together the
ginger, lemon juice, and pepper. Slowly drizzle in the
oil, whisking constantly, until the mixture is emulsified.
Season with salt to taste. Add the cabbage and carrot
and toss thoroughly to evenly coat with the dressing.
Garnish with the nuts.

CHINESE SPICY NOODLE SALAD
▼▼▼

*One winter when we were living in Ithaca, New York, my
husband and I spent snowy Saturday mornings studying
Chinese vegetarian cooking with Stella Fessler, a renowned Chinese cook who lives there. The class consisted
almost entirely of cooks from the vegetarian restaurants
in town. At the end of class, we all eagerly consumed the
morning's lessons. This noodle salad is a slight modifica-
tion of one we made. I never seem to tire of this versatile,
quickly prepared dish; it continually reappears on my table in one or another of its many guises. CHINESE
SCALLION BREAD (page 126-27), MANDARIN PAN-
CAKES (page 124-25), or SESAME TORTILLAS (page
116) make interesting companions. You can make the
dressing and get the vegetables ready ahead of time.*

YIELD: 2 to 4 servings

PREPARATION TIME: 30 to 40 minutes

⅓ cup unsalted peanut butter, or 3 tablespoons
   peanut butter plus 2 tablespoons tahini
1 tablespoon brown rice vinegar
1 tablespoon tamari
½ teaspoon hot chili oil, or ⅛ teaspoon ground red
   pepper seeds
⅓ cup vegetable stock or water
½ to 1 cup vegetables cut into thin strips—
   cucumber, Chinese cabbage, bok choy, radish,
   snowpeas, broccoli, carrot, or kohlrabi
6 to 8 ounces soba noodles or whole wheat
   spaghettini
1 tablespoon roasted sesame oil
2 to 3 cups finely shredded dark greens or spinach
3 green onions, finely chopped
4 ounces tofu, well pressed and cut into small
   strips (for extra firmness, blanch or steam it
   briefly)

Thoroughly whisk together the peanut butter, vinegar,
tamari, chili oil, and stock.

Lightly steam any vegetables that need cooking.
(You can do this first and use the stock for the dressing.)

Cook the noodles until they are just done, rinse
with cold water, drain well, and mix with the roasted
sesame oil.

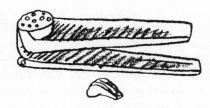

Arrange the shredded greens on individual plates, and sprinkle the green onion on next. Portion out the noodles, tofu, and vegetables, in that order, then ladle the dressing over all. Or mix the dressing with the noodles first and garnish with the vegetables and tofu.

NOTES

- Substitute tempeh for the tofu. Brown a 4-ounce cake of tempeh on both sides in a bit of sesame oil, add ¼ cup stock, cover tightly, cook until the pan is almost dry. Add ½ teaspoon tamari, finish steaming, and cut into strips or cubes.

- Substitute 1 to 2 cups of briefly blanched mung bean or lentil sprouts for the tofu.

- Substitute egg for the tofu. Heat a skillet or wok over moderately high heat and add enough sesame oil to coat. Beat 1 or 2 eggs, pour into the pan, and cook, lifting the edge with a spatula as necessary to allow the uncooked portion to run underneath. As soon as the egg has set, fold it into thirds, transfer it to a cutting board, and slice it into thin strips.

- Mustard greens are especially good in this dish; they impart a spicy pungency.

- Save soba noodle cooking water for breads, sauces, and soups, or use it for the dressing.

- Sprinkle some toasted sesame seeds on top.

PESTO PASTA SALAD
▾▾▾

Pesto makes an excellent dressing for a pasta salad, and it's a good way to use up leftovers—of pesto, pasta, and odds and ends of vegetables. Serve this salad with CROÛTES *(page 185) seasoned with garlic, an Italian bread spread with* ROASTED GARLIC *(page 133-34), or* FOCACCIA *(page 89).*

YIELD: 2 generous servings

PREPARATION TIME: About 45 minutes

> 1 tablespoon plus 1 teaspoon olive oil
> 1 small red onion, quartered and thinly sliced
> 1 clove garlic, pressed or minced
> Freshly ground black pepper—several grindings
> 1 small zucchini, halved lengthwise and sliced crosswise
> ¼ teaspoon kelp powder
> 1 small carrot, thinly sliced on the diagonal
> 2 small potatoes, halved or quartered and sliced
> 1¼ cups diagonally sliced green beans

> 2 ounces fusilli or other short cut of pasta
> 1 cup quartered cherry tomatoes
> ¼ cup minced fresh parsley
> ½ cup pesto (page 141–43)
> ¼ teaspoon sea salt, or to taste
> Lettuce leaves

Heat 1 tablespoon oil in a medium-sized skillet over moderate heat and briefly sauté the onion and garlic. Add the pepper, zucchini, and kelp powder and continue to sauté until the vegetables are just tender. Transfer the sauté to a medium-sized mixing bowl and cool.

Steam the carrot slices until just tender. Boil the potato slices until just tender; drain well. Blanch the beans. Add these to the bowl.

Cook the pasta al dente, drain it, and toss with the remaining teaspoon olive oil. Add to the vegetables, along with the tomatoes and parsley. Mix gently. Thoroughly fold in the pesto and season with salt. Serve on the greens. If you make the salad ahead of time, add the tomatoes just before serving.

BLACK-EYED PEA SALAD
▾▾▾

Black-eyed peas on New Year's are said to bring luck. During the summer, I like to renew the bid for good fortune by preparing this salad with fresh black-eyed peas; their superlative flavor even makes up for the tedium of shelling them. If your summer farmers' market isn't overflowing with fresh ones, substitute cooked dried black-eyed peas (see page 238 for cooking directions). Serve this salad with a corn bread or biscuits.

YIELD: 2 to 4 servings

PREPARATION TIME: 30 to 40 minutes

> 2 cups shelled fresh black-eyed peas
> 1 tablespoon olive oil
> 1 medium-sized red onion, chopped
> 2 cloves garlic, pressed or minced
> 1 large bell pepper, chopped
> Freshly ground black pepper—several grindings
> 1 teaspoon ground cumin
> ½ teaspoon kelp powder
> 1 tablespoon lemon juice
> 1 tablespoon mellow barley miso
> 2 medium-sized tomatoes, cut into ½-inch dice
> ¼ cup minced fresh parsley

Steam the peas for 10 to 15 minutes, or until tender. Reserve the steaming water.

Heat the oil in a medium-sized skillet over moderate heat and sauté the onion and garlic briefly. Stir in the bell pepper, black pepper, cumin, and kelp powder and continue to sauté until the vegetables are just tender. Add the peas and ¼ cup of the steaming water and simmer for several minutes to blend the flavors.

Whisk the lemon juice and miso to a smooth paste and stir into the sauté. Remove from the heat. Cool, and chill if desired. Stir in the tomatoes and parsley just before serving.

MARINATED LENTIL SALAD
▼▼▼

Serve this savory, protein-rich salad warm or chilled on a bed of greens, stuff it into pita, or scoop or wrap it with other flat breads. Minced fresh basil or mint leaves, toasted nori flakes, tomato or avocado slices, and black olives are all good additional garnishes. Add some cooked pasta for an even heartier salad. Prepare the lentils in advance.

YIELD: 3 to 4 servings

PREPARATION TIME: 20 to 30 minutes, not including preparing the lentils

- 1   *cup dried lentils*
- 1   *2-inch strip kombu*
- 2   *tablespoons olive oil*
- 1   *medium-sized sweet onion, finely chopped*
- 1   *clove garlic, pressed or minced*
     Freshly ground black pepper—several grindings
- ¼   *teaspoon ground cloves*
- ½   *teaspoon ground cumin*
- 2   *tablespoons lemon juice*
- 1   *tablespoon mellow barley miso*
- ½   *teaspoon umeboshi vinegar, or more to taste*
- 2   *green onions, finely chopped*
- ⅓   *cup fresh parsley, finely chopped*

Rinse the lentils and soak in water to cover for several hours or overnight. Drain and add the kombu and fresh water to cover. Bring to a boil, cover, turn the heat to low, and cook about 45 minutes, until the lentils are tender. Partially uncover and continue to simmer gently until any remaining liquid cooks away. Cool to room temperature or chill.

In a small skillet, heat the oil over moderate heat and sauté the onion until it appears translucent. Add the garlic, pepper, cloves, and cumin and sauté briefly.

In a medium-sized bowl, whisk the lemon juice and miso to a smooth paste. Stir in the lentils, the sauté, and vinegar and mix thoroughly. Garnish with the green onions and parsley.

TABOULI
▼▼▼

This refreshing Middle Eastern salad features cracked wheat and fresh mint and parsley. There are many versions, though traditional ones tend to go heavy on the parsley and easy on the wheat. This tabouli is somewhere in between—light and lemony and laden with minced herbs, yet with enough wheat for some substance. It also includes nontraditional carrots and almonds. I reserve tomatoes and cucumbers for garnish, since I find that when they are mixed in they tend to dilute the flavor of the salad, particularly when it is left over. Prepare the bulgur several hours in advance and plan to let the salad marinate for an hour or so—minus the tomatoes and cucumbers—before serving. Serve it with pita or LEBANESE WRAPPER BREAD (page 121-22) and bean or vegetable dips.

YIELD: 4 servings

PREPARATION TIME: About 30 minutes, not including preparing the bulgur

- 1½   *cups water*
- ½   *teaspoon sea salt*
- 1   *cup bulgur*
- ¼   *cup lemon juice*
- ½   *teaspoon kelp powder*
- ¼   *cup olive oil*
- ½   *cup fresh mint leaves, finely chopped*
- 2   *cups fresh parsley, finely chopped*
- ½   *cup grated carrot*
- ½   *cup lightly toasted chopped almonds*
- 4   *cups torn crisp lettuce or spinach leaves*
- 1   *medium-sized cucumber, peeled and seeded, if necessary, and finely diced*
- 1   *large tomato, finely diced*

Heat the water to boiling, add the salt, and pour over the bulgur in a 2-quart glass or ceramic bowl. Cover tightly and set aside for an hour or more, until the grain has absorbed the water and cooled. Refrigerate until chilled.

Whisk together the lemon juice, kelp powder, and oil. Pour this over the bulgur and toss with a long-tined fork to coat the grains. Add the mint, parsley, carrot, and almonds, and thoroughly toss again.

Serve on the greens, garnished with the cucumber and tomato.

NOTES

- Substitute 1 cup coarse cracked wheat for the bulgur; see page 13-14 for cooking directions.

- Sliced or chopped radishes and Greek olives are other tasty garnishes.

```
▀▄▀▄▀▄▀▄▀▄▀▄▀▄▀▄▀▄▀▄▀▄▀▄▀▄▀▄▀▄
```

POCKETFUL OF HUMMUS AND TABOULI
▼▼▼

This compact Middle Eastern combo was one of the most popular sandwiches at the natural foods deli where I worked in Atlanta.

YIELD: 1 sandwich

PREPARATION TIME: 15 minutes

> 1 pita (page 120-21)
> 6 lettuce leaves
> 1/2 cup HUMMUS (page 137)
> 1 cup TABOULI (page 219)
> 1/4 cup chopped cucumber
> 1/4 cup chopped tomato

To warm the pita, wrap it in foil and place in a 300-degree oven for a few minutes. Cut the pita in half to form two pockets.

Line each pocket with 3 lettuce leaves (position 1 along the bottom to keep the bread from getting soggy). Spread half the hummus in each pocket. Stuff half the tabouli into each one, and pack the cucumber and tomato on top.

NOTES
- Substitute BABA (page 134), MEDITERRANEAN BEAN SPREAD (page 138), or WHITE BEAN SPREAD (page 138) for the HUMMUS.

- Substitute ANASAZI BEAN SPREAD (page 138-39) for the HUMMUS and TEXABOULI (page 220) for the TABOULI.

```
▀▄▀▄▀▄▀▄▀▄▀▄▀▄▀▄▀▄▀▄▀▄▀▄▀▄▀▄▀▄
```

TEXABOULI
▼▼▼

This is a Tex-Mex variation of tabouli for anyone with pecans and plenty of cilantro. Serve it with SPICY BEAN BREAD (page 68) or any kind of tortillas and ANASAZI BEAN SPREAD (page 138–39) or REFRITOS (page 136). Tomatoes are a good garnish for this salad, or stuff the salad into scooped-out tomatoes. Soak and cool the bulgur ahead of time.

YIELD: 4 servings

PREPARATION TIME: About 30 minutes, not including preparing the bulgur

> 1 1/2 cups water
> 1/2 teaspoon sea salt
> 1 cup bulgur

> 1/4 cup lime juice
> 1/4 cup olive oil
> 1/2 cup lightly toasted pecans, finely chopped
> 4 cups fresh cilantro leaves, coarsely chopped
> 1/4 to 1/2 cup minced green onions, to taste
> 1 ripe avocado, peeled and cut into 1/2-inch chunks
> Dark greens

Heat the water to boiling, add the salt, and pour over the bulgur in a 2-quart glass or ceramic bowl. Cover tightly and set aside for an hour or more, until the grain has absorbed the water and cooled. Refrigerate until chilled.

Whisk together the lime juice and oil. Pour this over the bulgur and toss with a long-tined fork to coat the grains. Add the pecans, cilantro, and 1/4 cup green onions and thoroughly toss again. Taste and add additional green onions if desired. Stir in the avocado chunks (if you anticipate leftover salad, use the avocado as a garnish). Serve immediately on a bed of greens.

NOTES
- Substitute 1 cup coarse cracked wheat for the bulgur; see page 13-14 for cooking directions.

MEMORABLE MEDITERRANEAN RICE SALAD
▼▼▼

Make this when fresh basil, tender spinach, and ripe tomatoes are plentiful. The rice adds a bit of staying power. Serve this salad with LEBANESE WRAPPER BREAD (page 121-22) or pita (page 120-21).

YIELD: 4 servings

PREPARATION TIME: 20 to 30 minutes

> 4 cups cooked long-grain brown rice
> 8 cups torn or coarsely chopped fresh spinach leaves
> 1/2 cup lightly toasted pine nuts
> 2 large tomatoes, diced
> 1/4 cup finely chopped fresh parsley
> 3/4 cup BASIL DRESSING (page 224)

If the rice is cold, sprinkle it lightly with about a teaspoon of olive oil, warm it slightly in a double boiler, and fluff with a fork.

Just before serving, assemble individual salads. On each plate, layer 1 cup spinach, 1 cup rice, the rest of the spinach, 1 tablespoon pine nuts, the tomatoes, parsley, and remaining pine nuts. Drizzle the dressing over all.

NOTES

▪ If you use freshly cooked rice, allow it cool almost to room temperature before fluffing it with a fork.

CURRIED RICE AND TEMPEH SALAD

▀▀▀

You'll need to give yourself a head start on this dish by cooking and cooling the curried rice in advance; the rice should be room temperature for the salad rather than chilled, however. Basmati rice is especially good for this. Don't be put off by the long list of ingredients; the salad is quick to assemble once you've prepared the dressing, vegetables, tempeh, and garnishes, which you can also do ahead of time. It can be adapted to the season and the items you have on hand: for instance, in place of the carrot, substitute other root vegetables, such as parsnips, turnips, or sweet potatoes; substitute a diced tart apple for the bell pepper; try out other combinations of vegetables, perhaps cauliflower, tomatoes, and summer squash. This salad is a complete meal by itself, but I like to serve it with some sliced fresh fruit and an especially compatible bread—CRACKED WHEAT BREAD (page 72-73), GINGERY CARROT BREAD (page 69-70), CHAPATIS (page 117-18), and PARATHAS (page 117-18) are good choices.

YIELD: 4 to 6 servings

PREPARATION TIME: 30 to 40 minutes, not including rice preparation

2 *whole cloves*
1/2 *teaspoon each cumin seeds, turmeric, coriander, and chili powder*
1/4 *teaspoon each cardamom, cinnamon, and cayenne*
1/8 *teaspoon fenugreek*
4 *to 5 tablespoons sesame oil*
1/2 *teaspoon black mustard seeds*
3 *cloves garlic, pressed or minced*
1 *tablespoon grated or minced fresh ginger root*
1 *cup long-grain brown rice, rinsed and drained*
1 *teaspoon sea salt*
1 3/4 *cups water*
2 *tablespoons lemon juice*
2 *tablespoons cider vinegar*
1 *large carrot, thinly sliced or finely diced*
1 *cup fresh peas or sugar snap peas*
1 *8-ounce cake tempeh*
1/2 *cup vegetable stock*
1 *teaspoon tamari*
1 *large red bell pepper, chopped or thinly sliced*
3 *large green onions, finely chopped*
1/4 *cup raisins*
4 *cups torn dark greens—dark lettuces, spinach, etc.*
1/2 *cup lightly toasted cashew pieces or chopped almonds*
1/2 *cup lightly toasted flaked coconut (optional)*

With a mortar and pestle or spice grinder, pulverize the cloves, cumin, turmeric, coriander, chili powder, cardamom, cinnamon, cayenne, and fenugreek.

Heat 1 tablespoon of the oil in a 1- to 1 1/2 quart saucepan over low heat and add the mustard seeds. Cook until they begin to pop. Add the garlic and ginger and sauté briefly. Stir in the spice mixture and cook, stirring constantly, for a minute or two. Stir in the rice and sauté briefly. Add 1/2 teaspoon of the salt and the water and bring just to a boil. Stir once, cover tightly, turn the heat as low as possible, and cook 40 minutes. Remove the pot from the heat with the lid in place and set aside to cool.

Whisk together the lemon juice, vinegar, and remaining 1/2 teaspoon salt. Gradually whisk in 2 tablespoons of the oil, emulsifying the mixture.

Lightly steam the carrot and peas until they are crisp tender. Save the steaming water to use as stock.

Heat 1 tablespoon oil in a medium-sized skillet over moderate heat and brown the tempeh on both sides, adding additional oil if necessary. Add 1/2 cup stock, cover tightly, and steam until the liquid has almost cooked away. Add the tamari and cook until the pan is dry. Cut the tempeh into small cubes or strips.

In a large bowl, toss together the cooled rice, carrots, peas, tempeh, bell pepper, green onion, and raisins. Drizzle the dressing on top and fold it in thoroughly. Serve the salad on a bed of torn greens, garnished with the nuts and coconut.

CAPONATA

▀▀▀

This is an eggplant salad with a slightly sweet-and-sour cast. Caponata is traditionally baked in the oven to a very soft consistency, but I like it with a crisper texture. This benefits from some marinating, so you can make it a day ahead. Serve it at room temperature or chilled on torn or

chopped greens—arugula is especially compatible. SOCCA *(page 123) and good black olives are perfect partners.*

YIELD: 4 servings

PREPARATION TIME: About 1 hour

    2 *pounds eggplant*
    1 *tablespoon olive oil, plus extra for brushing the eggplant*
    2 *large bell peppers*
    1 *medium-sized red onion, coarsely chopped*
    2 to 3 *cloves garlic, pressed or minced*
    2 *small zucchini, cut into ½-inch dice*
    Freshly ground black pepper—several grindings
    ¼ *teaspoon ground dried thyme, or ½ teaspoon minced fresh thyme*
    ¼ *teaspoon kelp powder*
  1½ *tablespoons cider vinegar*
    1 *tablespoon mirin*
    2 *tablespoons capers*
  ⅜ *teaspoon sea salt, or more to taste*
    ¼ *cup finely chopped fresh basil leaves*
  3 to 4 *medium-sized tomatoes*

Cut the eggplant into ½-inch slices. Layer them in a colander, sprinkling salt between each layer. Put a weight on top and press for about 30 minutes. Rinse and pat dry. Brush both sides of each slice with olive oil and arrange on a baking sheet (an easy way to do this is to pour some oil onto the sheet and dip the slices into it). Bake at 350 degrees for 15 to 20 minutes, until very tender. Cut the eggplant into ½-inch dice and transfer to a large bowl.

Roast and peel the peppers as described on page 130; cut them into ½-inch squares. Add to the eggplant.

Heat the 1 tablespoon oil in a medium-sized skillet over moderate heat and sauté the onion, garlic, and zucchini until the onion is just tender. Add the black pepper, thyme, and kelp powder and cook, stirring, a couple of minutes longer. Add this to the eggplant.

Stir in the vinegar, mirin, capers, salt, and basil and set aside for 30 minutes or so, or cover and refrigerate

for several hours or overnight, stirring occasionally.

Just before serving, cut the tomatoes into ½-inch dice and stir them into the salad.

NOTES

- If you use Oriental eggplants, you don't need to salt and press them.

- Substitute other varieties of summer squash for the zucchini and pimientos for the bell peppers.

PICKLED BEETS
▾▾▾

Use these in a SALADE COMPOSÉE *(page 214-15) or* TEMPEHTATION SALAD *(page 215-16), or simply slice or cube them and sprinkle on some minced fresh dill weed and perhaps a drizzle of* VINAIGRETTE *(page 223). Fixed any way, they are good with rye breads. Save the marinade and marinate hard-boiled eggs in it: you'll end up with purple pickled eggs!*

YIELD: 2 to 4 servings

PREPARATION TIME: 10 minutes, not including cooking the beets

    4 *large or 8 to 12 small beets*
  ½ *cup cider vinegar*
    6 *black peppercorns*
    4 *whole cloves*
  ½ *teaspoon mustard seed*

Scrub the beets well, cover with water in a pot, and bring just to a boil. Cover, reduce the heat, and simmer until just tender—10 to 20 minutes, depending on the size of the beets. Drain, reserving the stock. Cut the ends off the beets and slip off the skins. Place the beets in a large jar or glass or ceramic bowl.

In a saucepan, combine 1 cup reserved beet stock, vinegar, peppercorns, cloves, and mustard seed and bring just to a boil. Immediately pour over the beets and marinate for several hours. If the marinade does not quite cover the beets, add additional beet stock. Use the extra beet stock in breads, soups, and sauces.

These will keep well in the refrigerator for a week or two.

PICKLED OKRA
▾▾▾

There's not much middle ground with okra; you either love it or you wouldn't touch it with a ten-foot pole. Its slippery sap is the issue. Pickling keeps the sap in check while allowing okra's tantalizing flavor through, so it's a good preparation technique for dubious tasters. Red okra makes particularly attractive pickles, though green ones taste just as good. Whatever the color, choose straight, slender, firm pods. Serve these crisp pickles with Southern- or Middle Eastern-style salads and sandwiches; I also like them with Mexican meals. These will keep a couple of weeks in the refrigerator.

YIELD: 1 pint

PREPARATION TIME: 20 to 30 minutes

> *Several small dill stalks with seeds*
> 12 *peppercorns*
> 1/2 *teaspoon mustard seed*
> 1 *small clove garlic, peeled*
> 1 *small hot pepper (optional)*
> 6 *to 8 ounces small, tender okra pods*
> 1/2 *cup apple cider vinegar*
> 1/2 *cup water*

Put the dill, peppercorns, mustard seed, garlic, and hot pepper in the bottom of a sterile pint jar. Rinse the okra and pack tightly into the jar vertically.

Combine the vinegar and water in a saucepan, bring to a boil, and pour over the okra in the jar. Cap and cool. Refrigerate for a day or two before eating the pickles.

To process the pickles, set the jar on a rack in a kettle of rapidly boiling water—with at least an inch of water above the top of the jar—cover, and keep the water boiling constantly for 5 minutes. Remove the jar to a rack to cool and seal.

NOTES
- Omit the dill and add 10 to 12 whole coriander seeds.

VINAIGRETTE
▾▾▾

This is a basic dressing that suits a wide variety of salads, from tossed greens to steamed vegetables, chef's salads to composed ones. Here it is in its simplest form; feel free to add pressed garlic, minced fresh or crushed dried herbs, or other extras to taste. Flavored vinegars are another way to add character. Directly multiply the ingredients to increase the amount. This will keep indefinitely in a covered container in the refrigerator.

YIELD: 2 servings

PREPARATION TIME: 10 to 15 minutes

> 1 *teaspoon prepared mustard (preferably Dijon-style)*
> *Freshly ground black pepper—several grindings*
> 1/4 *teaspoon kelp powder*
> 1 *tablespoon lemon juice or vinegar*
> 1 *tablespoon vegetable stock or water*
> 1 *tablespoon olive oil or another oil*

Whisk together the mustard, pepper, kelp powder, lemon juice or vinegar, and liquid. Slowly dribble in the oil while whisking constantly to form an emulsion.

NOTES
- The liquid lightens this dressing; omit it or substitute olive oil or a light vegetable oil, such as sunflower or sesame oil, for a thicker, richer dressing.

TOFU-SESAME DRESSING
▾▾▾

This is a creamy topping for a crisp salad—or for steamed vegetables, cooked grains, or baked potatoes. You can also use it as a dip for raw vegetables.

YIELD: About 1 cup

PREPARATION TIME: About 10 minutes

> 1/2 *cup (about 3 ounces) mashed tofu*
> 1/4 *cup tahini*
> 3 *tablespoons lemon juice*
> 1 *clove garlic*
> 1 *teaspoon roasted sesame oil*
> 1 *teaspoon tamari*
> 1/2 *teaspoon umeboshi vinegar*
> 4 *to 6 tablespoons vegetable stock or water*

In a blender or in a food processor fitted with the metal blade, combine the tofu, tahini, lemon juice, garlic, oil, tamari, and vinegar and blend until thoroughly smooth. With the blender or processor running, gradually add the stock or water until the dressing reaches the desired consistency. This dressing will thicken a bit upon standing; thin it by blending or whisking in additional liquid, a tablespoon at a time. Covered and refrigerated, it will keep for several days.

SESAME-LEMON DRESSING
▾▾▾

Miso balances the oil and goes well with the sesame and lemon flavors in this smooth and mellow yet lively blend. This dressing adds a special touch to even the simplest green salad.

YIELD: About 1/2 cup

PREPARATION TIME: 10 minutes

> 2 *tablespoons tahini*
> 1 *tablespoon lemon juice*
> 1 *teaspoon roasted sesame oil*
> 1/4 *cup vegetable stock or water*
> 1 *teaspoon hatcho miso, or to taste*

Blend or whisk together the tahini, lemon juice, oil, and liquid. Blend or whisk in miso to taste.

Tightly covered and refrigerated, this will keep indefinitely.

NOTES

- Add a small clove of pressed or minced garlic.

ZESTFUL MISO DRESSING
▼▼▼

Lemon zest makes this dressing especially perky. It keeps well when refrigerated and has lots of applications; use it to dress tossed or arranged vegetable salads or grain salads.

YIELD: About ½ cup

PREPARATION TIME: 10 to 15 minutes

> 2 tablespoons lemon juice
> ¼ teaspoon kelp powder
> Freshly ground black pepper—several grindings
> 1 tablespoon mellow barley miso
> 1 tablespoon vegetable stock or water
> 2 tablespoons sesame oil or other vegetable oil
> ½ to 1 teaspoon finely grated lemon zest

Whisk together the lemon juice, kelp powder, pepper, miso, and stock or water. Slowly dribble in the oil, whisking constantly, to emulsify the mixture. Whisk in lemon zest to taste.

If the dressing is too thick, add additional liquid.

TANGY TAHINI DRESSING
▼▼▼

This piquant sesame dressing is a refreshing alternative to vinaigrette for tossed or composed vegetable salads. It is a good keeper when covered and refrigerated. For extra zing, add a small clove of pressed or minced garlic and/or a bit of minced fresh ginger root.

YIELD: About ½ cup

PREPARATION TIME: 10 minutes

> 1 tablespoon roasted sesame oil
> 2 tablespoons tahini
> 1 tablespoon brown rice vinegar
> ¼ teaspoon umeboshi paste
> 4 tablespoons vegetable stock or water
> Sea salt or tamari, to taste

Whisk together the oil, tahini, vinegar, and umeboshi paste. Gradually whisk in the stock or water. Season with salt or tamari to taste.

BASIL DRESSING
▼▼▼

Stimulating in color as well as flavor, this refreshing bright green topping is a seasonal star! Use it to dress tossed salads and to prepare MEMORABLE MEDITER-RANEAN RICE SALAD (page 220-21).

YIELD: About ¾ cup

PREPARATION TIME: 10 minutes

> 1 cup loosely packed fresh basil leaves
> 2 tablespoons lemon juice
> ¼ cup vegetable stock or water
> 1½ teaspoons mellow barley miso
> 1 small clove garlic
> ¼ cup olive oil

Combine all ingredients except the oil in a blender and blend thoroughly. While the machine is still running, gradually add the oil.

Extra dressing will keep for several days in a tightly covered jar in the refrigerator. Reblend if it separates.

CHAPTER 16

Baked Desserts

UNQUESTIONABLY, DESSERTS DELIGHT the senses and, perhaps more than any other type of food, become the stuff of memories. I never eat a gingerbread man without thinking of my grandmother and the long evenings we spent together rolling, cutting, and decorating cookies at Christmastime. Candlelit cakes recall my mother fulfilling my wish for a blue birthday cake, complete with tiny boat candleholders riding the waves of swirled blue meringue frosting. And the sight of a handsome fruit tart transports me back to the pâtisseries of Paris. Certain friends often mention to me how vividly they remember their first gratifying taste of some of the desserts that I have served them.

One of my greatest hopes is that at least a few such fond memories are born when patrons bite into the various cookies and bars, cakes, and pies that are offered at Breadfellows, my fanciful bakery-tearoom. Years from now, they may describe the heavenly nondairy cheesecake or the wonderfully moist, spicy carrot cake in mouth-watering detail to their grandchildren and taste these delectable baked desserts all over again.

Few adults retain their childhood sweet tooth, yet something sweet can end a meal on just the right note or appease our hunger until the next meal. My rule of thumb for desserts is that they can be elegant and somewhat sweet, but not cloying, sugary concoctions. Whole-grain flours, unrefined sweeteners, fresh and dried fruits, and nuts compose tasty treats that will satisfy a craving for richness yet won't throw your pancreas and liver into shock. In a pinch, they are even healthy enough to stand on their own.

Look to the Breadfellows pastry case to gratify your desire for dessert and you're in for a sweet reward; it will be filled with baked goods made from the recipes that follow. Also, don't forget about dessert items that appeared in earlier chapters, including sweet quick breads and yeasted pastries, dessert crêpes, fruit-topped pizzas and coffee cakes, and sweet bread puddings.

NUT BUTTER COOKIES
᙭᙭᙭

These crisp, nutty cookies will melt in your mouth; the almond butter variety are my all-time favorite cookies.

YIELD: About 1½ dozen cookies

PREPARATION TIME: 15 to 20 minutes to prepare; 25 minutes to bake

> ¼ cup sunflower, sesame, or corn oil
> 1 cup unsalted (preferably crunchy) peanut butter or almond butter, at room temperature
> ¼ cup maple syrup
> ½ teaspoon pure vanilla extract
> 1 cup sifted whole wheat pastry flour
> ¼ teaspoon sea salt

Preheat the oven to 300 degrees. Lightly grease a large baking sheet or line it with baking parchment.

In a medium-sized bowl, beat together the oil and nut butter until they are thoroughly combined. Beat in the maple syrup and vanilla.

Sift together the flour and salt. Stir into the wet mixture—a soft dough will come together into a ball and leave the sides of the bowl. Cover and refrigerate for about 10 minutes.

Roll the dough into 1-inch balls. Arrange the balls on the prepared sheet and flatten them with a fork—dipping it into water occasionally keeps·it from sticking.

Bake in the preheated oven for about 25 minutes—until the bottoms are lightly browned.

Cool the cookies on the sheet for a few minutes, then transfer them to a rack.

NOTES
- Substitute a mild-flavored honey for the maple syrup.

SAND DOLLARS
᙭᙭᙭

These are delicate almond wafers—just right as a light dessert or as an accompaniment to fresh fruit or ice cream or sorbet.

YIELD: About 3 dozen cookies

PREPARATION TIME: 20 to 30 minutes to prepare; 30 minutes to bake

> 1 cup unsalted soy margarine or butter, softened
>   A pinch of sea salt
> ⅓ cup mild-flavored honey
> 1 teaspoon pure vanilla extract
> 2 cups whole wheat pastry flour
> ½ cup finely ground almonds

In an electric mixer or in a medium-sized bowl with a wooden spoon, cream the margarine or butter. Beat in the salt, honey, and vanilla. Thoroughly mix in the flour and almonds to form a soft dough. Chill the dough until firm.

Preheat the oven to 275 degrees.

Roll the dough into small balls and place them at generous intervals on ungreased baking sheets. Flatten the balls into thin circles.

Bake in the preheated oven for 30 minutes or until they are lightly browned. Cool on the sheets for a few minutes, then carefully transfer to a rack to finish cooling.

Store in a loosely covered container to maintain crispness.

NOTES
- Substitute maple syrup for the honey, and ground walnuts, pecans, or hazelnuts for the almonds. Rub the skins off hazelnuts while still warm from toasting before grinding them.

OUTSTANDING OATMEAL COOKIES
᙭᙭᙭

Oatmeal cookies usually disappointed me until I worked out this recipe. These are crisp on the outside, chewy on the inside, and supremely satisfying.

YIELD: About 1½ dozen cookies

PREPARATION TIME: 15 to 20 minutes to prepare; 20 to 25 minutes to bake

> ⅔ cup rye flour
> 2 tablespoons soy flour
> ½ teaspoon sea salt
> ½ teaspoon baking soda
> 2 tablespoons wheat germ
> 1½ cups rolled oats
> ½ cup sunflower oil
> ⅓ cup maple syrup
> 1 egg
> ¼ cup chopped dates
> ¼ cup lightly toasted chopped pecans

Preheat the oven to 325 degrees. Line a large baking sheet with baking parchment or grease it lightly.

Sift the flours, salt, and soda into a medium-sized mixing bowl. Stir in the wheat germ and rolled oats.

In another bowl, whisk together the oil and syrup. Whisk in the egg. Stir in the dates. Add the dry mixture and nuts and fold gently until the ingredients are combined.

Drop spoonfuls of the dough onto the prepared sheet. Flatten with a fork or the back of the spoon to form rounds about ½ inch thick.

Bake in the preheated oven for 20 to 25 minutes, until lightly browned on top and browned on the bottom. Transfer to a cooling rack.

NOTES

- Substitute raisins or other dried fruits for the dates; substitute walnuts, almonds, or other nuts for the pecans.

SESAME SHORTBREAD
▰▰▰

Shortbread is a tender, rich bar cookie that is usually made with lots of butter and sugar. In this recipe, tahini adds protein and a sesame flavor that goes well with the rye flour. Use a mild-flavored honey for a delicate sweetness.

YIELD: 1 8-inch square or 9-inch round pan

PREPARATION TIME: About 15 minutes to prepare; 30 minutes to bake

    1 *cup unsalted tahini*
    ¼ *cup unsalted soy margarine or butter, softened*
    ⅓ *cup honey*
    ¼ *teaspoon sea salt*
    1½ *cups rye flour*

Preheat the oven to 300 degrees. Grease an 8-inch square or 9-inch round baking pan.

In an electric mixer or in a medium-sized bowl with a wooden spoon, blend together the tahini, margarine or butter, and honey until thoroughly combined and smooth. Mix in the salt. Incorporate the flour gradually—until the dough holds together and leaves the sides of the bowl.

Press the dough evenly into the prepared pan. Bake for 20 to 25 minutes, until very lightly browned. Cut into pieces while still hot. Cool in the pan on a rack.

APRICOT-ALMOND BARS
▰▰▰

A smooth dried-apricot purée is sandwiched between two crunchy layers in these yummy bars. You can substitute other fruits and nuts for the apricots and almonds.

YIELD: 1 8-inch square pan

PREPARATION TIME: About 45 minutes to prepare; 40 to 45 minutes to bake

    1 *cup dried apricots*

    1 *cup unsweetened apple juice or cider*
    ⅓ *cup lightly toasted almonds*
    1 *cup rolled oats*
    1 *cup whole wheat pastry flour*
    ¼ *teaspoon sea salt*
    ¼ *cup sunflower oil*
    ¼ *cup mild-flavored honey*

Combine the apricots and juice in a saucepan and cook over low heat until the apricots have absorbed the juice and are swelled and soft. Purée in a blender or food processor and set aside.

In a food processor fitted with the metal blade, briefly blend the almonds. Add the oats, flour, and salt, and blend briefly again. Drizzle in the oil and pulse to distribute it evenly throughout the crumbly mixture. Drizzle in the honey and pulse again.

Preheat the oven to 350 degrees. Grease an 8-inch square baking pan. Firmly press half of the crumbly mixture into the bottom of the pan. Spread the fruit purée over the pressed layer, sprinkle the remaining crumbly mixture evenly over the fruit filling (it helps to dip your fingers in water occasionally while you do this), and press it down gently.

Bake in the preheated oven for 40 to 45 minutes—until the top is golden brown and crisp.

Cool in the pan on a rack. Cut into bars and serve warm or cooled.

NOTES

- Substitute maple syrup or brown rice syrup for the honey.

- Substitute lightly toasted walnuts, pecans, or hazelnuts for the almonds. (Rub the skins off the hazelnuts after roasting them in a 325-degree oven for about 10 minutes.)

- For *DATE BARS*, substitute pitted dates for the apricots—I particularly like Medjool dates; add the finely grated zest of a lemon to the purée.

- For *PRUNE-ORANGE BARS*, substitute pitted prunes for the apricots. Finely grate the zest of 1 orange, then juice the orange and add apple juice to the orange juice to equal 1 cup. Simmer the prunes in the orange-apple juice. Add the zest to the purée.

CAROB BROWNIES
▰▰▰

Carob is often used as a chocolate substitute because it has a somewhat similar flavor, especially when roasted—which is one way that it is sold. Unlike chocolate, carob is naturally sweet. It is also a healthier alternative than chocolate, since it contains significant amounts of protein, vitamin A, B vitamins, calcium, and other minerals, and it is lower in fat and calories than chocolate, too. Despite carob's positive nutritional profile, these fudgy bars are truly luscious!

YIELD: 1 8-inch square pan

PREPARATION TIME: About 45 minutes, including baking

    2/3 cup roasted carob powder, sifted
    1/2 cup sunflower oil
    1/2 cup tahini
    1/2 cup maple syrup
    2 eggs
    2 teaspoons pure vanilla extract
    1 cup sifted whole wheat pastry flour
    1/2 teaspoon sea salt
    1/2 teaspoon baking powder
    1 cup lightly toasted pecans or walnuts, coarsely chopped

Preheat the oven to 325 degrees. Grease an 8-inch square baking pan.

In a medium-sized bowl, thoroughly whisk the carob powder into the oil. Whisk in the tahini and maple syrup. Beat in the eggs and vanilla until thoroughly smooth.

Sift the flour with the salt and baking powder. Add it to the liquid mixture and stir gently—just until combined. Fold in the nuts. Spread evenly in the prepared baking pan.

Bake in the preheated oven for 20 minutes or a few minutes longer if you prefer drier, cakier brownies. Cool on a rack. Cut into bars and serve warm or cool.

NOTES

- Substitute raisins for 1/2 cup of the nuts.

- For very thin brownies, divide the batter between two pans and bake for 10 or 15 minutes.

- For eggless brownies, omit the eggs. Thoroughly blend 2 ounces of tofu with 1/4 cup unsweetened apple juice and whisk this mixture with the other wet ingredients in place of the eggs.

APPLE CAKE
▾▾▾

This is a simple and delicious dessert or coffee cake for brunch; I especially like it served warm.

YIELD: 1 8-inch square or 9-inch round cake

PREPARATION TIME: About 30 minutes to prepare; 40 minutes to bake

    2 eggs
    1/2 cup sunflower oil or melted unsalted soy margarine or butter
    1/3 cup maple syrup
    3 cups finely diced, peeled apple (4 to 5 medium-sized apples)
    1 3/4 cups whole wheat pastry flour
    1/2 teaspoon sea salt
    1 teaspoon baking soda
    1/2 teaspoon cinnamon
    1/2 teaspoon nutmeg

Preheat the oven to 350 degrees. Grease an 8-inch square glass or ceramic baking pan.

In a medium-sized mixing bowl, beat the eggs well. Beat in the oil and syrup and stir in the prepared apples.

Sift the flour, salt, soda, and spices. Add to the liquid mixture and stir gently, just until a batter forms.

Spread the batter evenly in the prepared pan. Bake in the preheated oven for 40 minutes, or until a tester inserted into the center comes out clean.

Cool on a rack; serve warm or cooled.

NOTES

- Substitute firm pears for all or part of the apples and add a pinch of allspice to the dry ingredients.

GINGER UPSIDE-DOWN CAKE
▾▾▾

Serve this delicately spiced cake "bottom-up," with the fruit on top. Without the fruit, this makes a delicious gingerbread; serve it topped with **LEMON GLAZE** (page 112) or apple sauce or pear sauce (see page 136).

YIELD: 1 8-inch square cake

PREPARATION TIME: About 30 minutes to prepare; 40 minutes to bake

    2 to 3 large ripe pears or peaches
    4 ounces tofu
    1 cup unsweetened apple juice
    Grated zest of one lemon
    1/3 cup sunflower oil
    1/3 cup plus one tablespoon maple syrup
    2 cups sifted whole wheat pastry flour

½ teaspoon sea salt
1 teaspoon baking soda
1 teaspoon ground ginger
¼ teaspoon ground allspice

Preheat the oven to 350 degrees. Grease an 8-inch square glass or ceramic baking pan. Drizzle one tablespoon syrup over the bottom.

Peel and core or pit the pears or peaches. Cut lengthwise into slices ¼ inch thick. Arrange in even rows on the bottom of the prepared pan.

In a blender, thoroughly blend the tofu and apple juice. Whisk with the lemon zest, oil, and ⅓ cup syrup in a medium-sized bowl.

Sift together the flour, salt, baking soda, ginger, and allspice. Gradually add to the wet mixture, whisking gently, just until a smooth batter forms. Pour evenly over the fruit slices.

Bake in the preheated oven for 40 minutes or until a tester inserted into the center comes out clean.

Cool the cake briefly on a rack, then invert it onto a plate. Serve warm or at room temperature.

NOTES

- To easily peel peaches, briefly immerse them in boiling water and then in cold water; the skins will slip off readily.

MOTHER'S CARROT CAKE
᭢

This recipe was inspired by an eggless, dairy-free cake served at Mother's Cafe & Garden, a vegetarian restaurant in Austin, Texas. I like to top this moist, spicy cake with SESAME-MAPLE ICING *(see box).*

YIELD: 1 8-inch square or 9-inch round cake

PREPARATION TIME: 20 to 30 minutes to prepare; 40 to 45 minutes to bake

2 tablespoons poppy seeds
⅓ cup sunflower oil or other light vegetable oil
⅓ cup maple syrup
   Grated zest of 1 orange
1 cup orange juice
⅓ cup raisins
2 cups grated carrots
2 cups whole wheat pastry flour
½ teaspoon sea salt
1 teaspoon baking soda
1 teaspoon baking powder
½ teaspoon each cinnamon, nutmeg, and allspice
⅔ cup lightly toasted pecans or walnuts, coarsely chopped

Preheat the oven to 350 degrees. Grease an 8-inch

▸▸▸▸▸▸▸▸▸▸▸▸▸▸▸▸▸▸▸▸▸▸▸▸

SESAME-MAPLE ICING
᭢

Spread this sweet, smooth frosting on MOTHER'S CARROT CAKE *(page 229) or any other moist spice cake or cupcakes.*

¼ cup maple syrup
¼ cup tahini
¼ teaspoon orange zest

Heat the syrup in the top of a double boiler. Whisk in the tahini. Remove from the heat and whisk in the zest. Set aside to cool and thicken before spreading it on the cake.

▸▸▸▸▸▸▸▸▸▸▸▸▸▸▸▸▸▸▸▸▸▸▸▸

square baking pan. Sprinkle in the poppy seeds and tilt the pan to coat the bottom and sides.

In a medium-sized mixing bowl, whisk together the oil and syrup. Whisk in the zest and juice. Stir in the raisins and carrots.

Sift the flour, salt, baking soda, baking powder, and spices. Add the sifted mixture all at once to the liquid mixture and stir gently, just until a thick batter forms. Gently fold in the nuts.

Spread the batter evenly in the prepared pan. Bake in the preheated oven for 40 to 45 minutes—until a tester inserted into the center comes out clean.

Cool the cake in the pan for at least 15 minutes before turning it out directly onto the rack to finish cooling.

Serve the cake slightly warm or at room temperature, plain or iced.

NOTES

- Substitute a mild-flavored honey for the maple syrup; orange blossom honey is especially good.

- Substitute unsweetened apple juice, milk, or soy milk for half to two-thirds of the orange juice.

FRUITCAKE

I've been making these cakes for the holidays since grade school. They are great to have on hand for serving to guests and giving as gifts. I make them just after Thanksgiving, so they'll be ready for Christmas.

YIELD: 4 2-pound cakes

PREPARATION TIME: About 30 minutes, plus several hours to soak the fruit; 2 hours to bake

> 2 cups each raisins and currants
> 1 cup each chopped figs, pitted dates, and pitted prunes
> ½ cup chopped dried fruit (dried apricots, apples, etc., or more figs, dates, or prunes)
> 3 to 4 cups unsweetened apple juice or apple cider
> 1 orange
> ½ lemon
> 3 cups whole wheat pastry flour or rye flour
> 1 tablespoon baking soda
> 1 teaspoon sea salt
> 2 teaspoons cinnamon
> ½ teaspoon nutmeg
> 1 teaspoon each mace, allspice, cloves, and ginger
> 1 cup softened unsalted soy margarine or butter, or light oil
> ½ cup honey
> ¼ cup molasses
> 4 eggs
> ½ cup each lightly toasted, coarsely chopped walnuts, almonds, Brazil nuts, and hazelnuts
> Brandy

In a large bowl, combine all the dried fruit and add enough apple juice or cider to cover. Cover the bowl and leave it in a cool place for several hours or overnight—until the fruit has swelled and softened. Drain the fruit, reserving the juice.

Preheat the oven to 275 degrees. Thoroughly grease the bottom and sides of four 8×4-inch loaf pans. Line the bottom and sides of the pans with waxed paper and thoroughly grease the paper.

Leaving the peel on, remove the seeds from the orange and lemon half and cut the fruit into small dice. Combine with 1 cup of the reserved juice in a blender, and blend well. Set aside.

Sift together the flour, baking soda, salt, and spices. Stir back in any bran that remains in the sifter.

In a large bowl, beat together the margarine, honey, molasses, and eggs until they are thoroughly combined. Alternately add the blended mixture and the dry mixture to the bowl, folding them in gently, just until a batter forms. Gently but thoroughly fold in the dried fruits and nuts.

Divide the batter equally among the four prepared pans, and spread it evenly. Arrange the pans in the preheated oven and place a pan of water on the rack underneath them. Bake for 2 hours. Cool in the pans on a rack for about 30 minutes. Remove the cakes from the pans, peel off the waxed paper, and cool thoroughly.

Wrap the cooled cakes in cheesecloth or muslin. Drizzle several tablespoons of brandy over each wrapped cake and put the cake in a plastic bag. Store in a cold pantry or in the refrigerator. Add more brandy two or three times more at weekly intervals.

NOTES
- Stored properly, these cakes will keep well for several months; for longer storage, freeze them.

TEASECAKE

This nondairy cheesecake has a wonderfully rich flavor and a splendidly smooth texture. It is so light and creamy, it's hard to believe that it is made with tofu rather than cream cheese. For the best flavor, use the freshest tofu you can find. This is a nutritious dessert: high in protein, minerals, and vitamins; cholesterol free and low in fat. Serve it plain or garnish with a fruit glaze (page 112) or a seasonal fruit topping or thinly sliced fresh fruit.

YIELD: 1 8-inch springform pan (6 to 8 servings)

PREPARATION TIME: About 1 hour, including baking but not cooling or chilling

> ¼ cup rolled oats
> ½ cup whole wheat pastry flour
> ¼ teaspoon plus a pinch of sea salt
> 3 tablespoons cold unsalted soy margarine or butter
> 6 tablespoons maple syrup
> 1 teaspoon kuzu powder
> ¾ cup plus 1 teaspoon unsweetened apple juice
> 1 pound tofu
> 1 tablespoon light vegetable oil
> 3 tablespoons tahini
> 3 tablespoons lemon juice
> 2½ teaspoons pure vanilla extract

Preheat the oven to 350 degrees. Grease the bottom of an 8-inch springform cake pan.

In a food processor fitted with the metal blade, blend the oats to a coarse flour. Add the flour and a pinch of salt and blend again. Cut in the margarine or butter evenly, until the mixture has a mealy consistency. Thoroughly blend in 2 tablespoons of maple syrup.

Press this mixture evenly on the bottom of the prepared pan and bake for 15 minutes. Cool on a rack.

Combine the kuzu and 1 teaspoon apple juice. Set aside until the kuzu has dissolved.

In a food processor fitted with the metal blade, blend the tofu well. With the machine still running, add ¼ teaspoon salt, the oil, tahini, 4 tablespoons maple syrup, lemon juice, vanilla, and dissolved kuzu. Gradually add ¾ cup apple juice and blend until thoroughly smooth. It should be rather liquid—if it is too thick, add additional apple juice, a tablespoon at a time, until the mixture readily drips off of a spoon.

Preheat the oven to 300 degrees. Lightly grease the sides of the pan.

Pour the filling evenly over the prebaked crust. Bake for 30 minutes.

Cool in the pan on a rack, then chill in the refrigerator for several hours before serving.

NOTES

- Substitute a mild-flavored honey for the maple syrup in the crust and filling.

- The water content of tofus is variable; this recipe is based on moderately firm tofu. As indicated, use the consistency of the filling mixture as your guide when adding the apple juice.

- For *GINGER TEASECAKE*, use a mild-flavored honey in the crust and filling, reduce the lemon juice in the filling to 1 tablespoon, omit the vanilla extract, and add 2 teaspoons finely grated fresh ginger root.

WHOLE WHEAT PASTRY CRUST
▼▼▼

Light and flaky and wholesome as well, this is an all-purpose pastry dough. Secrets to making it tender are cold ingredients (I use the flour and margarine or butter directly out of the freezer) and a light, quick hand. I like to use apple juice in dessert crusts.

YIELD: 1 9-inch pie shell

PREPARATION TIME: About 20 minutes to prepare; 1 hour to chill

  1 cup whole wheat pastry flour, well chilled
  Pinch of sea salt

  5 tablespoons unsalted soy margarine or butter, well chilled
  3 to 4 tablespoons cold water, unsweetened apple juice, or vegetable stock

Sift together the flour and salt. Stir back in any bran that did not pass through the sifter.

In a medium-sized bowl with a pastry blender or in a food processor fitted with the metal blade, quickly cut the margarine or butter into the dry ingredients until the mixture reaches a mealy consistency. If you use a processor, transfer the mixture to a bowl.

Dribble in the liquid a tablespoon at a time and stir gently with a fork or your fingers until the dough begins to pull away from the sides of the bowl and ball up in the center. The amount of liquid will vary with the absorbability of the flour; judge by the consistency of the dough rather than a measured amount.

Form the dough into a compact ball, sprinkle it lightly with flour, wrap in waxed paper, and refrigerate for about an hour. Chill the pie plate as well.

Flatten the chilled ball on a lightly floured work surface. Gradually roll the dough out into a circle about 2 inches larger than the pie plate, stopping several times to lightly flour the dough and the work surface and to turn the dough over—work quickly but carefully.

Fold the circle in half, position it in the pie plate, and unfold. Roll the edge of the pastry under, even with the edge of the pan. Flute the edge.

If time permits, chill the pastry shell well before filling it.

NOTES

- For a 9-inch double crust, use:

  1⅔ cups whole wheat pastry flour
    Pinch of sea salt
  8 tablespoons unsalted soy margarine or butter
  6 to 8 tablespoons liquid

Prepare the dough as described above, and divide the dough into two balls, one slightly larger than the other. Roll out the larger ball to fit the pie plate and the smaller one into a circle about 1 inch larger than the pan. To assist in sealing the top and bottom crusts, dab cold water around the edge of the bottom crust before placing the top crust on and press the edges together before rolling them under and fluting the edge. Slash the center of the top crust to allow steam to escape during baking.

- For a latticed crust, roll dough for the top crust and cut it into ten ½-inch wide strips. Using every other strip, lay strips across the filled pie shell, pressing one end of each to adhere it to the edge; a little water will help it stick. Fold back the second and fourth strips and lay one of the two shortest remaining strips of dough across the pie; lay the folded strips back down over it and fold back the other three strips (middle and two sides). Now lay one the next-longest remaining strips across these folded strips. Continue weaving the pastry strips in this manner until the lattice is complete. Decoratively crimp the edges of the pie, sealing bottom and top crusts in the process.

CALL IT PUMPKIN PIE
▰▰▰

This is a delicately flavored version of a spicy old favorite—pumpkin pie. I prefer the consistently sweet, non-watery quality of baked winter squash to pumpkin, and butternut squash is best. If you just have to have pumpkin, substitute an equal amount of drained, cooked pumpkin for the squash.

YIELD: 1 9-inch pie

PREPARATION TIME: About 1 hour, plus about 45 minutes to bake the squash

    1   medium-sized butternut squash (20 to 24
        ounces)
    2   eggs
    1/3 cup maple syrup
    1/2 teaspoon sea salt
    1/4 teaspoon each cinnamon, mace, and cloves
    1/2 teaspoon ground ginger, or 1 to 2 teaspoons
        finely grated fresh ginger root
    1 1/2 cups milk or soy milk
    1   unbaked 9-inch whole wheat pie shell, chilled
        (see page 231)

Cut the squash in half lengthwise and place it, cut side down, on a lightly greased baking sheet. Bake at 375 degrees until tender, about 45 minutes. Remove the seeds. Scoop out the pulp and mash it.

In a food processor fitted with the metal blade or in a blender, purée 1 3/4 cups of the squash. With the machine still running, add the eggs, maple syrup, salt, and spices. Gradually add the milk and blend until thoroughly smooth.

Preheat the oven to 450 degrees. Pour the filling into the pie shell and spread it evenly. Bake for 15 minutes. Cover the fluted edge of the crust with a ring of foil, shiny side up. Reduce the heat to 300 degrees and bake the pie 30 to 40 minutes longer—until the tip of a knife inserted into the center comes out clean.

Cool on a rack. Serve at room temperature or chilled.

NOTES
- Substitute 1/4 cup of a mild-flavored honey for the maple syrup.
- Substitute allspice for the mace.

MINCE-TREAT PIE
▰▰▰

I developed this recipe at the request of a friend who wanted to take an unrefined, vegetarian mincemeat pie to his family's holiday gathering. My husband claims that this is the best pie he has ever eaten. I often prepare the filling the day before I make the pie and chill it overnight.

YIELD: 1 9-inch pie

PREPARATION TIME: 30 to 40 minutes to prepare; 45 to 55 minutes to bake

    1 1/2 teaspoons kuzu powder
    2   teaspoons brandy
    1/2 cup unsweetened apple juice
    1   cup raisins
    1/2 cup currants
    4   medium-to-large apples, peeled, cored, and
        finely diced
        Finely grated zest of 1 orange
    1/3 cup orange juice
    1   tablespoon lemon juice
    1/2 teaspoon each cinnamon, cloves, nutmeg, and
        mace
    1/4 teaspoon ground ginger
    1/4 cup honey
    1   tablespoon dark barley miso
    1   cup lightly toasted, coarsely chopped walnuts
        Pastry for a 9-inch double crust (page 231),
        chilled

Combine the kuzu and brandy and set aside until the kuzu dissolves.

Combine the apple juice and raisins in a blender and blend briefly, just until the raisins are chopped.

In a medium-sized saucepan, stir together the blended mixture, currants, prepared apples, orange zest and juice, and lemon juice. Cover and bring to a simmer over medium heat, stirring occasionally. Add the spices and honey, reduce the heat, and cook until the apples are soft.

Thoroughly stir the miso into the kuzu and add it to the pot. Cook briefly, stirring, just until the mixture thickens. Cool completely.

Preheat the oven to 425 degrees.

Roll out the bottom crust and fit it into a 9-inch pie plate; leave the edges unfinished, extending about an inch beyond the upper edge of the pan, and refrigerate.

Roll out the top crust and cut it into strips for a lattice top.

Remove the pie shell from the refrigerator. Scatter about ⅓ of the walnuts on the bottom of the shell. Stir the remaining nuts into the filling and spread the filling evenly in the pie shell. Cover with a pastry lattice, as described on page 231-32, then roll and flute the edge.

Bake at 425 degrees for 15 minutes. Cover the edges of the crust with a ring of foil, shiny side up. Reduce the heat to 325 degrees and bake for 30 to 40 minutes, until the juice is bubbling up through the lattice.

Cool on a rack. Serve the pie warm or at room temperature.

NOTES

- Increase the honey to ½ cup and stir 1 cup fresh or frozen cranberries into the filling near the end of cooking.

CRANAPPLE-CURRANT PIE
▼▼▼

Serve this festive pie for dessert in autumn and winter when apples and cranberries are at their peak. I often make the filling the day before or early on the day that I make the pie and thoroughly cool and chill it.

YIELD: 1 9-inch pie

PREPARATION TIME: 30 to 40 minutes to prepare; 45 to 55 minutes to bake

> 1   teaspoon cold unsweetened apple juice
> 1   teaspoon kuzu powder
>   Finely grated zest of 1 orange (about 1½ teaspoons)
>   Juice of 1 orange (⅓ to ½ cup)
> 3   large tart apples, cored, peeled, and cut into small chunks
> ½   cup currants
> 1   cup fresh or frozen cranberries
> 6   tablespoons maple syrup
> ¼   teaspoon cinnamon
>   Pastry for a 9-inch double crust (page 231), chilled

Combine the apple juice and kuzu and set aside until the kuzu has dissolved.

In a saucepan, combine the orange zest and juice, apples, and currants. Bring just to a boil, reduce the heat to low, cover, and simmer gently for several minutes, until the apples begin to juice. Stir in the cranberries, maple syrup, and cinnamon and continue to cook, stirring occasionally, until the apples are barely tender. Add the dissolved kuzu and cook, stirring, until the juice thickens. Set aside to cool.

Preheat the oven to 450 degrees. Roll out the bottom crust and fit it into the pie plate, leaving the edge of the pastry extending about an inch over the rim. Roll out the top crust and cut it into strips. Spread the filling evenly in the pie shell. Weave a lattice on top with the pastry strips as described on page 231-32, then roll and flute the edge.

Bake at 450 degrees for 15 minutes. Cover the edges of the crust with a ring of foil, shiny side up. Reduce the heat to 325 degrees and bake 30 to 40 minutes, until the juice is bubbling up through the lattice and the apples are tender.

Cool on a rack. Serve the pie warm or at room temperature.

TARTE TATIN
▼▼▼

This upside-down apple pie is practically a national institution in France. It was originated, some say accidentally, by the Tatin sisters, innkeepers in a village on the Loire in the nineteenth century. Apples arranged on the bottom of the pan caramelize during the cooking process while a pastry crust laid on top becomes brown and crisp; the tart is reversed onto a plate and served with the fruit on top. My recipe for this French tradition is maple-sweetened. You'll need a 2-inch deep, ovenproof 9-inch skillet for making this tart.

YIELD: 1 9-inch tart

PREPARATION TIME: About 45 minutes to prepare plus 30 minutes to marinate the apples; 45 minutes to bake

>   Finely grated zest of 1 lemon (½ to 1 teaspoon)
>   Juice of 1 lemon (3 to 4 tablespoons)
> 4   large Pippin apples (2 pounds)
> ½   cup maple syrup
> 1   tablespoon unsalted soy margarine or butter, softened
>   Pastry for a 9-inch single crust (page 231), chilled

Combine the lemon zest and juice in a medium-sized mixing bowl. Peel, core, and quarter the apples. Slice the quarters lengthwise into wedges about ¼ inch thick at their widest part. Carefully but thoroughly mix the apple slices with the lemon zest and juice. Drizzle in ¼ cup of the maple syrup and fold with a rubber spatula to coat the apples. Set aside for 30 minutes to allow the apples to juice.

Preheat the oven to 425 degrees. Liberally coat the inside of a heavy-bottomed, ovenproof skillet, 9 inches in diameter at the top edge and 2 inches deep, with the margarine or butter. Drizzle 1 tablespoon of the maple syrup over the bottom of the pan. Decoratively arrange a layer of apple slices in the bottom of the pan and drizzle a tablespoon of syrup on top. Continue to layer the apples evenly—other than on the bottom, they do not have to be artfully placed—and drizzle the remaining syrup between the layers. Reserve any juices remaining in the bowl in a small saucepan.

On a lightly floured surface, roll the chilled pastry dough into a 9½-inch circle. Lay the pastry on top of the skillet, tucking the excess inside the rim of the pan. With a sharp knife, pierce the pastry in several places to allow steam to escape during baking.

Set the skillet over moderate heat on top of the stove for about 5 minutes. Then bake in the preheated oven for 30 minutes, until the pastry is brown and crisp. Remove the pan from the oven (but leave the oven on) and place it back on a burner over moderate heat for about 10 minutes, lifting and shaking the pan occasionally to be sure the apples are not sticking to the bottom—this is to cook down any remaining juice. If, by tipping the skillet, you determine that a lot of juice still remains, hold a lid or plate on top of the skillet and carefully pour excess juice into the saucepan containing the reserved marinade.

Place the skillet back into the oven and turn off the oven. In 5 to 10 minutes, when the crust has become crisp again, remove the pan to a cooling rack. Shake the pan once again to be sure that the apples on the bottom are not sticking. Place a plate upside down over the skillet and then invert the tart onto the plate.

Over moderate heat, bring the reserved liquid just to a boil, and simmer until it becomes syrup. Pour this evenly over the cooling tart.

APPLE CRISP
▼▼▼

This is a fitting end to a meal, especially in cool weather. It is sweet and succulent underneath and crunchy on top.

YIELD: 8 servings

PREPARATION TIME: About 2 hours, including baking

> 3 *pounds apples, peeled, cored, and cut into small dice*
> 3 *tablespoons lemon juice*
> ¼ *cup whole wheat pastry flour*
> ¼ *teaspoon cinnamon*
> ¼ *teaspoon nutmeg*
> ¼ *cup maple syrup*
> 1½ *cups oat flakes*
> ⅓ *cup wheat germ*
> ⅓ *cup brown rice flour*
> ⅓ *cup barley flour*
> ½ *cup lightly toasted, coarsely chopped almonds*
> ½ *cup date sugar or Sucanat*
> ½ *cup soy margarine or butter, melted (or a light vegetable oil, such as sunflower)*

Preheat the oven to 325 degrees. Grease a 10-inch square glass or ceramic baking dish (or a pan of comparable size).

Mix the diced apple with the lemon juice. Sift the pastry flour and spices over the apples and stir. Mix in the maple syrup. Spread the mixture in the prepared pan; cover and bake in the preheated oven for about 30 minutes, until the fruit is almost tender and is juicing. Set aside.

Mix together the oats, wheat germ, rice and barley flours, almonds, and date sugar. Drizzle the margarine or butter into this mixture and stir with a fork to distribute it evenly. Sprinkle this crumbly mixture evenly over the baked fruit and press down lightly. Bake, uncovered, until the topping is lightly browned and crunchy, about 45 minutes.

NOTES

- Substitute other fruits, such as pears, peaches, blueberrries, strawberries, rhubarb, or cranberries, for all or part of the apples. For rhubarb or cranberries, use ½ cup of honey in place of the maple syrup.

- Using the same proportions, substitute different grains and nuts in the topping mixture.

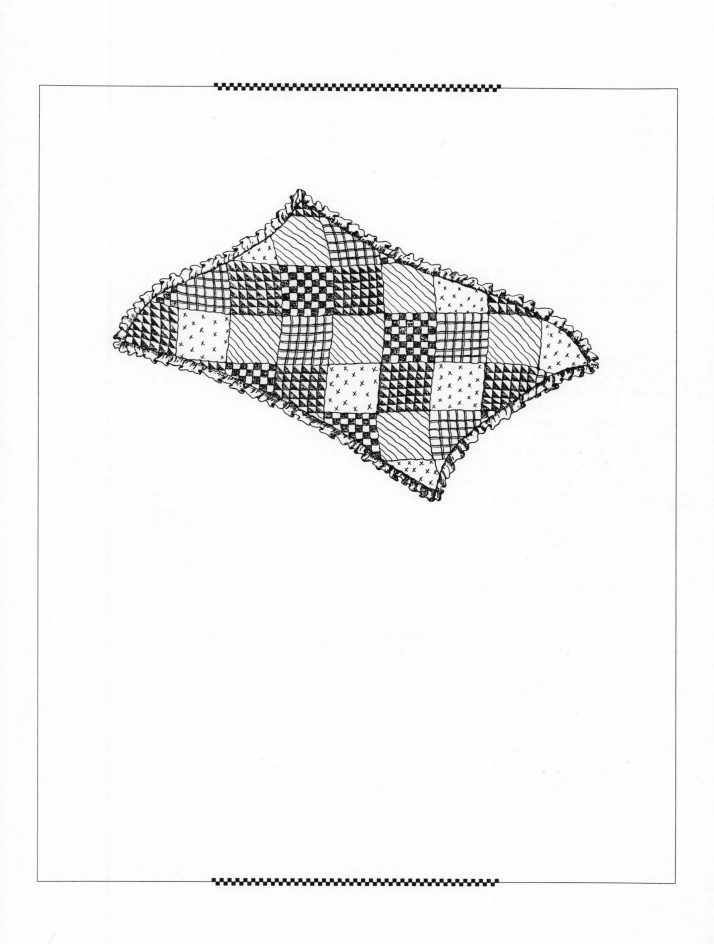

GLOSSARY

Aduki beans (also known as *adzuki* or *azuki* beans) are small, dark red beans. Until recently, they were always imported from Asia; now it is possible to find less expensive ones that are grown in the United States. These beans are renowned for their digestibility. Refer to **Beans** for cooking directions.

Amaretto is a sweet, almond-flavored, Italian liqueur. I like its flavor in combination with carob.

Anaheim peppers. *See* **Chili peppers.**

Anchos. *See* **Chili peppers.**

Anasazi beans are the unhybridized forebears of pinto beans. They resemble pinto beans in size and shape but are maroon with white patches. Anasazi beans taste somewhat like pinto beans, but the flavor is fuller and sweeter. Refer to **Beans** for cooking directions.

Arugula, sometimes called roquette or rocket, is a spicy salad green. It is dark green in color and has rather narrow leaves with deep lobes. This pungent green adds character to salads and its flavor blends especially well with tomatoes, eggplant, and basil. It is rich in calcium.

Bean curd. *See* **Tofu.**

Beans come in many different shapes and sizes, and have long been staples in most cuisines around the world. Beans are an excellent source of protein, particularly when consumed with grains. They are also a good source of complex carbohydrates, vitamins, minerals, and fiber. Dried beans are economical and easy to store, and they have many culinary uses.

Cooked dried beans are often associated with flatulence and indigestion, but certain preparation techniques can eliminate or minimize these effects. Soaking the beans before cooking them enhances their digestibility and also helps to maintain their shape, which may be important if you are using them in a salad or another dish where their appearance counts. Add enough water so that the beans will still be covered when they expand.

If it is particularly warm, refrigerate the beans to prevent them from fermenting. An alternative method is to bring the beans to a boil, turn off the heat, cover, and soak for two hours. Add a piece of kombu (about 2 inches long for one cup of dried beans) when you begin cooking the beans; it will have nearly disintegrated by the time they are done. Extra minerals and other nutrients from the sea vegetable are a bonus. A bay leaf cooked with beans also promotes digestibility. Miso is another digestive aid; in addition, it augments the rich, full flavor of beans. Add miso to taste after beans are thoroughly cooked.

See also individual names.

COOKING BEANS

Always sort through dried beans or peas to pick out any pebbles or other foreign matter; though somewhat tedious, this step may prevent a broken tooth. Rinse the beans to remove any grit and dust, and soak as described above. Drain the soaked beans, add fresh water to cover, and bring the beans to a boil. Skim off any foam that forms on the surface and reduce the heat to low. Cover and simmer, checking occasionally to be sure there is enough water. Cook until tender. Do not add salt before the beans are cooked or they won't soften. If you don't have difficulty digesting beans, cook them in their soaking water to preserve nutrients.

One cup of dried beans yields about 2½ to 3 cups cooked. The following chart shows the amount of water and cooking times for various kinds of beans. Older beans take longer to cook. Pressure-cooking saves time and preserves flavor. Cook black beans and soybeans over particularly low heat to prevent them from foaming up and clogging the vent of the cooker.

Black mustard seeds are used in Indian dishes, especially in curries. Add them to heated oil in a pan and toast them until they pop before adding onion and other ingredients. Their flavor is somewhat milder than yellow mustard seeds.

BEAN PREPARATION CHART

Beans (1 cup dry)	REGULAR COOKING		PRESSURE COOKING	
	Water	Preparation Time	Water	Preparation Time
Aduki	4 cups	1 hour	2¾ cups	30 minutes
Anasazi	3 cups	2 to 2½ hours	2¾ cups	1 hour
Black turtle	4 cups	2 to 3 hours	2¾ cups	1 hour
Black-eyed peas	3 cups	45 to 60 minutes	2½ cups	40 minutes
Chickpeas	4 cups	2 to 3 hours	2¾ cups	1 hour
Kidney	3 cups	1 hour	2½ cups	45 minutes
Lentils	3 cups	45 to 60 minutes	2½ cups	25 minutes
Navy	3 cups	1 hour	2½ cups	40 minutes
Pinto	3 cups	2 to 2½ hours	2¾ cups	1 hour
Soybeans	4 cups	3 hours	3 cups	2 hours
Split peas	3 cups	45 minutes	2½ cups	20 minutes

Black pepper is the dried fruit of a tropical vine indigenous to India. Pepper is definitely best freshly ground; a pepper grinder is well worth the investment. My favorite all-purpose peppercorn is *tellicherry*.

Black turtle beans, also known simply as black beans, are a member of the kidney bean family and are native to Mexico. They have an oval or very slight kidney shape and a matte rather than shiny black surface. Their flavor is sweet but hearty. Black beans tend to foam considerably, especially at the beginning of cooking. Refer to **Beans** for cooking directions.

Black-eyed peas are oval or kidney-shaped beans, dull white in color with a black spot on one side. Indigenous to Africa, black-eyes are now a popular dish in the southern United States. They are sometimes called cowpeas or China beans. Refer to **Beans** for cooking directions.

Calamata olives are large, black Greek olives with a pronounced briny flavor—a welcome contrast to most California olives, which are rendered relatively tasteless by extensive processing.

Carob powder is made from the dried, roasted, ground pods of the locust tree, an evergreen indigenous to the Mediterranean. The longer carob is roasted, the darker it is and the richer its flavor. It is sold both roasted and unroasted. Carob is exceedingly high in calcium and contains other minerals and vitamins. It is low in fat and naturally sweet. Carob is sometimes considered a chocolate substitute, but true "chocoholics" would never endorse it. In any case, carob deserves to be judged on its own merits. Store it in a cool, dry spot and sift it through a strainer if it becomes caked.

Chia seeds appear somewhat like flattened poppy seeds. They grow in Mexico and the Southwest. Long ago, they were valued by Native Americans as a highly energizing food which provided endurance for stressful activities. Add them to bread doughs or sprinkle them on top.

Chickpeas, also known as garbanzos, are lumpy, roundish beans about ½ inch in diameter. Tan chickpeas are most familiar in this country, though other varieties are red, white, brown, or black. They have a somewhat nutty flavor and hold their shape when cooked. Refer to **Beans** for cooking directions.

Chili peppers contain a substance called capsaicin which creates a burning sensation upon contact with skin. I always wear rubber gloves when I handle chilies to avoid irritating my hands. To tone down the fire of chili peppers, remove their membranes and seeds, since these are the areas where most of the capsaicin is concentrated.

There are many species of hot peppers. Following is a brief description of some of the most common ones:

Poblanos are mildly hot, dark green peppers, usually 3 to 5 inches long. They are shaped something like bell peppers, though a bit more triangular—wide at the stem end and narrowing to somewhat of a point. Their skin is relatively thick; I usually char and peel these peppers before adding them to dishes.

Anchos are ripe, dried poblanos, deep reddish-brown in color. They are the major ingredient in commercially prepared chili powder.

Serranos are 1 to 2 inches in length, elongated, and smooth sided; they vary in color from green to bright red-orange. Whatever their shade, these are sizzling hot.

Jalapeños resemble serranos in shape though they are somewhat larger—up to about 3 inches long. They are also extremely hot.

Anaheims are 6 to 8 inches long and about 2 inches wide. They turn from green to red as they mature and can be used at either stage. These peppers are mildly hot.

Chili oil. *See* **Hot chili oil**.

Coconut milk is the liquid inside the coconut. To extract it, puncture at least two of the three "eyes" located at one end of the coconut with an awl or similar implement and drain the liquid through a fine-mesh strainer into a cup; it should taste fresh and sweet. If the milk tastes fermented or moldy, the coconut has spoiled. Clues to a good coconut are weightiness and a hard, dry, intact surface; shaken, it should sound as if it contains a substantial amount of liquid.

To separate the meat from the shell, heat the drained coconut in a moderate oven for 10 to 15 minutes and then give it a hard blow with a hammer or mallet. It will fall apart into several pieces and the meat should be easy to pry from the shell.

Commercial-style coconut milk (available in some Asian and natural foods stores) is prepared by blending either fresh or soaked dried coconut with hot water and then straining the purée. Use equal parts of fresh coconut and hot water or 1 part dried, unsweetened coconut to 1½ parts hot water; in either case, 1 cup of coconut will yield about 1 cup of coconut milk. Freeze the liquid to keep it longer than a couple of days.

Daikon is a long, white, Japanese radish with a sweet yet pungent flavor. Cooking daikon, such as in stir-fries or stews, tones down its hotness. Daikon may also be pickled. I have heard that this radish aids digestion.

Fenugreek is the seed of a leguminous plant indigenous to southern Europe and Asia. It has a pleasantly assertive flavor, resembling a cross between anise and celery. It is commonly used in curries and African dishes.

Five-spice powder is a mixture of ground star anise, cloves, Chinese cinnamon, fennel, and Szechuan pepper. Sometimes ground ginger is added to it, too. It is used in Chinese cooking.

Five-spice tofu is sometimes available in Asian food stores. To prepare it at home, gently simmer well-pressed tofu in a mixture of ½ cup tamari or shoyu, 1 teaspoon sea salt, 1½ teaspoons star anise, ¼ teaspoon five-spice powder, and 1½ cups water for about 5 minutes. Remove the pan from the heat and marinate for

several hours. Drain the tofu and reserve the marinade to use again.

Garbanzos. *See* **Chickpeas**.

Garlic is a member of the allium family (along with onions, chives, shallots, leeks, and scallions). Its outstanding flavor ranges from strong and pungent when raw to mild and mellow when braised or baked. Its natural general antibiotic properties are widely recognized.

Keep unpeeled garlic in a well-ventilated container, such as a small basket, in a cool, dry place. To preserve it longer, separate the cloves, cover them with oil, and refrigerate, or place the cloves in a container in the freezer and remove and peel them while frozen as needed.

Administering a blow to the side of a garlic clove with a cleaver makes peeling it much easier. I usually put the peeled garlic through a press and then finely chop whatever remains in the press with a knife.

Elephant garlic, a giant-sized cousin of regular garlic, has become popular recently. The flavor of this variety is a bit sweeter and milder. The large size of the cloves makes the peeling process less tedious.

Ghee is the Indian term for clarified butter, the fat that is left when milk solids and water are taken out of butter. To prepare ghee, heat unsalted butter over low heat until it melts; carefully skim off the foam on the surface and throw it away; strain the remaining golden oil through a fine mesh or muslin, taking care to separate any sediment on the bottom of the pan. Clarified butter does not burn at high temperatures and it keeps indefinitely. You can substitute an oil with a high smoking point, such as sesame oil, for ghee.

Herb vinegars can be made with a variety of fresh herbs, such as dill, basil, garlic, tarragon, or pericon. Simply add a few sprigs of the freshly cut, rinsed herb to a jar, fill it with vinegar (I use red wine vinegar or apple cider vinegar), and let it steep for several weeks. The more herbs used and the longer they steep in the vinegar, the more prominent their flavor will be. When the herbs soften and turn brown, strain the vinegar and discard the herbs. Herb vinegars add a hint of summer to winter salads.

Hot chili oil is oil flavored with hot pepper seeds. It is available commercially or you can make your own by putting dried red chili peppers or their seeds in a jar and adding heated sesame, peanut, or another vegetable oil. Of course, the more peppers you use, the hotter the oil will taste. Strain the oil after it is well flavored and keep it refrigerated to prevent it from becoming rancid. Hot oil is used as a flavoring in Oriental cuisines.

Hot sherry is sherry flavored with chili peppers. This is a lively addition to vegetable stir-fries and other preparations. Simply add about a dozen ripe serrano peppers to a fifth of dry sherry and let them steep for about a week or two before using the sherry in cooking. Remove the peppers if you wish.

Jalapeños. *See* **Chili peppers**.

Jicama is a large, turnip-shaped root vegetable. It has a tough brown skin that must be cut away. The flesh, which can be eaten raw or cooked, is slightly sweet and combines well with both fruits and vegetables. Raw jicama is crispy, somewhat like water chestnuts or apples. Keep it in the refrigerator.

Kelp. *See* **Seaweeds**.

Kidney beans have a rather sweet flavor and hold their shape quite well when cooked. Refer to **Beans** for cooking directons.

Koji is grain—usually rice or barley, or soybeans—that has been cultured with an aromatic mold called *Aspergillus Oryzae*. It is used to ferment miso, amasake, sake, rice vinegar, shoyu, tamari, and certain pickles. You may find it at natural foods stores, or order it from mail order sources. I use koji to prepare AMASAKE (page 106).

Kombu. *See* **Seaweeds**.

Kuzu is a vine native to Japan, but it is now prevalent in the southeastern United States, where it is called kudzu and is generally viewed as an undesirable weed. The powdered root, which is also called kuzu, is used as a thickening agent in cooking; it is a white, tasteless starch that becomes colorless when cooked. Dissolve kuzu powder in a cold liquid before adding it to a hot liquid that you wish to thicken. Though it is more expensive than arrowroot and cornstarch, kuzu is more effective. It also has medicinal properties. Kuzu is often lumpy; grind the chunks with a mortar and pestle before dissolving it.

Lentils look like small flattened spheres with convex surfaces. The two most familiar varieties in this country are either greenish-tan or bright red-orange in color. Both require little or no soaking and cook relatively quickly. Refer to **Beans** for cooking directions.

Marsala is a rather sweet dessert wine which originated in Marsala, Sicily. It is an interesting addition to tomato sauces or tomato dishes.

Mirin is a sweet cooking wine prepared with sweet brown rice, rice koji, and water. This Oriental flavoring can be used as a subtle seasoning for Western-style dishes as well.

Miso is fermented soybean paste. Most misos contain a fermented grain, such as rice or barley, in addition to the soybeans. Different types of miso vary in color, flavor, saltiness, and texture. Light-colored misos, such as mellow barley or mellow rice miso, contain proportionately less soybeans, more grain, and less salt than dark misos and are fermented for a shorter period of time. I use miso as a seasoning in many dishes in lieu of salt. Miso is high in protein and its enzymes promote digestion. To preserve these beneficial enzymes, do not boil a mixture after adding miso. Like other salty substances, miso enhances the flavor of foods, but miso also adds a special depth and richness. Shop for miso in natural foods stores or Oriental groceries.

Mustard seeds. *See* **Black mustard seeds**.

Navy beans are small oval white beans with a mild flavor. They are a variety of kidney bean and were once a staple in the United States Navy diet. Great Northern beans are larger versions of navy beans. Refer to **Beans** for cooking directions.

Nori. *See* **Seaweeds**.

Nutritional yeast is a food supplement prepared by growing yeast on a molasses or wood pulp medium and then pasteurizing the culture to kill the yeast. It is exceedingly rich in protein, B vitamins, and some minerals. Though similar to brewer's yeast, a by-product of the beer industry, it has a much more agreeable taste. Nutritional yeast is also known as food yeast or primary-grown yeast.

Okara is the nutritious, high-fiber soy pulp that remains as a by-product of making soy milk or tofu. It has a moist, mealy consistency and a mild soy taste. There are many uses for okara, from protein-rich livestock or pet food or organic mulch or fertilizer to an ingredient in breads, burgers, or pâtés.

Olive oils vary considerably depending on how they are processed. "Extra virgin" on the label indicates that the oil has resulted from the initial pressing of olives and is unrefined. Extra virgin olive oil has a delectable fruity flavor. Other virgin olive oils result from later pressings and have more acidity and less pronounced flavor. "Pure" olive oil is extracted from the pulp and pits of pressed olives; chemical solvents are sometimes used in this process. Pure olive oil is generally refined to remove unpleasant flavors. There may be subtle differences in the flavors of olive oils, especially extra virgin oils, depending on the type of olives, the region where they are grown, and the season in which they are harvested. Olive oil is a particularly nutritious oil since it is a monosaturated fat and appears to contribute to a healthy cholesterol balance in the body. It is high in vitamin E, making it less susceptible to rancidity than other oils.

Pericon, also called sweet marigold, is a perennial herb well suited to the hot, dry climate of Texas and the Southwest, and this is where you're most likely to find it. Pericon's long, narrow, spear-shaped leaves have an intense anise scent and flavor and make a good substitute for tarragon. In autumn, pericon bears golden blossoms which make attractive edible garnishes as well as bright spots in bouquets.

Pimientos, also called pimentos, are perhaps best known as the stuffing for green olives. These medium-sized, smooth-sided, dark red peppers are plump at the stem end and taper to a bit of a point at the other end. Their flesh and skin are both relatively thick and their flavor is superbly sweet. I almost invariably roast and peel them.

Pinto beans are a member of the kidney bean family. They are pinkish-tan and speckled and have a sweet, mild flavor. They are a common ingredient in Southwestern cuisine. Refer to **Beans** for cooking directions.

Poblanos. *See* **Chili peppers**.

Rice wine is commonly used in both Japanese and Chinese cooking. Chinese rice wine, which is aged longer than most Japanese sakes, tends to have a mellower flavor. Look for Chinese Shaoxing rice wine in liquor stores or Oriental groceries.

Roasted sesame oil. *See* **Sesame oil**.

Seaweeds are mineral storehouses and are super sources of protein and vitamins—including vitamin B$_{12}$, which is notoriously scarce in vegetarian diets. Sea vegetables bestow many medicinal and cosmetic benefits on their human consumers; they even show a capacity for detoxifying radioactive elements. Most seaweeds are sold in a dried form, and they keep well in a cool, dry storage area. I have used several different sea vegetables throughout the book; descriptions of these follow.

Thin, papery sheets of dried **nori**, or **laver**, as it is also called, turn from a dark purplish color to an olive green when toasted over a burner. Nori has a nutty flavor which complements many other foods, and its form makes it an ideal wrapper for grains and vegetables, as in sushi rolls. An enzyme which breaks down cholesterol is prevalent in nori.

Kelp is a giant-sized underwater plant which may grow as long as 1,500 feet. There are close to 1,000 varieties of kelp. It is said that kelp promotes healing and maintains vigor in those who eat it. Kelp is usually sold as a fine greenish powder. I use kelp powder as a nutritious salt substitute in many of my recipes.

Kombu and **wakame** are members of the kelp family, although they are sold as discrete items. They come in dried strips and are available in packaged form in natural foods stores. Kombu contributes flavor to soup stocks and tenderness to cooked dried beans. Wakame, somewhat more delicate than kombu, is a favorite addition to miso soups.

Serranos. *See* **Chili peppers**.

Sesame oil has a deliciously nutty flavor and can be used for baking or sautéing, and in salad dressings. Since it is highly stable, it is a good choice for deep-frying too. Roasted sesame oil, extracted from roasted sesame seeds, is darker than regular sesame oil and has a particularly enticing fragrance and rich flavor; it is typically used as a seasoning rather than as a cooking oil.

Sesame salt, or *gomasio* as it is called in Japanese, is a mildly salty, highly nutritious seasoning consisting of lightly roasted, ground sesame seeds blended with sea salt in a ratio of about 16 to 1. To prepare it, roast sesame seeds in a heavy skillet (I use a cast-iron one) and then grind them, together with a good quality sea salt, in a *suribachi* (Japanese mortar) or in a food processor. For even fresher sesame salt, combine whole roasted sesame seeds and sea salt in a sesame seed grinder—a small, inexpensive utensil—and grind it as needed. Sesame salt is a delicious topping for poached eggs and steamed or sautéed vegetables.

Shiitake mushrooms are valued for their nutritional content and cleansing and strengthening properties as well as for their delicious, unique flavor. Though expensive in both fresh or dried form, just a small amount of shiitakes will impart their special rich, full flavor to soups, stir-fries, and other dishes. To rehydrate dried shiitakes, soak them in boiling water to cover for several hours. Save the soaking water to enrich soups and sauces. Fresh shiitakes are more delicate in flavor than the dried. Both are commonly used in Japanese, Chinese, and Korean cooking. Keep fresh mushrooms —of any kind—in a paper bag in the vegetable compartment of your refrigerator; mushrooms rapidly become slimy when stored in plastic.

Shoyu is a particular type of soy sauce that is made from soybeans, wheat, salt, and water. It is aged for one to two years, during which time it acquires a full, mellow flavor. Add shoyu near the end of cooking to preserve its flavor. It can also be used as a dipping sauce. *See also* **Soy sauce** and **Tamari**.

Soba are fine, spaghetti-like noodles that are made either solely with buckwheat flour or with a combination of buckwheat and wheat flours. This Japanese-style pasta may also contain additional ingredients, such as wild yam (*jinenjo*), lotus root, mugwort, or green tea. Soba are available in natural foods stores and Oriental markets.

Soybeans are an excellent source of protein and other nutrients but are difficult to digest due to certain enzymes that are present in the whole beans. Various preparation techniques, especially those that involve fermentation, render these beans more digestible. Shoyu, tamri, miso, soy milk, tofu, and tempeh are some of the most familiar soy-based foods. There are both yellow and black varieties of soybeans. Refer to **Beans** for cooking directions.

Soy milk, a beverage prepared from soybeans, is increasingly available commercially in a variety of forms. While aseptically packaged soy milks keep and travel well, fresh soy milk from a local soy dairy is preferable for consumption on a regular basis, since it is subject to much less processing. Soy milk is an excellent dairy-free substitute for cow's milk. It has an equal amount of protein and considerably more iron but is totally cholesterol free. On the other hand, cow's milk is higher in calcium, vitamin B_{12}, and riboflavin.

Making soy milk is a bit of a production, but the process becomes a routine if you make it regularly. Measure out 1 cup of dried beans and sort through it to pick out foreign matter. Rinse the beans and soak them in cool water to cover and then some—since they will expand considerably—for several hours or overnight. Refrigerate the beans if it is particularly warm. Drain the beans and blend them with 6 cups fresh boiling water for 2 to 3 minutes. Be sure to preheat the blender jar with hot water—to keep the temperature up and, in the case of a glass jar, to guard against cracking. Swathe the blender jar in a towel to hold in the heat. Line a strainer with a piece of muslin and set it over a bowl. Pour the blended mixture into the muslin and stir to urge the liquid through, then gather up the muslin and squeeze out as much liquid as possible. Measure the liquid and pour it into the top of a double boiler. Cook over gently simmering water, stirring occasionally, for about 30 minutes. This step makes the bean protein digestible by destroying the enzymes. Again measure the soy milk and add water to compensate for evaporation. Cool the hot liquid quickly and store it in sterile jars in the refrigerator; it will keep for several days to a week. You may flavor soy milk with a sweetener, vanilla extract, or a sweet spice such as nutmeg.

Soy sauce is used extensively as a seasoning in Oriental cuisines. It is commercially produced by exposing refined soybeans to hydrochloric acid to break them down further, heating the mixture, neutralizing the acid with sodium carbonate, and adding caramel coloring, salt, corn syrup, water, and perhaps a preservative. Naturally fermented shoyu and tamari are far superior in flavor and nutrition. *See also* **Shoyu** and **Tamari**.

Split peas are dried peas that have been split in half. There are both green and yellow varieties, either of which cooks quicker than any other legume. Refer to **Beans** for cooking directions.

Sprouts of grains, beans, herbs, and vegetable seeds are highly nutritious foods—rich in protein and vitamins, and low in fat and calories. Though sprouts are readily available commercially, with little effort, you can obtain fresher, cheaper, and more varied ones by growing them yourself. Be sure to use seeds which have not been treated with pesticides or herbicides. Pick over the seeds and remove any foreign matter. Place up to ¼ cup of seeds in a quart jar and fill it with warm water. Cover the jar with cheesecloth or a nonmetallic screen and secure it with a rubber band or use a special plastic mesh screw-on cap made for this purpose. Soak for 8 to 12 hours and drain. Wrap the jar in a towel or set it in a dark spot and lay it on its side. About every 12 hours, rinse and drain the seeds until the sprouts are the length you desire; most take about 3 days.

Star anise is the star-shaped fruit of an aromatic eastern Asian tree, a relative of the magnolia. It is one of the spices in Chinese five-spice powder and is used in other Asian cuisines. Look for star anise in dried form in Asian markets and natural foods stores.

Sweet marigold. *See* **Pericon**.

Tahini is a smooth, creamy paste made from hulled sesame seeds. It has a delicious sesame flavor. Try to find tahini made from organically grown, mechanically hulled sesame seeds to avoid chemical residues from pesticides or processing solvents. Tahini is available in natural foods stores, ethnic markets, and many supermarkets. Refrigerated after opening, it will keep for several months. Use it for spreads, sauces, salad dressings, and soups.

Tamari originally referred to the liquid that comes to the surface of hatcho miso as it aged; it was taken off for use as a seasoning. Now, the term generally refers to naturally fermented soy sauce that is wheat-free and contains only soybeans, salt, and water. The flavor of tamari is stronger than that of shoyu and is best when added early in cooking. Look for it in natural foods stores and Oriental markets. *See also* **Shoyu** and **Soy sauce**.

Tempeh is a cultured and fermented cooked soybean preparation that usually comes in flat, square cakes about ½ inch thick. Sometimes it contains grains, seeds, or other beans as well as soybeans. Tempeh has a "meaty" texture. Raw, it has a wonderfully enticing aroma sometimes likened to yeasted bread dough. Like tofu, tempeh is a willing recipient of many types of seasonings and is an extremely versatile culinary resource. It can be sautéed, simmered, grilled, steamed, or fried. Unlike tofu, freezing does not alter tempeh's texture and is a good way to keep it on hand. Tempeh is high in protein and B vitamins, contains no cholesterol, and is easy to digest. My first tempeh was homemade, but it is now widely available commercially; look for it in the refrigerator or freezer case in natural foods stores. *See also* **Tofu**.

Tequila is a clear, potent liquor made from a species of Central American century plant called Agave tequilana.

Tofu, or bean curd, is a white, rather soft, cheese-like substance prepared by curdling soy milk with a coagulant, straining the whey, and applying pressure to the remaining curds to mold them into solid cakes. It is an economical source of cholesterol-free protein, and is also low in sodium and saturated fat. Tofu is rich in calcium if a calcium-containing compound, such as calcium chloride or calcium sulfate, is used as a coagulant.

Fresh homemade tofu is a treat. Commercial tofu, however, is quite acceptable and is widely available in natural foods stores, Oriental markets, and many supermarkets. You may find tofu available in varying degrees of firmness—soft or "silken," firm, and extra firm. I have used firm tofu in the recipes in this book. Keep tofu refrigerated, in water to cover, and change the water daily to maintain its fresh flavor; it will keep for several days. If the water yellows and the tofu tastes sour and feels slimy, it has spoiled. Tofu is sometimes sold in vacuum-packed containers stamped with an expiration date; once open, keep as above.

By itself, tofu is rather bland, but it readily sops up seasonings of all sorts. It may be pressed and blanched to achieve a firmer texture; it can be mashed, or blended to a light and creamy consistency. It can also be steamed, simmered, sautéed, deep-fried, or baked. Freezing tofu (in a plastic freezer bag or container) turns it an off-white color and renders it spongy, chewy, and especially absorbent once it has thawed. Tofu is also available in a freeze-dried form and in many commercial preparations, from mayonnaise and dips to "hot dogs" and "burgers." In other words, this is an extraordinarily versatile food in terms of both flavor and texture.

To press a block of tofu, place it in a colander or strainer or sandwich it between paper or cloth towels on a tray and set a flat-bottomed pan and a weight of some kind on top. To blanch tofu, immerse it in boiling water and simmer for a few minutes; drain well.

Tomatillos resemble small green tomatoes with light brown papery wrappers. They have a tart, lemony flavor and a gelatinous texture which functions as a thickener in sauces. Tomatillos are available in the produce section of supermarkets and, in season, at farmers' markets in the Southwest. Select firm ones and leave the husk on until you're ready to use them. They will keep for several weeks in the refrigerator.

Umeboshi are tart, salty, pickled plums. They are made by packing the small, unripe Japanese plums in sea salt along with the leaves of an iron-rich herb called *shiso* or *perilla*, a natural preservative that turns the plums a deep pink. In addition to their use as a zesty flavoring in the kitchen, umeboshi plums are effective digestive aids; strange as it may sound, sucking on a pickled plum and on its pit will quickly cure an upset stomach.

Umeboshi paste is made by puréeing the pickled plums. It is available commercially, or you can make your own. I use it in salad dressings and sushi rolls.

Umeboshi vinegar is the liquid that remains after the plums are pickled. It is both salty and tart. Use it sparingly in salad dressings and sauces; a shake or two of umeboshi vinegar is a lively addition to miso soup or steamed vegetables.

Umeboshi plums, paste, and vinegar are available in natural foods stores and Oriental markets. In tightly closed containers, these products will keep indefinitely. If salt crystals form on plums or paste, just scrape them off before using.

Vermouth is a white wine that contains aromatic herbs and spices. It ranges in flavor from sweet to dry.

Wakame. *See* **Seaweeds**.

MENUS

WHEN IT COMES TO planning menus, bread is typically an afterthought—an appealing extra not essential to the meal. In this cookbook, I'm proposing an alternative approach, one that turns the usual process inside out by beginning with bread and making it the foundation of a meal rather than an accessory. This approach should appeal to any enthusiastic baker who regards baking as an essential culinary skill. Even if it is simply a base for a spread, structure for a sandwich, or accompaniment to a soup or salad, bread should be viewed as an integral part of a meal and as a flexible starting point for creative menu planning.

Let's begin with pumpernickel bread as an example; it is typical in its versatility. In wintertime you might serve thick slices with a hearty beet or cabbage soup, along with a simple salad and something like apple cake for dessert. If the weather is warm, you might slice the bread extra thin and serve it with a vegetable pâté, chilled soup, or some kind of a potato salad and a light dessert. Pumpernickel dough may also be used as the crust for a cabbage or onion kuchen or for a pizza topped with mustard sauce, sauerkraut, and juicy strips of tempeh—unusual, but wonderful!

Or, consider the possibilities of corn tortillas. Hot off the griddle, these soft breads are delightful with or without a spread, and they are fine accompaniments to chilis, soups, and salads. They can be stuffed and rolled, stacked flat between layers of filling, or folded over it. Soft tortilla strips can be scrambled with eggs or tofu. Fried or baked until crisp, whole corn tortillas become edible plates; tortilla pieces become chips for dips and soup and salad garnishes. Start with any of these tortilla-based dishes and add a complementary soup or salad, and maybe dessert. Olé! You have a tasty, well-rounded meal.

In using breads as a basis for meals, you should be restrained only by a few basic principles that apply to all menu planning. First and foremost, use the freshest ingredients you can find. Focus on seasonal vegetables and fruits, and select dishes that match the weather and mood of the season. In cold weather, there's nothing more welcome than a hearty bean soup with a substantial chunk of bread; in summer, beans might be more appealing in a salad, served with a flat bread. Decide on a format: well-designed meals don't necessarily require a main dish but may consist of several dishes of equal import. The appropriate format often depends upon which meal of the day you are planning for, where and how it will be served—indoors or out, as separate courses or altogether, and so on—and, of course, the tastes and appetites of the particular individuals you will be serving. Consider the interplay of flavors, textures, and even colors when you plan a meal. Traditional ethnic combinations work well, but don't be limited by them; strike on your own in mixing and matching dishes.

The following sample menus are presented to illustrate how breads may be used to shape menus from recipes in this book. They are not provided as a comprehensive guide to bread-based meals but as a point of departure for creating your own innovative, delicious combinations. Menus in which bread plays a similar role are grouped together.

Bread and soup or a vegetable stew—and perhaps dessert—may be enough for a satisfying light meal.

- Japanese Vegetable Pancakes
  Miso Soup
  Ginger Teasecake

- Chinese Scallion Bread
  Oriental Noodle Soup
  Apricot-Almond Bars

- Cauliflower-stuffed Parathas
  Indian Lentil Soup
  Ginger Upside-down Cake

- Spoonbread
  Ratatouille
  Lemon Crêpes with Lemon Glaze

- Corn Bread
  Chili
  Apple Crisp

Bread, soup, and salad form a classic partnership in which each of the members shares equal weight.

- Chapatis
  Cashew-Carrot Soup
  Curried Rice & Tempeh Salad
  Sand Dollars

- Alan's French Bread
  Soupe au Pistou
  Boston Lettuce Composée
  Tarte Tatin

- Basic Biscuits
  Southwestern Sweet Potato Soup
  Black-eyed Pea Salad
  Peanut Butter Cookies

- Focaccia
  Minestrone
  Tossed Greens with Vinaigrette
  Teasecake

- Natural-rise Rye Berry Bread
  Madeira-Mushroom Soup
  Dilled Beet & Potato Salad
  Apple Cake

Bread combined with a dip, spread, or filling and soup or salad and dessert is another type of complete meal.

- Amalthea's Pita
  Mediterranean Bean Spread
  Baba
  Tabouli
  Sesame Shortbread

- Pain Pour Nicol
  Mushroom Pâté
  Borscht
  Call-It-Pumpkin Pie

- Mushroom-stuffed Crêpes
  Boston Lettuce Composée
  Cranapple-Currant Pie

- Mexican Bean Burgers in True Grits Bread Buns
  Pico de Gallo
  Tortilla Soup
  Carob Brownies

- Socca
  Caponata
  Glorious Gazpacho
  Fruit Sorbet

Pizzas, turnovers, or bread-crusted tarts are substantial main dishes to build a meal around.

- Pissaladiere
  Pimiento Purée
  Salade Composée
  Almond Butter Cookies

- Breakfast Pizza
  Cantaloupe À L'Orange
  Streusel Coffee Cake

- Indian Turnovers
  Indian Coleslaw
  Outstanding Oatmeal Cookies

- Knishes
  Best Butternut Squash Soup
  Pickled Beets
  Mother's Carrot Cake / Sesame-Maple Icing

- Cabbage Kuchen
  Sesame-Potato Soup
  Mince-Treat Pie

INDEX

NOTES

NOTES

NOTES

NOTES

NOTES